# Sexual Abuse Litigation: A Practical Resource for Attorneys, Clinicians, and Advocates

*Sexual Abuse Litigation: A Practical Resource for Attorneys, Clinicians, and Advocates* has been co-published simultaneously as *Journal of Aggression, Maltreatment & Trauma,* Volume 3, Number 2 (#6) 2000.

# Sexual Abuse Litigation: A Practical Resource for Attorneys, Clinicians, and Advocates

Rebecca Rix, MALS
Editor

*Sexual Abuse Litigation: A Practical Resource for Attorneys, Clinicians, and Advocates* has been co-published simultaneously as *Journal of Aggression, Maltreatment & Trauma,* Volume 3, Number 2 (#6) 2000.

Routledge
Taylor & Francis Group
NEW YORK AND LONDON

First published 2000 by The Haworth Press, Inc.

This edition published 2011 by Routledge
605 Third Avenue, New York, NY 10017
4 Park Square, Milton Park, Abingdon, Oxon OX14 4RN

*Routledge is an imprint of the Taylor & Francis Group, an informa business*



*Sexual Abuse Litigation: A Practical Resource for Attorneys, Clinicians, and Advocates* has been co-published simultaneously as *Journal of Aggression, Maltreatment & Trauma*™, Volume 3, Number 2 (#6) 2000.

Cover design by Thomas J. Mayshock Jr.

**Library of Congress Cataloging-in-Publication Data**

Sexual abuse litigation: a practical resource for attorneys, clinicians, and advocates/Rebecca Rix, editor.

p. cm.

"Co-published simultaneously as Journal of aggression, maltreatment & trauma, volume 3, number 2 (#6) 2000."

Includes bibliographical references and index.

ISBN 0-7890-1174-3 (alk. paper)–ISBN 0-7890-1175-1 (alk. paper)

1. Child sexual abuse–United States. 2. Adult child sexual abuse victims–Legal status, laws, etc.–United States. 3. Recovered memory. I. Rix, Rebecca. II. Journal of aggression, maltreatment & trauma.

KF9325.S495 2000
345.73′02536–dc21 00-040763

ISBN 13: 978-0-7890-1175-6 (pbk)

# Sexual Abuse Litigation: A Practical Resource for Attorneys, Clinicians, and Advocates

## CONTENTS

## ABOUT THE EDITOR

**Rebecca Rix, MALS,** has a Master's Degree in Liberal Studies from Reed College and is working toward a doctorate in American History at Yale University. She has published and presented on topics of intellectual and cultural history as well as sexual abuse litigation. She became interested in the role cultural beliefs play in the political controversies surrounding sexual abuse litigation while working as a legal assistant for Michael Morey. Her current research interests include the interactions of ideas, culture, and gender in the formation of political structures such as law and public policy.

## ABOUT THE CONTRIBUTORS

**Brooks Cooper, JD,** is an associate with the Oregon law firm Sam Hochberg & Associates, where his practice focuses on intellectual property and tort litigation. He is a governor of the publications, legislative and public education committees of the Oregon Trial Lawyer's Association. He has authored numerous articles on scientific evidence and appellate developments for legal periodicals, including a regular column, "Between the Sheets," for *Trial Lawyer* magazine.

**Julian J. Hubbard, JD,** is a California attorney specializing in psychiatric and psychological malpractice, sexual abuse cases, and insurance coverage litigation. He represented the plaintiff in the first fully litigated civil cases involving childhood sexual abuse and delayed memory in California, for which his client was awarded $1.1 million, and has received other substantial verdicts in insurance bad faith litigation. He serves on the Editorial Board of the *California Insurance Law & Regulation Reporter* and *The Insurance Litigation Reporter*, and has authored numerous articles on insurance coverage-related matters.

**Barbara Jo Levy, JD,** is a partner in the Washington law firm Sindell & Levy, specializing in plaintiff's personal injury including sexual abuse cases. Since representing an adult survivor of childhood sexual abuse in the first such Washington case in 1980, Ms. Levy has represented numerous clients and assisted in obtaining legislation to extend the Discovery Rule for adult survivors of child sexual abuse in Washington in 1988. She has served on numerous advisory boards dealing with child abuse issues in the law, and co-authored "Childhood Sexual Abuse–The Plaintiff's Perspective," *Shepard's Expert and Scientific Evidence Quarterly*, Vol. 2, No. 2, Fall 1994. She currently serves as an arbitrator, judge *pro tem,* and mediator, and is a regular speaker at legal education seminars and conferences.

**Michael S. Morey, JD,** is an Oregon attorney who represents adult and child victims of sexual abuse, in addition to his practice in personal injury and product liability litigation. Originally a prosecutor who specialized in rape and child sex abuse prosecutions, Mr. Morey has over 15 years of experience in representing victims of sexual abuse in civil litigation in Oregon, Washington, Alaska, California, Arizona, Idaho and South Dakota. He sponsored Senate Bill 234 which repealed Oregon's 40 year age limitation for delayed discovery child sexual abuse cases in 1992. He co-authored "Childhood Sexual Abuse–The Plaintiff's Perspective," *Shepard's Expert and Scientific Evidence Quarterly*, Vol. 2, No. 2, Fall 1994.

**Janet L. Sonne, PhD,** is a Professor in the Department of Psychology, Loma Linda University Graduate School and the Department of Psychiatry, Loma Linda School of Medicine where she teaches and supervises graduate students in clinical psychology and medical students, provides clinical services, and conducts research focusing on sequelae of childhood sexual abuse and sexual misconduct of professionals. Dr. Sonne serves as a consultant to licensing boards and to clergy committees on issues of psychotherapist and clergy misconduct. She has also served on the ethics committees of the American Psychological Association and the California Psychological Association.

**Mary R. Williams, JD,** is a California attorney specializing in representing adult victims of childhood sexual abuse in civil suits to recover damages for their injuries. She filed the first such action in California in 1982, pioneering application of the "delayed discovery of injury" doctrine to actions by adult survivors of CSA. Since then she has successfully represented victims in approximately 150 such actions. Ms. Williams also drafted California's landmark legislation extending the statute of limitations for such actions (Code of Civil Procedure section 340.1) and led the legislative efforts that resulted in the enactment of and subsequent amendments to this legislation. Ms. Williams has authored two published articles on the current legal and scientific controversy regarding adult claims of "recovered memory" of CSA: "Suits by Adults for Childhood Sexual Abuse: Legal Origins of the Repressed Memory Controversy," *Journal of Psychiatry and Law*, Vol. 24, pp. 207-228, Summer 1996; "Memories of Childhood Sexual Abuse: Legal Issues for Psychotherapists," in Prozan, C., editor, *Construction and Reconstruction of Memory*, Jason Aronson, 1997.

# Foreword

Few mental health issues have captured more attention in professional and public circles recently than human memory and psychotherapy. The number of articles in professional and lay journals and other publications has exploded over the last half decade. What has become most clear from this explosion of information is that the clinical, research, and legal issues that bear on the relationship of memory and psychotherapy are complex, the data are often contradictory or unclear, the motives of authors not always apparent, and the conclusions reached are often overly simplified, one-sided, or, on occasion, misleading.

Many historical, cultural, and political forces have combined to bring attention to this issue. The recent controversy has been precipitated, at least to a considerable degree, by concerns arising from civil law suits in which adult children, sometimes with a period of memory loss (and sometimes without such periods), sue their alleged abusers for psychological damages. The advent of this litigation illuminated and intensified a serious debate among academic professionals and advocates of different scientific approaches over which theories and bodies of research most appropriately inform understanding about human behavior and psychotherapy. Deep-seated cultural views about sexual abuse, the nature of interpersonal helping, and the liberation of women and children, as well as personal motives, have also shaped how the issue is framed and driven the extreme ends of the debate.

Given the central role that the law and the courtroom have played in framing this complex issue and the fact that these issues bring therapists and lawyers so often into contact with each other, a need has

[Haworth co-indexing entry note]: "Foreword." Conte, Jon. Co-published simultaneously in *Journal of Aggression, Maltreatment & Trauma* (The Haworth Maltreatment & Trauma Press, an imprint of The Haworth Press, Inc.) Vol. 3, No. 2 (#6), 2000, pp. xix-xx; and: *Sexual Abuse Litigation: A Practical Resource for Attorneys, Clinicians, and Advocates* (ed: Rebecca Rix) The Haworth Maltreatment & Trauma Press, an imprint of The Haworth Press, Inc., 2000, pp. xv-xvi. Single or multiple copies of this article are available for a fee from The Haworth Document Delivery Service [1-800-342-9678, 9:00 a.m. - 5:00 p.m. (EST). E-mail address: getinfo@haworthpressinc.com].

 

emerged for information about the knowledge base, roles, and responsibilities of professionals helping survivors in this area of the law. This volume provides clinicians, attorneys, and other advocates with just such an understanding about litigation and the adult survivor.

*Jon Conte*

# Preface

How have "repressed" memories of childhood sexual abuse (CSA) been transformed from one of many elements in the delayed discovery lawsuit to one of the most controversial topics in the professional and popular media? More importantly, how can helping professionals responsibly and effectively advocate on behalf of adult CSA survivors interested in civil litigation in the midst of this heated controversy? *Sexual Abuse Litigation: A Practical Resource for Attorneys, Clinicians, and Advocates* answers these and other questions in clear language and in a format designed for use both as a substantial legal guide and a practical reference. Its balanced, multifaceted approach is ideal for lawyers, clinicians, and advocates who work with CSA survivors, as well as for survivors considering legal action.

While there are certainly false allegations of abuse, many more allegations are true: the American Psychological Association recently estimated that 16 to 34% of girls and 10 to 20% of boys are sexually abused, usually by a family member or a trusted adult.[1] The psychological and physical injuries associated with such abuse call for legal redress, but the partial or total traumatic amnesia experienced by many CSA survivors often precludes timely legal action against abusers. In recognition of these facts, many state legislatures have provided "delayed discovery" statutes of limitations as a means of legal redress for adult CSA survivors. Such litigation–and the social change it represents–has provoked a heated debate over the reliability of "repressed" memories. This litigation-related focus on the issue of "repressed" memories is troubling insofar as it distracts attention from the myriad practical challenges involved with formulating political and legal responses to the troubling realities of CSA, in the media as well as the courtroom.

---

[Haworth co-indexing entry note]: "Preface." Rix, Rebecca. Co-published simultaneously in *Journal of Aggression, Maltreatment & Trauma* (The Haworth Maltreatment & Trauma Press, an imprint of The Haworth Press, Inc.) Vol. 3, No. 2 (#6), 2000, pp. xxi-xxv; and: *Sexual Abuse Litigation: A Practical Resource for Attorneys, Clinicians, and Advocates* (ed: Rebecca Rix) The Haworth Maltreatment & Trauma Press, an imprint of The Haworth Press, Inc., 2000, pp. xvii-xxi. Single or multiple copies of this article are available for a fee from The Haworth Document Delivery Service [1-800-342-9678, 9:00 a.m. - 5:00 p.m. (EST). E-mail address: getinfo@haworthpressinc.com].

 

*Sexual Abuse Litigation* offers practical information to meet the challenges of CSA advocacy. Its authors place the current memory controversy in historical context and examine how various psychological and medical conceptions of trauma have shaped public opinion and the construction of delayed discovery statutes of limitations. Experienced litigators guide the reader through case evaluation and development, the pitfalls and opportunities of professional cooperation between therapists and lawyers, the effective use of plaintiff expert witnesses, and the identification of insurance benefits for injuries related to CSA. After analyzing the "false memory" defense, the authors offer strategies for sustaining the admissibility of the CSA survivor's testimony and maintaining focus on the central question of whether abuse occurred. Appendices include ground-breaking tabulations of CSA statutes of limitations for all fifty states, actual defense expert witness deposition and cross-examination testimony to demonstrate effective litigation techniques, and vital networking resources for the lawyer, clinician, advocate, or survivor.

In the first chapter, Rebecca Rix traces the history of traumatic memory studies from nineteenth-century Europe to present-day America. Noting that controversies over traumatic neurosis and CSA have recurred since the mid-nineteenth century, she argues that the current "repressed" memory controversy is distinguished by the presence of litigation that challenges longstanding cultural assumptions about CSA. Ms. Rix provides an overview of five stages of traumatic memory studies, as well as outlining the confluence of social, medical, and legal developments that have provided the context for recent political and legal responses to CSA. Revisiting the cultural legacies of early scientific studies sheds light on the reluctance of the public to see CSA as a public policy issue, as well as clarifying the concepts and cultural traditions represented in the current memory controversy.

In the second chapter, attorney Mary Williams discusses the problems encountered when the scientific and social awareness of CSA is translated into public policy as she reviews and analyzes delayed discovery statutes of limitations in adult survivor litigation. While CSA cases contain factual similarities to cases for which delayed discovery, mental incapacity, equitable estoppel, and other legal doctrines were created, the unusual social dynamics and long-term psychological effects do not fit precisely with any of these legal doctrines. Ms. Williams explores the historical development of delayed discovery statutes of limitations, evaluates the different types of statutes and applicable case law, and analyzes the problematic use of the concept of repression in legislation. Her chapter references and interprets her exhaustively researched state-by-state tabulations of delayed-discovery statutes of limitations and relevant appellate decisions, which are published in this volume as appendices A, B, and C.

The problematic "fit" between the different aims and languages of psychology and law can create difficulties not only for legislatures, but also in the working relationships of therapists and lawyers involved in delayed discovery CSA litigation. In the third chapter, however, psychologist Janet Sonne and attorney Julian Hubbard demonstrate how, in the emotionally-charged environment of this litigation, these professional differences can actually optimize the ability of each professional to assist their common client, the CSA survivor. Dr. Sonne reviews the psychological and behavioral sequelae of CSA and identifies six elements of the client's psychological functioning key to the litigation process, as well as posing questions for the attorney's self-evaluation for the unique demands of CSA litigation. Mr. Hubbard addresses what survivors and therapists need to know about how the litigation process can exacerbate the client's psychological problems.

Given the complex and demanding nature of delayed discovery litigation, the legal viability of a case should not be the only consideration in deciding whether to pursue litigation on behalf of a CSA survivor. In the fourth chapter, attorney Michael S. Morey explores the legal and non-legal issues related to the lawyer's initial case evaluation. After analyzing how evaluation of CSA cases differs from other types of personal injury cases, he presents a model for non-suggestive yet thorough client interviewing and case evaluation to help both survivor and lawyer decide whether to pursue legal action. Mr. Morey demonstrates how lawyers can make the case evaluation process a valuable resource for survivors, whether or not legal action is ultimately taken, with practical tips and a reproducible intake form.

If legal action is pursued, retaining and working with expert witnesses becomes an important part of developing the case and preparing for litigation. In the fifth chapter, attorney Barbara Jo Levy examines the essential role of plaintiff's expert witnesses in countering the "false memory" defense. Their assistance in preliminary case evaluation, education of the judge and jury, and critical evaluation of defense expert testimony will help maintain focus on whether sexual abuse occurred, rather than allowing analysis of the facts to become mired in debates over memory science. Ms. Levy identifies the distinct roles of the treating therapist and the expert witness, outlines criteria for choosing a qualified expert witness, and reveals three key objectives of successful cross-examination. In appendices D, E, F, and G, Ms. Levy provides questions for the direct and rebuttal examination of plaintiff's expert witnesses, as well as actual deposition testimony and subsequent cross-examination of a defense witness to illustrate these strategies in action.

Anticipating and countering the recent defense strategy of engaging in pre-trial evidentiary hearings is another important element of countering the "false memory" defense. In the sixth chapter, attorney Brooks Cooper illuminates how admissibility standards governing scientific evidence complicate delayed-discovery CSA cases. Recent developments in law, such as the pre-trial evidentiary hearings that invoke the "gatekeeper" function of the judge enunciated in *Daubert v. Merrell-Dow Pharmaceuticals,* have found favor among defense lawyers attempting to bar delayed memory testimony by characterizing it as the product of unreliable science. To overcome this litigation hurdle, Mr. Cooper contextualizes the present controversy in the history of scientific evidence admissibility, tracing emerging trends in judicial opinion on scientific evidence given by expert witnesses from the 1923 case *Frye v. United States* through the present, and offers strategies and techniques to maintain evidence admissibility before and during the trial.

Despite the frequently significant damages in CSA cases, the plaintiff's ability to collect any settlement or judgment award is often precluded by the limited financial resources of the defendant(s). In the seventh and final chapter, attorney Julian Hubbard offers a primer on individual and corporate insurance coverage issues and reviews the development of limited coverage for CSA injuries in statutory and case law. While direct coverage for CSA injuries is rare, indirect coverage may be found, especially if negligent acts of individuals other than the perpetrator facilitated the abuse. Mr. Hubbard delineates a practical model for research and legal strategies to ensure reaching any available insurance coverage, and explores the benefits and drawbacks of drawing on administrative resources to finance survivors' medical and mental health care.

Much remains to be done to prevent and redress childhood sexual abuse, and it is the hope of the authors that this book will contribute to this ongoing process by documenting what has and has not worked in the recent and not-so-recent past. While academic and clinical researchers continue to develop scientific knowledge of traumatic memory loss and recall, lawyers and other advocates need essential, practical information in order to act on the knowledge currently available. In that spirit, we offer the reader a "usable past," hopeful that new analyses will clarify some of the issues around this most complex subject.

*Rebecca Rix*
*June 1999*

## NOTE

1. See *Violence and the Family: Report of the American Psychological Association Presidential Task Force on Violence and the Family* (Washington, DC: American Psychological Association, 1996) 11.

# Trauma, Science, and the Law: A Brief History of Trauma Research and the Social Response

Rebecca Rix

**SUMMARY.** In this chapter, the author shows that while debates over trauma and neurosis surfaced and disappeared in nineteenth-century Europe and America, the current debate is unique in that it involves innovative legal remedies for child abuse survivors. The history of traumatic memory studies from the nineteenth century to the present are traced, different theories of traumatic memory impairment and their cultural influence are surveyed, and the confluence of social, scientific, and political developments that led to legislative and legal responses to CSA are examined. The semantic correlation of the "false memory" defense with recognized stages of memory and PTSD are evaluated. *[Article copies available for a fee from The Haworth Document Delivery Service: 1-800-342-9678. E-mail address: <getinfo@haworthpressinc.com> Website: <http://www.haworthpressinc.com>]*

**KEYWORDS.** Hysteria, combat fatigue, combat neurosis, shell shock, soldier's heart, dissociation, repression, seduction theory (Sigmund Freud) traumatic amnesia related to childhood sexual abuse, Posttraumatic Stress Disorder (PTSD), Central Nervous System (CNS), impairment of in PTSD, implicit versus explicit memory, false memory syndrome, cultural and historical underpinnings of the false memory controversy

---

Address correspondence to: Rebecca Rix, Law Office of Michael S. Morey, Lakeside Plaza, 8 N. State Street, Suite 301, Lake Oswego, OR 97034.

[Haworth co-indexing entry note]: "Trauma, Science, and the Law: A Brief History of Trauma Research and the Social Response." Rix, Rebecca. Co-published simultaneously in *Journal of Aggression, Maltreatment & Trauma* (The Haworth Maltreatment & Trauma Press, an imprint of The Haworth Press, Inc.) Vol. 3, No. 2 (#6), 2000, pp. 1-47; and: *Sexual Abuse Litigation: A Practical Resource for Attorneys, Clinicians, and Advocates* (ed: Rebecca Rix) The Haworth Maltreatment & Trauma Press, an imprint of The Haworth Press, Inc., 2000, pp. 1-47. Single or multiple copies of this article are available for a fee from The Haworth Document Delivery Service [1-800-342-9678, 9:00 a.m. - 5:00 p.m. (EST). E-mail address: getinfo@haworthpressinc.com].

 

> Amongst all the many victims of medical ignorance clad in authority the poor hysteric has hitherto fared the worst; and her gradual rehabilitation and rescue will count among the philanthropic conquests of our generation.[1,2]
>
> *-William James, 1894*

Law plays an essential but problematic role in maintaining public dialogue about childhood sexual abuse (CSA).[3] CSA has become a political issue partly due to legislation allowing "delayed discovery" lawsuits against alleged perpetrators in recognition of the fact that traumatic amnesia frequently precludes more timely legal action. The presence of legal responses to the problem of CSA distinguishes the current debate over the existence and reliability of traumatic amnesia from earlier, similar, and all-but-forgotten debates. The controversy of clashing scientific and cultural traditions are now brought into the public sphere for adjudication on a case-by-case basis, rather than permitting the debate to rage only in professional and academic circles as before. Yet if law has altered this controversy over memory and trauma, cultural traditions derived from these earlier controversies have inexorably defined the contours of this debate's legal discourse. This chapter places the current controversy in cultural and historical context by revisiting some of the forgotten controversies and examining how they have shaped current understanding of trauma and neurosis in medicine and the law.

One such controversy occurred a century ago, when several different medical and mental health investigators, working independently, discovered the "etiology of hysteria," the root of neurosis, in the disruption of memory caused by traumatic experience. These investigators believed this discovery would result in a completely new perspective on hysteria. They argued that the hysteric was not malingering, genetically inferior, or demonically possessed, but a victim of prior traumatic experience. For the American philosopher and psychologist William James, this discovery meant that the right-minded society could proceed with an appropriately philanthropic social response. However, controversy soon engulfed the emerging science. Within a decade, hysteria fell out of fashion as a topic of scientific inquiry and the hysteric was again viewed by many as one whose suffering was either imaginary or conceived for personal gain.

Despite the advance in medical knowledge, no "philanthropic conquest" took place.

Legal and social responses to the problem of CSA required nearly a century of research on the psychological aftermath of trauma, medical acceptance of traumatic amnesia and trauma-related neuroses, and a more progressive legal and social environment. Child abuse generally, and CSA specifically, reached the legislative agenda in the 1980s, due to growing public awareness of the pernicious legacies of abuse for both the individual victim and society.[4] The effort to obtain legal protections and remedies for abused children and adults abused as children came from a movement of activists, including survivors of abuse, lawyers, clinicians, researchers, and leaders of social service organizations. As public awareness of the prevalence and injurious effects of CSA increased, tolerance for child abuse decreased. Legal provisions such as the delayed discovery statute of limitations established an unprecedented response to this public concern, by codifying this "philanthropic conquest" in the legal sphere.

Since laws represent a codification of existing rules of social conduct, they contain many cultural assumptions.[5] Changes in law (and therefore, challenges to underlying rules of social conduct) are thus often contested both legally and socially. This is particularly true when the matter is as sensitive as CSA. The adversarial nature of litigation has added further controversy to this public and scientific dialogue, with defense experts calling delayed memories into question in an attempt to foster disbelief of CSA victims in the courtroom and in the public mind.[6] Their attacks on the incomplete scientific understanding of the precise mechanisms of memory disruption, coupled with their alternative explanations for the plaintiff's memories ("false memory syndrome") and skepticism toward victims of CSA, echo earlier reactions to advances in traumatic memory awareness.

While often invoked as a defense in CSA litigation, "false memory syndrome" is not a medical diagnosis, but rather a phrase coined by the False Memory Syndrome Foundation.[7] Its popular appeal–aside from the benefits it offers a legal defense–stems from its resemblance to familiar threads of popularized psychology that echoes the later work of Sigmund Freud. Seen in the most favorable light, "false memory" studies raise old but important questions about the reliability of normal memory and bring attention to poorly trained therapists and advocates.[8] Seen in the worst light, "false memory" studies attempt to distract the judge, jury, and society at large from the issue of CSA by invoking traditional explanations of the fantasy-based origins of CSA allegations. These old explanations ring true both because they contain seeds of scientific truth (e.g., that normal memory can be imperfect) and because they resonate with European and American cultural traditions about the origins of neurosis. Thus, the lawyer who handles delayed discovery cases must not only be cognizant of the vast body of scientific literature on posttraumatic memory loss and recall, but must also be aware of persistent, alternative explanations for neurosis with deep cultural roots that can distract attention away from CSA.

The scientific literature on traumatic neurosis is vast, and as this chapter seeks to overview the history of the science and the cultural reception of that science, only a brief survey is included here. Such a historical survey permits the tracing of the cultural patterns of science and law of the present memory controversy in CSA cases; for more thorough coverage of the scientific literature, the reader should refer to several of the many literature reviews currently available.[9] The first section of this chapter traces the development of medical awareness of traumatic neurosis and the concurrent development of a language of conflict over the awareness and denial of that reality. The second section argues that the terms of the current memory debate have been influenced by the legacy of past memory debates and the advent of legal-defense deconstruction of traumatic memory studies. The reader should take note that different disciplines use different terms and explanations for essentially the same phenomena. If the advocate is unfamiliar with the confused semantics in this area of research, the defense may confound the judge or jury with references to studies that have little or nothing to do with traumatic memory.

## *A CENTURY OF POSTTRAUMATIC NEUROSIS STUDIES*

Two key points have emerged from the past century of studies on posttraumatic neurosis. First, there is a consensus among researchers from a variety of disciplines that memory loss, sometimes with later recall, is a common feature of the human response to psychological trauma.[10] Such trauma appears to cause an alteration in the way the mind encodes, stores, and retrieves memory.[11] This impairment of memory processes can lead to partial or total amnesia and various forms of related neurosis. Second, cultural traditions have historically offered alternative explanations for the origins of posttraumatic neurosis (e.g., demonic possession, ethnic inferiority, inferiority of the "weaker sex," mental weakness, fantasy, and suggestibility). These explanations deflect attention from the social problem of traumas such as CSA by locating the origins of neurosis in the weak mind, rather than in the traumatic experience, of the trauma survivor.

This section traces the forging of traumatic memory studies and cultural responses in five diverse and overlapping stages.[12] The first occurred at the end of the nineteenth century, when researchers established that hysteria was a psychological phenomenon with roots in dissociated or repressed traumatic experience. The second stage also began in the nineteenth century and spanned most of the twentieth, when studies on soldiers' "shell shock," "combat fatigue," and the traumatic neuroses of war culminated in the medical acceptance of posttraumatic stress disorder (PTSD). Mid to late twentieth-century feminists played a pivotal role in the third stage by raising awareness of sexual violence via research, public education, and legal reforms, creating an environment of reform activism. The fourth stage began in the 1980s, when researchers studied the psychological aftermath of CSA, including traumatic amnesia and neurosis, extending trauma studies to include the experiences of children. The fifth stage, a growing body of research on the neurological and physiological responses to overwhelming stress, has provided important findings that may illuminate the physiological underpinnings of the posttraumatic symptoms documented regularly since the mid-nineteenth century.

### *The Nineteenth Century: Seeking the Etiology of Hysteria*

At the 1993 Convention of the American Psychological Association, psychologist John Briere quipped in a debate with psychologist Elizabeth Loftus that World War II, so far as he could recall, occurred prior to the publication of *The Courage to Heal*, a popular self-help book for CSA survivors.[13] Here, Briere responded to the notion that memory loss and posttraumatic neurosis were novel pseudo-scientific ideas derived from self-help manuals, rather than longstanding subjects of social scientific and medical research. In fact, the mysterious malady called "hysteria" (with its striking resemblance to PTSD) preceded World War II by 25 centuries.[14] As the name hysteria implies (the Greek *hysterikos* means "suffering in the uterus"), its origins were associated with women and with internal mental or moral flaws, rather than external causes.[15]

As with hysteria, CSA has been documented since well before the nineteenth century. Physicians, government investigators, reformers' exposés, court records, and popular folklore documented incidents of CSA as early as the eighteenth century.[16] Although CSA was recognized, cultural rationalizations minimized and changed its nature and effects. Incest and CSA were linked with overcrowding and poverty, while their negative psychological effects were deemed the result of constitutional defect (especially among the "weaker sex") and considered autogenic in nature, "arising from heredity, bad habits or the self-imposed conditions of urban living."[17] Hysteria and CSA were thus discredited among medical professionals, as well as the public; understanding a causal link between the two would not be possible until the traumatic origins of hysteria were identified.

The psychiatrist Bessel van der Kolk and his co-authors have argued that the correlation between psychological trauma and hysteria was discovered as psychiatry became a scientific discipline in the mid-to-late nineteenth century.[18] As soon as such correlative theories identified an etiological role of CSA in the development of hysteria, some critics argued that false memories ("*pseudologica phantastica*") were common in children's accusations of incest against parents.[19] Beginning in 1856, a French public health journal was the forum for a forensic/medical debate about the prevalence of CSA and the truthfulness of victims' reports. On one side, some physicians argued that

> sexual acts against children were very frequent, that assaulted children often showed no physical signs, that children's reports were largely truthful, that fathers and brothers were often the molesters and that "higher education" did not inhibit men from committing such acts.[20]

These assertions sound strikingly modern, and indeed, psychiatrist Roland Summit comments that Ambrose Tardieu, the dean of forensic medicine in France, described in 1860 what is recognizable today as the Battered Child Syndrome.[21] However, Tardieu's successor, Alfred Tournier, attacked Tardieu's assertions by arguing that children regularly lied about CSA. Another contemporary, Paul Brourdel, claimed that 60 to 80% of CSA claims were unfounded, and could be viewed as young girls' deliberate attempts to gain the emancipation that would allow them to live a life of unfettered debauchery. The mother's ignorance and the child's "extreme suggestibility" facilitated the manufacture of such "slander."[22] This discrediting of CSA reports discouraged research and reform for several decades.

That the mid-century debate was forensic as well as scientific and medical is telling, for, as psychiatrist Judith Herman has argued persuasively, advances in understanding human responses to trauma have historically been associated as much with favorable political and cultural conditions as with able scientific investigators.[23] Herman traces the modern awareness of trauma and neurosis to the work (dating to the 1870s) of the French neurologist Jean-Martin Charcot, whose interest in hysteria was as political and cultural as scientific. Intrigued by the Catholic notion that hysterics were women possessed by demons, Charcot saw the possibility of undermining clerical authority by demonstrating the psychological, rather than the spiritual, basis of hysteria. In seeking a rational, scientific explanation for the apparent possession of hysterics, Charcot aimed to debunk the clerical argument that these women proved the existence of demonic possession. In short, Herman argues, Charcot intended to "claim hysterical women for science."[24] His "laboratory"–the Salpêtrière–was, she notes,

> an asylum for the most wretched of the Parisian proletariat: beggars, prostitutes, and the insane. Charcot transformed this neglected facility into a temple of modern science, and the most gifted and ambitious men in the new disciplines of neurology and psychiatry journeyed to Paris to study with the master. Among the many distinguished physicians who made the pilgrimage to the Salpêtrière were Pierre Janet, William James, and Sigmund Freud.[25]

Charcot's prestige thus lent credibility and dignity to the study of the hysteria, while his Salpêtrière offered many of the founders of modern psychiatry and neurology a grounding in the emerging science on hysteria.[26] By 1880, Charcot demonstrated that hysterical symptoms resembling neurological damage ("motor paralyses, sensory losses, convulsions and amnesias"[27]) were in fact psychological, since they could be induced and relieved with the aid of hypnosis.[28]

Charcot's students Pierre Janet and Sigmund Freud took up the work where Charcot left off, by seeking the etiology of these psychological disturbances. Working independently, Janet and Freud (with his collaborator Josef Breuer) engaged in intensive interviewing and treatment of hysterics. By the mid-1890s, these investigations revealed a common pattern of prior traumatic experience resulting in memory disruption, amnesia, and somatic symptoms.[29] Janet termed the phenomenon the "dissociation" of "subconscious fixed ideas," while Freud and Breuer called it "double consciousness," noting that "hysterics suffer mainly from reminiscences."[30] The discovery of "dissociation" and "double consciousness" represented the beginning of the end of medical ignorance about hysteria, or at least so it seemed.

*Freud and the Etiology of Hysteria*

In developing what one patient called the "talking cure," Freud and Breuer discovered that the "reminiscences" from which many hysterics suffered were of "premature seduction," or CSA.[31] In his resulting "seduction theory," presented in his 1896 paper, "The Etiology of Hysteria," Freud argued that

> at the bottom of every case of hysteria there are one or more occurrences of premature sexual experience, occurrences which belong to the earliest years of childhood, but which can be reproduced through the work of psycho-analysis in spite of the intervening decades. I believe this is an important finding, the discovery of a *caput Nili* in neuropathology.[32]

Freud's identification of CSA as the cause of hysteria reflected his clinical experience, but it also revisited the work of the French investigators at mid-century. In fact, Freud owned many of the essays and books written by investigators on both sides of the French CSA/hysteria debate.[33] Unlike Charcot's belief in the hereditary origin of hysteria and its identification as an essentially feminine malady, Freud's seduction theory held that hysteria was rooted in CSA, with its betrayal of power relations and the "forgetting" of a trauma leading to neurosis.[34] Boundary violations by the adult "seducer" confused and disrupted the child victim's psychological development.[35] Freud believed that memories retrieved after years of absence were not fantasies, but recollections of an actual event, "with all the feelings that belonged to the original experience."[36] His experience treating middle-class hysterics demonstrated that CSA was shockingly common and that its incidence was unrelated to poverty, social class, or ethnicity as was commonly assumed.[37] Freud argued that the higher incidence of hysteria in women resulted from the more frequent sexual exploitation of girls than boys as children.[38] Finally, Freud asserted that fathers (and in the case of his clinical practice, often well educated, respected, middle-class fathers) were the likely "seducers."[39]

Freud's seduction theory met with an icy reception from the Society for Psychiatry and Neurology in Vienna.[40] Preferring traditional explanations of hysteria, the Society dismissed the theory, and apparently Freud's credibility with it. The theory that Freud believed would earn him a place in history instead wrought havoc in his professional life. Freud held firm for a discouraging year, although personal letters reveal his profound disappointment and anger toward the medical establishment. He wrote his friend and colleague Wilhelm Fliess: "I am as isolated as you could wish me to be: the word has been given out to abandon me, and a void is forming around me."[41] Despite professional censure and financial difficulties, Freud stood by the seduction theory. However, after the death of his own sexually abusive father in October of 1896, Freud underwent a psychological crisis that he described in letters to Fliess as his "neurosis" or "hysteria."[42]

The historian William McGrath argues that the death of Freud's father was especially troublesome for Freud, given the impossibility of reconciling the filial respect appropriate to mourning with his belief that his father was responsible for his and his siblings' "hysterical symptoms."[43] The seduction theory placed blame primarily on fathers for "premature seduction" of their children, and while Freud did not publicly blame his own father, in private correspondence he identified him as "one of those perverts" who was "responsible for the hysteria of (Freud's) brother and several younger sisters."[44] Freud's own hysterical symptoms and his difficulty getting established professionally (which he attributed as much to rising nationalism and anti-semitism in Vienna, as to the chilly professional reception of the seduction theory) impelled him to reach a different, less provocative, conclusion about the etiology of hysteria.[45]

Freud located in the Greek tragedy *Oedipus Rex* a means of absolving the guilt of the "seducer" in the infliction of hysteria; hysteria, he theorized, could be caused by a child's repression of "Oedipal" sexual and violent impulses, rather than actual sexual violence perpetrated on the child.[46] As Freudian psychoanalysis developed from classical literary themes, "repression" of these guilty impulses (or fantasies) became central to the formation of hysteria.[47] Such a formulation resolved Freud's personal and professional dilemmas by offering an explanation of hysteria that retracted the indictment of his father, and middle class respectability, implicit in his seduction theory. Psychological, cultural, and professional exigencies thus trumped the lessons of empirical science.

The retraction of the seduction theory, then, was as much a cultural act as a scientific one. While the seduction theory was clearly overstated (its failure to include forms of trauma other than CSA oversimplified the etiology of hysteria), it did contain an important truth (that the trauma of CSA can create lasting psychological injuries). Freud had scientific concerns about the theory, including his uncertainty over how to discern the veracity of his patients' self-report and how to account for retractions of CSA allegations,[48] yet these issues were cause for circumspection, not retraction. Nor did the retraction result from additional empirical observation: on the contrary, in the period before the retraction, Freud had engaged in the non-empirical methodology of analyzing his own dreams in a period of psychological distress.[49] His return to traditional explanations for his patients' hysteria (*e.g.*, suggestibility or "*pseudologica phantastica*," albeit with a neoclassical twist)[50] permitted Freud an accommodation to professional, social, and political exigencies, as well as an uneasy resolution of his own psychological distress.

Problematically, by retracting rather than modifying the seduction theory, Freud absolved the sins of all his patients' fathers as well as "forgetting" the molestation of his siblings at the hands of his own father. Freud's explanation of his retraction to Fliess revealed a sentiment that has become an enduring tradition in the study of traumatic neurosis: when Freud's methodology was inadequate to illuminate the precise mechanisms involved in traumatic neurosis, his frustratingly incomplete understanding of the causal correlation of trauma and neurosis turned to denial of that correlation.[51] The weight of Freud's doubt, not additional evidence, was the crucial factor in his retraction of the seduction theory. As Freud concluded, "[n]ow I have no idea where I stand because I have not succeeded in gaining a theoretical understanding of repression and its interplay of forces."[52]

While Freud was uncertain about abandoning the seduction theory at first, his ambivalence was edited out during the publication of his letters and writings, by Freud himself and by his followers.[53] When subsequent Freudians attempted to address the connection between CSA and neurosis, they were met with the same reception Freud received in 1896, except that they could expect such treatment from Freud himself.[54] The heart of neurosis, Freudians insisted, was not traumatic experience, but fantasy. In the words of Anna Freud in 1981:

> Keeping up the seduction theory would mean to abandon the Oedipus complex, and with it the whole importance of phantasy life, conscious or unconscious phantasy. In fact, I think there would have been no psychoanalysis afterwards.[55]

Thus, the abandonment of the seduction theory was perceived as critical to the formation and maintenance of psychoanalytic doctrine. Freud's increasingly popular psychoanalysis obscured the link between hysteria and CSA by popularizing the notion of Oedipal fantasies as the cause, and psychoanalysis as the cure, of neurosis. The social and political implications of CSA were thereby hidden in the apolitical, private office of the psychoanalyst, absolving the public of the obligation to fashion the "philanthropic conquest" anticipated by another of Charcot's students, William James. Freud's replacement of the traumatic experience etiology with the fantasy etiology created a more palatable explanation of the origins of neuroses, and, through the subsequent popularization and cultural acquisition of psychoanalytic ideas, his theories continue to inform Western thought.

### *Janet's "Dissociation"*

The popularity of Freudian psychoanalysis also tended to obscure Pierre Janet's work on dissociation. Another student of Charcot, Janet worked independently from Freud and Breuer in the 1890s to discover the cause of hysteria. Janet argued that normal memory was, "like all psychological phenomenon," an action; the action of normal memory was essentially that of "telling a story."[56] Trauma, he hypothesized, disrupted the process that permitted the "liquidation" of sensory data into the "story" told by normal memory. During a traumatic event, sensory data was recorded differently than during a non-traumatic event and was stored as a dissociated or "fixed" idea. These "fixed" or "unliquidated" ideas formed the nucleus of hysteria. Such "unliquidated" ideas could be retrieved and integrated into normal consciousness using hypnosis, resulting in decreased hysterical symptoms. The satisfactory liquidation of such a "fixed" idea into normal memory, he argued, required the achievement of "an inward reaction through the words we address to ourselves, through the organization of the recital of the event to others and to ourselves, and through the putting of this recital in its place as one of the chapters in our personal history." Until that narrative liquidation process had taken place, he continued, "one who retains a fixed idea of a happening cannot be said to have a 'memory.'. . . it is only for convenience that we speak of it as a 'traumatic memory.'"[57]

The psychiatrist Bessel van der Kolk has noted that while Janet's work was well known in the early twentieth century by trauma researchers, it was subsequently obscured by psychoanalytic ideas and virtually forgotten:[58]

> For the past 75 years psychoanalysis, the study of repressed wishes and instinct, and descriptive psychiatry, virtually ignored the fact that actual memories may form the nucleus of psychopathology and continue to exert their influence on current experience by means of the process of dissociation.[59]

Recent research in neuroscience, however, has returned to a study of trauma as the precipitating event of dissociation and posttraumatic neurosis. Over the past three decades, psychobiologists, neuroscientists, and psychiatrists have found evidence that traumatic memory is encoded, stored, and retrieved differently than "normal" memory, and that these "memories" are qualitatively different.[60] Thus, scientific inquiry has challenged the profound medical and cultural influence of psychoanalysis, renewing interest in Janet's century-old hypotheses about the uniqueness of traumatic memory.

### *Legacies of the Studies on Hysteria*

Studies of trauma and neurosis in the nineteenth century left important legacies. The mid-century debate over incest and hysteria, and true and false memories, offered the first modern memory controversy. A few decades later, Charcot began the investigation of the psychological origins of hysteria, and his students Janet and Freud made important scientific and cultural contributions to the field. While Freud's seduction theory found a "premature seduction" at the core of nearly every case of hysteria, Janet theorized that trauma-induced disruption of normal memory processes caused hysteria. Freud's subsequent retraction of his seduction theory and development of psychoanalysis provided a non-traumatic explanation of neurosis and its treatment by substituting fantasy for experience at the core of memory. Freud's retraction, however, was an act of cultural accommodation as much as one of scientific judgment. Psychoanalysis and the ideas of "repression," "fantasy," and "suggestibility" would provide an alternative, increasingly popular explanation for the origins of neurosis. This alternative explanation developed from uncertainty over the precise interplay of forces in the mind, to a prevailing suspicion that the mind could not be trusted.

*Studies From Combat*

Studies that linked traumatic experience and neurosis began on another front during the nineteenth century, that of wartime combat. Combat neurosis was initially studied during the Civil War, but it was not until World War I that "shell shock" or "combat neurosis" was prominently studied.[61] "Combat neurosis" led soldiers to exhibit symptoms resembling those of hysteria, including memory loss, mutism, sensory loss, and motor paralysis.[62] Remedies were required in order to return able-bodied soldiers to combat as quickly as possible, as well as to maintain morale.[63] Before the turn of the century, one medical tradition held that posttraumatic symptoms were organic and physical in origin. Physicians in this tradition named posttraumatic maladies "cardiac neuroses," "irritable heart," and "soldiers' heart," likely due to the frequency of cardiac problems in traumatized soldiers. Such names seem to have anticipated the connection between mind and body demonstrated by recent psychobiological and neuroscientific studies, as well as destigmatizing the posttraumatic symptoms of soldiers.[64]

The organicism of the nineteenth century, however, did not characterize the theories of combat neurosis in the early twentieth century. During World War I, for example, medical personnel believed that soldiers' symptoms were caused either by moral or emotional infirmity or from the physical shock of being near explosions (hence the name "shell shock").[65] Early treatments included electric shock "therapy" and attempts to make the soldier feel ashamed of his symptoms. However, as it became clear that the syndrome was common among men of unquestioned bravery, American psychiatrists J. W. Appel and G. W. Beebe realized there was "no such thing as 'getting used to combat,'" noting that,

> [e]ach moment of combat imposes a strain so great that men will break down in direct relation to the intensity and duration of their exposure. Thus psychiatric casualties are as inevitable as gunshot and shrapnel wounds in warfare.[66]

For Appel and Beebe, combat neurosis was the predictable result of psychological wartime trauma.

The American psychiatrist and anthropologist Abram Kardiner was first to correlate Janet's studies of hysteria and dissociation with combat neurosis.[67] Kardiner's important work helped bring about a renaissance of trauma studies.[68] He recognized that the study of combat neurosis should build on the foundation provided by Janet's studies of hysteria, but he found the word "hysteria" had become pejorative.[69] Kardiner began treating veterans in the 1920s and compiled his findings in his 1941 *The Traumatic Neuroses of War.*[70] Kardiner's work continued through World War II and the war in Vietnam, culminating in his outline of the constellation of symptoms that reflected both Janet's influence and anticipated the current conception of PTSD.[71] World War II saw the application of Kardiner's scientific theories on war neuroses. Therapeutic interventions were as brief as possible and were accomplished near the soldier's fighting unit. Like Janet and Charcot, military psychiatrists found the use of altered states of consciousness effective in gaining access to memories of traumatic events in order to diminish symptoms. Both sodium amytal and hypnosis were used on the front to expedite the retrieval of traumatic memories for psychotherapeutic purposes.[72]

In the Vietnam era, notes psychiatrist Judith Herman, scientific research was complemented by actions taken by veterans on their own behalf. The efficacy of recounting experiences in alleviating posttraumatic symptoms led Vietnam veterans to form "rap groups" in the 1970s. These groups served both psychological and political needs, offering members emotional support as well as raising public awareness about the psychological aftermath of combat.[73] The insistent lobbying of Vietnam veterans prompted not only treatment of, but research on, posttraumatic neurosis, including an investigation commissioned by the Veterans Administration.[74] This and other research led to the inclusion of PTSD in the American Psychiatric Association's diagnostic manual in 1980.[75]

Although much research had been done since *The Traumatic Neuroses of War*, the posttraumatic phenomenon is recognizably the same disorder outlined by Kardiner, and before him, Pierre Janet.[76] Most of its clinical features fall into three main categories: hyperarousal, intrusion, and constriction (e.g., numbing and avoidance).[77] According to the DSM-IV, hyperarousal includes:

> difficulty falling or staying asleep, irritability or outbursts of anger, difficulty concentrating, hypervigilence, and exaggerated startle response.

Intrusive symptoms include:

> recurrent and intrusive distressing recollections of the event,[78] including images, thoughts or perceptions; recurrent distressing dreams of the event;[79] acting or feeling as if the traumatic event were recurring (includes a sense of reliving the experience, illusions, hallucinations, and dissociative flashback episodes, including those that occur on awakening or when intoxicated);[80] intense psychological distress at exposure to internal or external cues that symbolize or resemble an aspect of the traumatic event, and physiological reactivity on exposure to internal or external cues that symbolize or resemble an aspect of the traumatic event.

Constriction includes:

> efforts to avoid thoughts, feelings, or conversations associated with the trauma; efforts to avoid activities, places or people that arouse recollections of the trauma; inability to recall an important aspect of the trauma; markedly diminished interest or participation in significant activities; feeling of detachment or estrangement from others; restricted range of affect (e.g., does not have loving feelings); sense of a foreshortened future (e.g., does not expect to have a career, marriage, children or a normal life span).[81]

PTSD, like hysteria, involved the disruption (through dissociation) of normal memory processes during the traumatic event. Memories could be present at inappropriate times in the form of intrusive thoughts, or memories might be lost or avoided.[82] Posttraumatic symptoms masked full awareness of the trauma, yet the survivor's symptoms made the traumatic past all too present.

### The Role of Feminism

Just as awareness of the traumatic neuroses of war was brought home by outspoken combat veterans, the prevalence and effects of domestic and sexual violence were made public by feminists in the 1960s and 1970s.[83] The feminist movement made inroads into the problems of violence against women through local organizations, grass-roots political action, and public education about the nature and effects of domestic and sexual violence. Women began to form "consciousness raising" groups in which they talked about traumatic experiences in a supportive and confidential environment. These groups provided support to individual participants who sought to develop a new understanding of violence against women, and who shared this new understanding with the public through political action.[84]

Judith Herman notes that the decades of the 1970s and 1980s brought a host of social and political changes including "speakouts" on rape, tribunals on crimes against women, and rape reform legislation. In 1971, feminists formed the first rape crisis center, and its success encouraged the formation of many others across the United States. Investigations into the problem of rape brought attention to other types of domestic and sexual violence, including CSA, and their psychological aftermath. In 1972, two researchers, Ann Burgess and Lynda Holmstrom, interviewed 92 women and 37 children rape victims and noted that "in the aftermath of rape, victims complained of insomnia, nausea, startle responses and nightmares, as well as dissociative or numbing symptoms," symptoms which resembled those described in studies of combat veterans.[85] Burgess and Holmstrom named this constellation of symptoms "rape trauma syndrome."[86] In the mid-1970s, feminists worked to redefine rape as a violent act, a necessary task given that rape was portrayed as a potentially fulfilling sexual experience at all levels of discourse, from "pornography to academic texts."[87] In 1975, the National Institute of Mental Health responded to feminist pressure by creating a center for rape research. The resulting studies revealed that children, as well as women, were victimized at an alarming rate and that both suffered lasting psychological damage as a result of the experience.[88]

The convergence of medical research and social awareness caused by feminists' efforts at public education provided a powerful catalyst for understanding the devastation caused by sexual trauma. The addition of PTSD to the DSM-III legitimated the posttraumatic psychological symptoms associated with combat neurosis, the modern study of which had built on Janet's nineteenth-century studies of hysteria. That the symptoms of combat neurosis were also present among survivors of sexual violence helped to legitimate the medicalization of posttraumatic neurosis in this population as well. Now, feminists and researchers could invoke the authority of the DSM-III to lend credence to syndromes such as the rape trauma syndrome. In the 1980s, researchers revisited the findings of the nineteenth-century work on hysteria, particularly that done by Janet and Freud prior to the retraction of the seduction theory, bringing more sophisticated methodology to bear on the same fields of inquiry.[89] The medical, social, and political environment in which these developments took place, meanwhile, created the seedbed in which innovative legal remedies for CSA would take root.

### *Studies on CSA and Traumatic Amnesia*

Numerous recent studies demonstrate a correlation between CSA and traumatic amnesia.[90] These studies indicate that a significant population of those sexually traumatized as children experience a period of partial or total amnesia for one or more episodes of CSA.[91] This "forgetting" seems to be correlated with the following:

1. more violent sexual abuse or sexual abuse coupled with physical abuse;
2. abuse which took place at an earlier age;
3. repeated acts of abuse; and
4. a close relationship to the abuser (for example, a family member instead of a stranger).

The studies also indicate that a significant portion of those who experience partial or total amnesia for the event recall it at a later date.[92] Independent corroboration of self-reported CSA histories were available for subjects in several of the studies.[93]

In their 1993 study, John Briere and Jon Conte noted that modern research affirmed the central tenet of Freud's retracted "seduction theory"; that is, "the role of childhood sexual trauma in the development of later symptomology."[94] They noted that CSA is relatively common, that "incidence rates in outpatient clinical populations may parallel those first reported by Freud in his clinical practice," and that

> such victimization has been associated with a variety of long-term impacts, including depression and anxiety, sexual problems, suicide attempts, somatization and dissociation; many of which would have been subsumed under Freud's original conception of hysteria.[95]

In Briere and Conte's study of 450 men and women who reported a history of CSA, 59.3% reported experiencing amnesia for their first molestation experience for a time before age 18.[96] This study found that the presence or fear of violence, younger age of victimization, and repeated instances of abuse were associated with amnesia.[97] Briere and Conte voiced concern that self-report might result in the underreporting of CSA, since CSA survivors might be amnesic.[98]

These findings are consistent with other studies of abused children. In 1987, Judith Herman and Emily Schatzow found that 64% of women with a history of CSA reported a period of partial or total amnesia of their abuse, associated with more violent episodes of abuse and younger age at the time of the abuse.[99] In 1994, Elizabeth Loftus, Sara Polonsky, and Mindy Thompson Fullilove found that 31% of their sample of 105 women in outpatient substance abuse treatment had experienced partial or total amnesia of their CSA history.[100] Also in 1994, Shirley Feldman-Summers and Kenneth Pope reported that 40% of their psychotherapist subjects who self-identified as survivors of physical or sexual abuse reported a period of partial or total amnesia of the abuse, corresponding to especially violent or frightening abuse.[101]

Despite the passage of many years between the actual abuse and the studies, external evidence corroborated the reported abuse memories of many subjects. In Herman and Schatzow's study, 74% of the subjects who could recall both abuse and a period of partial or total amnesia for the abuse were able to corroborate their memories with information from the perpetrator or family members (including siblings abused by the same perpetrator), or with physical evidence.[102] In Feldman-Summers and Pope's study, 47% reported some form of corroboration for the abuse memories.[103]

Williams' (1994) study investigated 129 women whose CSA was conclusively documented in the emergency room medical records of a public hospital, thereby avoiding the problem of retrospective corroboration. Seventeen years after their emergency medical treatment for injuries related to CSA, 12% of those interviewed reported that they were never abused in childhood, and 38% did not report the abuse that sent them to the hospital (the "index abuse").[104] Sixteen percent of those who reported the index abuse also reported experiencing a period of amnesia for the event.[105] Two additional findings suggest that amnesia, and not shame or some other factor, explains failure to report the index abuse. First, among those who did not report the index abuse, 35% reported other events of CSA perpetrated by family members. Second, there was no correlation between disclosing other very personal matters, such as previous abortions, prostitution, or contraction of sexually-transmitted diseases, suggesting that shame was not preventing disclosure.[106] The study also found a correlation of total amnesia with younger age at time of abuse, and with familiarity with the abuser.[107]

Williams' study also addressed the issue of false reporting of CSA. She noted that "the best research suggests that between 4% and 8% of reports of CSA today are fictitious."[108] To address that concern, she conducted further analysis of her subjects, restricting her analysis to girls who met two additional criteria: first, a record of medical evidence of genital trauma in the emergency room report, and second, documentation of being given the highest credibility rating (based on a four point, subjective interviewer rating scale) in the 1970s. Of the original 129 subjects, only 23 met both these criteria. "Interestingly," she notes,

> . . . in the 23 cases that meet this high standard for the validity of the original abuse allegation, over half (52%) of the women did not recall the abuse when interviewed in 1991-1992. This suggests that the .38 rate of no recall is not an inflated figure attributable to originally false or mistaken reports. Indeed, there was a tendency for the women who did not recall the abuse to have actual medical evidence of genital trauma (37% vs. 24%) and to have a high credibility rating (87% vs. 84%).[109]

The 52% rate of total amnesia for the abuse in these well-documented cases is striking, and again raises the concern over the underreporting of CSA due to amnesic victims.

While the common methodological hurdle of verifying the self-report of study subjects was not an issue for Williams, she did note that she was unable to address whether amnesia was more or less likely with repeated abuse.[110] Other research, however, indicates that a previously traumatized person may be more adept at dissociating than a person not previously traumatized. Dr. Lenore Terr, a clinical psychiatrist, suggests that at first the traumatized person somewhat actively "suppresses" memory of the traumatic event; if traumatic events continue to occur, the victim passively "suppresses" memory of the traumatic events, and they become "repressed."[111] In 1988, she studied 20 children whose traumatic experiences had been witnessed by police or other eyewitnesses. In this sample, she found that children who had experienced a stream of traumas prior to the "index trauma" were unlikely to remember the index trauma as accurately as those children whose first traumatic experience had been the index trauma.[112] The single event trauma, which Terr refers to as "Type I" childhood trauma, is thus more likely to result in vivid memories of the event. Type I memories may be suppressed but are not as likely to be completely repressed as is the case with repeated traumas. However, if a child is exposed to a stream of traumatic events, which Terr refers to as Type II childhood trauma, he or she becomes "well rehearsed in terror, a child prone to losing memory of an ordeal."[113] Bessel van der Kolk notes that in the DSM-IV field trials (1991), research showed that hypermesia (*i.e.*, intrusive thoughts, nightmares) was more common after one-time traumatic events, while "chronic amnesias tend to occur after repeated traumatization in childhood."[114] These studies corroborate Appel and Beebe's hypothesis that the length of exposure to trauma is the critical factor in the development of traumatic neurosis. The traumatized mind appears to adapt to repeated ordeals by employing defense mechanisms that prevent the events from being fully acknowledged.

### *The Psychobiology and Neuroscience of Posttraumatic Stress*

Recent psychobiological and neuroscientific research has found that specific trauma-related disruptions of the Central Nervous System (CNS) may provide a physiological explanation for traumatic memory loss and PTSD.[115,116] Building on over thirty years of research on the physiological response to overwhelming stress,[117] recent research has linked changes in two structures of the limbic system, the amygdala and the hippocampus, with PTSD symptoms.[118] Research indicates that the amygdala, which has been called an "emotional computer,"[119] is important in assigning meaning (especially fear and other negative emotions) to incoming sensory data. The hippocampus functions to classify that sensory data and its assigned emotional connotations by "comparing" it to previous experience.[120]

Language plays a critical role in this hippocampal classification. Bessel van der Kolk argues that the maturation of the CNS brings a shift in memory storage from "primarily sensorimotor (motoric action) and perceptual representations to symbolic and linguistic organization of mental experience."[121] This mature ability to represent memory in symbolic and linguistic forms, rather than those of sense and emotion, remains vulnerable to disruption under overwhelming psychological stress. The defensive response to such stress is not a loss of data recording, but a disruption of its normal process:

> [W]hen stress interferes with hippocampally mediated memory storage and categorization, some mental representation is probably laid down by means of a system that records affective experience but has no capacity for symbolic processing or placement in space and time.[122]

Thus, overwhelming stress appears to cause regression to a pre-verbal form of memory. Just as infantile amnesia is related to immaturity of the limbic system (particularly the hippocampus), argues psychologist Susan Reviere, traumatic amnesia is likely related to the trauma-related disruption of normal adult hippocampal functioning.[123] The emotions and sensory data of the traumatic experience are thereby dissociated from the process of linguistic classification that would translate the experience into a memory that could be recalled and recounted.[124] This failure to associate the traumatic experience with a particular space and time also predisposes the trauma survivor to "re-experiencing" the traumatic experience (in the form of PTSD-like symptoms) if presented with a "cue" reminiscent of the original traumatic experience.[125]

The peculiar way in which memories are encoded during periods of extreme stress, and their subsequent vulnerability to being triggered by reminiscent cues, may be mediated by the behavior of endogenous stress neurohormones.[126] Under extreme stress, the secretion of some neurohormones (such as oxytocin and endogenous opioids) inhibit memory consolidation and probably "play a role in creating the amnesias that are often seen in PTSD."[127] Such amnesia, numbing, or "stress-induced analgesia," which correlates highly with the victim's belief that the stressor is uncontrollable, appears to be a component of the dissociative response.[128] Other neurohormones (such as norepinephrine and vasopressin[129]) appear, conversely, to "overconsolidate" traumatic memories.[130] In the case of overconsolidation, the traumatized brain responds to cues of the original trauma with a proclivity to accessing memory "traces" of the trauma "at the expense of other memories, and to 'remember' the trauma whenever aroused."[131] Such "remembering" precipitates the physiological arousal associated with the original event, making the survivor feel as though they are re-experiencing the traumatic event. This psychological and physiological re-experiencing "re-kindles" and strengthens the memory trace, rendering the survivor more vulnerable to subsequent intrusive symptoms and hyperarousal, which in turn trigger further re-kindling.[132]

Despite intrusive symptoms, the trauma survivor may not be able to recall and recount the traumatic event due to trauma-related impairments in cognitive functioning and language production. Recent studies on combat veterans and CSA survivors have shown reduced hippocampal volume in subjects who experienced PTSD symptoms versus those subjects who did not.[133] Bessel van der Kolk notes that the cause of this size reduction is unclear; it is possible that a smaller hippocampus may predispose a person to PTSD, but van der Kolk believes that characteristically heightened levels of cortisol, known to be toxic to the hippocampus, may cause the reduction through dendrite atrophy or cell death.[134] Further, van der Kolk notes that previously traumatized subjects performed 40% worse on a test of verbal memory than did their peers of "comparable age and education."[135] Researchers have also used positron emission tomography (PET scans) to gain visual data of the autonomic responses associated with subjects' flashbacks of traumatic experiences. The researchers observed heightened activity in the part of the paralimbic system located in the right hemisphere and associated with the amygdalla, while Broca's area ("the part of the left hemisphere that is responsible for translating personal experiences into communicable language") appeared to be "turned off."[136] This is particularly interesting since, as van der Kolk notes, psychologists and neuroscientists generally agree that "whereas the left hemisphere is specialized for cognitive analysis and language production, the right hemisphere plays a central role in the perception and expression of emotion, particularly of negative emotion."[137] Thus, this research offers physiological explanations for the "speechless terror" associated with dissociation and may demonstrate a physiological inability in trauma survivors to translate sensory emotional memories into communicable language, even to themselves; they may, van der Kolk notes, quite literally be "out of touch with their feelings."[138]

Recent psychobiological and neuroscientific studies thus suggest physiological explanations for the view, well-accepted by the psychiatric and psychological communities, that there are different types of memory. What we usually think of as "remembering" is what the American Psychiatric Association (APA) refers to as "explicit" (or declarative) memory, which is the "ability to consciously recall facts or events."[139] Psychologist Daniel Brown and his co-authors note that such explicit (declarative) memory is the type that false memory or pseudomemory researchers study, in contrast with the traumatic memory associated with the limbic system.[140] Implicit (or procedural) memory refers to "behavioral knowledge of an experience without conscious recall."[141] To illustrate, the APA notes that implicit memory functions in demonstration of a skill without (explicit) recall of how one learned the skill (*e.g.*, bicycle riding), as well as in the case of the traumatic memory of, for example,

> an adult who has an affective reaction to an event without understanding the basis for that reaction (*e.g.*, a combat veteran who panics when he hears the sound of a helicopter, but cannot remember that he was in a helicopter crash which killed his best friend).[142]

In the case of overwhelming distress, it appears that dissociation separates the traumatic experience from conscious thought, rendering it an implicit memory.[143]

The explicit recollection of an implicit memory of a traumatic event appears to be highly state-dependent, requiring an effective interaction between the encoding and retrieval functions of memory.[144] Lenore Terr argues that the necessary conditions include both a "ground" and a "cue."[145] The "cue" is something reminiscent of the traumatic event. Many clients have described recalling memories of abuse upon the disclosure of a family member or friend abused by the same person, hearing about the abuse of others, going through major life transitions, and so on. The "ground" is a measure of psychological comfort, such as being out of the home of the abuser.

Given the conditions known to facilitate explicit recall, the criticism that psychotherapy implants false memories of abuse is problematic: if the therapist's office provides a measure of comfort, it is quite possible (and, given the current understanding of psychological healing, clinically desirable) that troublesome implicit memories *will* become explicit in the course of therapy. If Terr and others are correct about the "cueing" necessary for rendering implicit memories explicit, then inquiring about a possible history of abuse would seem a responsible and reasonable course. Allowing the patient to verbalize fragments of implicit memories in order to facilitate the language-based integration of traumatic memories thought to be key to diminishing symptoms seems, also, to be part and parcel of the professional function of psychotherapists who deal with the traumatized. The difficulty, of course, arises when newly explicit memories become part of a legal case. The problematic relationship of traumatic memory science and the legal realm are the subject of the next section.

### *Summary*

Since the middle of the nineteenth century, researchers have been interested in the human response to overwhelming stress, and a large body of scientific literature has developed from their investigations. Building on studies of hysteria and combat neurosis, modern researchers have employed empirical, psychobiological, and neuroscientific methodology to study the role of memory impairment in posttraumatic neurosis. These studies indicate that traumatic memory is qualitatively different from normal memory in its disruption of communications between encoding and retrieval functions of the CNS. When implicit traumatic memories exist, triggers reminiscent of the original trauma can precipitate debilitating symptoms without explicit memory for the cause. For explicit recall to occur, there must be a measure of psychological comfort as well as a cue. Yet given the psychological damage caused by trauma, the presence of explicit memories does not bring immediate relief; the liquidation of previously "fixed" or dissociated memories through the "talking cure," first recognized by Freud and Breuer, is often necessary for reducing the symptoms of PTSD.

The past century and a half of medical awareness of the correlation of trauma and neurosis has also been peppered with an explanatory dialectic; advances in the understanding of the lasting psychological effects of trauma have routinely been met with controversy and alternative explanations. These alternative explanations have traditionally focused on the role of fantasy and inherent flaws (such as cowardice, weakness, or biological inferiority) as the causes of neurosis. Such explanations were offered in the mid-nineteenth century, with Fournier's *pseudologica phantastica*, in the late-nineteenth and early twentieth century with Freud's substitution of "phantasy" for "premature seduction" in psychoanalysis, and with the allegations of cowardice against soldiers who broke down under the stress of warfare.

The recent advances in the science of delayed memory have met with the most dramatic social response to an increase in traumatic memory science yet. These scientific advances occurred in a social and political context in which concerns over the prevalence of child abuse has become a public policy issue, in which feminism has sensitized the public to the devastation caused by all-too-common sexual violence, and in which lawyers and legislators have been willing to employ innovative strategies to find legal redress for the victims of a type of violence previously considered too private for the state's intervention, despite its high social cost. In particular, delayed discovery statutes of limitations responded to new information about delayed memory by making legal remedies available to CSA survivors whose psychological injuries demand redress and whose previous lack of explicit recall prevented them from making an earlier claim against their abuser. That a new, albeit familiar, controversy should have met delayed memory litigation, then, should come as no surprise.[146]

## *TRAUMATIC MEMORY STUDIES AND THE LAW*

When traumatic memory studies entered the legal realm, defense lawyers and their experts responded by focusing on incompletely-answered questions in those studies. In effect, this strategy calls traumatic amnesia itself into question. It also works to change the substance of the lawsuit from an inquiry as to whether or not the plaintiff was abused, to debating the precise mechanisms by which "repression" occurs.[147] "False memory" experts raise the issues of suggestibility, the reliability of memories after a period of amnesia, and the veracity of self-report to discredit the plaintiff's allegations of abuse. The following sections explore how these issues align with the well-accepted stages of memory: encoding, storage, retrieval, and recounting.[148]

### *Encoding and Suggestibility: Was the Encoded Data "Experience" or "Fantasy?"*

Psychotherapy has been used successfully with trauma survivors for many decades. Recently, however, psychotherapists have come under fire for "implanting" memories of CSA that never occurred in unwitting patients by means of what false memory experts deem "highly suggestive" therapy techniques. False memory experts suggest that reading self-help books like *The Courage to Heal* and engaging in psychotherapy are "important sources" of false memories of CSA.[149] A number of third-party malpractice claims have been made against therapists for allegedly implanting false memories of CSA, often by the person accused of committing the abuse, although most courts do not permit such actions.[150]

Some studies used to support the suggestibility theory involve inaccuracies in "flashbulb" memory and the incorporation of erroneous details into explicit memory. Psychologist Daniel Brown and his coauthors explain that this represents a fundamental flaw in generalization on both counts. First, explicit memory is distinct from dissociated, implicit traumatic memory (even if the memory is of direct experience).[151] Second, flashbulb memory is not an implicit memory of a trauma experienced directly, but "rather an explicit memory for the otherwise incidental personal circumstances taking place in the individual's personal life at the time of hearing the shocking public news."[152] Unlike traumatic memory studies, most false memory studies involve observational, not direct, experience.[153] In one such study, Elizabeth Loftus demonstrated that laboratory subjects inaccurately reported peripheral details of a depiction of a filmed car accident after deliberately suggestive questioning.[154] In her article, "The Reality of Repressed Memories," Loftus cites other flashbulb memory studies of subjects' faulty recollections of hearing about the *Challenger* explosion,[155] the faulty memory of a baseball outfielder whose face was smashed by a baseball,[156] and the faulty memory of football spectators six years after observing a player suffer cardiac arrest on the field.[157] Interestingly, none of the subjects in the studies cited forgot that they had seen a film of a car accident, that *Challenger* had exploded, that they had been hit in the face with a baseball, or that a football player had fallen on the field, respectively. In that sense, their explicit memory for these events was good, but as Lenore Terr has commented, Loftus uses the phrase "false memory" to "describe a misreported detail within a memory. A grade of 'B – ' is an 'F,' as far as Loftus and a number of her fellow experimentalists are concerned."[158]

Loftus and others have sought to learn if it is possible not simply to change a peripheral detail in an explicit memory, but to induce the manufacturing of an entire memory for a traumatic event that did not occur. In one study, Loftus and Coan attempted to implant memories of a "traumatic" event in an adolescent boy, by directing his older brother to convince him that he had memories of a particular event of being lost in a mall at age five, although this event never occurred.[159] This one-subject study was offered as an indication that a "traumatic" memory can be implanted, despite the fact that getting lost in a shopping mall is hardly traumatic when compared to CSA or combat. Several years later, Loftus and Coan followed up this study with a five-person study in which each subject was insistently told by a trusted relative of an experience of being lost at age five; four of the five subjects acquired a false memory for the event.[160] These false memories of getting lost, along with false memories of other, more innocuous events (such as "touching one's toes or crossing one's arms"[161]) are seen by Robert Belli and Elizabeth Loftus as "[raising] questions about the veridicality of some reports of repressed sexual abuse memories 'recovered' through the assistance of a therapist or self-help guide."[162] "The experimental literature," they argue, "highlights the ease with which subjects can be encouraged to misattribute the source of their remembered experiences, so that events that were either suggested or imagined are remembered as having actually occurred."[163]

While these studies point out the pitfalls of suggestibility or "source misattribution" in explicit memory among some subjects, they do not shed light on traumatic memory. As Lenore Terr has argued, when these "false memories" do occur, they are not psychological traumas but "simply stories," unaccompanied by clinical characteristics of psychological trauma such as "returning perceptions, behavioral reenactment, trauma-specific fears, and futurelessness."[164] Daniel Brown and his collaborators note, similarly, that "the false memory position fails to take into consideration that traumatic memory is associated with psychobiological features and cognitive characteristics that are quite different from ordinary memory."[165] The author knows of no studies that indicate that memory for a traumatic event can be implanted with associated memory disruption and a host of psychological and physiological symptoms consistent with PTSD.[166] Given the important differences between normal autobiographical memory and traumatic memory, it is simply incorrect to theorize about the implantation of traumatic memories in the clinical setting from laboratory tests on a non-traumatized population.[167] As Jon Conte has commented, false memory science is not bad science as far as it goes, but it goes too far when it draws conclusions about delayed memories of trauma.[168]

### *Storage and Reliability: Are Delayed Memories Inherently Less Reliable?*

The author knows of no studies that demonstrate that memories recalled after a period of traumatic amnesia are less reliable than normal memories. Since memory–whether normal or delayed–undergrids the testimony of all victims and witnesses, it would seem that the issues surrounding the reliability of testimony in delayed recall sexual abuse cases would be similar to that in other types of litigation. It should be noted, however, that some courts have held that delayed memories are inseparable from the methods used to retrieve them. For example, in *State of New Hampshire v. Joel Hungerford* (1997), the court acknowledged the novelty of "treating the testimony of a percipient witness to a crime as scientific evidence," yet held that the court's role as "gatekeeper" of scientific evidence, not jury evaluation of the facts, was the proper method of evaluating recovered memory evidence.[169]

Lawyers handling delayed discovery cases must balance what is known about the reliability of delayed memories of trauma with practical legal considerations. Rather than demonstrating the unreliability of delayed traumatic memories, recent neuroscientific and psychobiological studies suggest that due to their "overconsolidation," traumatic memories may be especially lasting. Other studies of delayed traumatic memories are generally accurate for the central event but may be mistaken on peripheral details. Of course, the veracity of these peripheral details may become important to a legal case. In practice, lawyers must simultaneously respect the survivor's therapeutic sense of narrative truth (e.g., how the traumatic event affected the survivor psychologically) while gaining direct or indirect coroborative evidence of the historical truth of the traumatic event. Further, the lawyer should investigate the methods being used in the client's therapy. In some jurisdictions, testimony concerning any memory recalled after hypnosis is barred. These issues should be explored with the client early on, and clarity reached about the sometimes-conflicting roles of the lawyer and the therapist.[171]

### *Retrieval and Recounting: How Reliable Are Studies Based on Survivors' Self-Report?*

The ability to render an implicit traumatic memory explicit appears to be contingent on the successful interaction between the encoding and retrieval functions of memory. The ability of the subject of a scientific study to recount a memory accurately can be influenced by a number of variables, including partial or total amnesia, misunderstanding, embarrassment, fabrication, the "Hawthorne Effect" (the tendency of subjects to "tell researchers what they think investigators want to hear"[172]), and so on. Nonetheless, since it is impossible to traumatize children in order to prospectively study traumatic amnesia, investigators have often relied on retrospective, self-reported evidence. The questions raised by such a study are predictable: (1) Is the content of the memory actual experience or fantasy? (2) Can a memory be accurately recalled after years of amnesia? and (3) Is the report given by the subject accurate? The first two questions have been addressed, but the accuracy of self-report requires attention.

False memory studies assert that false memories arise from suggestive questioning and heavy-handed therapeutic techniques, and lead to inaccurate reporting of abuse and false accusations.[173] The brochure of the FMSF claims that "false memory syndrome" is "a condition . . . centered around a memory of traumatic experience which is objectively false but in which the person strongly believes."[174] False memory advocates have pointed to recanters of CSA allegations as evidence of this phenomenon. In one study of the development of "pseudomemories," subjects were interviewed about the development of the memories they later retracted.[175] The researchers found that many of these memories defied credibility (e.g., those for molestations that occurred prior to birth or during infancy) and that questionable therapeutic practices were used to elicit these memories.[176] Interestingly, the authors comment that many of these recanters had "experienced molestation or abuse as well as pseudomemories of sexual abuse," although the study does not reveal the means by which the researchers discerned one from the other.[177]

Given the methodological problems with self-report, it is impossible to know what, precisely, recanters are recanting. A "false memory?" A deliberate fabrication? Or, perhaps, a real memory? The APA cautions that retractions are not uncommon in cases where abuse actually did occur.[178] Additionally, the bad therapist/implanted memory hypothesis may offer the survivor an alternative, potentially less upsetting explanation for memories of incest or CSA by placing blame on his or her therapist.

The methodological issues that call self-report into question require that the lawyer handling a delayed discovery CSA case conduct a thorough investigation in order to gain direct or indirect corroboration of their client's self-report and to rule out questionable therapy.[179] Lawyers must be familiar with the scientific literature on traumatic neurosis and memory, and must also be careful about asking leading questions that might contaminate the client's answers.[180] These precautions, however, should not overshadow knowledge of the significant underreporting of CSA. They should also not suggest that the self-report of CSA survivors is less reliable than that of other plaintiffs or that competent therapy is incompatible with the litigation process. Indeed, one study has demonstrated that CSA memories recalled in therapy are as accurate as CSA memories that had never been forgotten.[181] Rather, the issues raised by the reliability of self-report serve here as a reminder that, in delayed discovery cases as in any other type of legal case, the lawyer must work to discern and verify the credibility of her client as well as considering the possibility of another explanation of the events that led the client to her office.

### *The Language of Silence: Semantic and Cultural Issues*

The way in which language is used by false memory experts may seem to be an esoteric issue, but its ability to confuse key issues should not be underestimated. Words such as "memory," "scientific," and "repression" can be used to mean very different things. Most confusing of all, the "symptoms" of "false memory syndrome" might be mistaken for PTSD, but for the false memory expert's assertion that the source of these symptoms is fantasy.

The word "memory" is clearly key to the "false memory" controversy. Very often, no distinction is drawn between traumatic memory and "normal" (explicit) memory. Generalizing the conclusions drawn from laboratory studies on "normal" memory to advance speculations about the reliability of traumatic memory is flawed. It is scientifically incorrect and very misleading to generalize conclusions about one type of memory to a very different type while ignoring fundamental differences between the two.

The argument that there is no cogent "scientific" evidence for repression betrays a bias against the clinical, retrospective methodology generally used by traumatic memory researchers. Clearly, traumatic memory cannot be studied in a prospective, laboratory fashion; one cannot traumatize humans in order to study their psychological response. However, history has provided more than enough traumatized subjects for study, the vast majority of which have had nothing to do with the so-called "recovered memory movement."

The quantity and diversity of traumatic memory studies renders problematic false memory experts' focused use of the word "repression." As a result of the long and varied history of scientific literature on the psychological response to trauma, a confusing professional jargon has emerged, reflecting the distinct subjects and disciplinary differences of researchers in this area (e.g., hysteria, combat fatigue, repression, dissociation, PTSD, etc.).[182] Different terminology has been used by various researchers with respect to different kinds of trauma, and sometimes, the same word has been used to mean different things. The word "repression" is particularly fraught with confusion. Freud's use of the term, for example, ranged from signifying an involuntary dissociation of a memory for traumatic experience during the experience, to a conscious "pushing away" of a traumatic experience after the experience, to a defense against forbidden desires, emotions, and thoughts.[183] Currently, "repression" may be defined as semi-unconscious blocking of external experience,[184] although most researchers use the terms "dissociation," "psychogenic amnesia," or "PTSD."[185] This seems academic only until one notes that the "no cogent scientific evidence for repression" argument forwarded by false memory advocates rests on the fact that "dissociation" and

"PTSD" are the terms preferentially used in traumatic memory literature. Further, while "repression" is not as scientifically meaningful (given its wide variety of meanings) as other, more specific terms for traumatic memory loss, it is culturally meaningful due to the popularization of psychoanalytic theory and legally meaningful due to the use of the term in delayed discovery statutes of limitations.[186] By choosing the word "repression," false memory experts respond to the statutory language implicit in delayed discovery cases, as well as engaging in a "semantic sidestep" of over a century of scientific evidence of psychogenic amnesia, dissociation, and PTSD.[187]

Perhaps the most confusing issue is the parallel between the symptoms of PTSD and "false memory syndrome." "False memory syndrome" is, according to False Memory Syndrome Foundation literature, a condition characterized by preoccupation with the idea that one has been abused, an unwillingness to discuss anything that might contradict this hypothesis with the alleged abuser, and impaired ability to function because of this chronic concern with the fantasized abuse. This "syndrome" is allegedly a common product of therapy and self-help books.[188] Interestingly, these symptoms mimic the DSM-IV description of PTSD. Intrusive thoughts about the trauma, avoidance of reminders of the abuse (including persons who inflicted or facilitated the abuse), and psychological injuries (often leading the sufferer to seek help from therapy and self-help texts) are common elements of PTSD.

### *Summary*

"False memory syndrome" offers an alternative explanation for the delayed memories of CSA. False memory advocates suggest that the sensory data encoded by the survivor is fantasy, not traumatic experience. They attack the reliability of delayed memories by arguing that because we do not understand precisely how an implicit memory becomes explicit after a period of amnesia, the resulting explicit memory cannot be trusted. While lawyers should conduct investigation to locate corroborative evidence of memories and must be aware of the type of therapy in which their client has been and is engaged, they should also be aware that the most serious demonstrable problem with relying on the self-report of CSA survivors is the fact that amnesia probably contributes to under-reporting of CSA, rather than an epidemic of objectively false but strongly believed allegations. False memory strategies follow the Freudian rejection of productive ambiguity in traumatic memory science in favor of affirmative denial, and engage semantic strategies to obscure over a century of trauma studies to support this position. "False memory syndrome" is a culturally appealing alternative to the reality of CSA, especially as it invokes such familiar ideas as psychoanalytic repression and fantasy. This goes a long way to explain why a "syndrome" not recognized by the mental health profession is so popular as a legal defense and in the popular media.

## *CONCLUSION: THE CRUCIAL ROLE OF THE LEGAL SYSTEM*

A century ago, William James believed that a scientific understanding of hysteria would be followed by appropriate philanthropic social action. In reality, however, social responses to the hysteria problem required more than enlightened philanthropy. They required the convergence of a developing medical understanding of posttraumatic neurosis, a feminist analysis of the politics of sexual trauma, and grass roots political efforts beginning in the 1960s and continuing to the present. While researchers have employed modern methodology to study the link between CSA and neurosis, survivors, activists, legislators, and lawyers have taken political action to redress and ameliorate the devastating psychological and social problems caused by CSA.

Yet this philanthropic conquest is not secure. While legal remedies have helped to define CSA as a public problem, defense lawyers and their experts have used scientific uncertainty and inapplicable research to cast doubt on the well-established phenomenon of trauma-related memory loss. The memory debate has spread from the courtroom to the mass media, where sensational cases distract attention from the realities of CSA. The APA voiced concern that "the passionate debates about [delayed memories of CSA] have obscured the recognition of a body of scientific evidence that underlies widespread agreement among psychiatrists regarding psychiatric treatment in this area."[189] They also expressed hope that "the public confusion and dismay over this issue and the possibility of false accusations not discredit the reports of patients who have indeed been traumatized by actual previous abuse."[190] While lawyers investigating CSA allegations must of course consider the possibility of false accusations, wholesale discrediting of those with delayed memories of CSA must be protested.

Active, informed, and responsible legal advocacy is essential to raising the public awareness of CSA so crucial to solidifying positive social change. Familiarity with the developing scientific literature on traumatic memory and PTSD is crucial to effective advocacy, as is awareness of the cultural and historical context of the "false memory" debate. Recent studies have illuminated the link between childhood trauma and adult mental illness in ways that call for social and political change. The laws that have, however imperfectly, worked to actively respond to this new awareness, have challenged cultural norms in far-reaching and profound ways. In such a contentious environment, legal advocates for CSA survivors play a key role not only in helping redress the injuries of the past, but also in ensuring that the reality of CSA is not hidden from the public sphere once again by a polarized political debate over the science of traumatic memories.

## NOTES

1. William James in *Review of Janet's Essays, 'L'etat mental des hysteriques' and 'L'amnesie continue,'* PSYCHOLOGICAL REVIEW 1 (1894) 195, cited in JUDITH HERMAN, TRAUMA AND RECOVERY: THE AFTERMATH OF VIOLENCE–FROM DOMESTIC VIOLENCE TO POLITICAL TERROR (New York: Basic Books, 1992) 16.

2. While the word "hysteria" has become pejorative, the symptoms of hysteria, combat fatigue, and other posttraumatic syndromes are largely the same.

3. In this chapter, I have followed the lead of other writers in abbreviating Childhood Sexual Abuse as CSA (thereby sacrificing the nineteenth-century language of "seduction" and "debauchery" for the sake of clarity and brevity) and Posttraumatic Stress Disorder as PTSD. Psychoanalysis is a kind of psychotherapy originating in the work of Sigmund Freud, while psychotherapy may draw on many different schools of psychological thought (*i.e.*, behaviorist, psychodynamic, cognitive, and so forth). False Memory Syndrome (FMS) is a name coined by the False Memory Syndrome Foundation (FMSF), an advocacy group for people accused of committing acts of CSA. FMS studies may also be called "pseudomemory" studies.

4. See BARBARA J. NELSON, MAKING AN ISSUE OF CHILD ABUSE: POLITICAL AGENDA SETTING FOR SOCIAL PROBLEMS (Chicago: The University of Chicago Press, 1984).

5. See H.L.A. Hart, *Law as the Union of Primary and Secondary Rules*, THE NATURE OF LAW: READINGS IN LEGAL PHILOSOPHY, (M. P. Golding, ed., New York: Random House, 1966) 144-160.

6. Elizabeth Loftus explains this in the "Jurors' Reactions to Repressed Memory Cases" section of her article, *The Reality of Repressed Memories*: "How do

people in general and jurors in particular react to repressed memory cases? Are memories that were once previously repressed as credible as memories that were never repressed? Understanding laypeople's reactions and credibility judgment is important not only for theoretical reasons but for practical ones as well. Theoretically speaking, laypeople's implicit or intuitive theories about repressed memories guide society's thinking on this topic." *The Reality of Repressed Memories*, 48 AMERICAN PSYCHOLOGIST 5, 522, 518-537 (1993).

7. Defined by John F. Kihlstrom in FMS Foundation Brochure, Philadelphia, PA. (1994) Lenore Terr notes that the False Memory Syndrome Foundation, a political advocacy group, has "garnered so much publicity for [its] cause that this cause is being confused today with a diagnosis . . . There is no such disorder. It is just a name taken by an organization representing parents, uncles, grandfathers, and siblings who believe they have been falsely accused." LENORE TERR, UNCHAINED MEMORIES (New York: Basic Books, 1994) 164.

8. For discussion and analysis of the "false memory" controversy, see DANIEL BROWN, ALAN W. SCHEFLIN & D. CORYDON HAMMOND, *The False Memory Debate* and *the Contours of the False Memory Controversy*, MEMORY, TRAUMA TREATMENT, AND THE LAW (New York: W.W. Norton & Company, 1998) 43.

9. For extensive treatments of studies on the psychological aftermath of trauma (including memory disruption), *see* BESSEL A. VAN DER KOLK, ALEXANDER C. MCFARLANE & LARS WEISAETH, eds., TRAUMATIC STRESS: THE EFFECTS OF OVERWHELMING EXPERIENCE ON MIND, BODY, AND SOCIETY (New York: The Guilford Press, 1996); DANIEL BROWN, ALAN W. SCHEFLIN & D. CORYDON HAMMOND, *The Nature of Memory* and *Trauma Memory* in MEMORY, TRAUMA TREATMENT, AND THE LAW, *supra*; Alan W. Scheflin & Daniel Brown, *Repressed Memory or Dissociative Amnesia: What the Science Says*, THE JOURNAL OF PSYCHIATRY AND THE LAW (Summer, 1996) 143-188; Arieh Y. Shalev, *Acute to Chronic: Etiology and Pathophysiology of PTSD–A Biopsychological Approach* and Steven M. Southwick, Rachel Yehuda & Dennis S. Charney, *Neurobiological Alterations in PTSD: Review of the Clinical Literature*, in POSTTRAUMATIC STRESS DISORDER: ACUTE AND LONG TERM RESPONSE TO TRAUMA AND DISASTER (Washington D.C.: American Psychiatric Press, 1997); Peter Brown, *Toward a Psychobiological Model of Dissociation and Post-Traumatic Stress Disorder*, DISSOCIATION: CLINICAL AND THEORETICAL PERSPECTIVES Steven Jay Lynn & Judith W. Rhue, Eds., (New York: The Guilford Press, 1994); 94-122 (SUSAN L. REVIERE, MEMORY OF CHILDHOOD TRAUMA: A CLINICIAN'S GUIDE TO THE LITERATURE (New York: The Guilford Press, 1996); KENNETH S. POPE & LAURA S. BROWN, RECOVERED MEMORIES OF ABUSE: ASSESSMENT, THERAPY, FORENSICS (Washington D. C.: American Psychological Association, 1996); LINDA M. WILLIAMS & VICTORIA L. BARYARD, eds. TRAUMA AND MEMORY (Thousand Oaks, CA: Sage Publications, 1999). *See also*, DIAGNOSTIC AND STATISTICAL MANUAL OF MENTAL DISORDERS, FOURTH EDITION (DSM-IV) (Washington, D.C., American Psychiatric Association, 1994).

10. For reviews of scientific literature that address memory loss or disruption as a result of traumatic experience, *see* VAN DER KOLK, MCFARLANE & WEISAETH, TRAUMATIC STRESS: THE EFFECTS OF OVERWHELMING EXPERIENCE ON MIND, BODY, AND SOCIETY, *supra*; BROWN, SCHEFLIN & HAMMOND, *The Nature of Memory* and *Trauma Memory* in MEMORY, TRAUMA TREATMENT, AND THE LAW, *supra*; Scheflin & Brown, *Repressed Memory or Dissociative Amnesia: What the Science Says, supra*; Shalev, *Acute to Chronic: Etiology and Pathophysiology of PTSD–A Biopsychological Approach* and Southwick, Yehuda & Charney, *Neurobiological Alterations in PTSD: Review of the Clinical Literature*, in POSTTRAUMATIC STRESS DISORDER: ACUTE AND LONG TERM RESPONSE TO TRAUMA AND DISASTER, *supra*; Brown, *Toward a Psychobiological Model of Dissociation and Post-Traumatic Stress Disorder*, DISSOCIATION: CLINICAL AND THEORETICAL PERSPECTIVES, *supra*; REVIERE, MEMORY OF CHILDHOOD TRAUMA: A CLINICIAN'S GUIDE TO THE LITERATURE, *supra*; POPE & BROWN, RECOVERED MEMORIES OF ABUSE: ASSESSMENT, THERAPY, FORENSICS, *supra*; WILLIAMS & BARYARD, TRAUMA AND MEMORY, *supra*. *See also*, DIAGNOSTIC AND STATISTICAL MANUAL OF MENTAL DISORDERS, FOURTH EDITION (DSM-IV), *supra*.

11. For reviews of scientific literature that address the physiological underpinnings of traumatic forgetting, *see* Bessel van der Kolk, *The Body Keeps the Score: Approaches to the Psychobiology of Posttraumatic Stress Disorder* and *Trauma and Memory* in TRAUMATIC STRESS, *supra*; Bessel A. van der Kolk, *The Body Keeps the Score: Memory and the Evolving Psychobiology of Posttraumatic Stress*, HARVARD REVIEW OF PSYCHIATRY 1 (1994), 1253-65; van der Kolk and van der Hart, *The Intrusive Past: The Flexibility of Memory and the Engraving of Trauma*, 48 AMERICAN IMAGO 4 (1991), 425-454; BROWN, SCHEFLIN & HAMMOND, *The Nature of Memory* and *Trauma Memory* in MEMORY, TRAUMA TREATMENT, AND THE LAW, *supra*, esp. pp. 91-97; Brown, *Toward a Psychobiological Model of Dissociation and Post-Traumatic Stress Disorder, supra*; Reviere, *Neurophysiological Substrates of Traumatic Memory*, in MEMORY OF CHILDHOOD TRAUMA, *supra*, 85-95.

12. For useful histories of traumatic memory studies, *see*, HERMAN, *supra*; Erna Olafson, David Corwin & Roland Summit, *Modern History of Child Sexual Abuse Awareness: Cycles of Discovery and Suppression*, CHILD ABUSE & NEGLECT 17 (1993)7-24; Bessel A. van der Kolk, Lars Weisaeth & Onno van der Hart, *History of Trauma in Psychiatry*, 47-74 in TRAUMATIC STRESS, *supra*; WILLIAM J. MCGRATH, FREUD'S DISCOVERY OF PSYCHOANALYSIS: THE POLITICS OF HYSTERIA (Ithaca: Cornell University Press, 1986); Michael L. Trimble, *Post-Traumatic Stress Disorder: History of a Concept*, TRAUMA AND ITS WAKE: THE STUDY AND TREATMENT OF POST-TRAUMATIC STRESS DISORDER (Charles R. Figley, ed., New York: Brunner/Mazel, Publishers, 1985).

13. John Briere in his debate with Elizabeth Loftus at the 101st Annual Convention of the American Psychological Association in Toronto, Ontario, Canada (August, 1993), cited in David Harrison, Barbara Jo Levy, Michael S. Morey, Sherry A. Quirk, Rebecca A. Rix & Anne P. DePrince, *Childhood Sexual Abuse: The Plaintiff's Perspective*, 2 SHEPARD'S EXPERT AND SCIENTIFIC EVIDENCE QUAR-

TERLY 2 (Fall 1994) 405, 399-415. THE COURAGE TO HEAL is a self-help book for CSA survivors by Ellen Bass and Laura Davis and frequently has been the target of FMSF criticism. ELLEN BASS & LAURA DAVIS, THE COURAGE TO HEAL (New York: Harper & Row, 1988).

14. *See* HERMAN, *supra*, 10.

15. WEBSTER'S NEW TWENTIETH CENTURY DICTIONARY OF THE ENGLISH LANGUAGE UNABRIDGED, 2nd ed. (New York: The World Publishing Company, New York: 1971).

16. Olafson, Corwin & Summit note that in eighteenth century London, it was believed by some that sexual congress with a child would cure venereal disease. Between 1730 and 1789, 25% of capital rape prosecutions at the Old Bailey involved victims younger than 10. Tardieu reported a similar French superstition a century later; in France, between 1858 and 1869, three quarters of those charged with rape were accused of raping children. *See* Olafson, Corwin & Summit, *supra*, 8.

17. *See id.* 10.

18. See van der Kolk, Weisaeth & van der Hart, supra, 49.

19. *See id.* 49.

20. *See* Olafson, Corwin & Summit, *supra*, 10.

21. Roland Summit, *Hidden Victims, Hidden Pain: Societal Avoidance of Child Sexual Abuse*, in LASTING EFFECTS OF CHILD SEXUAL ABUSE (Newbury Park: Sage Publications, 1988). 39-61, 45.

22. *See id.* 46.

23. *See* HERMAN, *supra*, 9.

24. *See* HERMAN, *supra*, 15.

25. *See id.* 10.

26. Sigmund Freud noted that Charcot "threw the whole weight of his authority on the side of the genuineness and objectivity of hysterical phenomenon" in his essay *Charcot* (1893), cited in HERMAN, *supra*, 11.

27. *See id.* 11.

28. *See id.* 11.

29. *See id.* 11-12.

30. *See id.* 12.

31. This patient was Anna O. (*See* HERMAN, *supra*, 12-13) The early theorists discovered the key role of language in liquidating the "fixed ideas" of traumatic memory. As psychiatrist and researcher Bessel van der Kolk explains, "Traumatic memories are the unassimilated scraps of overwhelming experiences, which need to be integrated with existing mental schemes, and transformed into narrative language. It appears that, in order for this to occur successfully, the traumatized person has to return to the memory often in order to complete it." See van der Kolk & van der Hart, *The Intrusive Past, supra*, 447.

32. Sigmund Freud in *The Aetiology of Hysteria* (1896), cited in HERMAN, *supra, 13*. Freud analyzed eighteen cases of hysteria to come to this conclusion and was "able to discover this connection in every single symptom, and, where the circumstances allowed, to confirm it by therapeutic success . . . these eighteen cases are at the same time all the cases on which I have been able to carry out the work of analysis . . . I therefore put forth the thesis that at the bottom of every case of hysteria there

are one or more occurrences of premature sexual experience (seduction)." Jeffrey Masson, *Freud and the Seduction Theory*, THE ATLANTIC MONTHLY, February 1984 46, 33-60.

33. *See* Olafson, Corwin & Summit, *supra*, 10.

34. William McGrath notes Charcot's belief that certain ethnic groups were mentally inferior and predisposed to hysteria. McGrath further explains that German psychiatrists held an organic origins theory of nervous disease, which emphasized racial and ethnic "degeneracy," which, more than any "supposed puritanism on the part of the medical establishment," explains their resistance to the sexual abuse origins of hysteria. Simply stated, they "regarded hysteria as an 'un-Germanic' disease." *See* MCGRATH, *supra*, 161-162.

35. "All the strange conditions under which the incongruous pair continue their love relations–on the one hand the adult, who cannot escape his share in the mutual dependence necessarily entailed by a sexual relationship, and who is at the same time armed with complete authority and the right to punish, and can exchange the one role for the other to the uninhibited satisfaction of his whims, and on the other hand the child, who in his helplessness is at the mercy of this arbitrary use of power, who is prematurely aroused to every sort of sensibility and exposed to every sort of disappointment, and whose exercise of the sexual performances assigned to him is often interrupted by his imperfect control of his natural needs–all these grotesque and yet tragic disparities mark the later development of the individual and of his neurosis, with countless permanent effects which deserve to be traced in the greatest detail." Sigmund Freud in *The Etiology of Hysteria*, cited in Masson, *supra*, 35.

36. Freud argued that "the behavior of patients while they are reproducing these infantile experiences is in every respect incompatible with the assumption that the scenes are anything else than a reality which is being felt with distress and remembered with the greatest reluctance." Quoted in Masson, *supra*, 35.

37. *See* Olafson, Corwin & Summit, *supra*, 10.

38. *See id.* 11. This is borne out by recent studies which indicate the prevalence of sexual abuse in girls is higher than that of boys. 16 to 34% of girls to 10 to 20% of boys are abused by a family member or trusted friend, according to VIOLENCE AND THE FAMILY: REPORT OF THE AMERICAN PSYCHOLOGICAL ASSOCIATION PRESIDENTIAL TASK FORCE ON VIOLENCE AND THE FAMILY (Washington, D.C.: American Psychological Association, 1996) 11.

39. *See* HERMAN, *supra*, at 14 and Olafson, Corwin & Summit, *supra*, 11.

40. Not long after giving his paper before the society, he wrote Wilhelm Fliess: "A lecture on the etiology of hysteria at the Psychiatric Society met with an icy reception from the asses, and from Krafft-Ebbing [the professor and head of the Department of Psychiatry at the University of Vienna] the strange comment: It sounds like a scientific fairy tale. And this after one has demonstrated to them a solution to a more-than-thousand-year-old problem, a 'source of the Nile!'" Excerpted in Masson, *supra*, at 35.

41. *See* Masson, *supra*, 36.

42. *See* MCGRATH, *supra*, 185.

43. *See id.* 186.

44. *See id.* 186.

45. *See id.* 175-187.

46. *See* id. 217.

47. Repression referred to a process whereby an individual actively pushed unacceptable wishes from consciousness. *See* van der Kolk and van der Hart, *The Intrusive Past, supra*, 437.

48. According to the American Psychiatric Association, retraction is not a fail-safe indication that abuse did not occur; "recanting following the report can occur in victims of documented abuse." *APA Issues Statement on Memories of Sexual Abuse*, PSYCHIATRIC TIMES, February 1994, 26.

49. *See* MCGRATH, *supra*, 230.

50. Freud's library included books by medical writers on both sides of the French debate over children's reports of sexual abuse. *See* Olafson, Corwin & Summit, *supra*, 10.

51. In this letter, Freud enumerated four reasons for abandoning the seduction theory, since Fliess found the theory credible and would, Freud noted, probably not find the retraction "intelligible without an explanation." After listing them, he noted that his "continual disappointment" with gaining a "complete resolution of a neurosis and the certain knowledge of its etiology in childhood" were key to his retraction of his theory. First, he was frustrated by the lack of "complete successes on which [he] had counted as well as the possibility of explaining . .. the partial successes in other ways, in the usual fashion." Second, he was shocked at the high incidence of paternal perversion implied by the "unexpected frequency of hysteria." Third, he noted the impossibility of distinguishing "between truth and fiction that has been cathected with affect." Fourth, he noted that "even in the most deep-reaching psychosis the unconscious memory does not break through, so that the secret of the childhood experiences is not disclosed even in the most confused delirium. If one thus sees that the unconscious never overcomes the resistance of the conscious, the expectation that in treatment the opposite is bound to happen to the point where the unconscious is completely tamed by the conscious also diminishes." Freud's ambitions for a complete and comprehensive theory of neurosis thus foundered on the issues of clinical frustration, his disbelief about the prevalence of "premature seduction," the problem of discerning truth in a patient's self-report, and what appears to be his unwieldy generalization of his etiology theory to a broad range of mental disorders. Freud quoted in Masson, *supra*, 53.

52. *See id.* 53.

53. Jeffrey Masson, the former provisional projects director at the Freud Archives, published previously unpublished letters and writing of Sigmund Freud in the 1980s against the wishes of Anna Freud. He argues that Ernst Jones, Freud's biographer and Anna Freud had been careful to present and preserve a tradition of Freud as consistent and confident about the foundations of psychoanalysis by careful editing of his writings. *See id.* 34.

54. As was the case with Saldor Ferenczi. *See* Olafson, Corwin & Summit, *supra*, 11-12.

55. Letter from Anna Freud to Jeffrey Masson, September 10, 1981, cited in Masson, *supra*, 59.

56. Pierre Janet in PSYCHOLOGICAL HEALING (1919), cited in HERMAN, *supra*, 37.

57. Janet cited in HERMAN, *supra*, 37.

58. *See* van der Kolk and van der Hart, *The Intrusive Past, supra,* 426.

59. *See id.* 426.

60. *See, e.g.*, Bessel van der Kolk, *The Body Keeps the Score: Approaches to the Psychobiology of Posttraumatic Stress Disorder* and *Trauma and Memory* in TRAUMATIC STRESS, *supra*; Bessel A. van der Kolk, *The Body Keeps the Score: Memory and the Evolving Psychobiology of Posttraumatic Stress, supra*; van der Kolk and van der Hart, *The Intrusive Past, supra;* BROWN, SCHEFLIN & HAMMOND, *The Nature of Memory* and *Trauma Memory* in MEMORY, TRAUMA TREATMENT, AND THE LAW, *supra,* esp. pp. 91-97; Brown, *Toward a Psychobiological Model of Dissociation and Post-Traumatic Stress Disorder, supra;* Reviere, *Neurophysiological Substrates of Traumatic Memory,* in MEMORY OF CHILDHOOD TRAUMA, *supra,* 85-95.

61. *See* Trimble, *supra,* 7-8.

62. *See* HERMAN, *supra,* 20-21.

63. *See id.* 20.

64. *See* van der Kolk, Weisaeth & van der Hart, *supra,* 48.

65. *See* Trimble, *supra,* 7-8.

66. J. W. Appel, and G. W. Beebe in *Preventive Psychiatry: An Epidemiological Approach,* JOURNAL OF THE AMERICAN MEDICAL ASSOCIATION 131 (1946), 1468-71, 1470, cited in HERMAN, *supra,* 25.

67. *See* HERMAN, *supra,* at 22-23; Bessel A. van der Kolk, *The Body Keeps the Score: Memory and the Evolving Psychobiology of Posttraumatic Stress, supra,* 1254.

68. *See id.* 1254 ("Starting with Kardiner and closely followed by Lindmann, a vast literature on combat trauma, crimes, rape, kidnapping, natural disasters, accident and imprisonment has shown that the trauma response is bimodal: hypermnesia, hyperreactivity to stimuli, and traumatic re-experiencing coexist with psychic numbing, avoidance, amnesia and anhedonia. These responses to extreme experiences are so consistent across the different forms of traumatic stimuli that this bimodal reaction appears to be the normative response to any overwhelming and uncontrollable experience.")

69. Kardiner observed that "[w]hen the word 'hysterical' . . . is used, its social meaning is that the subject is a predatory individual, trying to get something for nothing. The victim of such a neurosis is, therefore, without sympathy in court, and . . . without sympathy from his physicians, who often take . . . 'hysterical' to mean that the individual is suffering from some persistent form of wickedness, perversity, or weakness of will." *See* HERMAN, *supra,* 24.

70. *See id.* 24.

71. *See id.* 24.

72. *See id.* 25. Hypnosis and amytal are recognized as "specialized interview techniques" by the American Psychological Association in their statement on memories on sexual abuse, which require special knowledge and experience on the part of the clinician who administers them. *See* APA, *Statement on Memories of Sexual*

*Abuse, supra,* at 26. While they are recognized by the medical and psychological profession as useful in treating the sexual abuse survivor by gaining access to traumatic memories, these modalities may create complications for the legal case, depending on jurisdiction. These practices will likely be attacked as inherently suggestive techniques by the defense, and some legal jurisdictions memories bar the testimony of memories recalled under hypnosis.

73. *See* HERMAN, *supra,* 27.

74. *See id.* 27.

75. *See id.* 27. PTSD was included for the first time in the 1980 edition of the American Psychiatric Association's DIAGNOSTIC AND STATISTICAL MANUAL OF MENTAL DISORDERS, THIRD EDITION (DSM-III) (Washington, D.C.: American Psychiatric Association, 1980).

76. Kardiner and Spiegel in WAR, STRESS, case 40, 381-89, cited in HERMAN, *supra,* 28.

77. *See* DIAGNOSTIC AND STATISTICAL MANUAL OF MENTAL DISORDERS, FOURTH EDITION (DSM-IV) (Washington, D.C.: American Psychiatric Association, 1994), 428. *See also,* HERMAN, *supra,* 35.

78. The DSM-IV notes that in the case of children, "repetitive play may occur in which themes or aspects of the trauma are expressed." DSM-IV, 428. Some investigators have posited a dual system of "behavioral memory" and "verbal or narrative autobiographical memory." Behavioral memory is an early development of the brain, while verbal autobiographical memory is associated with the maturing brain. In short, children do not have the same verbal capacities with regard to memory, and their memories are "expressed primarily in the form of behavioral reenactment and imagery." *See also* BROWN, SCHEFLIN & HAMMOND, *supra,* 89.

79. In the case of children, "there may be frightening dreams without recognizable content." DSM-IV, 428.

80. The DSM-IV notes that in the case of young children, "trauma-specific reenactment may occur." DSM-IV, 428. *See also* footnote 78 herein.

81. It should be noted that there are specific indications in the DSM-IV relative to diagnosis of PTSD and other dissociative disorders. This is intended as an overview only; the reader is referred to both the DSM-IV and to experts in the mental health sciences.

82. Such memory loss has been reported between 8.6 to 39% for veterans in various studies. *See* BROWN, SCHEFLIN & HAMMOND, *supra,* at 156, as well as studies related to sexual abuse in the next section of this chapter.

83. When the Seattle lawyer Barbara Jo Levy took her first sexual abuse case in 1980 (defendant was the father of 19-year-old plaintiff, and admitted the abuse), the doctrine of parental immunity still stood: children were effectively considered chattel of their fathers. (Wives were also effectively considered chattel of their husbands.) A 1905 case (*Roller v. Roller*) still controlled Washington state law on incest, asserting the state's duty to "preserving harmony in domestic relations" by denying a child the "right to appear in court in the assertion of a claim to civil redress for injuries suffered at the hands of the parents." There were no cases in which adults had brought cases against their parents in the civil arena, demonstrating recent and revolutionary nature of delayed discovery legislation and litigation. *See* Barbara Jo Levy, *Legal Is-*

*sues Facing the Therapist Who Treats Sexually Abused Clients* (Seminar Presentation, Washington State Psychological Association, 1994), audiocassette.

84. One participant explained that "[t]he decision to emphasize our own feelings and experiences as women and to test all generalization and reading we did by our own experience was actually the scientific method of research. We were in effect repeating the seventeenth century challenge of Science to Scholasticism: 'Study nature, not books,' and put all theories to the test of living practice and action." *See* HERMAN, *supra,* 29.

85. *See id.* 31.

86. *See id.* 31.

87. *See id.* 30.

88. *See id.* 30. Interestingly, Linda Meyer-Williams' study of adult survivors of CSA uses the hospital emergency room records generated by one of these rape studies. Linda Meyer-Williams, *Recall of Childhood Trauma: A Prospective Study of Women's Memories of Childhood Sexual Abuse,* 62 JOURNAL OF CONSULTING AND CLINICAL PSYCHOLOGY 6 (1994) 1167-76.

89. *See* HERMAN, *supra,* 32.

90. In addition to the studies reviewed in this section, see Scheflin & Brown's analysis and useful reference chart of 25 studies demonstrating dissociative amnesia among CSA victims, in Scheflin & Brown, *Repressed Memory or Dissociative Amnesia: What the Science Says, supra,* 180-181.

91. John Briere & Jon Conte, *Self-Reported Amnesia of Childhood Sexual Abuse in Adults Molested as Children,* 6 JOURNAL OF TRAUMATIC STRESS 1 (1993) 21-31; Shirley Feldman-Summers & Kenneth S. Pope, *The Experience of 'Forgetting' Childhood Abuse: A National Survey of Psychologists,* 62 JOURNAL OF CONSULTING AND CLINICAL PSYCHOLOGY 3 (1994) 636-639; Judith L. Herman & Emily Schatzow, *Recovery and Verification of Memories of Childhood Sexual Abuse Trauma,* 4 PSYCHOANALYTIC PSYCHOLOGY 1 (1987) 1-14; Elizabeth F. Loftus, Sara Polonsky & Mindy Thompson Fullilove, *Memories of Childhood Sexual Abuse: Remembering and Repressing,* 18 PSYCHOLOGY OF WOMEN QUARTERLY 1 (1994) 67-84; *see also* TERR and Williams, *supra.*

92. *See* especially Williams, *supra.*

93. *See* Herman & Schatzow, Feldman-Summers & Pope, and Williams, supra.

94. *See* Briere & Conte, *supra,* 3.

95. *See id.* 3-4.

96. *See id.* 8.

97. *See id.* 8.

98. *See id.* 9.

99. *See* Herman & Schatzow, *supra,* 4.

100. *See* Loftus, Polonsky & Fullilove, *supra.* This may seem confusing since Elizabeth Loftus is one of the most prominent defense experts in the "false memory" movement and frequently asserts the lack of "cogent scientific evidence" for the repression of sexual abuse memories. In a book review of Loftus" THE MYTH OF REPRESSED MEMORY, however, Bessel van der Kolk commented that Elizabeth Loftus is an "equal opportunity witness for the defense: She ignores both her own and other people's research that contradicts the point of her book." *The Minefields of*

*Memory: When Experts Dispute Delayed Recall, Are They Forgetting Something?* BOSTON GLOBE, 26 November 1994, B19-B21.

101. *See* Feldman-Summers & Pope, *supra,* 636.

102. *See* Herman & Schatzow, *supra,* 10-11.

103. *See* Feldman-Summers & Pope, *supra,* 638.

104. *See* Williams, *supra,* 16.

105. *See id.* 16.

106. *See* Williams, *supra,* 10.

107. *See id.* at 2.

108. Everson and Boat interviewed Child Protective Service Workers, who estimated that 4.7% to 7.6% of all child and adolescent sexual abuse allegations are fictitious. *See* Mark D. Everson and Barbara W. Boat, *False Accusations of Sexual Abuse by Children and Adolescents,* 28 JOURNAL OF AMERICAN ACADEMY OF CHILD AND ADOLESCENT PSYCHIATRY 230-235 (1989).

109. *See* Williams, *supra,* 11-12.

110. This is due to the fact that when the data was collected in 1973-1975, information on repeated assaults by the same offender was not collected. *See* Williams, *supra,* 14.

111. *See* TERR, *supra,* 9-10.

112. *See id.* 11. Her conception of traumatic forgetting is based on her considerable research on children's psychological response to trauma. *See e.g.,* Lenore Terr, *Psychic Trauma in Children: Observations Following the Chowchilla School-bus Kidnapping,* 138 AMERICAN JOURNAL OF PSYCHIATRY 14-19 (1981); Lenore Terr, *Chowchilla Revisited: The Effects of Psychic Trauma Four Years After a School-bus Kidnapping,* 140 AMERICAN JOURNAL OF PSYCHIATRY 1543-1550 (1983); Lenore Terr, *Childhood Traumas: An Outline and an Overview,* 148 AMERICAN JOURNAL OF PSYCHIATRY 10-20 (1991); Lenore Terr, *What Happens to the Memories of Early Trauma? A Study of Twenty Children Under Age Five at the Time of Documented Traumatic Events,* 27 JOURNAL OF THE AMERICAN ACADEMY OF CHILD AND ADOLESCENT PSYCHIATRY 96-104 (1988).

113. *See* TERR, *supra,* 30.

114. *See* van der Kolk & van der Hart, *The Intrusive Past, supra,* 443.

115. *See, e.g.,* van der Kolk, *The Body Keeps the Score: Approaches to the Psychobiology of Posttraumatic Stress Disorder* and *Trauma and Memory* in TRAUMATIC STRESS, *supra;* van der Kolk, *The Body Keeps the Score: Memory and the Evolving Psychobiology of Posttraumatic Stress, supra*; van der Kolk & van der Hart, *The Intrusive Past, supra*; BROWN, SCHEFLIN & HAMMOND, *The Nature of Memory* and *Trauma Memory* in MEMORY, TRAUMA TREATMENT, AND THE LAW, esp. 91-97; Shalev, *supra;* Southwick, *supra*; Brown, *supra*; Reviere, *Neurophysiological Substrates of Traumatic Memory,* in MEMORY OF CHILDHOOD TRAUMA: A CLINICIAN'S GUIDE TO THE LITERATURE, *supra,* 85-95.

116. A full treatment of the emerging literature on the psychobiology and neuroscience of traumatic neurosis is beyond the scope of this chapter. The reader is encouraged to read the reviews cited herein as well as staying abreast of emerging studies for further information.

117. *See* Brown, *supra,* 110.

118. *See id.* 110.

119. *See* BROWN, SCHEFLIN & HAMMOND, *supra,* 94.

120. *See* van der Kolk, "The Body Keeps the Score: Memory and the Evolving Psychobiology of Posttraumatic Stress," *supra,* 260-261.

121. *See id.* 261.

122. *See id.* 261.

123. *See* Reviere, *supra,* 86-87.

124. *See* BROWN, SCHEFLIN & HAMMOND, *supra,* 95.

125. *See id.* 97, 103.

126. *See* van der Kolk, *The Body Keeps the Score: Approaches to the Psychobiology of Posttraumatic Stress Disorder, supra,* 228; *see also* Brown, *supra,* 111.

127. *See* van der Kolk, *The Body Keeps the Score: Approaches to the Psychobiology of Posttraumatic Stress Disorder, supra,* 229.

128. *See* Brown, *supra,* 101.

129. *See* van der Kolk, *The Body Keeps the Score: Approaches to the Psychobiology of Posttraumatic Stress Disorder, supra,* 220.

130. *See id.* 229.

131. *See id.* at 229.

132. *See* van der Kolk, *The Body Keeps the Score: Memory and the Evolving Psychobiology of Posttraumatic Stress, supra,* 261; van der Kolk, *The Body Keeps the Score: Approaches to the Psychobiology of Posttraumatic Stress Disorder, supra,* 229; Brown, *supra,* 112; BROWN, SCHEFLIN & HAMMOND, *supra,* 95-96.

133. *See* van der Kolk, *The Body Keeps the Score: Approaches to the Psychobiology of Posttraumatic Stress Disorder, supra,* 232. It is important to note that there is variation among trauma survivors with respect to the development of posttraumatic neurosis and symptomatology; for a discussion of the complexity of individual response, *see, e.g.,* Alexander C. McFarlane and Rachel Yehuda, *Resilience, Vulnerability, and the Course of Posttraumatic Reactions* and Bessel van der Kolk, *The Complexity of Adaptation to Trauma: Self-Regulation, Stimulus Discrimination, and Characterological Development,* in TRAUMATIC STRESS, *supra,* 155-181, 182-213. However, while there is "a great deal of individual variability for any single physiological response, .. . the presence of an overall pattern of disturbed response appears to be constant." *See* Brown, *supra,* 102.

134. *See* van der Kolk, *The Body Keeps the Score: Approaches to the Psychobiology of Posttraumatic Stress Disorder, supra,* 233.

135. *See id.* 233.

136. *See id.* 233.

137. *See id.* 234.

138. *See id.* 234.

139. *See* APA, *Statement on Memories of Sexual Abuse, supra,* 26.

140. *See* BROWN, SCHEFLIN & HAMMOND, *supra,* 94.

141. *See* APA, *Statement on Memories of Sexual Abuse, supra,* 26.

142. *See id.* 26.

143. *See* BROWN, SCHEFLIN & HAMMOND, *supra,* 97.

144. Explicit recollection requires "the interaction between encoding and retrieval conditions, or compatibility between the engram and the cue. . . . (M)emories are

reactivated when a person is exposed to a situation, or is in a somatic state, reminiscent of the one when the original memory was stored." *See* van der Kolk and van der Hart, *The Intrusive Past, supra,* 445. *See also,* Brown, *supra,* 104; BROWN, SCHEFLIN & HAMMOND, *supra,* 97.

145. *See* TERR, *supra,* 30.

146. For a discussion and analysis of the various arguments of the false memory controversy, *see* BROWN, SCHEFLIN & HAMMOND, *The False Memory Debate* and *The Contours of the False Memory Controversy* in MEMORY, TRAUMA TREATMENT, AND THE LAW, *supra.*

147. *See,* in particular, the case of *Ramona v. Rose,* where the jury foreman expressed concern that the nature of the psychotherapy was used to dismiss Holly Ramona's case for CSA against her father: "It doesn't seem right. [In the Napa trial] we didn't have to determine if she had or hadn't been abused. What we were discussing was a malpractice case." Cited in Cynthia Grant Bowman & Elizabeth Mertz, *A Dangerous Direction: Legal Intervention in Sexual Abuse Survivor Therapy,* 109 HARVARD LAW REVIEW 3 (1996) 566 (note 94), 551-639.

148. *See* APA, *Statement on Memories of Sexual Abuse, supra,* 26.

149. Loftus citing the work of false memory advocates George Ganaway, Hollida Wakefield, and Ralph Underwager on the self-help book and therapist origins of false memories, in Elizabeth Loftus, *The Truth About Repressed Memories,* 48 AMERICAN PSYCHOLOGIST 5 (1993) 525, 518-537.

150. For discussion of these issues, *see* Bowman & Mertz, *A Dangerous Direction, supra; see also* Mary R. Williams, *Suits by Adults for Childhood Sexual Abuse: Legal Origins of the "Repressed Memory" Controversy,* THE JOURNAL OF PSYCHIATRY & LAW (Summer 1996) 212-215, 207-228.

151. *See* BROWN, SCHEFLIN & HAMMOND, *supra,* 94.

152. *See id.* 117.

153. *See id.* 127.

154. *See* Elizabeth Loftus, *When a Lie Becomes Memory's Truth: Memory Distortion After Exposure to Misinformation,* 121 CURRENT DIRECTIONS IN PSYCHOLOGICAL SCIENCE 1 (1992).

155. *E.g.,* N. Harsch and U. Neisser, *Substantial and Irreversible Errors in Flashbulb Memory of the Challenger Explosion,* Poster Presentation at the meeting of the Psychonomic Society, Atlanta Georgia (November, 1989); U. Neisser and N. Harsch, *Phantom Flashbulbs: False Recollections of Hearing the News about* Challenger, in E. WINOGRAD & U. NEISSER, eds., AFFECT AND ACCURACY IN RECALL: STUDIES OF "FLASHBULB" MEMORIES 9-31 (New York: Cambridge University Press, 1992), cited in Elizabeth Loftus, *The Reality of Repressed Memories, supra,* 531.

156. Outfielder Tony Conigliaro mistakenly believed this event took place during a day game rather than a (presumably well-lit) night game, demonstrating an error in "flashbulb" memory. L. F. Loftus and L. Kaufman, "Why do Traumatic Experiences Sometime Produce Good Memory (Flashbulbs) and Sometimes no Memory (Repression)?" in WINOGRAD & NEISSER, AFFECT AND ACCURACY IN RECALL: STUDIES OF "FLASHBULB" MEMORIES, *supra,* 212-223, cited in Loftus, *The Reality of Repressed Memories, supra,* 531.

157. J. Abhold [Unpublished doctoral dissertation data], University of Arkansas (1992), cited in Loftus, *The Reality of Repressed Memories, supra,* 531.

158. *See* TERR, *supra,* 163.

159. E. F. Loftus & D. Coan, *The Construction of Childhood Memories,* in THE CHILD WITNESS IN CONTEXT: COGNITIVE, SOCIAL AND LEGAL PERSPECTIVES. D. Peters, ed. (New York: Klewer, in press when cited), cited in Loftus, *The Reality of Repressed Memories, supra,* 532.

160. Loftus & Coan study cited in Robert F. Belli & Elizabeth Loftus, *Recovered Memories of Childhood Abuse: A Source Monitoring Perspective,* in Lynn & Rhue, DISSOCIATION: CLINICAL AND THEORETICAL PERSPECTIVES, *supra,* 420, 415-433.

161. *See id.* 420.

162. *See id.* 421.

163. *See id.* 421.

164. *See* Terr, *supra,* 163.

165. *See* BROWN, SCHEFLIN & HAMMOND, *supra,* 47.

166. Bessel van der Kolk notes that despite her reputation as a careful laboratory researcher, Elizabeth Loftus "makes the extraordinary leap that her capacity to 'implant' this memory suggests that it is easy for therapists to make a person have vivid memories of having been raped as a child. In this facile application of her laboratory research to people's real traumas, she is blind to the well-established differences between memories of laboratory studies of events (such as [yet another] violent scene on TV) and the memory processes involved in having been raped or having witnessed the murder of one's best friend." *See* van der Kolk, *The Minefields of Memory: When Experts Dispute Delayed Recall, Are They Forgetting Something?, supra.*

167. On the other hand, it has been known for some time that people can, under certain circumstances, be "brainwashed." Barbara Jo Levy notes that counsel may want to explore with expert witnesses the characteristics of brainwashing, which may more accurately describe a process of "implanting memories," and if appropriate, share that description with the factfinder. Personal communication with Barbara Jo Levy.

168. Jon Conte, *Memory, Research, and the Law,* in Williams & Baryard, TRAUMA AND MEMORY, *supra,* 77-92, 81. This chapter is a useful primer on critical readings of memory science.

169. See e.g. *State of New Hampshire v. Joel Hungerford,* 142 N.H. 110; 697 A.2d 916; N.H. LEXIS 64 (1997), 13, and *State of New Hampshire v. David Walters,* 142 N.H. 239; 698 A.2d 1244; N.H. LEXIS 81 (1997). On the issues associated with such pre-trial evidentiary hearings in sexual abuse cases, see Brooks Cooper, *Delayed Memories and Scientific Evidence: Maintaining the Pretrial Admissibility of Delayed Memory Evidence,* in this volume.

170. *See* TERR, *supra,* 163-164.

171. For further discussion of this issue, see Janet Sonne and Julian Hubbard's chapter on the professional relationship between lawyers and therapists, *Sexual Abuse Litigation: A Difficult Journey Through Unfamiliar Territory,* in this volume.

172. *See* Conte, *supra,* 78.

173. *See* Harold I. Lief & Janet Fetkewicz, *Retractors of False Memories: The Evolution of Pseudo-memories,* THE JOURNAL OF PSYCHIATRY & LAW (Fall 1995) 411-435. All the retractors profiled in this study were located through the False Memory Syndrome Foundation, *see* Lief & Fetkewicz, *supra,* 415.

174. John Kihlstrom quoted in the False Memory Syndrome Foundation Brochure (Philadelphia: 1994).

175. *See* Lief & Fetkewicz, *supra.*

176. *See id.* 418 (for pre-infantile and infantile memories which would be unlikely due to infantile amnesia) and 422-423 (for descriptions of problematic therapeutic practices).

177. *See id.* 414.

178. *See* APA, *Statement on Memories of Sexual Abuse, supra,* 26.

179. Attorney Barbara Jo Levy argues that plaintiff's lawyers should involve their expert witnesses in this investigation. *See* Barbara Jo Levy, *Plaintiff and Defense Expert Witnesses,* in this volume.

180. *See* BROWN, SCHEFLIN & HAMMOND, *supra,* 86. For a model of case evaluation, see Michael S. Morey, *Evaluation of the Delayed Discovery Case,* in this volume.

181. *See* Scheflin & Brown, *Repressed Memory or Dissociative Amnesia: What the Science Says, supra,* 176.

182. Studies have also been made of the psychological response of prisoners of war, political prisoners, survivors of the Holocaust, survivors of physical abuse and battering, survivors of natural disasters, and so on. *See* HERMAN, *supra.*

183. *See* van der Kolk and van der Hart, *The Intrusive Past, supra,* 437.

184. *See, e.g.,* Lenore Terr's use of "repression," in TERR, *supra,* 9-10.

185. *See* Scheflin & Brown, *Repressed Memory or Dissociative Amnesia: What the Science Says, supra,* 144.

186. Mary Williams argues that repression was favored in delayed discovery statutes of limitations because, of the various conceptions of memory loss, it was the most congruent with existing legal theories that provide for delays in bringing legal action. For this discussion, *see* Mary Williams, *A History and Analysis of Delayed Discovery Statutes in Adult Survivor Litigation,* in this volume.

187. *See* Harrison, Levy, Morey, Quirk, Rix & DePrince, *Childhood Sexual Abuse, supra,* 404. *See also* Scheflin & Brown, *Repressed Memory or Dissociative Amnesia, supra,* 143.

188. False Memory Syndrome Foundation Brochure; *see also* BROWN, SCHEFLIN & HAMMOND, *The False Memory Debate* and *The Contours of the False Memory Controversy* in MEMORY, TRAUMA TREATMENT, AND THE LAW, *supra.*

189. *See* APA, *Statement on Memories of Sexual Abuse, supra,* 26.

190. *See id.* 26.

# History and Analysis of Delayed Discovery Statutes of Limitations in Adult Survivor Litigation

Mary R. Williams

**SUMMARY.** In this chapter, attorney Mary R. Williams examines how while Childhood Sexual Abuse (CSA) cases share many of the types of facts for which delayed discovery, mental incapacity, equitable estoppel and other legal statutes of limitations doctrines were created, the combination of factors of CSA cases, including unusual social dynamics and long-term psychological effects, does not fit exactly with any of these legal doctrines. She explores the historical development of delayed discovery statutes of limitations, evaluates the different types of statutes and case law, and analyzes the problematic use of the concept of repression in legislation. This chapter interprets her ground-breaking state-by-state tabulations of delayed discovery statutes of limitations and reported appellate decisions on limitations in CSA actions, published in this volume as appendices A, B, and C. *[Article copies available for a fee from The Haworth Document Delivery Service: 1-800-342-9678. E-mail address: <getinfo@haworthpressinc.com> Website: <http://www.haworthpressinc.com>]*

**KEYWORDS.** Social and psychological dynamics of CSA, cognitive aspects of sexual abuse recollection ("re-cognizing"), Type I Discovery, Type II Discovery, legislative history, fiduciary duty, retroactivity of CSA Statutes, applicability to actions against non-perpetrators, in-

---

Address correspondence to: Mary R. Williams, JD, Law Office of Mary R. Williams, The Creamery Building, Post Office Box 1375, Point Reyes Station, CA 94956-1375.

[Haworth co-indexing entry note]: "History and Analysis of Delayed Discovery Statutes of Limitations in Adult Survivor Litigation." Williams, Mary R. Co-published simultaneously in *Journal of Aggression, Maltreatment & Trauma* (The Haworth Maltreatment & Trauma Press, an imprint of The Haworth Press, Inc.) Vol. 3, No. 2 (#6), 2000, pp. 49-71; and: *Sexual Abuse Litigation: A Practical Resource for Attorneys, Clinicians, and Advocates* (ed: Rebecca Rix) The Haworth Maltreatment & Trauma Press, an imprint of The Haworth Press, Inc., 2000, pp. 49-71. Single or multiple copies of this article are available for a fee from The Haworth Document Delivery Service [1-800-342-9678, 9:00 a.m. - 5:00 p.m. (EST). E-mail address: getinfo@haworthpressinc. com].

 

tentional and non-intentional torts, "False Memory Syndrome" movement, "repression" as the basis for delayed discovery legislation, problems with

When an adult client is interested in pursuing a civil suit for damages for childhood sexual abuse (CSA), one of the first questions an attorney will need to evaluate is whether the action is barred by the statute of limitations applicable to it. The governing statutes and case law on this issue vary greatly from state to state, making it difficult to formulate general guidelines on the subject.

In the absence of a special statute of limitations for actions based on CSA, such actions are governed by the personal injury statute of limitations of the state whose law governs the action. Most personal injury statutes provide only one or two years in which to bring an action. In the case of one injured as a child, the statute is tolled during the victim's minority[1] and begins to run when plaintiff reaches the age of majority, which in most states is 18. Thus, under personal injury statutes CSA victims would be barred from pursuing a civil remedy by the time they reached the age of 19 or 20, unless they could claim the benefit of some additional exception to the running of the statute.

The main additional exceptions available are tolling for mental incapacity, equitable estoppel for fraud and/or duress, and the more modern doctrine of "delayed discovery" accrual. Like tolling for minority, tolling for mental incapacity or insanity is provided by statute in most states. Equitable estoppel is a judicially developed doctrine, by which a defendant may be held estopped from benefiting by the statute of limitations if his own wrongful conduct, such as fraudulent concealment of the injury or intimidation and duress of the plaintiff, have both actually and reasonably prevented the plaintiff from being able to file suit within the required time period. The doctrine of "delayed discovery of injury" has been developed to accommodate situations in which the nature of the injury, such as medical malpractice or exposure to toxins, is such that the victim may not reasonably be able to discover the injury and/or its cause within the short time period provided by personal injury statutes. The discovery rule delays "accrual" of the action, and thus delays the starting of the statutory time clock, until the plaintiff has, or reasonably should have, become aware of all the essential elements of the cause of action, including the defendant's identity, the nature of the wrongful conduct, and the fact of having been injured by it.

Because most victims of CSA do not become aware of their long-term psychological injuries, or of the causal connection between the earlier abuse and those injuries, until sometime in their twenties or thirties, they would be barred from suing before they had a reasonable chance to do so unless they could invoke one of these additional exceptions to the running of the statute. In the early 1980s, as adult victims of CSA began to speak out and to seek to hold their abusers accountable in the courts, a movement began and quickly spread across the country to extend the time period in which CSA victims could file suit. Attorneys for "adult survivors" requested that the courts apply existing, judicially-fashioned exceptions to the running of the statutory time period, such as the exception for "delayed discovery of injury," and/or sought to enact new statutes of limitations for CSA actions.

To date, thirty-one states have enacted special statutes of limitations applicable to actions based on CSA. Twenty-six of these statutes provide that the limitations period does not begin to run until the plaintiff has in some manner "discovered" the injury or the causal connection between the injury and the earlier abuse, while five simply provide an extended number of years beyond the date of plaintiff's majority in which to commence legal action. There is considerable variation in the statutory language defining what constitutes discovery of an action for CSA, and most CSA statutes have not yet been definitively interpreted on this issue.

Twenty states (including the District of Columbia) have as yet no special statute of limitations for CSA actions. In seven of these states, the courts have held discovery accrual applicable in certain cases. One state court fashioned a narrow exception, based on the doctrine of "fraudulent concealment of injury," in actions against the plaintiff's parent. Another state court applied an exception for mental incompetency where the plaintiff alleged repression of memory of the abuse. Of the remaining eleven states, nine have refused to apply any exception to the running of the personal injury statute of limitations in CSA actions, while two states have as yet no case law on the issue.

This article will review the history of the movement to extend statutes of limitations for adult survivors of CSA, discuss the major issues currently being litigated, and offer some suggestions for dealing with these issues. Appendix A compiles and presents, for each state including the District of Columbia, the statutes of limitations governing CSA actions, reported appellate decisions on limitations issues in CSA actions, and a brief analysis of the "state of the law" on CSA limitations issues in each state.[2] Appendices B and C condense this information into chart form for quick reference.

## *HISTORY OF EXTENSIONS OF TIME FOR CSA ACTIONS BY ADULTS*

In the early 1980s, some adults who had been sexually abused in childhood sought to file civil actions for damages against the persons who had abused them, despite the barriers presented by the short statutes of limitations governing personal injury actions in each state. Psychological research and clinical literature on the long-term effects of CSA made it clear that children who are sexually abused typically accommodate to it psychologically by coping mechanisms such as denial, minimization, dissociation, and/or traumatic amnesia regarding the abuse itself or its damaging effects, and as a result often do not disclose the abuse or begin to be able to perceive its long-term effects on their lives until many years later in adult life, often in their mid-twenties or early thirties.[3] Based on these findings, attorneys representing adult CSA plaintiffs argued that because survivors of CSA typically were not psychologically able to recognize their long-term injuries and file suit until many years later, courts should apply exceptions such as delayed discovery accrual, tolling for mental incapacity, or equitable estoppel for fraud and duress, to delay the running of the statute until the effects of these coping mechanisms had reasonably worn off.[4] The movement to extend statutes of limitations for adult CSA actions was thus premised on the belief that most victims of CSA are psychologically unable to bring suit for their injuries until later in adult life. To understand the evolution of judicial and statutory extensions of time for these actions, and effectively argue regarding the justifiability of plaintiffs' delay, one must have a good understanding of the social and psychological dynamics of CSA that relate to the need for an extension of time to sue.

## *Social and Psychological Dynamics of CSA*

CSA generally is accomplished through the offender's use of a socially sanctioned position of authority and trust *vis-a-vis* the child to induce the child's compliance with the sexual contact and to keep it a secret. In CSA, there is a fundamental imbalance of power between the offender and the child, which implicitly gives rise to intimidation, coercion and duress. Often the offender also explicitly threatens or physically intimidates the child, or threatens to harm others upon whom the child is dependent. In most instances the acts of sexual abuse are intimidating and frightening to the child.

Often the offender will explicitly misrepresent to the child the nature of his conduct,[5] such as by telling the child that it is an expression of his love but must be kept a secret because others would not understand, or that it is the child's fault and will get the child in trouble if others knew. Implicitly the offender's manipulation of the child's dependency and trust is a fraud upon the child. This fraud continues into her adult life because of the psychological effects of the abuse, which cause the child to internalize feelings of badness and low self-worth, and to grow up with such self-images without knowing why.

Because the child experiencing CSA usually perceives herself as unable to change or get out of the situation, she needs to adapt and accommodate to it psychologically, and as a result develops varying degrees of psychological coping and/or blocking mechanisms, described in the clinical literature as denial, minimization, dissociation, and/or various forms of traumatic amnesia. The child's ability to cognize and remember the abuse is also impaired by the fact that the child typically does not discuss it with others while growing up, and therefore does not incorporate an awareness of it into a conscious self-recollection narrative. These awareness-inhibiting and memory-inhibiting mechanisms, developed in childhood, continue to operate into adulthood, causing the adult survivor to be delayed in "re-cognizing" the abuse as abuse, or in perceiving that the abuse is causally connected to psychological and emotional problems in adult life. Sometimes these mechanisms prevent active recollection of the incidents of sexual abuse, or even awareness that the abuse happened, for a period of many years.

### *Legal Responses*

The social dynamics and long-term psychological effects of CSA present a unique factual pattern. Although having strong similarities to the types of facts for which "delayed discovery," mental incapacity, equitable estoppel and other doctrines were created, the combination of factors presented by CSA does not exactly fit any of them. The exception for insanity or mental incapacity generally requires that the plaintiff have been unable to conduct his or her affairs, and is not available if the plaintiff has in most respects been functional. The long-term psychological effects of CSA generally do not cause this level of impairment. The doctrines of equitable estoppel for fraud or duress generally require that the defendant have engaged in affirmative acts of misrepresentation or fraud, or have exerted both overt and continuing duress on the plaintiff. The psycho-social dynamics of CSA usually are more implicit in the nature of the sexual abuse and the relationship between the defendant and the child. And, although the CSA victim's typical inability to recognize his or her long-term psychological injuries until later is closely analogous to situations to which courts have applied the "delayed discovery of injury" doctrine, the subjective, psychological nature of the factors causing this delay do not fit easily with some of the traditional requirements of that doctrine. For example, the doctrines generally require that the plaintiff used "due diligence" to discover the injury and its cause, and holds that their knowledge of some injury is sufficient to start the running of the statutory time period, while an inability to appreciate the full extent of one's injuries will not further delay accrual.

Although some courts have been willing on their own to apply these exceptions to at least some adult CSA actions,[6] many have been reluctant to do so in the absence of legislative direction.[7] Therefore, in the late 1980s and early 1990s, advocates for adult survivors turned to state legislatures to enact special statutes of limitations for civil actions based on CSA. To date, thirty-one states have enacted such statutes. Of these, twenty-six provide in some manner for delayed accrual of the action,[8] while five provide an extended period of time to sue with no delayed accrual.[9]

Among the twenty states (including the District of Columbia) having as yet no CSA statute, seven have applied discovery accrual to at least some adult survivor actions,[10] and two have fashioned limited exceptions on other grounds.[11] Thus, to date, forty states have either legislatively or judicially provided an extension of time for at least some CSA actions by adults, and in thirty-three of these the basis for the extension is some form of delayed discovery accrual.

Where discovery accrual has been applied, one of the most litigated issues has been whether it should be applied only where the plaintiff had completely "repressed" the incidents of abuse until a date within the statutory period–so-called "Type 2" discovery–or whether it should also be applied where the plaintiff had always had some knowledge or recollection of the abuse but had been delayed in being able to recognize that the abuse was causally connected to his or her adult psychological injuries until a date within the statutory period–so called "Type 1" discovery.[12] In addition, where there is a CSA statute there are also frequently issues regarding its retroactive operation and its applicability to causes of action against persons other than the perpetrator of the abuse. These issues will be discussed in detail next.

## *CURRENT ISSUES IN CSA ACTIONS*

### *Retroactive Operation of CSA Statutes*

Where an extension of time to sue is created by judicial interpretation, the question of retroactive operation generally does not arise. However, where the change is made by enactment of a special statute, the question arises whether the new statute can be applied to revive an action that had lapsed or technically expired under the previous limitations period before the new law was enacted.

Issues of retroactivity have been decided differently in different states, due sometimes to differences in statutory language and sometimes to differences in traditional approaches to statutory interpretation and retroactivity in general. For example, despite the lack of any express language of retroactivity, Connecticut's CSA statute has been held to revive lapsed actions, due to Connecticut's general rule that statutory extensions of time to sue are presumed to operate retroactively unless otherwise specified.[13] In California and many other states, retroactive operation is not presumed but may be accomplished by the use of express language in the statute.[14] In these states, the courts have held that the legislature has the power to revive a civil action by retroactive extension of a limitations period, because a civil statute of limitations grants the defendant only a procedural rather than a substantive right. However, some states adhere to the minority rule that to revive an action that had previously lapsed is to deprive a defendant of a substantive right without due process. In these states, even express language of revival in the CSA statute has been invalidated as unconstitutional.[15] In states where retroactive operation has been denied, due either to a lack of express language of revival in the statute, or to a holding that revival is unconstitutional, legislation may still be pursued for revival of lapsed claims, as has been done in California and Virginia. In states where the issue has not been decided, it will turn on the wording of the statute, its legislative history, and the state's traditional rules regarding retroactive operation of statutes, and particularly of extensions of time to sue.

In states which permit revival, issues have arisen regarding what statutory language indicates that the Legislature intended to revive lapsed actions. In California and Iowa, a statement that the statute shall apply to all actions filed on or after its effective date was held not sufficiently "express" to indicate an intent to revive lapsed claims.[16] In Minnesota, language applying the statute to "all cases pending" and establishing an immediate effective date was held to overcome the presumption against retroactive application.[17] In Montana, language providing that the statute applied to all actions commenced on or after its effective date, regardless of when the cause of action arose, was held sufficient to revive lapsed claims.[18] In California and Oregon, language applying the statute to all actions filed on or after its effective date "including any action that would have been barred by application of" the period of limitations in effect prior to its effective date, was held sufficient to revive lapsed claims.[19]

As shown in Appendix C, many states with CSA statutes have either legislatively defined or judicially interpreted the issue of revival by now. However, a significant number have not, and in those states practitioners need to research the issue by looking to the wording of the statute, its legislative history, and judicial interpretations of comparable statutory language in other states.

### *Applicability to Actions Against Non-Perpetrators*

In states with CSA statutes, another issue that arises is whether the statute is applicable to causes of action against persons other than the perpetrator, such as for negligence in permitting the abuse to occur.

Connecticut and Iowa have held their CSA statutes applicable to any persons or entities who might be legally liable for the resulting harm, despite the absence of statutory language regarding the issue.[20] Some statutes expressly state that they are applicable to actions against persons who have negligently or knowingly permitted the abuse to occur. For example, Minnesota's CSA statute contains an express provision for legal action against "a person who caused the plaintiff's personal injury either by (1) committing the sexual abuse against the plaintiff, or (2) negligently permitting sexual abuse against the plaintiff to occur."[21] New Jersey's CSA statute provides that, as used therein, a person standing *in loco parentis* within the household commits sexual abuse for purposes of the statute if he or she "knowingly permits or acquiesces in sexual abuse by any other person;" thus, it applies to actions against relatives or household members who knowingly fail to report or stop the abuse.[22] Oregon's statute expressly applies to any action based on child abuse or on "conduct knowingly allowing, permitting or encouraging child abuse."[23] Utah's statute applies to intentional or "negligent" sexual abuse and defines the latter as a failure on the part of a family or household member to prevent or report the abuse.[24] Virginia's statute applies to "actions for injury to the person, whatever the theory of recovery, resulting from sexual abuse."[25]

Some statutes specify that they govern actions against the perpetrator of the abuse, thereby implicitly excluding actions against non-perpetrators.[26] Others state they govern actions "based on" sexual abuse or intentional conduct.[27] While the Rhode Island Supreme Court has interpreted the latter language as implicitly excluding causes of action against persons other than the perpetrator of the abuse, Montana's Supreme Court has held that this language includes such actions.[28]

Some statutes apply to actions for injuries or damages "resulting from," "caused by" or "arising from" CSA.[29] This language focuses on the injuries for which the action seeks relief, rather than on the acts constituting the tort. This language may have been a factor in the decisions in Connecticut and Iowa which held their CSA statutes applicable to actions against persons other than the perpetrator whose negligence made them partially liable for the injuries.[30] However, this same difference of language was ignored in California, where the court noted that if the legislature had intended the statute to apply to non-perpetrators, it would have indicated it more expressly.[31]

In this tort-reform era many legislators and judges may not favor the idea of including non-perpetrators within the purview of a special statute of limitations for CSA. However, there are many reasons why it is important as a matter of justice and social policy. While negligence in permitting CSA to occur may not seem as reprehensible as committing the abuse itself, it often occurs within families and institutions (such as schools and churches), and so long as there is little potential liability for it due to short statutes of limitations, there is little legal deterrent to such behavior. Indeed, in terms of social policy, extending the time period for such causes of action may have more deterrent and thus preventive effect than the extension of time to sue the perpetrator, as the existence of potential civil liability would be an incentive for schools, churches and other institutions to act promptly and responsibly on complaints of CSA.

In states where the statute appears not to apply to causes of action against non-perpetrators, it may be possible to argue that judicial discovery accrual ought to be applied to these ancillary causes of action.[32] Also, where there is evidence that the non-perpetrating person or entity had notice but concealed the information or engaged in a "cover-up," one could argue that there was either "intentional" conduct coming within the terms of the CSA statute, or that the conduct gave rise to a cause of action for fraud or concealment that did not accrue until discovery of the essential facts.

### *Applicability of Delayed Discovery Accrual or Tolling*

By far the most litigated issue with regard to limitations for CSA actions is whether or not delayed discovery accrual or other exceptions apply, and if so under what circumstances. There are now only two states that have neither a CSA statute nor any reported decisions on adult CSA actions.[33] Nine states without a CSA statute have refused to apply delayed discovery accrual or other judicially created exceptions.[34] The remaining forty jurisdictions (including the District of Columbia) have provided some kind of relief for adult CSA actions, either by statute, case law, or both. Of these, two have rejected application of the judicial discovery rule but have fashioned other exceptions. Indiana's court has provided a limited exception for fraudulent concealment only in an action against a parent.[35] A North Carolina court has held that repression of memory tolls the statute for mental "incompetence."[36] Five states–Connecticut, Georgia, Idaho, Louisiana and Texas–have enacted CSA statutes which extend the time to sue without providing for delayed discovery accrual.[37]

The remaining thirty-three jurisdictions (including the District of Columbia) have provided either judicially or legislatively for some type of delayed discovery accrual in adult CSA actions. In thirteen states delayed accrual has been held applicable to Type 1 discovery,[38] and in ten more states the language of the CSA statutes appears intended to apply to Type 1 discovery, but has not yet been interpreted in any reported decisions.[39] Of the ten remaining discovery accrual jurisdictions, six appear to limit application of discovery accrual to Type 2 situations. Two of these, Oklahoma and Utah, have enacted statutes that appear to limit discovery accrual to Type 2 discovery. The courts of the District of Columbia and Ohio have limited application of the judicial discovery rule to Type 2 discovery, and the New Hampshire court appears to lean in that direction.[40] Minnesota, which enacted a CSA statute that appeared to apply to Type 1 discovery, has interpreted the statute in a manner that in fact precludes such application.[41] In the remaining four states, Maine, Missouri, Nebraska and Wyoming, the statutory language and/or court decisions are too unclear to hazard a guess at how this issue will ultimately be decided.

Although there appear to be more states that permit delayed accrual for Type 1 discovery than limit it to Type 2, there are twelve CSA statutes that appear to have been intended to apply to Type 1 discovery that have not yet been interpreted on this issue. The *Blackowiak* and *W.J.L.* decisions in Minnesota, discussed *infra,* illustrate the pitfalls of categorizing CSA statutes before they have been interpreted. In addition, some courts give theoretical recognition to the possibility of Type 1 discovery, but apply the reasonableness requirement in a way that could effectively eliminate much of what is intended to be covered by Type 1 accrual.[42]

Issues of discovery accrual also appear to be suffering from the recent controversy over so-called "recovered memories" of CSA. Recent rulings in Alabama,[43] Michigan,[44] Pennsylvania,[45] South Carolina,[46] Texas,[47] and Maryland[48] have refused to apply the judicial discovery rule even to Type 2 discovery of CSA. The decisions appear to have been based primarily on the perception that the psychological profession is at best very divided about, and at worst mainly skeptical of, the reliability and trustworthiness of so-called repressed and later recovered memories of CSA. To understand this current trend it is helpful to examine the historical interplay between the initial responses of many courts to adult survivor actions and the subsequent development of the "false memory syndrome" movement.[49]

Although scientific issues certainly exist regarding the existence, causes, and parameters of traumatic amnesia among adult survivors of CSA, it is doubtful whether the current controversy would have arisen, would have generated such media coverage, or would have become as intense and vitriolic as it has, had adult survivor litigation never occurred. The very substance of the current debate has been influenced and to some extent skewed by the legal system's need to articulate the delay experienced by CSA survivors in terms that fit into traditional legal doctrines regarding what does and does not justify delay.

The distinction made early on between Type 1 and Type 2 discovery in adult CSA actions is in many ways an unfortunate one. While based to a certain extent on clinical realities, it arose in part because of the need to define discovery of CSA in terms that would fit into the traditional judicial doctrine of delayed discovery, and distorts the psychological realities by making it appear that these two "types" exist as separate and distinct entities, rather than points on a continuum of experience.

Under the judicial discovery rule, a plaintiff's knowledge of facts necessary to constitute the cause of action, or of facts which would put a reasonable person in plaintiff's position on notice to investigate and discover these facts, constitutes legal "discovery" of the cause of action. A plaintiff with knowledge or notice of his or her injury is also under an obligation to use "due diligence" to investigate and discover its cause. Obviously, a plaintiff who blamelessly lacks knowledge or awareness of the abuse itself more easily fits into the judicial doctrine of discovery accrual than a plaintiff who always knew of the abuse but claims to have been delayed in discovering or realizing that the abuse was causally connected to psychological problems in his or her adult life.[50]

As a result, the legal system has an inherent bias in favor of Type 2 over Type 1 discovery of CSA. This has probably contributed to an excessive emphasis on "repressed" memory as the basis for delay, and thus to the attack on the validity and reliability of such memories by defense attorneys and their experts. In turn, the focus on the "repressed" memory issue has facilitated continued judicial ignorance of the much more common basis for delay in CSA actions, which might best be described as a psychological or emotional inability to "re-cognize" the abuse as abuse, and in this sense to discover the cause of action. In order to provide justice to the majority of victims of CSA, who do not fit into the Type 2 category, there is a great need for legal arguments and rulings that more accurately and fairly accommodate Type 1 delay.[51] This would, in turn, de-emphasize and put into better perspective the debate over the role of "repressed" memory or traumatic amnesia in such actions.

The judicial policy question regarding the propriety of extending the time for adult CSA actions really comes down to the question of whether, as a general rule, such delayed actions are likely to be so lacking in probative evidence as to render them unfit for the judicial process.[52]

In the 1980s and early 1990s, most courts and legislatures considering the issue struck a balance in favor of permitting adult survivors to sue. This may have been based in part on recognizing that CSA actions by adults were not, in fact, likely to be more difficult to prove or disprove than such actions filed during the victim's minority. In the latter there is rarely physical evidence or eyewitness testimony, and they often fail or flounder due to the difficulty of relying on a child's testimony. Actions by adults are arguably in some ways more appropriate for the judicial process, due to the greater clarity and reliability of the adult victim's testimony over that of the child. In addition, the passage of time may enhance rather than detract from the availability of witnesses and other evidence, as family members and other witnesses may be more willing to testify when the victim is an adult than when the victim is still a child and the family is going through crisis as a result of disclosure. In light of the fact that, without an extension of time most victims of CSA are deprived of a meaningful opportunity to sue for their injuries, most courts and legislatures that have addressed the problem so far have agreed that an extension of time is appropriate.

Since the early 1990s, however, the controversy over whether recovered memories are scientifically accepted or reliable has revived judicial reluctance by adding new scientific, or quasi-scientific, arguments to the "stale-evidence/faded-memories" position. The reliability of recovered memories and whether testimony about recovered memories should be admissible in court is dealt with elsewhere and will not be discussed here. Aside from the reliability issue, those who use this argument against extending the limitations period for CSA actions appear to assume that adult CSA actions are always or mostly based on such recovered memories. Indeed, the focus on the recovered memory issue has obscured, and thus contributed to continued judicial ignorance of, the main reason for delay in CSA actions, which is not repressed memory or traumatic amnesia regarding the abuse itself, but the clinically significant impairments of memory and understanding that cause most victims of CSA not to "recognize"–literally, not to "re-cognize" and in this sense discover–their long-term psychological and emotional injuries until later in adult life.

Unfortunately, early judicial rulings distinguishing between Type 1 and Type 2 discovery (as though these were so easily and neatly categorized in the clinical or the real world), and indicating that Type 2 was a better fit with the existing judicial discovery rule, probably contributed to the emphasis on repressed memory as a basis for delayed accrual, and thus to the ultimate emergence of the "repressed memory" controversy in its present, litigation-driven form.

In addition, many CSA statutes were drafted without sufficient awareness of the importance of providing for Type 1 discovery, or of the fact that it is necessary to draft statutory language that clearly provides for it. Many statutes have simply provided for accrual upon the date the plaintiff discovered or reasonably should have discovered the injury, without making it clear that knowledge of the abuse is not synonymous with discovery of the injury for purposes of accrual.

The problem is illustrated by recent decisions of the Minnesota court, *Blackowiak v. Kemp*[53] and *W.J.L. v. Bugge*,[54] interpreting the discovery provision of that state's CSA statute. Minnesota's CSA statute defines discovery accrual as "the time the plaintiff knew or had reason to know that the injury was caused by the abuse." Although it would appear that the Legislature intended to allow for discovery accrual based on a delayed recognition of the causal connection between the injury and the abuse (which is Type 1 discovery), Minnesota's Supreme Court held in *Blackowiak* that the phrase "reason to know" implies that the reasonableness of the CSA plaintiff's delay should be determined by the standard of an objective, reasonable person, *not* the standard of a person who had been subjected to the abuse and therefore might have reasonably have developed certain psychological coping mechanisms that interfered with the ability to make this connection. Under the objective, reasonable person standard, it is not reasonable for there to be a delay between knowing that one had been abused and knowing that one had been injured, and thus Type 1 discovery is effectively precluded by the use of this standard.[55]

Justice Gardebring's strong dissent in *Blackowiak* and again in *W.J.L.* contends that this interpretation by the majority elevates semantics over substance and thwarts the clear intent of the Legislature.

The *Blackowiak* decision points to key interpretive issues that may be of critical importance in the future in states with CSA statutes apparently providing for Type 1 discovery: What constitutes reasonable delay in a Type 1 action, and by what standard is reasonableness ascertained. These issues are sometimes framed in terms of whether to apply an objective reasonable person standard or a more subjective standard that takes into account the effects of the CSA on the victim.[56]

Some courts have held that in order to be subject to delayed accrual the injury itself must be "inherently unascertainable" or "inherently unknowable." Reasoning that repression is the victim's subjective response to the CSA, rather than an objective characteristic of CSA itself, these courts have rejected application of discovery accrual even in Type 2 actions.[57] This reasoning seems strained, and also seems to serve no legitimate social purpose. If a characteristic of a tort is that it usually causes psychological reactions in the victim that prevent the victim from perceiving the tort until years later, is this any different, from a social policy point of view, from a tort that causes inherently hidden injury (such as asbestosis)? Is there any legitimate, social policy reason to blame the victim of CSA for failing to discover the tort earlier, but not the victim of medical malpractice or product liability?

Perhaps the underlying difference is not that one is inherently or objectively unascertainable and the other not, but rather that the reasons for Type 1 delay in CSA actions are foreign to the experience of most judges, who consequently view those reasons as unusual and subjective.

While most courts have found Type 2 delay to fulfill the requirement of objective reasonableness in CSA actions, the same cannot be said of Type 1. Here a tendency to label the unfamiliar as unreasonable can be seen most clearly. Some courts have held all Type 1 delay unreasonable as a matter of law on grounds that, sexual abuse being injurious as a matter of law, knowledge of sexual abuse is knowledge of injury as a matter of law.[58] A related but different basis for rejecting Type 1 delay is the legal doctrine that awareness of any appreciable injury commences the limitations period, and inability to appreciate the full extent of injury does not further delay accrual.[59] Both positions are part of the judicial doctrine of discovery accrual, which may be overcome by a CSA statute that clearly provides for Type 1 discovery.[60]

Even where courts have been willing to consider Type 1 delay as potentially reasonable, it is clear that they often struggle with stereotypes and preconceptions as to the reasonableness of such delay. In general, courts have appeared to be more willing to find the delay potentially reasonable if the plaintiff was a female abused at a tender age, as opposed to a male homosexually abused in his early teens.[61] For example, in *Ernstes v. Warner*, the court held the alleged Type 1 delay of a male plaintiff, molested repeatedly by his junior high science teacher when he was between the ages of thirteen and fifteen, unreasonable as a matter of law, stating that it based its decision on the minor's age at the time of the abuse and the nature of the abuse itself.[62] The court added, "/i/f the victim had been younger or the abuse more threatening, perhaps this might be a different case."[63]

Not all Type 1 delays by male plaintiffs are considered unreasonable, nor all such delays by females reasonable.[64] The trend is a reflection, however, of some of the difficulties inherent in the attempt to apply a delayed discovery exception to Type 1 CSA actions. While a plaintiff's failure to understand the causal connection between medical treatment or product exposure and subsequent injuries is easily understandable to judges and laymen, most people find it difficult to understand, and thus to find reasonable, an adult's inability to make the connection between known CSA and some injury.

Judges, who often must rule on whether a particular Type 1 delay is reasonable or unreasonable as a matter of law, bring to this task their own sense of reasonableness based on their education and life experience. Moreover, they must try to decide each case on the basis of general principles that can be followed consistently, and thus create a "bright line" for future legal reference. The difficulty of doing this in Type 1 actions is probably a factor in the reluctance of courts to find Type 1 delays reasonable, even where a CSA statute provides for it.[65]

Colorado's statutory language, referring to a psychological inability to acknowledge the offense and the harm resulting therefrom, is in many ways a better description of the phenomenon for which relief is being sought in Type 1 cases (and perhaps in Type 2 as well). However, we have not yet had the benefit of any court interpretations of this language, and perhaps when those occur it may be evident that this language does not solve the problem either. California has had success by specifying in its CSA statute that the injury, discovery of which triggers accrual, is "psychological injury or illness occurring after the age of majority," thereby making it clear that it is discovery of the causal connection between adult psychological injuries and the earlier CSA, not knowledge of the CSA itself, that triggers accrual.[66]

The decisions examined earlier illustrate the "catch-22" facing advocates for victims of CSA. Courts are reluctant to permit plaintiffs who have always known of the abuse to sue on a delayed accrual basis, while courts are also viewing with increasing skepticism plaintiffs who claim to have "repressed" and recently recovered memories of CSA. The issues do not appear close to being resolved and are likely to be fought out in our courtrooms and legislatures for years to come.

Practitioners representing Type 1 plaintiffs should put evidence before the court regarding the unique characteristics of CSA that give rise to and thus justify this kind of delay, and make it clear that these characteristics are not subjective or unique to the plaintiff but are general to most victims of CSA. Where there is a statute providing for discovery accrual, it may be helpful to argue that the statutory rule supersedes the judicial discovery rule and provides for a type of discovery accrual that would otherwise not be possible. It may also be useful to point out that most arguments concerning the unreasonableness of Type 1 delay are based on an inability to understand it and/or a tendency to "blame the victim" for not having acted on his or her rights sooner, and that it is this kind of injustice that the CSA statute was intended to correct. It is also important to present the court with a rationale that contains guidelines for determining the objective reasonableness of Type 1 delay in general. This may be done by pointing to facts in one's case which can form the basis for a general rule that can be consistently applied in other cases of Type 1 delay.

## NOTES

1. Only one state, Delaware, does not provide tolling for minority.

2. Appendix A no doubt contains errors and omissions. The author hopes that readers will notify her of any mistakes, as well as any new information to be added.

3. See, e.g., K.C. Meiselman, INCEST: A PSYCHOLOGICAL STUDY OF CAUSES AND EFFECTS WITH TREATMENT RECOMMENDATIONS (San

Francisco: Jossey-Bass, 1991); J. Herman, FATHER-DAUGHTER INCEST (Cambridge: Harvard University Press, 1981); R. Summit, *Beyond Belief: The Reluctant Discovery of Incest,*in WOMEN'S SEXUAL EXPERIENCE, M. Kirkpatrick, ed. (New York: Plenum Press, 1982); D. Gelinas, *The Persisting Negative Effects of Incest,* 46 PSYCHIATRY 312-332 (1983); J. Blake-White and C. M. Kline, *Treating the Dissociative Process in Adult Victims of Childhood Incest,* SOCIAL CASEWORK: THE JOURNAL OF CONTEMPORARY SOCIAL WORK (September 1985) 394-402; D. Russell, THE SECRET TRAUMA: INCEST IN THE LIVES OF GIRLS AND WOMEN (New York: Basic Books, 1986); J. Briere and M. Runtz, *Symptomatology Associated with Childhood Sexual Victimization in a Nonclinical Adult Sample,* 12 CHILD ABUSE & NEGLECT 51-59 (1988).

4. See, e.g., M. G. Salten, *Statutes of Limitations in Civil Incest Suits: Preserving the Victim's Remedy,* 7 HARV. WOMEN'S L. J. 189 (1984); D. M. DeRose, *Adult Incest Survivors and the Statute of Limitations: The Delayed Discovery Rule and Long-Term Damages,* 25 SANTA CLARA L. REV. 191 (1985); J. W. Harshaw, *Not Enough Time?: The Constitutionality of Short Statutes of Limitations for Civil Child Sexual Abuse Litigation,* 50 OHIO ST. L. J. 753 (1989); L. Bickel, *Tolling the Statute of Limitations in Actions Brought by Adult Survivors of Childhood Sexual Abuse,* 33 ARIZ. L. REV. 427 (1991).

5. Solely for convenience, the male pronoun will be used when referring to offenders and the female when referring to victims.

6. *See, e.g., Hammer v. Hammer,* 142 Wis.2d 257, 418 N.W.2d 23 (Wis.App. 1987); *Osland v. Osland,* 442 N.W.2d 907 (N.D. 1989); *Fager v. Hundt,* 610 N.E.2d 246 (Ind. 1993); *Farris v. Compton,* 652 A.2d 49 (D.C.App. 1994); *Ault v. Jasko,* 70 Ohio St.3d 114, 637 N.E.2d 870 (Ohio 1994); *Dunlea v. Dappen,* 83 Haw. 28, 924 P.2d 196 (Haw.1996); *Doe v. Roe,* 955 P.2d 951 (Ariz.1998).

7. *See, e.g., Tyson v. Tyson,* 107 Wash.2d 72, 727 P.2d 226 (Wash. 1986)/superceded by CSA statute/; *DeRose v. Carswell,* 196 Cal.App.3d 1011, 242 Cal.Rptr. 368 (Cal.App. 1987) /superceded by CSA statute/; *E.W. v. D.C.H.* 754 P.2d 817 (Mont. 1988)/superceded by CSA statute/; *Cassidy v. Smith,* 817 P.2d 555 (Colo. 1991)/superceded by CSA statute/; *O'Neal v. Division of Family Services,* 821 P.2d 1139 (Utah 1991) /superceded by CSA statute/; *Lovelace v. Keohane,* 831 P.2d 624 (Okla. 1992) /superceded by CSA statute/.

8. Alaska Stat., Title 9, Section 09.10.140. Arkansas Code Ann., Title 16, Section 16-56-130. California Codes Ann., Code of Civil Procedure, Section 340.1. Colorado Rev. Stat. Ann., Title 13, Section 13-80-103.7. Florida Stat. Ann., Title VIII, Section 95.11. Illinois Compiled Stat. Ann., Act 5, Article 13, Section 5/13-202.2. Iowa Code Ann., Title XXXI, Chapter 614, Section 614.8A. Kansas Stat. Ann., Chapter 60, Section 60-523. Maine Rev. Stat. Ann., Title 14, Section 752-C. Ann. Laws of Massachusetts, Part 3, Title V, Chapter 260, Section 4C. Minnesota Stat. Ann., Part IV, Chapter 541, Section 541.073. Ann. Missouri Stat., Chapter 537, Section 537.046. Montana Code Ann., Title 27, Chapter 2, Section 27-2-216. Nevada Rev. Stat. Ann., Title 2, Chapter 11, Section 11.215. New Jersey Stat. Ann., Title 2A, Chapter 61B, Section 2A:61B-1. New Mexico Stat. 1978 Ann., Chapter 37, Section 37-1-30. Oklahoma Stat. Ann., Title 12, Chapter 3, Section 95, Subsection 6. Oregon Rev. Stat., Title 2, Chapter 12, Section 12.117. Gen. Laws of Rhode Island, Title 9,

Section 9-1-51. South Dakota Codified Laws, Title 26, Chapter 26-10, Section 26-10-25. Utah Code Ann., Title 78, Chapter 12, Section 78-12-25.1. Vermont Stat. Ann., Title 12, Chapter 23, Section 522. Code of Virginia Ann., Title 8.01, Section 8.01-249. Rev. Code of Washington, Title 4, Section 4.16.340. Wisconsin Stat. Ann., Chapter 893, Section 893.587. Wyoming Stat. Ann., Title 1, Chapter 3, Section 1-3-105(b). Note that Colorado is included in this group, although its statute does not use delayed discovery terminology. It provides that a victim of CSA within a "trust-based relationship" may be subject to a psychological disability to sue, defined as being "psychologically and emotionally unable to acknowledge the assault or offense and the harm resulting therefrom," and where such disability is shown may file within six years of its removal. This terminology appears to be a different and perhaps better way of describing what is often meant by "Type 1" discovery in CSA actions. See discussion of "Type 1/Type 2" distinction, *infra*.

9. Connecticut Gen. Stat. Ann., Title 52, Section 52-577d. Code of Georgia Ann. (1994 Rev.), Title 9, Section 9-3-33.1. Idaho Code, Title 6, Section 6-1701 to 6-1705. Louisiana Stat. Ann. Rev., Title 9, Section 2800.9. Texas Codes Ann., Civil Practice & Remedies Code, Section 16.0045.

10. *Farris v. Compton, supra*; *McCollum v. D'Arcy*, 638 A.2d 797 (N.H. 1994), and *Conrad v. Hazen*, 665 A.2d 372 (N.H. 1995); *Florez v. Sargeant*, 185 Ariz. 521, 917 P.2d 250 (Ariz. 1996); *Osland v. Osland, supra; Ault v. Jasko, supra*; *Dunlea v. Dappen, supra*; *Teater v. State of Nebraska*, 252 Neb. 20, 559 N.E.2d 758 (Neb. 1997).

11. *Fager v. Hundt, supra*; *Leonard v. England*, 115 N.C.App. 103, 445 S.E.2d 50 (N.C.App. 1994) rev.grtd.

12. The "Type 1/Type 2" distinction was first made in *Johnson v. Johnson*, 701 F.Supp. 1363 (N.D.Ill. 1988), where discovery accrual was applied to Type 2 discovery. The distinction has since dominated judicial thinking on the issue, and the terminology has been adopted as a shorthand way of referencing it in many decisions.

13. *See, Roberts v. Caton*, 224 Conn. 483, 619 A.2d 844 (Conn. 1993).

14. *See, Liebig v. Superior Court*, 209 Cal.App.3d 828, 257 Cal.Rptr. 574 (Cal.App. 1989); *Lent v. Doe*, 40 Cal.App.4th 1177, 47 Cal.Rptr.2d 389 (Cal.App. 1995); *K.E. v. Hoffman*, 452 N.W.2d 509 (Minn.App. 1990); Cosgriffe v. Cosgriffe, 864 P.2d 776 (Mont. 1993); *A.K.H. v. R.C.T.*, 312 Or. 497, 822 P.2d 135 (Or. 1991).

15. *See, Wiley v. Roof*, 641 So.2d 66 (Fla. 1994); *Doe v. Roman Catholic Diocese of Jefferson City*, 862 S.W.2d 338 (Mo. 1993); *Kelly v. Marcantonio*, 678 A.2d 873 (R.I. 1996); *Starnes v. Cayouette*, 419 S.E.2d 669 (Va. 1992) /superceded by Constitutional Amendment, 1995, and legislative enactment, 1996/.

16. *David A. v. Superior Court*, 20 Cal.App.4th 281, 24 Cal.Rptr.2d 537 (Cal.App. 1993) /superceded by 1994 amendments adding express language of revival and making the language applicable to any action filed since the original effective date of the CSA statute/; *Frideres v. Schiltz*, 540 N.W.2d 261 (Iowa 1995).

17. *K.E. v. Hoffmann*, 452 N.W.2d 509 (Minn.App. 1990).

18. *Cosgriffe v. Cosgriffe*, 864 P.2d 776 (Mont. 1993).

19. *Liebig v. Superior Court*, 209 Cal.App.3d 828, 257 Cal.Rptr. 574 (Cal.App. 1989); *Lent v. Doe*, 40 Cal.App.4th 1177, 47 Cal.Rptr.2d 389 (Cal.App. 1995); *A.K.H. v. R.C.T.*, 312 Or. 497, 822 P.2d 135 (Or. 1991).

20. *Almonte v. New York Medical College*, 851 F.Supp. 34 (D.Conn. 1994); *Frideres v. Schiltz*, 540 N.W.2d 261 (Iowa 1995).

21. Minnesota Stat. Ann., Part IV, Chapter 541, Section 541.073.

22. New Jersey Stat. Ann., Title 2A, Chapter 61B, Section 2A:61B-1.

23. Oregon Rev. Stat., Title 2, Chapter 12, Section 12.117.

24. Utah Code Ann., Title 78, Chapter 12, Section 78-12-25.1.

25. Code of Virginia Ann., Title 8.01, Section 8.01-249.

26. Alaska Stat., Title 9, Section 09.10.060. Idaho Code, Title 6, Section 6-1701. Louisiana Stat.Ann.Rev., Title 9, Section 2800.9.

27. Arkansas Code Ann., Title 16, Section 16-56-130. Colorado Rev.Stat.Ann., Title 13, Section 13-80-103.7. Florida Stat.Ann., Title VIII, Section 95.11. Maine Rev.Stat.Ann., Title 14, Section 752-C. Gen. Laws of Massachusetts, Part 3, Title V, Chapter 260, Section 4C. Montana Code Ann., Title 27, Chapter 2, Section 27-2-216. New Mexico Stat. 1978 Ann., Chapter 37, Section 37-1-30. Oklahoma Stat.Ann., Title 12, Chapter 3, Section 95, Subsection 6. General Laws of Rhode Island, Title 9, Section 9-1-51. South Dakota Codified Laws, Title 26, Chapter 26-10, Section 26-10-25. Texas Codes Ann., Civil Practice & Remedies Code, Section 16.0045. Rev. Code of Washington Ann., Title 4, Section 4.16.340. Wyoming Stat.Ann., Title 1, Chapter 3, Section 1-3-105(b).

28. *See*, *Kelly v. Marcantonio*, 678 A.2d 873 (R.I.1996), and *Werre v. David*, 913 P.2d 635 (Mont.1996).

29. California Codes Ann., Code of Civil Procedure, Section 340.1. Connecticut Gen.Stat.Ann., Title 52, Section 52-577d. Code of Georgia Ann. (1994 Rev.), Title 9, Section 9-3-33.1. Iowa Code Ann., Title XXXI, Chapter 614, Section 614.8A. Kansas Stat.Ann., Chapter 60, Section 60-523. Ann. Missouri Stat., Chapter 537, Section 537.046. Nevada Rev.Stat.Ann., Title 2, Chapter 11, Section 11.215. Vermont Stat.Ann., Title 12, Chapter 23, Section 522. Wisconsin Stat.Ann., Chapter 893, Section 893.587.

30. *See* footnote 20, *supra*.

31. *Debbie Reynolds Studios v. Superior Court*, 25 Cal.App.4th 222, 30 Cal.Rptr. 2d 514 (Cal.App. 1994).

32. *See, e.g., Barquin v. Roman Catholic Diocese of Burlington*, 839 F.Supp. 275 (D.Vt. 1993).

33. Delaware and West Virginia.

34. Alabama: *Travis v. Ziter*, 681 So.2d 1348 (Ala. 1996); Kentucky: *Rigazio v. Archdiocese of Louisville*, *supra*, 853 S.W.2d 295. Maryland: *Doe v. Maskell*, 679 A.2d 1087 (Md. 1996). Michigan: *Lemmerman v. Fealk*, *supra*, 534 N.W.2d 695. New York: *Bassile v. Covenant House*, 152 Misc.2d 88, 575 N.Y.S.2d 233, (N.Y.Sup. 1991) aff'd, 191 A.D.2d 188, 594 N.Y.S.2d 192 (N.Y.App. 1993); and *Burpee v. Burpee*, 152 Misc.2d 466, 578 N.Y.S.2d 359 (N.Y.Sup. 1991). Pennsylvania: *E.J.M. v. Archdiocese of Philadelphia*, 424 Pa.Super. 449, 622 A.2d 1388 (Pa.Super. 1993); and *Seto v. Willits*, 432 Pa.Super. 346, 638 A.2d 258 (Pa.Super. 1994). South Carolina: *Doe v. R.D.*, 308 S.C. 139, 417 S.E.2d 541 (S.C. 1992); and *Roe v. Doe*, 28 F.3d 404 (4th Cir. 1994). Tennessee: *Doe v. Coffee County Board of Education*, 852 S.W.2d 899 (Tenn.App. 1992) /Type 1 case; decision did not address Type 2/.

35. *Fager v. Hundt, supra*, 610 N.E.2d 246; *Ernstes v. Warner*, 860 F.Supp. 1338 (S.D.Ind. 1994). Fager involved a "Type 2" plaintiff, and it is not clear from the decision whether the court would apply the exception to a Type 1 plaintiff suing a parent.

36. *Leonard v. England*, 445 S.E.2d 50 (N.C.App.1994). Per conversation with plaintiff's attorney, the State Supreme Court granted defendant's petition for review, then granted plaintiff's petition for dismissal of the action. As the decision was not ordered depublished, it appears to stand as citable authority.

37. Connecticut Gen. Stat. Ann., Title 52, Section 52-577d. Code of Georgia Ann. (1994 Rev.), Title 9, Section 9-3-33.1. Idaho Code, Title 6, Sections 6-1701 through 6-1705. Louisiana Stat. Ann. Rev., Title 9, Section 2800.9. Texas Codes Ann., Civil Practice and Remedies Code, Section 16.0045.

38. Arizona: *Doe v. Roe*, 955 P.2d 951 (Ariz.1998). California: *Lent v. Doe, supra*, 40 Cal.App.4th 1177, 47 Cal.Rptr.2d 389. Hawaii: *Dunlea v. Dappen, supra*, 83 Haw. 28, 924 P.2d 196. Illinois: *D.P. v. M.J.O., supra*, 640 N.E.2d 1323. Iowa: *Frideres v. Schiltz, supra*, 540 N.W.2d 261. Kansas: *Shirley v. Reif*, 920 P.2d 405 (Kan.1996). Massachusetts: *Flanagan v. Grant, supra*, 897 F.Supp. 637. Montana: *Cosgriffe v. Cosgriffe, supra*, 864 P.2d 776. New Mexico: *Martinez-Sandoval v. Kirsch, supra*, 884 P.2d 507, rev.den. North Dakota: *Osland v. Osland, supra*, 442 N.W.2d 907. Oregon: *Flaningam v. Flaningam*, 929 P.2d 1084 (Or.App.1996). Washington: *Oostra v. Holstine*, 86 Wash.App. 536, 937 P.2d 195 (Wash.App. 1997). Wisconsin: *Hammer v. Hammer*, supra, 418 N.W.2d 23.

39. Alaska, Arkansas, Colorado, Florida, Nevada, New Jersey, Rhode Island, South Dakota, Vermont, and Virginia.

40. *Cevenini v. Archbishop of Washington*, 707 A.2d 768 (D.C.App.1998); *Scott v. Borelli*, 666 N.E.2d 322 (Ohio.App.1995); *Conrad v. Hazen*, 665 A.2d 372 (N.Hamp.1995), and *Taylor v. Litteer*, 925 F.Supp. 898 (D.N.Hamp.1996).

41. *See, Blackowiak v. Kemp*, 546 N.W.2d 1 (Minn.1996), and *W.J.L. v. Bugge*, 573 N.W.2d 677 (Minn.1998).

42. *See, e.g., Flanagan v. Grant*, 897 F.Supp. 637 (D.Mass.1995); *Martinez-Sandoval v. Kirsch*, 884 P.2d 507 (N.Mex.App.1994).

43. *Travis v. Ziter*, 681 So. 2d 1348 (Ala. 1996).

44. *Lemmerman v. Fealk, supra*, 534 N.W.2d 695.

45. *E.J.M. v. Archdiocese of Philadelphia, supra*, 622 A.2d 1388, and *Seto v. Willits, supra*, 638 A.2d 258.

46. *Doe v. R.D., supra*, 417 S.E.2d 541, and *Roe v. Doe, supra*, 28 F.3d 404.

47. *S.V. v. R.V., supra*, 1996 WL 112206.

48. *Doe v. Maskell, supra*, 679 A.2d 1087.

49. The "false memory syndrome" movement contends that there is no scientific basis for the concept that memories of CSA are or can be totally repressed and later recovered by the victim, and claims that most if not all such allegations are the result of over-suggestive psychotherapy or other forms of influence. *See, e.g.*, False Memory Syndrome Foundation, *The False Memory Syndrome Phenomenon* (Philadelphia: False Memory Syndrome Foundation, 1992); H. Wakefield and R. Underwager, *Uncovering Memories of Alleged Sexual Abuse: The Therapists Who Do It* and R.A. Gardner, *Belated Realization of Child Sexual Abuse by an Adult, Issues in*

*Child Abuse Allegations*, vol. 4, no. 2, Fall 1992, 177-213; E. Loftus, & K. Ketcham, *The Myth of Repressed Memory* New York (St. Martin's Press, 1994); R. Ofshe, & E. Watters, *Making Monsters: False Memories, Psychotherapy, and Sexual Hysteria* (New York, Charles Scribners' Sons, 1994); C. Wassil-Grimm, *Diagnosis for Disaster: The Devastating Truth About False Memory Syndrome and Its Impact on Accusers and Families* (Woodstock, New York, The Overlook Press, 1995); Ofra Bickel, Public Broadcasting Service, and WGBH Television (Boston), FRONTLINE, "Divided Memories," first aired April 1995.

To date, no studies or case reports of "false memory syndrome" have been published in the peer-reviewed professional literature, nor is the "syndrome" being considered for inclusion in the APA's Diagnostic and Statistical Manual of Mental Disorders. Evidence for the existence of such a "syndrome," or even for the existence of a significant number of instances of therapy-induced memories of CSA that are essentially and verifiably false, is anecdotal and extremely slim. See, D., Brown, "*Pseudomemories: The Standard of Science and the Standard of Care in Trauma Treatment*," AMERICAN JOURNAL OF CLINICAL HYPNOSIS 37:3, January 1995. Nevertheless, the false memory movement has captured the public mind and greatly impacted recent judicial thinking on adult CSA actions.

50. Numerous decisions have reiterated these basic elements of the discovery rule as the reason for holding it inapplicable to Type 1 discovery of CSA. *See, e.g., DeRose v. Carswell, supra*, 242 Cal.Rptr. 368 /superceded by CSA statute/; *Cassidy v. Smith*, 817 P.2d 555 (Colo.App. 1991) /superceded by CSA statute/; *E.W. v. D.C.H., supra*, 754 P.2d 817 /superceded by CSA statute/; *O'Neal v. Division of Family Services*, 821 P.2d 1139 (Utah 1991) /superceded by CSA statute/.

51. For an excellent example of such arguments, see the Arizona courts' recent decisions in *Nolde v. Franke*, 949 P.2d 511, (Ariz.App.1997) rev.grtd., and *Doe v. Roe*, 955 P.2d 951 (Ariz.1998).

52. *See, e.g., Tyson v. Tyson, supra*, 727 P.2d 226 /superceded by CSA statute/.

53. 546 N.W.2d 1 (Minn.1996).

54. 573 N.W.2d 677 (Minn.1998).

55. *Blackowiak, supra,* 3.

56. *See Martinez-Sandoval v. Kirsch*, 884 P.2d 507 (N.Mex.App.1994); *Shirley v. Reif*, 920 P.2d 405 (Kan.1996); *Frideres v. Schlitz*, 113 F.3d 897 (8th Cir.1997).

57. *See, e.g., Tichenor v. Roman Catholic Church*, 32 F.3d 953 (5th Cir. 1994) /applying Mississippi law/; *Vandenheuvel v. Sowell*, 886 S.W.2d 100 (Mo.App. 1994), rev.den. /but see *Sheehan v. Sheehan*, 901 S.W.2d 57 (Mo. 1995), where Missouri high court appears to open door to delayed accrual for repression/; *Lovelace v. Keohane, supra*, 831 P.2d 624 /superceded by CSA statute/; *Seto v. Willits, supra*, 638 A.2d 258; *Roe v. Doe, supra*, 28 F.3d 404; *Sanchez v. Archdiocese of San Antonio, supra*, 873 S.W.2d 87; *S.V. v. R.V., supra*, 1196 WL 112206.

58. In addition to *Blackowiak, supra*, this reasoning is found in *DeRose v. Carswell, supra*, 242 Cal.Rptr. 368 /superceded by CSA statute/; *E.W. v. D.C.H., supra*, 754 P.2d 817 /superceded by CSA statute/.

59. *See, e.g., DeRose, supra* /superceded by statute/; *Cassidy v. Smith*, 817 P.2d 555 (Colo.App. 1991) /superceded by statute/; *Bock v. Harmon, supra*, 526 So.2d 292; *E.W. v. D.C.H., supra*, 754 P.2d 817 /superceded by statute/; *Doe v. First United*

*Methodist Church*, 68 Ohio St.3d 531, 629 N.E.2d 402 (Ohio 1994); *Doe v. Coffee County Board of Education*, *supra*, 852 S.W.2d 899; *O'Neal v. Division of Family Services*, 821 P.2d 1139 (Utah 1991) /superceded by statute/.

60. *See*, *Lent v. Doe*, *supra*, 47 Cal.Rptr.2d 389, rev.den.; *Cosgriffe v. Cosgriffe*, *supra*, 864 P.2d 776. But, *cf.*, *Blackowiak v. Kemp*, *supra*, 546 N.W.2d 1.

61. *See, e.g.*, *Snyder v. Boy Scouts of America* 205 Cal.App.3d 1318, 253 Cal.Rptr. 156 (Cal.App. 1988) /male molested by Boy Scout leader at ages 11 to 15/; *Ernstes v. Warner*, 860 F.Supp. 1338 (S.D.Ind. 1994) / male molested by male junior high teacher at ages 13 to 15/; *Bock v. Harmon* 526 So.2d 292 (La.App. 1988) /male molested by father at ages 12 to 18/. Cf., *D.P. v. M.J.O.*, 266 Ill.App.3d 1029, 640 N.E.2d 1323 (Ill.App. 1994) /females molested by father at ages 3 to 18, held Type 1 delay potentially reasonable/; *Sinclair v. Brill*, 857 F.Supp. 132 (D.N.Hamp. 1994) /female molested and abused by guardians at ages 11 to 18, held a reasonable person could find her delay reasonable/.

62. 860 F.Supp. 1338 (S.D.Ind. 1994).

63. *Id.*, 1340.

64. *See*, *Wimberly v. Gatch*, 635 So.2d 206 (La. 1994) /still minor male, molested at ages 9-10 by older boy, held delay in disclosure to others reasonable/; *Phinney v. Morgan*, 39 Mass.App.Ct. 202, 654 N.E.2d 77 (Mass.App. 1995) /females molested by father, had complained to mother who did not help, and had complained to siblings more than three years before filing, held Type 1 delay not reasonable/; *Flanagan v. Grant*, 897 F.Supp. 637 (D.Mass. 1995) /female molested by father at ages 14 to 18, disclosed at 18 and then retracted, held Type 1 delay unreasonable/; *Martinez-Sandoval v. Kirsch*, 118 N.M. 616, 884 P.2d 507 (N.Mex.App. 1994) /female molested by priest at ages 15 to 19, knew sexual contact had caused her venereal disease and pregnancy, held Type 1 delay unreasonable/.

65. *See, e.g.*, *Woodroffe v. Hasenclever*, 540 N.W.2d 45 (Iowa 1995); *Flanagan v. Grant*, *supra*, 897 F.Supp. 637; *Doe v. Redeemer Lutheran Church*, 531 N.W.2d 897, (Minn.App. 1995) rev.grtd.; *S.E. v. Shattuck-St. Mary's School*, 533 N.W.2d 628, (Minn.App. 1995) rev.den.; *Martinez-Sandoval v. Kirsch*, *supra*, 884 P.2d 507, rev.den.

66. *Lent v. Doe*, *supra*, 47 Cal.Rptr.2d 389, rev.den.; *Sellery v. Cressey*, *supra*, 48 Cal.App.4th 538.

# Sexual Abuse Litigation: A Difficult Journey Through Unfamiliar Territory

Janet L. Sonne
Julian J. Hubbard

**SUMMARY.** Practicing psychologist Janet Sonne and attorney Julian Hubbard illuminate how the different aims and languages of psychotherapy and law can be either an asset or a liability in the emotionally-charged environment of sexual abuse litigation. Properly understood, these differences can optimize the ability of each professional to assist their common client, the sexual abuse survivor, in the litigation process and beyond. Dr. Sonne reviews the psychological and behavioral sequelae of childhood sexual abuse and identifies six elements of the client's psychological functioning key to the litigation process, as well as posing questions for the attorney's self-evaluation for the unique demands of sexual abuse litigation. Mr. Hubbard then addresses what survivors and therapists need to know about the litigation process, exploring dynamics of legal strategy that can exacerbate the client's psychological problems. In the final section, both offer tips to enhance professionals' focus on education and communication as a means to better serving the sexually abused client. *[Article copies available for a fee from The Haworth Document Delivery Service: 1-800-342-9678. E-mail address: <getinfo@haworthpressinc.com> Website: <http://www.haworthpressinc.com>]*

---

Address correspondence to: Janet L. Sonne, PhD, Professor, Department of Psychology, Loma Linda University, 11130 Anderson Street, Loma Linda, CA 92350.

[Haworth co-indexing entry note]: "Sexual Abuse Litigation: A Difficult Journey Through Unfamiliar Territory." Sonne, Janet L., and Julian J. Hubbard. Co-published simultaneously in *Journal of Aggression, Maltreatment & Trauma* (The Haworth Maltreatment & Trauma Press, an imprint of The Haworth Press, Inc.) Vol. 3, No. 2 (#6), 2000, pp. 73-95; and: *Sexual Abuse Litigation: A Practical Resource for Attorneys, Clinicians, and Advocates* (ed: Rebecca Rix) The Haworth Maltreatment & Trauma Press, an imprint of The Haworth Press, Inc., 2000, pp. 73-95. Single or multiple copies of this article are available for a fee from The Haworth Document Delivery Service [1-800-342-9678, 9:00 a.m. - 5:00 p.m. (EST). E-mail address: getinfo@haworthpressinc.com].

 

**KEYWORDS.** Narrative versus historical truth, psychological and behavioral effects of CSA, ego strength of survivor, client's motivation to pursue litigation, support systems for client, psychological effects of litigation on client, emotional justice versus legal justice, attorney self-evaluation, costs of litigation, unpredictability of litigation, Adversarial, empirical nature of litigation, defendant's rights, defense strategies, right of privacy, professional boundaries, triangularization

Sexual abuse litigation is a journey through unfamiliar territory for most attorneys and other advocates. This new territory has a unique, sometimes treacherous terrain and a language which can sound foreign to litigators. This chapter provides attorneys, mental health professionals (psychiatrists, psychologists, social workers, and marriage and family counselors), and survivors "maps" and "translations" for this journey. It is based on Janet Sonne's experience as a clinical psychologist specializing in the treatment of survivors and perpetrators of sexual abuse and a consultant to attorneys regarding such cases, and on Julian Hubbard's experience as a plaintiff and defense attorney in sexual abuse cases.

## *BEFORE YOU BEGIN THE JOURNEY: MAPPING THE TERRAIN AND LEARNING THE LANGUAGE*

### *Psychological Sequelae of Sexual Abuse: Understanding Six Key Areas of the Survivor's Psychological Functioning*

An integral factor in the journey of sexual abuse litigation is the survivor. The survivor's psychological and behavioral functioning throughout the litigation process will necessarily influence the quality of "travel" for all involved. It is, therefore, imperative that the attorney be familiar with the nature and terminology of the psychological impact of sexual abuse on the survivor/client. Understanding the client's psychological functioning will facilitate the anticipation of potential "rocky roads" or missed communications. Only then can the attorney take appropriate measures to safeguard the welfare of the survivor. As tempting as it may be to begin the sexual abuse litigation journey without first consulting any "roadmaps" or "language guides," the potential client and the attorney are best served when that familiarity precedes the decision to file a public complaint.

Sexual abuse (whether experienced as a child or as an adult) can impose a variety of possible long-term psychological and behavioral sequelae on the survivor. Research findings suggest that the specific impact of sexual abuse on an individual varies according to the nature and context of the abuse experience and the individual characteristics of the survivor (e.g., the age at onset of the abuse, personality traits, etc.). Psychological sequelae of sexual abuse include: depression and suicidality, anxiety and fear, cognitive distortions (e.g., automatic assumptions that the world is a dangerous, threatening place), doubt and confusion regarding one's perceptions, identity confusion and psychological boundary issues, mistrust of and ambivalence about close interpersonal relationships, and post-traumatic stress disorder. Further, as an attempt to cope with such dysphoric symptoms, survivors tend to engage in ultimately maladaptive behaviors such as alcohol and drug abuse, self-mutilation, bingeing and purging, sexual promiscuity, gambling, and compulsive overinvolvement in work or sport endeavors.[1]

The attorney will benefit at the outset from consultation with a mental health professional–either the potential client's psychotherapist or an expert retained by the attorney–regarding the manifestations of such sequelae in the survivor's psychological and behavioral functioning. Such an assessment may impact the decision to file a complaint and will certainly aid the attorney during the process of the litigation. Accordingly, we recommend that the attorney immediately obtain the client's authorization to speak to his or her therapist and obtain a written release to do so at their first meeting. The mental health professional may assess several critical areas of functioning: ego strength and defenses, severity of acute symptoms, motivation to pursue litigation, emotional and social support systems, cycles of mistrust, and the ability to cope with a negative outcome of the litigation.

*Ego Strength and Defenses.* The mental health professional can provide the attorney with an assessment of the client's overall ego strength and characteristic psychological defenses. Simply defined, ego strength (or ego resiliency) refers to the capacity of the individual to: (1) control and regulate instinctual drives, (2) exercise appropriate judgment, (3) distinguish internal fantasy from external reality, (4) form and maintain mutually satisfying interpersonal relationships, and (5) form and maintain a coherent sense of self. Psychological (or ego) defenses provide a critical component of ego resiliency by operating to control and modulate unacceptable instinctual drives or feelings associated with the drives by allowing expression of the drives in a disguised and more acceptable manner. Some ego defenses are potentially more maladaptive for the individual than others. For instance, "acting out" is a defense through which the individual expresses an unconscious wish or drive through impulsive behavior to avoid being conscious of an accompanying feeling. The person who desires to express him- or herself in a sexually aggressive manner may act out by finding and engaging with multiple sexual partners. Dissociation (another defense) is a temporary but marked modification of an individual's character or sense of personal identity which occurs to avoid severe emotional distress. Victims of sexual abuse often describe first dissociating during the abuse event; for example, some have reported a sensation of floating out of their bodies up to a corner of a room's ceiling to observe the event as it occurred.

An individual's ego strength is most critical in circumstances in which the individual experiences external stress. As noted above, the experience of sexual abuse can negatively and seriously impact the survivor's ego functioning, leaving the individual less ego-resilient and, thus, vulnerable to serious complications in the face of stress in general and, specifically, the stress of litigation. Litigation stress can activate characteristic defenses for the client, such as acting-out and dissociation, which can severely complicate and even compromise the process of pursuing litigation. Litigation stress can also precipitate psychotic decompensation in the client with severely compromised ego strength. Such decompensation entails the overwhelming of the ego functions such that the individual can no longer distinguish internal fantasy from external reality; the individual experiences psychotic symptoms such as delusions or hallucinations.

*Severity of Acute Symptoms.* The survivor of sexual abuse may experience a variety of psychological and behavioral symptoms, as noted above. An assessment of the severity of those sequelae is imperative before the decision is made whether to proceed with litigation. The emotional and practical demands of such a process on the survivor can be overwhelming for the individual who is severely depressed and acutely suicidal, suffering from extreme symptoms of post-traumatic stress disorder (e.g., severe anxiety, flashbacks, nightmares), abusing illicit drugs and/or alcohol, or engaging in dangerous self-mutilative behavior. The client who experiences such severe symptoms is likely to have difficulty recounting, and even remembering, the specifics of the abuse experience–the very basis of the proposed claim.

*Motivation to Pursue Litigation.* The client's motivation to pursue litigation must be clarified. It is common for victims of abuse to have ambivalent feelings regarding the accused. On the one hand, the alleged abuser is likely to be someone the client has known, trusted, identified with, depended on, and even loved. On the other hand, the client is likely to experience feelings of marked anger and betrayal; those feelings typically trigger the client's initial pursuit of litigation. The client often experiences intense desires to punish the alleged perpetrator and to prevent the harm of others. The client also may experience feelings of terror of potential physical recrimination or attack by the accused. The client's feelings toward the alleged abuser are likely to remain mixed throughout the litigation journey; even the most angry client may have extended periods of wishing to withdraw from the case for fear of hurting or angering the accused, for fear of being hurt or overwhelmed by anger.

*Emotional and Social Support Systems.* A thorough assessment of the client's emotional and social support systems is critical to insure his or her well-being and, often, safety from retraumatization. The rigors of the litigation journey are notorious–finding and gathering data for interrogatories, consultation and decision-making with counsel, traveling and appearing for deposition and, if necessary, giving trial testimony. Further, the risk is high that the negative sequelae of the sexual abuse will remain active or even increase during the litigation process. Various aspects of the legal process can evoke the abuse trauma, triggering depression, panic attacks, posttraumatic recollections or flashbacks of the events, and other symptoms.

Counsel can and often does become the client's *de facto* support system. To minimize the risk of overburdening the professional relationship, however, counsel must evaluate whether the client can rely on others (a spouse or significant other, parents, siblings, friends, support group members) for active emotional, practical, and, if necessary, financial support during the process of litigation. Unfortunately, the simple presence of a relationship (e.g., a marriage) does not insure a supportive relationship with regard to litigation. Some spouses and family members may actively oppose the client's pursuit of litigation.

An assessment also must be made of the client's willingness to engage in counseling or psychotherapy. A therapist can carefully monitor the client for indications of suicidal intent and/or other forms of self-harm such as physical self-mutilation, substance abuse, or disordered eating (bingeing, purging). The therapist can also continue assessment of the client's reactivity in relation to the alleged perpetrator (e.g., monitoring their level of anger, even rage, at the defendant or at others perceived as "conspiring" with the defendant or as not protecting the victim). Should the therapist suspect that the client may act-out on his or her rage against an individual, the therapist may then have the legal responsibility in some states to issue a warning to that individual and to a law enforcement agency (in California, the duty to warn is codified in Civil Code Section 43.92).

The therapist also can monitor the effects of the litigation process on significant others in the client's life. Often the litigation stress affects the client's support system adversely, potentially compromising the client's welfare. Significant others must cope with their own feelings of blame, confusion, and anger as well as the emotionality of the client. They must cope with the social effects of media publicity and the financial stress litigation often involves. The mental health professional may conduct conjoint and/or family sessions to assess and to ease that stress. The privacy right of family members should be discussed and the divulgence of their personal issues protected from disclosure in the litigation. The attorney who is informed of the need for conjoint work can hold an informational meeting with the client and those individuals in his or her support system.

If the client is involved in psychotherapy prior to pursuit of litigation, the attorney must also consider the legal ramifications of the techniques used in that therapy in the initial assessment. Some therapeutic interventions designed to reduce severe anxiety may actually contaminate the litigation process. For example, if the client has been hypnotized or led through guided imagery exercises to desensitize feeling of fear or panic, all memories related to the abuse may be tainted and rendered inadmissible as a matter of law in many jurisdictions. Further, hypnotically refreshed memory has been treated with a great deal of suspicion by the court because of the potential for the distortion of the memory resulting from suggestion.[2]

The attorney must not assume that the client's involvement in individual psychotherapy is sufficient enough therapeutic support. Although such involvement is important and helpful, it is not, and cannot be, insurance of the broad band of support such clients need. First, the sexually abused client typically experiences many issues regarding trust of and safety around authority figures. Thus, the relationship with a therapist is likely to be tentative and conflicted. Second, the psychotherapist carries at all times the professional responsibility to operate within clear role boundaries. Such responsibility limits the therapist's interactions with the client to the psychotherapy sessions and some phone conversations and thus obviates participation in many of the client's extensive support needs. For instance, the therapist cannot ethically provide much practical support (e.g., baby-sitting children during the client's deposition or driving the client to trial). Other sources of therapeutic and practical support may be suggested by the attorney and/or the treating psychotherapist. For instance, the client may be referred to group psychotherapy, organized self-help activities, or child care groups.

*Cycles of Mistrust.* The pre-litigation assessment should establish the appropriate environment to develop the client's trust while ensuring the client's right to be assertive with the prospective attorney. Victims of sexual abuse have experienced betrayal of their trust by authority figures upon whom they depended. The resulting loss of a sense of power, control, and trust often permeates the client's life and emotional outlook, typically generalizing to and affecting the relationship with their attorney. If the sense of powerlessness and mistrust are very marked, the litigation journey becomes extremely difficult, if not impossible, for all concerned. The juxtaposition of powerlessness and mistrust often produces a curious counterpoint, in that the client's mistrust is all-too-often paired with a rather passive acceptance of an attorney's decisions and actions, at least until the attorney commits what the client perceives as "last straw" behavior. Abuse clients may experience a series of interactions with their attorneys in which their questions do not get asked and their objections to actions are neither raised nor resolved. Counsel may then be surprised by the client's apparently "sudden" decision to change attorneys.

The sexual abuse survivor's sense of powerlessness and mistrust often also extends to their relationship with their therapist. Thus, as noted previously, the relationship with the therapist can be just as tentative and conflicted as the relationship with counsel. It should be anticipated that the client may discuss concerns or difficulties that he or she is experiencing with either of the two professionals with the other. If such discussions are allowed or encouraged, triangulation may result in which tension in one dyad (e.g., the attorney-client dyad) is decreased by one member of that dyad pulling a third party (e.g., the therapist) into an alliance against the other member. It is also important for both professionals to be aware that some clients, as an expression of their psychopathology, may engage in a process called splitting with the attorney and the therapist which can rigidify the triangulation. Splitting is a psychological defense process through which one person is perceived, characterized, and presented by the client as "all bad" and the other as "all good." In these circumstances, the client should be supported and encouraged to confront the professional with whom there is an issue and to work for resolution to the client's satisfaction in a manner consistent with his or her best interests. Further, open communication between the two professionals must be maintained to check the client's perceptions of the "goodness" and "badness" of the conduct of each.

*Ability to Cope with a Negative Outcome of Litigation.* An assessment must be made of the client's ability to accept and cope with the possibility that the legal case may not result in a positive outcome. A loss carries with it several potentially very negative psychological, emotional, social, and economic results. Frequently, an abuse survivor is pursuing litigation for validation, desiring acknowledgment of the abuse from others, as well as to ensure that the perpetrator takes responsibility for his or her inappropriate behavior. During the course of seeking this validation, the survivor may experience an emerging sense of self and empowerment surrounded by therapists, experts, attorneys, and support group members who provide attention and support. When there is a defense verdict, the survivor may feel rejected, lacking in worth and credibility to the world at large, and, once again, powerless. The attention and support will fall away. The attorneys are likely to focus on other matters. The doubters will assure the survivor that they knew all along that none of the abuse ever happened.

The survivor may then begin to question his or her own sanity, the perceptions of the abusive behavior, and of experiences in general. The client may also feel confused regarding who is responsible for the abusive behavior and may feel guilty and ashamed. The legal loss can trigger many of the same sensations and feelings associated with the abuse–but the arena is now the social world which has become like a large mirror of his or her most negative self-image.

These particular problems can be exacerbated by the economic realities of losing. Sometimes, the client will become responsible for paying both the defense costs and his or her own costs. If experts are retained in the litigation, the resulting debt can be many thousands of dollars. If the client is working or has saved money, dollars that could have gone to therapy, education, or recovery will now be spent paying for the litigation. The debt may be sufficiently large that it will hover and shadow the client for a long time.

The client may have initiated the litigation partially out of a desire to regain control and a sense of empowerment and to see that the perpetrator is punished. Given the realities of losing, desperation and anger may overwhelm the survivor. The client may feel that the legal system failed or that the perpetrator is all-powerful and has gotten away with their abusive behavior. Under these conditions, when the client has poor ego strength and feels depleted of resources and support, he or she may act to personally exact the punishment of the defendant, for instance by injuring self or others, slashing tires, sending letters and news clippings to the alleged perpetrator's employers, obsessive phone calling, or engaging in an actual physical attack.

To avoid this result, the attorney must assist the client in understanding the fundamental difference between emotional justice and legal justice. Legal justice does not always permit emotional justice, even if there is a plaintiff decision. In a civil case, the compensation award may be very low and all of the causes of action may not prevail. In a criminal case, the defendant may avoid incarceration or gain a reduced punishment through plea-bargain. It is the province of the therapist to assist the client in discovering that emotional justice is inner work; that the highest and best result will always be the survivor's progress towards re-empowerment and, ultimately, psychological healing.

### *Meeting the Unique Challenges Posed by Sexual Abuse Litigation: Critical Issues for the Lawyer*

A second integral factor in the journey of sexual abuse litigation is the preparation of the attorney to meet the terrain's unique challenges. As a result, the initial case evaluation must include a likely unfamiliar facet: the attorney's realistic self-evaluation of his or her willingness and ability to undertake the demanding and challenging work associated with the sexual abuse survivor/client. The self-evaluation should include the abuse litigator's ability to understand and manage the client's psychological dynamics, the extra dimensions of responsibility assumed by the attorney, and the case preparation and emotional support costs of sexual abuse litigation.

*Ability to Understand and Manage the Client's Dynamics.* As discussed above, the abuse survivor is often dealing with issues related to authority and trust, sexual identity, memory, and boundaries far more intense than the attorney's usual clientele. The attorney may experience the survivor's exquisite sensitivity to the ordinary stresses of the attorney-client relationship as unpredictable and an uncomfortable departure from the norm. For example, the abuse client may resent the accepted and ordinary authority and trust afforded the attorney to handle the legal details, as she or he may feel vulnerable to manipulation. On the other hand, the client may rely too much on the attorney, checking critical faculties at the door, merging with the attorney's authority and becoming unable to make decisions. The client may dress inappropriately, request hugs and physical contact, or act suggestively with the attorney as a means of testing normalized boundaries. The client may express interest in the personal life of the attorney, attempt to adopt a caretaker role with him or her and then resent the resulting burden of the attorney's emotional issues

*An Extra Dimension of Responsibility.* The very fact that the abuse survivor has been damaged by an exploitative relationship often imposes a greater measure of responsibility on the litigator. In many cases, the attorney may represent one of the first real relationships for the abuse survivor, albeit a professional one, in which every secret and every raw motive is revealed. The relationship may become a potential model for the client's recovery and subsequent psychological outlook. As the litigation is pending, the abuse client may try to integrate more appropriate modes of interaction into deeply embedded patterns of defensive behaviors such as acting-out and self-destruction. As a result, the attorney-client alliance presents enormous metaphorical implications for the client's future well-being.

*Costs: Case Preparation and Emotional Support.* As part of the self-evaluation process, the attorney must also consider the costs of case preparation and emotional support associated with sexual abuse litigation. Case preparation is frequently complex and thus often expensive. Defense attorneys often attempt any means to discredit the survivor's memory or past. The defense may perform intensive investigation and discovery to paint the survivor in a particularly unfavorable light. Thus, the attorney may need to conduct a similarly exhaustive investigation to prepare the survivor's case, reviewing records, interviewing key percipient witnesses, and retaining expert witnesses. This process can amount to tens of thousands, in some cases even hundreds of thousands, of dollars in cost advances and hundreds of hours of professional time. Clients are often focused on winning their cases at any cost, while the attorney is footing the bill. The attorney must have a clear understanding of his or her limits in this area. Only then can the attorney discuss those limits with the survivor.

The sexual abuse survivor, who lives with or without a large support network during the course of the litigation, may rely on counsel heavily and become easily anxious about each phase of the case, drawing more and more time from counsel's practice for emotional reassurance. In order to avoid complicating his or her life and that of the client unnecessarily, the attorney must decide whether, and then to what degree, he or she can commit emotional support to each particular client and case given counsel's own limitations and needs. To avoid the creation of a time-costly and, ultimately potentially damaging dependency relationship, the survivor is best informed of reasonable limitations on the attorney's accessibility from the outset of the case.

## *AS THE JOURNEY UNFOLDS: TRAVEL HAZARD WARNINGS FROM A LITIGATOR*

After a sexual abuse complaint is filed and served, there is the temporary satisfaction, and even exhilaration, of opening a passage previously closed and of beginning the journey from secrecy to disclosure. However, inexorably, when the winding road of the standard legal process mixes with the unpredictable and sometimes stormy psychological dynamics of the sexual abuse survivor, travel hazards can ensue for the survivor, the litigator, and the psychotherapist.

Most likely, the sexual abuse survivor is uninformed regarding the standard processes involved in litigation. Counsel should explicitly describe the entire litigation process, including prospective timelines, specifically focusing on the factors most likely to impact the survivor: the unpredictability of the process, the exposure of the survivor's most private and personal matters to public scrutiny, the adversarial, empirical nature of the process, and common defense strategies.

### *Unpredictability of the Process*

The survivor/client needs to be informed from the outset about several factors which contribute to the unpredictability of the litigation journey. Such factors include the variable span of time for the litigation itself, the issues related to insurance coverage and the possibility of a declaratory relief action by the defendant's insurers, the potential for appeal at each step of the case, mediation and arbitration, settlement, and plea bargaining. Often survivors of sexual abuse experience a hypervigilant, anxious orientation towards all that happens around them with an exaggerated, even compulsive, need to control events to maintain a sense of safety. The client needs to be informed, and reminded that the normal litigation process is exactly what she or he fears most–unpredictable and, most often, out of his or her control.

### *Exposure of What Is Private*

Survivors of sexual abuse describe their feelings of having been exploited and exposed–of having what is most private about them forcibly "shared" by another. Aspects of the legal procedure can reiterate that experience and the client, again, is better oriented and prepared when forewarned. Counsel should explain that the survivor's psychotherapy records may be open to scrutiny by the defense, and subsequently, by the judge and jury and the open court, once any claim of damage to the survivor's mental status is made. As a result, every significant area and relationship initially exposed by the survivor in the safety and confidentiality of the therapeutic environment may now be discussed and debated, and even used to impeach his or her truthfulness. For example, as the survivor may struggle with articulating certain truths, any inaccurate description or account will give rise to a charge by the defense that the survivor is a liar or a distorter of fact. His or her sexual history and/or current sexual practices may be made public if the client is claiming damages for emotional distress and an injury to her sexual functioning in a civil case. The client also should be aware that he or she may be questioned in extensive detail regarding the specifics of the sexual abuse. (Further discussion of such areas of inquiry by the defense will follow under *Defense Tactics.*)

### *The Adversarial, Empirical Nature of the Litigation Process*

The survivor of sexual abuse typically wants to be understood and believed regarding his or her personal sense of the abuse experience (narrative truth); the survivor's feelings of self-worth and goodness are often linked to others' understanding and validation. Plaintiff and defense counsel, on the other hand, are charged with the responsibility to present their cases rigorously based on objective facts (historical truth). Unless the client is informed of this inherent disparity of expectations for the litigation process, significant risk ensues for retraumatization of the client. While the client is working through the narrative truth in therapy, when returning to the legal case at hand, she or he must refocus on developing clear, accurate details, dates, chronology, and documentation.

Defense counsel may be experienced as an angry, intrusive, powerful, ultimately abusive authority figure, not unlike the accused perpetrator. The dynamics are heightened when the client who has experienced abuse by a perpetrator of the opposite gender faces a defense attorney or, as is now often the case, a panel of defense attorneys of the same gender as the perpetrator. A significant effect may also occur, however, when the survivor faces a same-gender defense attorney; the attorney may evoke a re-creation of the survivor's past hope or expectation that he or she might be understood and believed about the abuse by a significant gender ally (e.g., parent, teacher, sibling, etc.), but is instead questioned, even attacked, and portrayed as the victimizer rather than the victim. The survivor should be advised that opposing counsel will likely present a vigorous defense and may act angrily and dismissively toward the client but that such behavior is reflective of counsel's professional responsibility and not of the client's worth or goodness. Most states have rules prohibiting attorneys for either side from engaging in harassive conduct. For example, in California, Business and Profession Code Section 6068 makes it the duty of an attorney "to abstain from all offensive personality, and to advance no fact prejudicial to the honor and reputation of a party or witness, unless required to do so by the justice of the cause with which he or she is charged." However, the survivor should also be advised that the defense can, unfortunately, sometimes become overzealous and offensive in their representation of sexual abuse cases. Such cases can stir up the most intense feelings for all parties involved; both authors of this chapter have witnessed attorney conduct (both defense and plaintiff) that crossed the line to harassment of the witness.

The defendant has a constitutional right to face his or her accuser and to be present in civil depositions and trial. For some survivors, this is the first interaction with the alleged abuser since the last incident of abuse. Clients have reported that even subtle aspects of these encounters can be impactful: the smell of an aftershave cologne, the tone of voice and the sounds of sighs, and the wide variety of nonverbal facial and bodily expressions of disapproval, anger, hurt, joint complicity and secret-making, or vulnerability. The anticipation of interaction with the defendant likely will stimulate emotional reactions to the original trauma. These reactions can paradoxically combine emotions such as fear, anger, sadness, confusing feelings of wanting to protect the defendant from pain or embarrassment, and/or a desire to heal and recover the former relationship.

Given these foreseeable stresses and strains, it is essential not only that the litigator educates the client in an effort to inoculate him or her against extreme reactions, but also that they work to develop strategies that provide the client needed support during these encounters. Such strategies might include breaks every hour during deposition, reviewing pictures of the defendant to desensitize the client to his or her appearance, encouraging the presence of other survivors or friends who understand and appreciate the stresses the client faces, and intensified contact with the therapist during difficult stretches of the legal process.

### *Defense Tactics*

It must be said at the outset that defense counsel vary widely with respect to level of skill, intelligence, ethics, compassion, and understanding. Sometimes defense attorneys immediately and openly acknowledge that what has happened was wrong and will work hard to resolve the case for the benefit of all concerned. Unfortunately, we have also observed very different behavior. One defense attorney attempted to first question the survivor's mother while opening a jackknife and then pointing it at her. Another stated many times on the record that he would be most civil and respectful during the process, that he would treat the plaintiff survivor as he would want his daughter to be treated in a similar situation, and then went on to question the survivor about her experiences in minute detail for more than twenty-five days of deposition.

Rigorous defense of the alleged perpetrator most often insures rough going for the plaintiff filing the complaint of sexual abuse and for plaintiff's counsel. In some such cases, defense may engage in what psychologist Kenneth Pope has described as a tripartite defense commonly, although crudely, known as "She's a slut; she asked for it; and she needed it (or benefited from it)."[3] Defense may file a motion with the court to offer a showing of good cause as to why information regarding the plaintiff's sexual history is required to argue the defense case. The argument is likely then to include that the client consented to or initiated the alleged abusive sexual contact, or did not suffer the damages claimed as a result of the abuse, or both. In California, for instance, Code of Civil Procedure Section 2017 (d) provides:

> In any civil action alleging conduct that constitutes sexual harassment, sexual assault, or sexual battery, any party seeking discovery concerning the plaintiff's sexual conduct with individuals other than the alleged perpetrator is required to establish specific facts showing good cause for that discovery, and that the matter sought to be discovered is relevant to the subject matter of the action and reasonably calculated to lead to the discovery of admissible evidence.

It has been our experience that the defense can obtain the right to inquire about a plaintiff's sexual history if sexual damage is an issue in the case, but may not necessarily obtain the right to know the identities of the individuals involved unless those individuals expressly consent. Foreseeably, such a defense strategy has a particularly complex effect on the victim of sexual abuse who likely suffers from characteristic low self-esteem, tends toward self-blame and shame in general, and/or has experienced specific blaming for the abuse by important figures in his or her life (e.g., the abuser, mother, police, church, etc.).

As noted previously, defense tactics can also include detailed questioning regarding the most intimate elements of the abuse experience and surrounding circumstances. In this respect, defense counsel can create upsetting and confusing patterns of questioning, jumping back and forth in time and context, focusing on specific distinct details during different events and reviewing any additional information the client offers about her life. This kind of questioning is difficult for the business client to follow, much less the abused client, who may be led through various events, backward and forward in time, all which have a negative impact on the client emotionally. The client may become extremely disoriented and upset under this form of examination.

Although the questioning may be presented in the service of "getting the facts," it may require offensive nonverbal and verbal responses from the plaintiff. In one case in Manhattan Criminal Court, a judge ordered a teenage sexual abuse victim to reenact her molestation while testifying in open court.[4] The judge ordered the 15 year old girl to clarify what she meant by "grabbing" or "fondling" by demonstrating on her own breast while on the stand. Defense questioning requiring verbal answers may also be deliberately coarse and humiliating, even while within the bounds of legal propriety. In one case with which we are familiar, a woman defense attorney asked the plaintiff how she could tell it was the perpetrator's penis inside her and "not a carrot" if she was truly a virgin when she was raped. In another case, during more than twenty-four days of the testimony of a survivor whose abuse was admitted by the defendant, the defense attorney frequently asked the plaintiff about "sucking the (defendant's) penis" and whether she always swallowed the semen ejaculated by the defendant into her mouth.

Another common defense strategy is to emphasize the client's pre-event psychopathology–either to reduce the client's credibility or to reduce the level of alleged damage or both. The defense argument is that the plaintiff is gravely disturbed psychologically and is either distorting reality unconsciously or deliberately. The client's history of psychological problems, sexual relationships, psychological treatment, hospitalizations, suicide attempts, substance abuse, self-mutilations, and legal difficulties are explored in detail and highlighted. The possible sources of any problems in the client's life are investigated and the defense may argue that the client's real damage arose from those sources. Such a defense tactic can have devastating effects on the sexually abused client by not-so-subtly reinforcing the survivor's tendency to perceive him- or herself as being bad or being insane.

Defense questioning regarding the survivor's past and current sexual practices, the abuse experience, and pre-event psychopathology may extend beyond the client to his or her family, friends, lovers, spouses, and therapy or support group members. Obviously, the defense will be interested in learning whether the survivor has changed his or her account of the abuse from person to person or group to group. Legal issues immediately emerge. Certainly, various individuals or groups may have a vital privacy interest in protecting against the disclosure of personal information. Accordingly, the attorney for the abuse survivor should assist the client in protecting the familial and support networks in keeping with the privacy rights of others. If necessary, proceedings should be halted if the defense insists on names and statements of third parties about intimate details of their private lives, including sexual contact with the client, and clarification sought with the court having jurisdiction over the claims.

The law on these issues is still developing in most jurisdictions.[5] In considering the rights of third parties and the defendant with respect to these issues, the courts are engaged in balancing conflicting interests–the right of innocent parties to maintain their privacy regarding the most intimate details of their lives, as against the rights of the accused to obtain any underlying basis for the claims against them in order to determine what information is discoverable. We believe the defense will often be afforded the right to inquire of the client what he or she said in the context of support group settings. However, we also believe that under most state constitutions, as well as the federal constitution, the right of privacy of these third parties will be upheld, including both identity and personal self-disclosures, unless there are compelling circumstances and a showing of good cause warranting some level of discovery.[6]

The attorney and the client's current psychotherapist should consult with one another and with the client on the appropriateness of various support groups. The attorney should also advise the client of the issues related to disclosure of personal information, particularly in regard to discussing attorney-client communications with other persons. If the client discloses an attorney-client communication to a third person, the client may end up waiving the attorney-client privilege.

Additionally, the defense may blame the survivor/client's current psychotherapist(s) for damages allegedly ensuing from the abuse of the accused perpetrator. The psychotherapist may be challenged regarding his or her competence to do assessment and/or treatment of clients alleging sexual abuse. The therapist's credentials and training may be publicly examined, as well as any previous professional difficulties with licensing or professional ethics agencies. Specific therapeutic techniques and interactions may be questioned. A particularly charged issue currently involves whether the therapist used hypnosis, sodium amytal, or guided imagery visualization techniques to "recover" forgotten memories of childhood abuse. Therapists have been accused by the defense of implanting false memories of abuse by using such suggestive methods, sometimes with very good reason. Further, plaintiff's memories of abuse may be declared inadmissible when recovered in therapy that is problematic in ways other than specific techniques used by the therapist. Recent New Hampshire Superior Court and Supreme Court decisions addressed just this issue.[7] The courts found that recovered memories could not be admitted as evidence not only because the memories were produced in response to suggestive techniques, but also because the memories were produced in the context of a therapy which "permeated the everyday structure of [the plaintiff's] . . . school and social life," thereby likely enhancing the suggestive power of the therapist.[8] Under the glare of such defense scrutiny, the survivor's already conflicted relationship with the therapist may become more conflicted, or in some cases, irrevocably damaged no matter how much help the therapist previously has rendered him or her.

### *The Limited Sources of Recovery*

Abuse perpetrators are rarely wealthy individuals. Very often the strong desire to exert power over a more vulnerable individual betrays the abuser's sense of powerlessness in their own personal and professional lives, including their lack of economic strength. There are other great difficulties in identifying resources for compensation. For example, there is a majority trend against insurance coverage for any sexual abuse of either children or adults and many state victims of crime programs are as relentlessly bureaucratic as the worst of the judicial system.

## *BUILDING BRIDGES THROUGHOUT THE JOURNEY*

Attorneys and mental health professionals are likely to find themselves thrown together as uncomfortable, even reluctant, "traveling companions" when they have in common a client engaged in the journey of sexual abuse litigation. Unfortunately, the all-too-common ensuing estrangement between the survivor's counsel and psychotherapist can interfere with each fulfilling his or her full fiduciary responsibility to the client, as well as with the efficiency and efficacy of the work each performs. Rather than each professional forging a separate, often parallel, road through this unfamiliar and treacherous territory, we advocate the building of many bridges between the attorney and the therapist. We have already discussed the advisability of assessment by the therapist of the client's capacity to withstand the rigors of litigation before filing the complaint. Once the decision is made to file, however, continuing communications and consultation between the two professionals should become part of a regularized routine through the process of the litigation. Such interaction can safeguard the emotional status of the client avoiding retraumatization of the client, as well as complication of or damage to the legal case.

The most critical point to be made regarding the ongoing collaboration between attorney and mental health professional is that each professional must clarify and maintain their professional roles and boundaries with each other and with the client. Each professional has duties and responsibilities to fulfill–the attorney to prepare and pursue the litigation, the therapist to plan and provide for the therapy. Although at times it will be tempting, each professional must resist engaging in the other's practice–the attorney making therapeutic suggestions or interventions and the therapist providing legal advice and strategy. The worst case scenario for the client occurs when one professional begins to openly second-guess with the client the work of the other. Such behavior is extremely confusing and anxiety-provoking for the sexual abuse survivor. It may also replicate common dynamics in abuse trauma where the victim is caught between two adults in conflict with all the attendant secrets to keep and loyalties to protect.

The maintenance of appropriate boundaries between the two professionals also requires that both understand from the outset that the attorney is not the *therapist's* attorney. The therapist should seek independent and separate legal advice regarding predictably thorny issues such as responses to subpoenas, fees, record productions, privileges, warning issues, and abuse reporting to the appropriate civil or criminal authorities.

Additionally, and at all times, both the attorney and the psychotherapist have the responsibility to remain objective and operate within clear role boundaries with the survivor/client. As described previously, many sexual abuse survivors have great difficulty with the establishment and maintenance of interpersonal boundaries subsequent to the destructive and invasive behavior of the perpetrator. That difficulty may be expressed by the client's hypervigilance for and insistence on very definite and, at times even rigid, boundaries. Or, conversely, the difficulty may be expressed by the client's behavior which blurs or overtly disregards boundaries. Simply stated, the professional must resist engaging in personal roles with the client. The professional must not socialize with the client (e.g., take the client out on a "date," play tennis with the client, become sexually intimate with the client). Other, more incidental involvement must also be carefully monitored. For example, each professional must monitor the levels of personal self-disclosure and of descriptions of activities in their personal life. A common complaint of clients is that their attorneys (and/or their therapists) disclose details of problems in their personal life similar to the client's (e.g., that they are recovering alcoholics and attend Alcoholics Anonymous, that they have been sexually abused, or that they are going through a divorce). While intended most often to be an effort to "connect" with a client, such disclosures typically upset, confuse, and may repel the client who has experienced traumatic intrusions of his or her personal boundaries by others. Further, as discussed previously, neither the therapist nor the attorney should provide financial (e.g., loans of money) or practical (e.g., baby-sitting) support to the client.

The therapist and attorney best serve their client when they actively develop and maintain their professional exchanges with each other throughout the litigation journey. The attorney can provide extremely valuable information to the therapist regarding the stages and processes of the legal process: when the client must respond to interrogatories, when the client can be expected to testify, when the therapist can be expected to testify, the expected breadth of testimony, the identification of the therapist's fees for deposition and trial, the likelihood that the therapist's records and charts will be subpoenaed, and the timing of other critical events, such as the defendants and defense witnesses' depositions. Such advance warning provides the therapist with the opportunity to monitor and support the client. For example, the therapist may need to increase the number of therapy sessions per week or decrease the intensity of any dynamic or uncovering work during the client's or defense witnesses' depositions or immediately preceding and during trial.

The therapist can inform the attorney regarding the ongoing psychological status of the client. In the course of psychotherapy, the mental health professional consistently assesses the client's reaction to the stress of litigation. The therapist can provide the attorney with information regarding warning signs or cues that the client may exhibit signaling acute anxiety reactions during the course of litigation. As discussed previously, sexual abuse survivors may suffer from symptoms of posttraumatic stress disorder which can become manifest while recounting the traumatic events of the abuse. Symptoms such as dissociation or panic attacks are likely to impair the client's memory of and ability to articulate those events in testimony. Further, the therapist may indicate to the attorney when the client's levels of self-blaming and ensuing depression increase risk for suicidal behavior or other forms of self-harm. In a civil case and within the constraints of the discovery time period, the attorney may use such information to make decisions regarding the time, the length, and importantly, the spacing of the client's deposition testimony. The therapist can also inform the attorney of the techniques employed during therapy sessions with the client. Such information opens the way for dialogue about and preparation by the attorney for potential defense challenges regarding the legal validity and admissibility of evidence ensuing from those sessions.

The value of collaboration and consultation between an abuse survivor's attorney and psychotherapist does not end with the settlement, dismissal, or decision of the legal case. An attorney who expects the progression usual in other types of legal cases–case completed, relationship completed, next case please–to hold true with the client in a sexual abuse case may be surprised. Regardless of the outcome of the litigation, abuse clients very often desire and pursue continued contact with their attorneys. The issue of continued contact is probably best addressed by the attorney at the outset of the litigation process, with the attorney informing the client about the limited scope of their professional role. However, given that the litigation process is emotionally charged, many strong emotional reactions may persist for the survivor. The attorney may find that the client continues to come in to "visit," to "check in," or to call periodically. Issues regarding a difficult termination of the attorney-client relationship may be explored in consultation with the client's therapist, again with the overarching goal of protecting the client's welfare. The therapist may advise the attorney of the valence of the client's emotional reactions (i.e., whether the client feels positively or negatively about the attorney) and plan with the attorney appropriate responses and a course toward termination. Further, the therapist who is informed of the relationship dynamics between the attorney and client can assess the therapeutic significance of such dynamics and guide the psychotherapy accordingly.

## *CONCLUSION*

Throughout this chapter we have discussed the rigors and risks inherent in the journey of sexual abuse litigation. Although the territory to be traversed is unfamiliar to most attorneys, it is not completely uncharted. Difficult terrain, language barriers, and travel hazards can be identified and managed. We argue that the best protection for all travelers is the building of bridges between the attorney and the mental health professional who are working toward a common goal: to re-establish the sexual abuse survivor's sense of empowerment and justice in the world. Such cooperation and consultation may effectively begin with the client's initial interactions with the attorney and proceed through the termination of the relationship between the client and the attorney. This model for sexual abuse litigation supports and enhances the fulfillment of each professional's fiduciary responsibility to the client. Ultimately, the by-products of this process can serve to assist the client in the discovery and forging of his or her continuing pathway to recovery long after the last mile of the actual litigation journey.

## NOTES

1. For excellent descriptions of these symptoms and behaviors, *see* John N. Briere, CHILD ABUSE TRAUMA: THEORY AND TREATMENT OF THE LASTING EFFECTS. (Newbury Park, CA: Sage Publications, 1992); Kenneth S. Pope, SEXUAL INVOLVEMENT WITH THERAPISTS: PATIENT ASSESSMENT, SUBSEQUENT THERAPY, FORENSICS. (Washington, D.C.: American Psychological Association, 1994); Lenore E.A. Walker, ABUSED WOMEN AND SURVIVOR THERAPY. (Washington, DC: American Psychological Association, 1994).

2. *See* B.L. Diamond, *Inherent Problems in the Use of Pretrial Hypnosis on a Prospective Witness,* 68 Cal. Rev. 313 (1980); *People v. Shirley*, 31 Cal. 3d 18, 181 Cal. Rptr. 243, 641 P2d 775, 783 (Cal. 1982).

3. Pope, 71.

4. *The New York Times*, October 14, 1995.

5. In California, most cases involving the right of privacy of innocent, nonparties arise in the context of divorce proceedings, where, in discovery, tax information is sought regarding the business activities of one spouse and some of the information relates to the private financial affairs of noninvolved individuals. *See, e.g., Schabel v. Superior Court of Orange County*, 5 Cal 4th 704 854 P2d 1117 (Cal. 1993); *Rifkin v. Superior Court*, 123 CA3d 1045, 177 Cal. Rptr. 82 (Cal. 1981). As stated by the California Supreme Court in *Valley Bank v. Superior Court*, 15 Cal 3d 652, 657,542 P.2d 977 (Cal. 1975): "When the interest of a private litigant in discovering relevant facts conflicts with the right of others to maintain reasonable privacy regarding their . . . affairs, a court must 'indulge in a careful balancing' before ordering disclosure." Just as the protection afforded by the right of privacy encompasses the financial affairs of nonlitigants, so the discussion of one's deepest vulnerabilities should be accorded the same safeguards. However, the argument will be strongest for member of support groups in which the survivor participated, rather than family members. Spouse's communications may also be protected by the spousal communication privilege.

6. We can foresee the possibility of a cult-like setting in a support group where a new member is encouraged, or even coerced, into "remembering" events that never occurred in response to peer pressure. However, such techniques could be identified and elicited without compelling innocent third parties to reveal their own stories.

7. *State v. Hungerford*, WL 378571 (N.H. Super., May 23, 1995); *State v. Hungerford* WL 358620 (N.H. Sup. Ct., July 1, 1995).

8. *Ibid*, 32.

# Evaluation of the Delayed Discovery Case

Michael S. Morey

**SUMMARY.** In this chapter, practicing lawyer Michael S. Morey guides the reader through the complex legal and non-legal issues involved in evaluating whether legal action should be pursued on behalf of an adult survivor of childhood sexual abuse. After analyzing how evaluation of sexual abuse cases differs from that in most other personal injury cases, he presents a model for non-suggestive yet thorough client interviewing and case evaluation to help both survivor and lawyer decide whether to pursue litigation. Viability of a case, determined by three critical legal issues, does not necessarily mean litigation ought to be pursued, and he explores how to make the initial interview a valuable resource to survivors, whether or not legal action is ultimately sought, with practical tips and a reproducible intake form. *[Article copies available for a fee from The Haworth Document Delivery Service: 1-800-342-9678. E-mail address: <getinfo@haworthpressinc.com> Website: <http://www.haworthpressinc.com>]*

**KEYWORDS.** Jurisdiction, statutes of limitations, collection on judgment/settlement, evidence, interviewing client, nonlegal issues in case evaluation, community resources, corroboration

The initial case evaluation is a very important stage of any personal injury claim. However, the initial evaluation of a case for a survivor of

---

Address correspondence to: Michael S. Morey, JD, Attorney at Law, Lakeside Plaza, 8 N. State Street, Suite 301, Lake Oswego, OR 97034.

[Haworth co-indexing entry note]: "Evaluation of the Delayed Discovery Case." Morey, Michael S. Co-published simultaneously in *Journal of Aggression, Maltreatment & Trauma* (The Haworth Maltreatment & Trauma Press, an imprint of The Haworth Press, Inc.) Vol. 3, No. 2 (#6), 2000, pp. 97-112; and: *Sexual Abuse Litigation: A Practical Resource for Attorneys, Clinicians, and Advocates* (ed: Rebecca Rix) The Haworth Maltreatment & Trauma Press, an imprint of The Haworth Press, Inc., 2000, pp. 97-112. Single or multiple copies of this article are available for a fee from The Haworth Document Delivery Service [1-800-342-9678, 9:00 a.m. - 5:00 p.m. (EST). E-mail address: getinfo@haworthpressinc.com].

 

sexual abuse is oftentimes more critical. It is essential to determine not only the legal viability of the claim but the relative benefits and drawbacks to the prospective client if he or she pursues a claim for damages. More so than in other personal injury claims, the simple determination of whether or not a case exists is not sufficient to determine whether a lawsuit is the best course of action.

The law does not provide redress for all cases of sexual abuse. However, in many cases a claim can and should be brought, allowing the survivor to take a stand against the abuser and recover monetary damages for the injuries caused by the abuse. The sensitive and complex nature of adult survivor cases is such that each case must be evaluated thoroughly on its own merits. It is vital to not give false hope about a weak case. However, if the facts and law support pursuit of a case, successful litigation against a perpetrator may well be the correct course of action.

Calling your office may be one of the first steps the survivor takes (other than, in many cases, initiating therapy) in dealing with the abuse. Professionalism in this area of law requires knowledgeable and sympathetic listening as the prospective client relates their experience during the evaluation interview. It is imperative to establish trust and rapport to obtain as much information as possible. If the case cannot (or should not) be pursued, you should be aware of the other resources available in your community, such as support groups or victims' assistance agencies. A referral to such an organization may be the best help you can provide the survivor. Such agencies often provide resources to help them identify alternative ways to proceed in dealing with the abuse. Thus, the intake interview can be an important step in the survivor's healing.

## *THE TELEPHONE INTERVIEW*

The initial contact with your office will likely be on the telephone. It is likely the person only recently mustered the courage to make the initial call. Therefore, the person who first speaks with the prospective client should be knowledgeable as well as sensitive to the survivor. Have an experienced legal assistant take these calls or make sure the receptionist can quickly identify the call as a sexual abuse case, so the prospective client can be quickly transferred to the lawyer.

It is in the best interest of both the caller and the lawyer to do an initial telephone interview of some depth. To begin with, it is often easier for the survivor to discuss the basic facts and circumstances of their abuse over the phone rather than in their first meeting in a lawyer's office. It is also important for the lawyer to spend sufficient time in an initial telephone interview to effectively screen cases that cannot be pursued. It is neither beneficial to the survivor, nor productive for the lawyer, to create false hope in a lawsuit that simply cannot, or should not, be pursued. Be sure to discuss with the potential client early on whether they have explored the issue of seeing a lawyer with their treating therapist, and whether that therapist agrees the client could benefit from discussing the issues with a lawyer.

The purpose of the initial telephone interview is to obtain sufficient information to determine whether or not the case warrants further evaluation and a personal client interview. A checklist of questions is helpful in helping the lawyer or legal assistant obtain the most important facts.[1] If it is clear from the beginning that the statute of limitations is insurmountable or that there is clearly no potential of making any financial recovery for the client, it may be better both for the survivor and the lawyer to come to that understanding over the telephone.[2]

If the decision is made to decline the case, the evaluation interview is still an important contact for the survivor. It is vital to refer them to other attorneys or other, non-legal resources.[3] By summoning the courage to call and reach out for help, they have taken a big risk. It is vital to meet them halfway in a genuine and helpful fashion, however brief the encounter.

If the lawyer believes the case merits further review, the client should be scheduled promptly for a personal interview in the lawyer's office. The author believes the prospective client should be encouraged to prepare and forward an extensive chronology of the facts and circumstances surrounding the abuse to the lawyer prior to the first meeting. This accomplishes two things: First, it allows the client to detail the abuse, a process which is often difficult to do in a meeting with a lawyer they have just met. Second, it allows the lawyer to become familiar with the facts which significantly improves the efficiency of the first interview. They should be encouraged to prepare and forward an extensive chronology of the facts and circumstances surrounding the abuse to the lawyer prior to the first meeting in order to familiarize the lawyer with the facts prior to their interview.[4]

## THE INITIAL CLIENT OFFICE INTERVIEW

### Introduction

There are a number of things a lawyer should consider in preparation for the office interview. First and foremost, the office interview needs to be as comfortable and non-threatening as possible. The receptionist, or whoever will greet the potential client, should be aware that there are special issues involved with this potential client. The lawyer should consider and discuss with the potential client, whether they would like to have someone else present during the interview. However, having another person present may impinge on the privileged exchange of information under the attorney-client privilege. The lawyer must be familiar with the specifics of the attorney-client privilege in their own jurisdiction. The lawyer should then review any potential breach of the privilege with the prospective client and explore the implications of having another party present.

The issue of gender also needs to be considered. Obviously, if a male lawyer is meeting with a female survivor who was abused by a male perpetrator, she may not feel comfortable talking about very personal issues in a private, unfamiliar room with a man she has just met. In such a situation, consider having a female legal assistant present during the interview. The important issue, however, is to establish rapport and trust. Conduct a thorough interview but do so with compassion, understanding the difficulty the survivor may be having discussing a very traumatic part of their past.

The interview process is likely to be quite different than in a standard personal injury case. In an automobile accident case, for example, after some rapport is established with the client, you start discussing the facts of the case. With the sexual abuse survivor, it is very important to spend additional time learning about the background of the potential client, whether they are presently in therapy, the nature of their family dynamics (especially in an incest case), and generally establishing trust and credibility with the client before discussing the details of the abuse. Keep in mind that while you may have heard a lot about sexual abuse, for them, it may still be loaded with secrecy and shame.[5] Your familiarity with sexual abuse issues will decrease their anxiety and build their trust in you as a knowledgeable advocate.

## *Summary of Critical Evaluative Criteria*

Issues of liability, statute of limitations, and collectibility are common to the evaluation of all personal injury claims. However, proper evaluation of a sexual abuse claim differs significantly from other types of cases in several ways. In the automobile accident case, for example, the fact that an accident occurred is almost never in dispute. Due to the nature of the crime of sexual abuse (particularly in delayed discovery cases), there is rarely any documentary evidence. Moreover, the defendant will typically deny, or at least minimize, any allegations of abuse. *The fact that abuse occurred is often the main dispute.* It is, therefore, imperative that the lawyer realize that proving the actual event or events is often the biggest hurdle.

Second, in most personal injury cases, determination of the statute of limitations is usually straightforward and simple to evaluate. Injured people rarely delay in reporting when and how they have been injured. In the sexual abuse survivor case, however, substantial delay in reporting is very common. For this reason, the practitioner must be familiar with the psychological issues which result in significant delay in reporting sexual abuse and, how partial or total traumatic amnesia can result in the client's failure to understand the link between the sexual abuse they suffered as a child and their adult psychological injuries.

Recognition of these unique litigation issues has resulted in many states adopting special statutes of limitations for the sexual abuse victim. These special statutes of limitations generally provide three avenues for the pursuit of litigation. First, they allow for a longer period for the juvenile disability extension. Second, for the traumatic amnesia survivor, it allows them a period of years to pursue a claim after they have remembered they were sexually abused as a child. Third, they allow a period of time for the victim who did not understand the link between the sexual abuse they suffered as a child and their adult psychological injuries. The attorney must be familiar with their individual state's statutes of limitations and able to identify the difference between delayed discovery of the abuse and the delayed causal connection of the harm.

The third critical issue of evaluation is on the potential collection of any judgment that is eventually obtained. Again, in the standard personal injury case, the issue of collection on the judgment is usually covered by insurance and generally fairly easy to determine. It is far more complicated, and uniformly more difficult to obtain insurance coverage on a judgment obtained for a sexual abuse victim. Therefore, the practitioner must fully evaluate whether or not a collection of any judgment from the defendant or any potential insurance carrier is feasible.[6]

Comparing the evaluation of the standard personal injury lawsuit to that of a delayed discovery sexual abuse case illustrates differences of which the lawyer must be aware in evaluating these types of cases. Ultimately, there are three critical questions. First, can you prove the case? Is there corroboration, admissions from the defendant, or other supporting evidence that will enable you to establish that the perpetrator committed the sexual abuse of your client? Second, can the case be pursued under the applicable statute of limitations? Third, does the perpetrator have sufficient assets to justify pursuit of the case against him or her, or are there insurance policies which provide coverage for the defendant, or other entities that bear responsibility?

## *EVALUATION OF THE THREE CRITICAL ISSUES*

### *Viability of the Case*

Although it may be a difficult process, it is imperative to discuss the facts of the abuse and the circumstances surrounding the abuse in detail with the potential client early on. This is often complicated by three issues. First, the abuse will almost invariably have taken place many years before. Second, rarely is there only a single incident; instead, the abuse generally occurs over the course of years, frequently at different locations. Third, the survivor was a child when the abuse occurred. In spite of those difficulties, it is important to determine not only what abuse was perpetrated on the survivor, but in what detail and how adequately can the survivor recount the abuse. A *caveat* is in order here, however. While the practitioner must get as much information as possible, it is necessary to avoid suggestive questioning. Ask many open ended questions and be supportive as the survivor recounts his or her history.

As mentioned previously, it is extremely helpful, not only to the lawyer but to the potential client, if in the initial telephone interview, the client was encouraged to prepare a written chronology of the abuse. It is often easier for a client to extensively recount the abuse in the privacy of their own home over the course of a week or two before meeting the lawyer in person. This not only insures that the client has spent sufficient time attempting to go through the abuse in as much detail as possible, but will assist the lawyer in clarifying the facts and circumstances surrounding the abuse. Provided the client is willing to do so, it is very beneficial to forward the chronology to the lawyer prior to the office interview so the lawyer will have a chance to review it in detail prior to the meeting.

Early on, it is vital to explore any and all avenues to corroborate the abuse. As was mentioned earlier, the core issue in dispute in sexual abuse cases is often whether or not the abuse occurred. The typical denial and minimizing of the abuser, coupled with affirmative defenses and the advent of false memory advocates, pose many challenges for the plaintiff's lawyer. While there is often a lack of documentary evidence due to the nature of the crime, frequently indirect corroboration of the survivor's claim does exist. There are four main areas of corroboration: witnesses, prior admissions by the defendant, admissions upon confrontation, and prior disclosures by the survivor.

First, were there any witnesses to the abuse itself? This is rare, although it does occur. Indirect corroboration is more likely to be obtained than any direct witnesses. Potentially useful information might include the following: what were the prevailing living conditions and relationships at the time of the abuse; were there other victims of this abuser (e.g., siblings, friends, neighbor children, etc.). This will often involve extensive follow-up, investigation and interviewing. Also, the perpetrator's spouse or ex-spouse(s) can sometimes be a link to corroboration. Rarely will the spouse admit that they knew the child was being abused, but if interviewed early, they may admit that there were substantial indications that the defendant was a sexual predator.

The second, and perhaps most critical form of corroboration, is whether the perpetrator has, at any time, admitted the abuse. This can take many forms. The perpetrator may have directly or tacitly admitted the abuse (or some inappropriate sexual activity with other children) to a third party (i.e., a family member). It is vital to get an idea of the survivor's family dynamics and conduct interviews with those who may have heard or seen something to corroborate his or her claim.

Although medical records of the perpetrator are protected by the physician-patient privilege, practitioners are advised to evaluate their individual state laws on this issue. For example, Washington State provides a statutory exception in civil cases involving child abuse if the perpetrator has been in therapy for committing sexual abuse. Discovery of such evidence will be extremely helpful in your discussions with the defense lawyer if the defendant now contends that he or she never committed sexual abuse.

Third, a direct confrontation with the abuser needs to be considered. This must be done before any lawsuit is filed for the obvious reason that an admission after a lawsuit has been filed is highly unlikely, and once represented by counsel, no contact with the defendant is permitted. It is imperative that no such confrontations (whether directly by the client or other family members) take place without fully discussing the same with the client's therapist and getting the therapist's approval. For obvious reasons, a confrontation between the survivor and the perpetrator can be very traumatic to the survivor and it is crucial that the therapist be involved in the discussion about any such confrontation.[7] However, provided the therapist agrees and the client is willing to do so, a confrontation may elicit a direct admission and/or apology. This not only substantiates the case but can be very important to the healing process.

There are a multitude of ways in which a confrontation can be accomplished. If the survivor is strong enough to do so, they can call the perpetrator directly on the telephone.[8] Setting up a meeting with the perpetrator that includes other family members, a clergy member who is familiar with the family, or the client's therapist, can also be a productive way to confront. Each survivor's situation is unique, however, and they, with their therapist's assistance, should be able to ascertain the best method of confrontation if one is advisable.

The fourth type of corroboration is whether the survivor confided in others while they were being abused as a child. This is often the most difficult type of corroboration to find because it usually consists of statements that were made many years, if not decades, before. However, ask the potential client about their siblings, best friends and/or confidantes during the time of the abuse, since they may have talked about the abuse while it was occurring. The survivor may have also confided in a doctor, teacher, or other authority figure and it is important to obtain copies of prior medical, school or other records. On occasion, the abuse may have been reported to law enforcement authorities. Obviously, this kind of documentation, while not available in most cases, is extremely valuable.

### *Statute of Limitations and Jurisdiction*

Due to the dynamics of childhood sexual abuse, the victim is frequently incapable of confronting the abuser or seeking legal help for the abuse for a significant period of time after the abuse. The victim is a child, while the perpetrator is generally an adult in a position of authority, such as a trusted family member. Further, sexual abuse, especially of young children, is very strongly correlated with traumatic amnesia.[9] For those reasons, it is often a matter of many years, sometimes decades, before survivors of childhood sexual abuse are capable of remembering, or of comprehending, the harmful nature of the sexual acts, and are psychologically capable of seeking redress for the injuries associated with those acts. In recognition of these dynamics and the terrible aftermath of sexual abuse, many state legislatures have passed statutes which allow survivors to bring civil actions within a period of time after they recall the abuse or understand the connection between the abuse and their injuries. Delayed discovery statutes of limitations are covered in depth in Mary Williams' chapter in this book, but the topic deserves revisiting here.

Many states have adopted specific, delayed discovery sexual abuse statutes of limitations. These statutes generally have three elements. First, they extend the juvenile exception to allow a sexual abuse survivor to pursue a claim for a certain number of years after reaching the age of majority.[10] Second, the statutes provide that the claim may be pursued within a certain number of years (three in Oregon, for example) from the time the survivor recovered memories of the abuse. This prong of the statute applies to the cases in which the survivor does not have conscious recollection of the abuse until some later triggering event. Third, the statues provide for the survivor who did not make the causal connection between the abuse and damages resulting from that abuse to bring the claim within a certain number of years of making that connection.

If your jurisdiction does not have a delayed discovery sexual abuse survivor statute, other theories need to be considered. Does the jurisdiction recognize delayed discovery in other types of cases such as medical malpractice or toxic torts? Does the jurisdiction recognize a continuing tort theory since occasionally the abuse has continued for many years and ended within a short period of time before the survivor came to see the lawyer? The lawyer should also consider other theories such as estoppel, especially in cases where the victim was threatened if they reported the abuse. The perpetrator should not benefit from his own wrongdoing if such threats prevented the abuse victim from seeking redress.

Once the lawyer has become familiar with the law of the jurisdiction in which the abuse occurred or where the defendant resides, an evaluation of the facts and application of the relevant jurisdiction's law is essential. This is often an evaluation that takes some time to complete. The lawyer must obtain the survivor's treating therapist's records and also records of any prior therapist or other medical provider who may have knowledge of the abuse, to determine if the victim previously discussed the abuse and/or sought therapy to help heal from the effects.

### *Defendant's Assets and Collectibility of Judgment*

The issue of collectibility on any judgment is a topic the lawyer must carefully evaluate and frankly discuss with the client. The lawyer must determine if this is a case with potentially applicable insurance coverage, or if collection will be made solely against the defendant's personal assets. A multitude of jurisdictions have issued appellate decisions holding that sexual abuse of a child is intended to cause harm as a matter of law, thus making the recovery against insurance far more difficult. For that reason, the lawyer must closely consider the extent of the defendant's assets which may be reachable after obtaining a judgment.[11]

The client is the primary source for information to determine the extent of the defendant's assets. However, use caution in accepting the client's assessment that the defendant has substantial assets. Discuss the matter with other family members who may have knowledge of the defendant's assets. The lawyer should obtain state-wide real estate information from a title company. Obtain copies of all credit reports available in the given jurisdiction. Have an experienced investigator do a background asset check on the defendant.

Once litigation is commenced, an extensive request for production should be prepared. Since the cases invariably justify pleading punitive damages, depending on the jurisdiction, the defendant should be required to produce asset documentation.

Depletion of the defendant's assets during the pendency of the litigation is a substantial concern. The lawyer needs to evaluate the status of prejudgment attachment law in the given jurisdiction. Written notice should be sent to the defense counsel informing the defendant that plaintiff will treat any transfer of assets after notice of the claim as a fraudulent transaction for purposes of avoiding the plaintiff as a creditor. In many jurisdictions an additional claim can be brought if the defendant does transfer assets.

The survivor's lawyer must also be aware of the consequences of a bankruptcy filing by the defendant. Although sexual abuse litigation involves intentional torts, the claim of a sexual abuse survivor can be discharged in a Chapter 13 Bankruptcy filing by the defendant. Full discussion of the consequences of bankruptcy is beyond the scope of this chapter and the practitioner is encouraged to discuss those issues with a bankruptcy lawyer in their jurisdiction.

Lastly, the plaintiff's attorney must be aware of the status of the garnishment and execution statutes in their given jurisdiction. Many assets the plaintiff believes the defendant has may be exempt from execution or garnishment. However, if the defendant is a present or former federal employee, their federal pension is not exempt from execution for claims related to childhood sexual abuse.[12]

## *DIFFICULT SITUATIONS*

### *Multiple Perpetrators*

It is not uncommon for a sexual abuse survivor to have been victimized by multiple perpetrators. This can be a substantial complicating factor in the legal case. A chronology of the perpetrators and a determination as to whether or not any of the perpetrators had knowledge of the survivor's prior abuse, are imperative in determining if the case can be successfully brought. For example, if the second perpetrator is the one that the survivor desires to pursue, and that perpetrator was aware of the prior abuse, the fact of multiple perpetrators should not be a substantial problem. The fact that the perpetrator was aware of the prior abuse and re-victimized the client aggravates the heinous nature of the abuse. When multiple perpetrators are involved, it is important to work with a qualified psychological expert, as well as the client's treating therapist, to deal with the issue of distinguishing damages between the multiple perpetrators.

### *Pending Criminal Litigation*

On occasion, the sexual abuse victim has the opportunity to pursue a criminal case against the perpetrator and may already have filed a police report. If that is the case, it is extremely important to allow the criminal prosecution to take its course prior to the commencement of any civil litigation. This is true for a number of reasons.

First, if civil litigation is commenced during the pendency of the criminal prosecution, it gives the criminal defense attorney a substantial opportunity to suggest motive in cross-examination of the victim. The criminal defense attorney can use the civil complaint to try to convince the jury that the only reason a criminal prosecution is being pursued is to facilitate the plaintiff in subsequently suing the defendant for financial gain.

Second, civil litigation will be far more economically feasible if the police agencies have conducted much of the investigation. Also, it is a very good way to determine whether or not the case can be proven. If the defendant is convicted, the plaintiff can use the conviction as collateral estoppel on the issue of liability in the civil case. If the defendant is not convicted, although it does not have direct collateral estoppel effect, as a practical matter it raises questions regarding ability to prove the civil case.

## *CONCLUSION*

The evaluation process in sexual abuse cases is complex. The viability of delayed discovery cases often centers around questions of whether or not there is some form of direct or indirect corroboration, the statute of limitations and the collectibility of judgment. The attorney and survivor must work together to decide the best course of action. Litigation is not suitable in all cases. In those where it is not, the service provided by the legal intake interview in giving the survivor an opportunity to fully explore the issues and in referring the survivor to other resources can be very valuable. In those cases where litigation is suitable, a careful, extensive and focused intake process is an invaluable part of successful legal representation of delayed discovery sexual abuse cases.

## NOTES

1. See the author's telephone intake interview sheet at the end of this chapter.

2. In the author's experience, many potential clients will indicate that making a financial recovery is irrelevant to them; they simply want to confront their abuser and have their day in court. While this is understandable and laudable, it is important for the lawyer to explain the realities of litigation. Litigation of this type is expensive and emotionally draining. If the case simply cannot be pursued, the potential client needs to be informed that it is in no one's best interest, especially theirs, to get involved in litigation that has no potential of success. On the other hand, the author does not want to discourage attorneys from taking on a case where the acts of abuse are aggravated and clearly established and there is no impediment such as the statute of limitations.

3. You may want to construct a Referral Resources notebook for ready reference. It should include the names of attorneys specializing in sexual abuse cases in other states, lawyers who specialize in custody issues, crisis lines for women and children in immediate danger (check with your local YWCA), low cost or sliding fee counseling centers for low income survivors who do not know who to go to for help, et cetera. See Appendix H, *Other Resources* for general guidelines.

4. It is imperative to instruct the client to write "Prepared for My Attorney" on each page of the document. That notation will make it clear that the document was intended to be a privileged attorney/client communication and therefore is not discoverable when a defense lawyer subsequently requests copies of chronologies, diaries, and other such writings of the survivor.

5. Books that are helpful in understanding the psychology of PTSD and the multitude of issues the survivor of sexual abuse encounters, include: Ellen Bass and Laura Davis, THE COURAGE TO HEAL (New York: Harper & Row, 1988); Judith Herman, TRAUMA AND RECOVERY: THE AFTERMATH OF VIOLENCE –FROM DOMESTIC VIOLENCE TO POLITICAL TERROR (New York: Basic Books, 1992); DIAGNOSTIC AND STATISTICAL MANUAL OF MENTAL DISORDERS, FOURTH EDITION (DSM-IV), (Washington, D.C.: American Psychiatric Association, 1994); Fay Honey Knopp and Anna Rose Benson, A PRIMER ON THE COMPLEXITIES OF TRAUMATIC MEMORY OF CHILDHOOD SEXUAL ABUSE, A PSYCHOLOGICAL APPROACH (Brandon, Vermont: Fay Honey Knopp & The Safer Society Press, 1996); Beverly Gomez-Schwartz, Jonathan M. Horowitz And Albert P. Cardarelli, CHILD SEXUAL ABUSE, THE INITIAL EFFECTS (Newbury Park, California: Sage Publications, Inc., 1990); Robert Geffner, Ph.D., Editor, JOURNAL OF CHILD SEXUAL ABUSE: RESEARCH, TREATMENT & PROGRAM INNOVATIONS FOR VICTIMS, SURVIVORS & OFFENDERS (Binghamton, New York: The Haworth Press, Inc., 1994).

6. See Julian Hubbard's chapter for a discussion of insurance coverage.

7. It is not uncommon, and the survivor needs to know it is not uncommon, for the perpetrator to deny the abuse. Also, often the most that is obtained is an indirect admission. However, even minimal or tacit admissions can go a long way to overcoming a subsequent denial or an attack by a "false memory" defense expert.

8. Under Oregon law, a person can tape-record an in-state telephone conversation *without* the other party's knowledge or consent. If that is not possible in your jurisdiction, consider using an independent third party (or perhaps a court reporter) to listen in on the conversation and corroborate the perpetrator's admission of what occurs.

9. Traumatic amnesia is the term used by the medical community whose treatment and research centers around the medical and psychological aftermath of trauma. Legislatures and lay people often use the terms repression and dissociation interchangeably, but this can result in confusion. It is critical that the practitioner be very familiar with traumatic memory studies. As a starting point, the overview of traumatic memory in Chapter 1 of this book is useful. Further, the publications in Footnote 5 of this article are excellent resources

10. For example, California provides eight years, Oregon provides six years, and Washington provides three years.

11. The issue of insurance coverage in sexual abuse cases is discussed by Julian Hubbard in this book.

12. If applicable, the "Child Abuse Accountability Act" amends federal law to permit the garnishment of retirement annuities of Federal employees for enforcement of a court order for the payment of monetary damages to victims of emotional, sexual or physical child abuse. 5 USCA § 8345, 8467

## CLIENT INTAKE FORM

*Photocopy and use this form when interviewing sex abuse victims over the telephone. Reassure them that all of the following information will be kept confidential.*

Date of Interview: ____________________

Name of Victim(s): ____________________

Address: ____________________

____________________

City and State: ____________________ Zip: ____________________

Home Phone: ____________________ Work Phone: ____________________

Age: ____________________ Date of Birth: ____________________

Referred By: ____________________

Have they consulted with another attorney about this issue? If so, who? ____________________

## DEFENDANT(S) INFORMATION

Name of First Defendant: ____________________

Address: ____________________

Relationship (parent, guardian, teacher, baby sitter, family friend, etc.) ____________________

Name of Second Defendant: ____________________

Address: ____________________

Relationship (parent, guardian, teacher, baby sitter, family friend, etc.) ____________________

When was the last time victim saw or spoke with the defendant(s)? ____________________

## DEFENDANT(S) FINANCIAL INFORMATION

Assets Owned by Defendant(s): (Houses, Property, Rental Properties, Businesses, Boats, Cars, Bank Accounts, Stocks, Bonds, Other) ____________________

## INFORMATION ABOUT THE ABUSE

City (Cities) and State(s) Where Abuse Occurred: ____________________

Date(s) of Abuse: ____________________

Description of the Abuse (Rape, Sodomy, Sexual Abuse, Fondling, Etc.): ____________________

## CORROBORATION

Has the abuse ever been reported to or by anyone in the family? No ____ Yes ____

If Yes, to or by whom? ____________________

Has the abuse ever been reported to or by anyone in the family? No ____ Yes ____

If Yes, to or by whom? (Police, School, Doctors, Counselors, Friend, Neighbors) ___________

Has the defendant been charged criminally for the abuse? No __ Yes __

If Yes, what state and country was the case tried in? ___________

What was the outcome of the criminal case? ___________

Name of prosecuting district attorney assigned to the case? ___________

Has there been discussion or confrontation with defendant(s) regarding the abuse? No__ Yes __
If Yes, was anyone else present? No __ Yes __ If Yes, who? ___________

Has there been any correspondence regarding the abuse? No __ Yes __

If Yes, describe correspondence, date sent/received, and who has possession of the correspondence now: ___________

Has Defendant(s) admitted the abuse? No __ Yes __

If Yes, what were the circumstances, and who, if anyone, was present? ___________

___________

## WITNESSES

Is/Are there any sibling(s) or other(s) who may have either seen the abuse occur or may know something about it? No __ Yes __

If Yes, identify witness and describe relationship: ___________

Was/were sibling(s) or other(s) abused also? No __ Yes __

Has the defendant ever been in therapy? No __ Yes __

If appropriate, relating to a parent or stepparent, what is the current relationship between the abuser and the non-abusing spouse? ___________

Is the non-abusive parent aware of the abuse? No __ Yes __

Is the non-abusive parent still married to or living with the defendant? No __ Yes __

Is the non-abusive parent supportive of the victim? No __ Yes __

## DISCOVERY AND THERAPY

Is this a case of delayed discovery? No __ Yes __

Is this a case of delayed causal connection? No __Yes __

When did the victim start discovering or making a causal connection about the abuse?

Date(s): ___________ Age: ___________ Other: ___________

What were the circumstances? ___________

Has caller ever been in therapy? No __ Yes __ Are they currently in therapy? No __ Yes __

If Yes, when did they start, and who is the therapist? ___________

What circumstances led them to seek therapy? ___________

How much memory do they have of the abuse? ___________

___________

# Plaintiff and Defense Expert Witnesses in the Sexual Abuse Case

Barbara Jo Levy

**SUMMARY.** Barbara Jo Levy presents strategies and techniques for countering the "false memory" defense through the effective use of plaintiff's expert witnesses. She argues that expert witnesses should assist in preliminary case evaluation, education of the judge and jury, and in critical evaluation of defense expert testimony. Plaintiff's experts are valuable allies in maintaining the focus of the case on whether or not sexual abuse occurred in the case at hand, rather than allowing the analysis of the facts to become mired in debates over memory science. She underlines the key distinction between the role of the treating therapist and the expert witness, gives important criteria in choosing an expert witness, and reveals three key objectives of successful cross-examination. Appendices provide questions for the direct and rebuttal examination of plaintiff's expert witness, as well as actual deposition testimony and subsequent cross-examination of a defense witness to illustrate these strategies in action. *[Article copies available for a fee from The Haworth Document Delivery Service: 1-800-342-9678. E-mail address: <getinfo@haworthpressinc.com> Website: <http://www.haworthpressinc.com>]*

**KEYWORDS.** Depositions, preparation for, qualifications of expert witnesses, distinct roles of treating therapist and expert witness, cross-examination of defense witness, "False Memory" defense, questionable therapeutic techniques, direct examination of plaintiff's witness, rebuttal examination of plaintiff's witness, roles of the expert witness,

---

Address correspondence to: Barbara Jo Levy, JD, Attorney at Law, Sindell & Levy, Howard Building, Suite 300, 614 First Avenue, Seattle, WA 98104.

[Haworth co-indexing entry note]: "Plaintiff and Defense Expert Witnesses in the Sexual Abuse Case." Levy, Barbara Jo. Co-published simultaneously in *Journal of Aggression, Maltreatment & Trauma* (The Haworth Maltreatment & Trauma Press, an imprint of The Haworth Press, Inc.) Vol. 3, No. 2 (#6), 2000, pp. 113-132; and: *Sexual Abuse Litigation: A Practical Resource for Attorneys, Clinicians, and Advocates* (ed: Rebecca Rix) The Haworth Maltreatment & Trauma Press, an imprint of The Haworth Press, Inc., 2000, pp. 113-132. Single or multiple copies of this article are available for a fee from The Haworth Document Delivery Service [1-800-342-9678, 9:00 a.m. - 5:00 p.m. (EST). E-mail address: getinfo@haworthpressinc.com].

 

expert evaluation of the survivor/client, traumatic memory studies, history of, traumatic memory studies, scientific

Expert witness testimony has become a focal point in childhood sexual abuse cases, particularly the now-controversial cases involving recovered memories. This chapter explores the effective use of plaintiff's expert witnesses and challenge to defense experts' positions in cases in which the plaintiff claims delayed discovery of childhood sexual abuse. Included are proposed questions for the plaintiff's experts, as well as the deposition and trial testimony of a defense expert. Careful selection and preparation of plaintiff's experts and cross-examination of defense experts are two of the critical factors that determine whether the trier of fact concludes that the plaintiff was victimized as a child or was subjected to an outside influence, such as improper therapeutic techniques.

## *PLAINTIFF'S EXPERTS*

Persuasive experts for the plaintiff are an essential ingredient of winning a delayed discovery case. The lawyer must convince the factfinder that the plaintiff's rendition of the case is the more credible one. Plaintiff's experts should assist the lawyer to explain why, given all the evidence and scientific knowledge about the sequelae of trauma, plaintiff's theory of the case makes the most sense. The competence and integrity of experts directly impacts their credibility.

In addition to being highly qualified, the plaintiff's experts must be open-minded. If the experts are "true believers" that all reports of sexual abuse are real, they will seem unreasonable. If the experts believe that there is no possibility of contamination or that suggestibility of sexual abuse memories is impossible, they will lose credibility. An effective expert must be willing to look at "alternative hypotheses"; that is, are there reasons that the plaintiff believes that she was sexually abused other than her memories? Then, taking a scientific approach, the expert should help the attorney demonstrate why, in this particular case, alternative hypotheses to actual abuse are unlikely explanations.

It is important to hire an expert *early* in the case. Although an initial evaluation may involve a substantial outlay of money, the cost of litigating a sexual abuse case will be many times higher. Therefore, early review of the case by an expert may save both time and money in the long run. It is preferable to hire an expert witness even before filing, perhaps only as a consultant at first. In some jurisdictions, a "consultant's" opinion is not discoverable, while an expert's opinion is. If the consultant's opinion is unfavorable, plaintiff may decide to drop or quickly settle the case. Lawyers may want to consider retaining experts known to be hostile to the plaintiff's position so that they are unavailable to the opposition.

### *Roles of Plaintiff's Forensic Expert*

*Educator.* Plaintiff's experts should be knowledgeable about the most recent research, as well as historical scientific literature on the psychological issues in the case. The experts should be able to articulate what research is scientifically significant and its strengths and weaknesses. The expert can provide citations to, or copies of, journal articles so that the plaintiff's attorney understands relevant psychological and biological research.

*Evaluator.* Your experts should be qualified to formulate opinions as to the plaintiff's alleged abuse, corroborating factors, the identity of potential abusers, the client's injuries, and her future needs resulting from the abuse. They should also alert plaintiff's attorney to problems in the case and suggest potential solutions.

*Legal Strategist.* Plaintiff's experts should be able to help with the litigation itself, providing:

1. Questions for depositions and interrogatories;
2. Interpretation and criticism of defense expert's reports, articles, depositions, etc.;
3. Questions for trial for plaintiff and defense experts and fact witnesses;
4. Analysis of the strengths and weaknesses of the defense experts' opinions; and
5. General strategy.

### *Choosing a Forensic Expert*

*The Treating Therapist Should not Be Used as an Expert Witness.* The roles of the treating therapist and the forensic expert witness are fundamentally different. The therapeutic alliance is based on helping clients work through issues and feelings related to past experiences and helping them develop more functional responses and behavior in their present lives. The treating therapist's job is to act in the best interest of the client. It is *not* the treating therapist's job to demand documentation supporting every statement a client makes. A treating therapist can testify about the facts of treatment, modalities utilized and what diagnoses were made, but should not have the additional burden of forensic insight.

Some treating therapists may have a sub-standard education, may not specialize in trauma issues, or may subscribe to unorthodox practices or beliefs, leaving their treatment and opinions open to attack by defense lawyers. A plaintiff may first consult with a lawyer after being treated by a therapist who is less than ideal. The attorney should not interfere with the ongoing therapeutic process, but can use an experienced forensic expert to demonstrate that the less than perfect therapy was not powerful enough to create false beliefs, as the defense will claim occurred. Even if the treating therapist's credentials are unimpeachable, it is probable that the therapist's credentials and methods will be attacked by the defense. For that reason, it is crucial to retain an *independent* forensic expert to objectively evaluate all psychological issues and to educate the finder of fact.

*The Forensic Expert's Role Differs from a Treating Therapist.* The forensic evaluator's role is to critically review psychological and factual evidence and determine what conclusion is most reasonable. She must consider whether there is any malingering, distortion, or fabrication, and be willing to explore and challenge the plaintiff's version of the facts. The forensic evaluator should analyze all documentation to determine what does and does not support the plaintiff's version of what occurred.

Plaintiff's experts should be asked to consider whether there were improper suggestions during therapy (or outside of therapy) which could have caused the plaintiff to develop false beliefs about being a victim of abuse, or any other factors which might make the plaintiff vulnerable to a "false memory" attack. At least one expert needs to meet with the plaintiff, take a history, and conduct and interpret psychological tests. This will necessitate some hours of actual interview time with the plaintiff in addition to psychological testing. Plaintiff's experts should also interview fact witnesses, including family of origin members, treating therapists, current friends, spouse, children, childhood friends and neighbors. The expert should review corroborating (or non-corroborating) information in records including:

1. school records;
2. medical records;
3. employment records;
4. statements/depositions/letters of parents and siblings;
5. journals;
6. literature relied on by the defense;
7. defense experts' reports;
8. deposition or trial testimony of defense experts in prior cases; and
9. interrogatories.

The plaintiff's expert may want to consult with the treating therapist to find out information that may not be in the record. Once a case is filed, the expert should review all pertinent depositions and attend, or listen to, the taped interview of the defense psychological/psychiatric examination of the plaintiff if permitted in the jurisdiction.

The plaintiff's attorney should consider hiring more than one forensic expert. The defense will likely have two, three, or more experts and it is a difficult burden for one plaintiff's expert to offset them alone. If the defense has four experts contradicting the plaintiff's lone expert, the plaintiff's burden of persuasion may be more difficult. The plaintiff's lawyer can consider experts who specialize in treatment, research or training, or who have substantial experience in all of these areas.

*It Is Important to Choose Expert Witnesses Carefully.* An extensive evaluation and records review represents a large investment of time by the experts, which will be expensive. The attorney, the client, and the experts should be aware that civil sexual abuse cases, especially those involving recovered memory, require a substantial investment of time and money. For these reasons, it is vital to *choose the experts carefully*: The plaintiff's attorney should look for an expert who has credentials (preferably a PhD or MD), experience, a research background, and the time and willingness to provide education on the issues and to strategize with plaintiff's counsel. Plaintiff's attorney should feel comfortable with the expert, have the freedom to ask questions, and be able to rely on him for assistance during those inevitably vexing times in litigation. Forensic experts should be familiar with and understand the rules of the legal system. They should have the ability to explain technical and psychological terms. The experts should be likeable and able to educate the trier of fact about the issues in a down-to-earth, non-pejorative, and sensible manner.

In selecting an expert witness for this type of case, plaintiff's lawyer might consider the following questions:

1. Is the expert specifically familiar with the topic of childhood sexual abuse?
2. Is the expert knowledgeable about the most recent literature which supports and challenges plaintiff's theory of the case?
3. Does the expert have clinical experience in the field of sexual abuse?
4. Is the expert familiar with research on memory, influence, and suggestibility, especially suggestibility in memory for trauma?
5. Does the expert have general familiarity with the field of interpersonal violence? Of trauma and traumatic memory?
6. What is the expert's experience and comfort in litigation?
7. What is the expert's research background?
8. What professional societies does the expert belong to?
9. Has the expert served on the editorial board of any professional journal, particularly journals specializing in trauma research?
10. Does the expert have time to evaluate the client, talk with witnesses, review all the records, participate in litigation strategy, and review depositions and other writings of the defense experts?
11. Is the expert familiar with the likely defense experts and defense arguments that will be raised?
12. Does the expert have the ability to educate, while demonstrating competence, integrity and credibility?

### *The Forensic Expert as Witness*

Appendices D and E contain a sample outline for the plaintiff's forensic expert's testimony. The testimony is divided into the following topics:

1. Background and credentials of the expert;
2. Review of the scientific literature on trauma and memory;
3. Evaluation of plaintiff in this case;

4. Opinions regarding defense experts and the foundations for their opinions; and
5. Rebuttal.

*Background of the Plaintiff's Expert.* In establishing the expert's background, the expert should list his extensive educational and research background in the area of human trauma and as many of the following credentials as possible: clinical experience, teaching experience, research experience, publications on the subject, and editorial positions on peer review journals. It is helpful if the expert has lectured at professional seminars for lawyers, judges, or other therapists, has been qualified as an expert in other cases, and has experience far beyond the courtroom.

*Expert's Knowledge of Scientific Literature, History of Trauma Studies, and Memory.* It is imperative that the plaintiff's expert detail the historical perspective of trauma and memory and establish that trauma theory is not a new development of the last ten or fifteen years, dealing only with sexual abuse trauma. The expert should discuss the history of trauma and memory research from the nineteenth-century studies of Freud, Charcot, and Janet, to the twentieth-century studies of combat veterans, concentration camp survivors, and survivors of physical and sexual trauma. The expert must establish that the phenomenon of traumatic amnesia, or dissociation, has been well-documented, and that the *real* issue is whether there was traumatic amnesia and subsequent recall of the trauma in *this* case.

Areas of questioning should include:

1. Are you familiar with the literature on the psychological and emotional consequences of trauma? (Has your expert published and reviewed articles in this field?)
2. Are you aware of scientific writings on memories of abuse? Are you aware of cases where an offender has corroborated sexual abuse or where there has been other independent corroboration of recovered memories?
3. In what capacities do you use research and knowledge about the subject of memory (e.g., as professor, therapist, writer, and/or researcher)? What do the studies tell us and *not* tell us on the subject?

4. Are different terms used to describe this phenomenon? (The expert can discuss traumatic amnesia and its mechanisms and explain how the terms "dissociation," "amnesia," and "forgetting" have been interchanged with the term "repression." This enables the plaintiff's lawyer to avoid the trap of arguing about the meaning of the word "repression." Defense experts try to entangle plaintiffs in the web of definitions.)
5. Have you had experience treating people who regain memories of abuse? What is that experience?
6. As part of your research and writing, have you looked into the issue of why children who are abused may not tell? What have you learned?
7. Based on your training, experience as a clinician, and knowledge as a researcher, do you have an opinion as to whether a child who has been sexually abused can reach adulthood without raising suspicion in others? Explain. (For example, a child in school may go to great lengths to hide abuse. Ask the expert witness to explore the recent change in attitudes about discussing abuse.)
8. Are there studies which show traumatic memory can be implanted? Are there studies which support the defense theory of "false memory syndrome?"

*Expert's Knowledge of the "False Memory" Controversy.* Plaintiff's lawyers should not be afraid to have their expert testify about the current controversy regarding recovered memories and discuss each side's positions. The experts should explain that although people can be convinced to believe in events that did not occur, there are necessary conditions for such beliefs to be instilled. These conditions may include the presence of a trusted authority figure, prolonged and repeated exposure to suggestion, group pressure, control of the person's environment, and psychological control through fear. The expert can later show that the required conditions did not exist in this case.

The experts should also discuss the research on which each side relies, and explain what the research does and does not establish. Areas for experts to discuss include:

1. The history and current status of memory research;
2. The historical disbelief of many in society that sexual abuse occurs, and that recovered memories are reliable;

3. That victims of sexual abuse started to be believed in the 1970s and 1980s;
4. That there is now a backlash and the reasons for that backlash;
5. That therapists have always had concern regarding the accuracy of self-reporting;
6. The history of the False Memory Syndrome Foundation; and
7. That the expert considered the potential of malingering and suggestibility in this case.

Plaintiff's experts should give examples of *proven* cases of recovered memories.

*Evaluation of Plaintiff in This Case.* The experts need to explain the details of the evaluation process they followed in the case and the reasons for using that process. The experts should list all people they interviewed and all documents they reviewed.

Plaintiff's experts should develop a DSM-IV diagnosis, with a detailed explanation supporting the diagnosis. The experts also need to state the bases for their determination that the plaintiff was sexually abused by the defendant, alternative hypotheses they have explored, and why those alternative hypotheses do not account for plaintiff's condition.

*Use Plaintiff's Expert to Pre-Empt Defense Expert's Testimony.* Plaintiff's counsel can use the direct exam of plaintiff's forensic experts as a pre-emptive strike against the defense experts. In plaintiff's case-in-chief, the lawyer should ask the plaintiff's experts if they have had a chance to review the defense experts' reports, depositions, journal articles, speeches, etc., and then ask the experts what they think of the defense experts' statements.

Example One:

Q. Have you read the works of Dr. Jones?

A. Yes, I have.

Q. And do you have an opinion on her works in the area of memory?

A. What I've read suggests to me that she is a good scientist, a very productive person, and very *knowledgeable* about memory processing.

Q. Do you have any opinions on how Dr. Jones' work in the area of memory is related to issues of childhood sexual abuse which have been forgotten?

A. Well, that's where I think the difficulty comes with Dr. Jones' work. I think that she has not studied and worked with clients who have experienced trauma. And to the extent that traumatic memory operates differently than non-traumatic memory, her work doesn't generalize. And also, I think that her lack of experience with treating or studying sexual abuse victims puts her at a serious disadvantage for understanding what happens to them and how they're affected by the abuser and how that effect manifests itself in the memory.

Example Two:

Q. Have you read the works of Dr. Smith or some of his writings?
A. I have.
Q. Do you have an opinion about his writings on the issues of repressed or forgotten memories?
A. In general, I find Dr. Smith's writings lacking in scientific merit and often using inflammatory and exaggerated language to express his position. That is not to say that everything that he says is wrong or has no merit. But his conclusions are often not based on any scientific evidence.
Q. Are Dr. Smith's opinions about the effect of therapy regarding influence or creating memories of sexual abuse generally accepted in the scientific community?
A. Well, they're not only not accepted, they are inconsistent with the research on psychotherapy process and psychotherapy outcome.

*Rebuttal by Plaintiff's Expert(s).* The plaintiff's lawyer should select a few areas where the defense experts may have raised questions in the mind of the trier of fact, and have plaintiff's experts answer those questions.

Example One:

Q: At least one of the defense experts has testified that scientific evidence shows that memories are unreliable and subject to influence under certain conditions and concluded from that, that memories without direct corroboration should not be accepted. Do you agree with that?
A: No.
Q: Why not?

Example Two:

Q: Some of the defense experts in this case testified that there are studies which demonstrate that people can be persuaded to believe they've had an experience they haven't had. Are you familiar with those studies?
A: Yes, I am.
Q: And can you tell us what conclusions can be drawn from these studies about adults who remember childhood sexual abuse after a period of forgetting?

## *QUESTIONS WHICH EXPERTS SHOULD ANSWER FOR THE TRIER OF FACT*

By the end of the expert's testimony, they should have answered the following questions for the trier of fact:

1. Did plaintiff intentionally create false or fabricated memories?
2. Were plaintiff's memories sufficiently reliable mental records of actual past occurrences to warrant the conclusion that plaintiff was more probably than not sexually abused by the defendant? In other words, are the facts in this case supportive of plaintiff's position that she was a victim of sexual abuse which she survived by dissociating the abuse from her conscious memory until time permitted the buried memories to resurface, rather than supporting the idea that these memories are a reaction to inappropriately suggestive therapy and environmental influences?
3. Is the human mind capable of storing data relating to childhood sexual abuse that is not accessible to conscious memory for a period of many years and then making it accessible to conscious memory?
   a. Although there may be no studies of trauma that *conclusively* demonstrate the psychological phenomenon of traumatic amnesia, there have been reports of its occurrence in the clinical experience over a long period of time, and it has been accepted in the relevant scientific community.
   b. The trauma to a defenseless young child is so confusing, threatening and frightening that a trauma-specific psychological defense is a normal response.

c. There are now biological studies which indicate that traumatic memories are stored differently in the brain than are non-traumatic memories.[1]

4. Is there any corroboration of the plaintiff's memories - siblings, records, friends, abuser's other behavior, or statements that may be probative on the issue of defendant's insensitivity to normal boundaries of sexual propriety?

## *DEFENSE FORENSIC EXPERTS*

There are two keys to cross-examination of the defense forensic expert. The first key is the presence of able and convincing plaintiff's experts as described in Section I of this chapter. The second is thorough preparation and analysis of the deposition testimony of the defense witness(es).

### *Deposition*

A lawyer cannot prepare too much for the defense expert's deposition. Plaintiff's counsel should read articles, prior depositions, trial testimony and speeches by the defense expert. Some frequently used defense experts have written numerous articles and/or books. Many have testified in prior cases, and it is important to read and analyze their previous testimony. In reading prior testimony, lawyers can search not only for the expert's weak points, but also for additional questions which should have been asked by the deposing attorney. (It is always easier for lawyers to criticize other attorneys' depositions and elicited testimony than their own.)

As discussed in the section on plaintiff's experts, plaintiff's counsel can obtain their own experts' suggestions for deposition questions that will highlight the defense expert's biases, weaknesses, insupportable positions, inconsistencies and extreme stances. The defense expert may testify the same way in all cases.

The deposition itself may be long. Plaintiff's counsel should be thorough, so that at the end of the deposition they know everything the expert is likely to assert and what admissions can be elicited at trial.

Example One:

Q. Do you have an opinion as to whether the plaintiff has deliberately fabricated any memories?
A. I don't know one way or the other; I assume that she is sincere in these beliefs.
Q. Do you agree that children who are sexually molested are likely to suffer emotional or psychological injuries?
A. There is evidence to that effect; yes.
Q. You are not going to testify in this case that memories cannot be repressed, are you, doctor?
A. No.
Q. And you are not going to testify that memories of childhood sexual abuse cannot be repressed, are you?
A. No.

Such admissions can be the foundation of cross-examination of defense experts at trial.

Example Two:

Q. Wouldn't you agree that sex abuse is common?
Q. Wouldn't you agree that sexual abuse is harmful?
Q. Sexual abuse is usually done in secrecy, isn't it?
Q. A lack of witnesses does not mean that sexual abuse didn't occur, does it?
Q. Abusers usually deny the abuse, don't they?
Q. Denial doesn't mean the abuse didn't occur, does it?

The defense experts almost have to admit these statements. If they do not, they appear biased.

The attorney can sometimes use one defense expert to challenge other defense experts. In one case I handled, a defense expert called another defense expert "rude." (The judge agreed with this analysis in his opinion.) In the same case, a defense expert on memory testified that a defense gynecologist who had examined the plaintiff 35 years earlier, could not, without records, possibly remember the details of the physical examination to which he testified.

If the defense experts are members of the False Memory Syndrome Foundation, their testimony may appear to be politically motivated. Questions should demonstrate that these experts always testify on the same side of cases, again demonstrating the defense experts' bias.

Often defense experts are paid handsomely (from $300.00 to $500.00 an hour) for their testimony. When they attempt to testify that the plaintiff's treating therapists are economically motivated, their own monetary incentive comes into question.

The deposition also allows the attorney to ascertain the expert's personality (if not already known). Is the expert straight-forward and engaging, or arrogant and hostile? This evaluation allows plaintiff's counsel to determine what tactics to use later in cross-examination.

## *BETWEEN DEPOSITION AND CROSS-EXAMINATION*

Trial preparation should include a summary of the defense expert's deposition, including all admissions which can be used at trial. Plaintiff's lawyer should review any research the expert has cited at deposition. Defense experts may misstate the literature, or relate only part of the story. By actually reading what the defense experts have quoted, attorneys can determine for themselves whether the defense expert's accounts are accurate. Demonstrating any misstatement at trial discredits the defense expert. If plaintiff's forensic experts read the defense expert's deposition, they can highlight admissions, misstatements, unsupported opinions, and research to impeach the defense experts at trial.

If there is a defense psychological examination, the session or sessions should be taped, if possible, and the tapes transcribed. Plaintiff's expert should read and/or hear the interview as well as read the resulting report. The plaintiff's expert can help demonstrate that the defense psychological examination may have been disjointed, slanted to obtain a certain kind of information, less than thorough, or that the report does not accurately reflect what actually occurred in the psychological exam. The defense examining psychological expert can then be impeached and his bias demonstrated.

## *TRIAL*

*Voir Dire.* In *voir dire,* plaintiff's counsel can elicit jurors' views on expert testimony, potential for experts being biased, and the importance of hearing the whole story, not half-truths.

*Opening Statement.* In opening statement, plaintiff's lawyers can underscore the importance of determining whether defense experts have the credentials to support their opinions, and/or whether they are presenting an accurate picture of the facts of this case.
Example:

> Dr. Johnson comes into every case stating that there is no such thing as forgetting multiple episodes of trauma. He looks only at what supports his pre-existing conclusion. He ignores or minimizes facts that oppose his opinion. Although he is not a therapist, he criticizes any therapist who recognizes forgetting and later remembering trauma as a real phenomenon. He states his opinions without any supporting scientific evidence.

*Pre-Empt the Defense Expert.* (See page 121 of this chapter.)

*Cross-Examination of the Defense Expert.* The three goals in cross-examination of the defense expert are:

> To elicit admissions;
> To neutralize the expert; and
> To highlight the expert's extreme positions.

Cross-examination should be short, with a goal of demonstrating that the defense experts are biased and untrustworthy.

Goal One: Eliciting Admissions. Hopefully, there will be certain admissions from the defense expert's deposition which support plaintiff's case, such as:

1. sexual abuse is harmful and common,
2. lack of witnesses does not mean the abuse did not occur,
3. abusers usually deny and denial does not mean abuse didn't occur,
4. and that abuse usually occurs in secrecy.

These are fairly well-known and accepted propositions, but it helps to have the defense experts support certain aspects of plaintiff's case.

Goal Two: Neutralizing the Defense Expert. This can be done especially with non-clinical experts. Example:

Q. You are not a licensed clinician, are you?

A. No.
Q. And you have never treated someone who was sexually abused, have you?
A. No.
Q. And you are not qualified to treat, are you?
A. No.
Q. And you have never diagnosed someone who was sexually abused, have you?
A. No.
Q. And you are not qualified to make such a diagnosis, are you?
A. No.
Q. You are not an expert in Post-Traumatic Stress Disorder, are you?
A. No.
Q. There is no evidence to show that clients are eager to discover that they were sexually abused, is there?
A. No.

Some defense experts seem proud of the fact that they are not clinicians. The lack of clinical experience, however, often diminishes such experts' credibility. If an expert has never diagnosed Post Traumatic Stress Disorder or worked with a person traumatized by sexual abuse, their ability to perceive the impact on a client can be challenged. How can these people be "experts" in cases involving sexual abuse allegations when they have never assisted a person trying to overcome the effects of traumatic experiences?

Goal Three: Highlight The Defense Expert's Extreme Positions. Some defense experts will offer what to many seem like extreme opinions. A recent trial transcript includes the following examples:

Example One:

Q: You don't know what else went on in the plaintiff's household when she was a child, do you, Doctor?
A: No, I don't.
Q: And yet you're certain that this abuse, or next to 100 percent certain that this abuse did not take place?
A: It is my professional opinion, based on the scientific literature on influence that it is virtually certain that this series of recollections are the product of influence and it is virtually certain that they are not based on memories of events that actually happened.

That's my professional opinion about the materials that I've reviewed.

Q: You never interviewed plaintiff, did you?
A: No, I didn't.
Q: You never interviewed any of her sisters?
A: No, I didn't.
Q: And you never interviewed the defendants, plaintiff's parents?
A: No, I did not.

Example Two:

Q: Doctor, is it your opinion that plaintiff's expert is in the subgroup of people, I think you said subculture of people, who believe in traumatic memories being forgotten and later remembered?
A: Oh, I think he definitely is.
Q: And so you think he's an extremist. Would that be fair to say?
A: Oh, I think he's one of the people who is promoting the idea that these influenced beliefs reflect real memories.
Q: And so he's being fooled?
A: He's making a mistake.
Q: And unless someone agrees with you, they're making a mistake. Is that correct?
A: Only about things that are this clear.

Example Three:

Q: And you're aware, aren't you now, Doctor, that on the last page of plaintiff's therapist's intake sheet, his plan with plaintiff was to have a short set of sessions and possibly only the one to encourage assertive action?
A: Well, that's what apparently he wrote in his plan, but apparently it turned out that they had about 90 sessions.
Q: In fact, you said in your deposition that plaintiff's therapist had turned plaintiff into a cash cow, didn't you?
A: Yes. Thank you for mentioning that. I restrained myself from repeating it, but since you brought it up, yes. I think that that's what happened.
Q: And are you aware that this therapist charged only $50 an hour?
A: I probably read that if it's in his deposition.

Q: And yet, Doctor, you charge *$3,000.00* for a day of testimony, don't you?
A: That's correct.

Rebuttal by Plaintiff's Expert. (See page 122 of this chapter.)

Closing. This is the time for plaintiff's counsel to demonstrate where the defense experts were inconsistent, biased and extreme, or told only half the truth.

Example:

> It's clear that Dr. Doe came into this case with a bias: that the abuse *didn't happen because, in his opinion, a person can't repress multiple episodes of trauma.* Then he constructs his *theory* of what must have happened–without ever talking to any party or therapist. He thinks that from looking at a list of memories, he can reconstruct the plaintiff's thought process. He decides the plaintiff's siblings are suggestible without ever meeting them. He somehow *knows* with close to *absolute certainty* that the abuse did not occur although he was never in the family household, does not know the effects of sexual abuse or how someone could cope with living in a household where abuse is occurring and without having an understanding of dissociation as a psychological defense mechanism. With no training in psychotherapy, he criticizes the therapists in this case.
>
> He testifies, with no evidence, that psychotherapy can manufacture out of nothing, elaborate memories of abuse. He sees a progression of memories into satanic cults where there has been no supporting testimony or evidence. He says if the plaintiff's siblings are having memories, it's because they've been influenced by the plaintiff, and if they don't have memories, that proves that the plaintiff's memories are not real.
>
> He tries to make us believe that the visual memories are not real memories. Think about being in law school–can you see yourself studying in the library, sitting in class–does the fact that you have visual memories mean to you that you did *not* go to law school? And so I have to ask, who is it that is fantasizing in this case–who is making unfounded assumptions?

> This is a man who equates working with memories of sexual abuse on a par with working with memories of space alien kidnaping and past life regression. And so I hope that's enough said about Dr. Doe.

Plaintiff's counsel should argue that their experts looked at *all* of the evidence rather than selected portions to reach their rational opinions. Closing is the time to reinforce the importance of looking at the facts *in this* particular case. The defense will continually try to generalize about memory. Plaintiff's counsel must detail the facts of *this* case that support the plaintiff's claims.

And hopefully in the end, the trier of fact will have the same opinions of the defense experts as did Judge Dennis Yule of one defense expert in *Crook v. Murphy,* Washington Superior Court, Benton County, WA. No. 91-2-001-2-5, March, 1994:

> Finally, Dr. _____ characterizes plaintiff's memories as a progress toward ritual, satanic cult images, which he states fits a pattern he has observed of false memories.
>
> It appears to the Court, however, that in this regard, he is engaging in the same exercise for which he criticizes therapists dealing with repressed memory. Just as he accuses them of resolving at the outset defining repressed memories of abuse and then constructing them, he has resolved at the outset to find a macabre scheme of memories progressing toward satanic cult ritual and then creates them.
>
> He testified that he began his work in this case by "trying to get an idea of the progression of interest and then the initial visualizations and then the development and elaboration of the visualization."
>
> Dr. _____ equates recovery of memories of early childhood sexual abuse with the recovery of past life traumas as memories of abduction of space aliens. He explains that he is the only one who has seen such a progression to satanic cults because he is perhaps "the only one who studied the record to the depth that I have studied it."

In my review of the plaintiff's collection of memories, the progression is not so apparent.

## *CONCLUSION*

Through direct examination of plaintiff's experts and cross-examination of defense experts, plaintiff's counsel wants to establish the credibility, objectivity and honesty of plaintiff's experts and the defense expert's biases and reliance on half-truths.

Expert testimony should establish that the phenomenon of traumatic amnesia or dissociation has been well documented historically and the *real issue* is whether there was traumatic amnesia and later recall of the trauma in *this* case. Finally, plaintiff's experts can demonstrate why the plaintiff's version of the facts is more credible than any alternative explanation.

## NOTE

1. See Bessel van der Kolk and Rita Fisler, *Dissociation and the Fragmentary Nature of Traumatic Memories: Overview and Exploratory Study*, JOURNAL OF TRAUMATIC STRESS 9 (1995), 505-25.

# Delayed Memories and Scientific Evidence: Maintaining the Pre-Trial Admissibility of Delayed Memory Evidence

Brooks Cooper

**SUMMARY.** In this chapter, practicing attorney Brooks Cooper illuminates how the legal tradition of applying different standards to the admissibility of expert and lay opinions as evidence in litigation complicates delayed-discovery sexual abuse cases. Admissibility standards have long been a source of controversy, and recent developments in law, such as the pre-trial evidentiary hearings that invoke the "gatekeeper" function of the judge under the standard enunciated in *Daubert v. Merrell-Dow Pharmaceuticals,* have become a favored strategy by the defense in an effort to bar delayed memory testimony by characterizing it as the product of unreliable science. To overcome this litigation hurdle, Mr. Cooper contextualizes the present controversy in the history of scientific evidence admissibility, tracing emerging trends in judicial opinion on scientific evidence from expert witnesses from the 1923 case *Frye v. United States* through the present, and offers strategies and techniques to maintain admissibility of the evidence before and during all phases of the trial. *[Article copies available for a fee from The Haworth Document Delivery Service: 1-800-342-9678. E-mail address: <getinfo@haworthpressinc.com> Website: <http://www.haworthpressinc.com>]*

**KEYWORDS.** Evidentiary hearings, expert witnesses, litigation strategies, history of scientific/expert testimony, "general acceptance" stan-

Address correspondence to: Brooks Cooper, JD, Attorney at Law, Sam Hochberg & Associates, 750 Morgan Building, 720 S.W. Washington Street, Portland, OR 97205.

[Haworth co-indexing entry note]: "Delayed Memories and Scientific Evidence: Maintaining the Pre-Trial Admissibility of Delayed Memory Evidence." Cooper, Brooks. Co-published simultaneously in *Journal of Aggression, Maltreatment & Trauma* (The Haworth Maltreatment & Trauma Press, an imprint of The Haworth Press, Inc.) Vol. 3, No. 2 (#6), 2000, pp. 133-145; and: *Sexual Abuse Litigation: A Practical Resource for Attorneys, Clinicians, and Advocates* (ed: Rebecca Rix) The Haworth Maltreatment & Trauma Press, an imprint of The Haworth Press, Inc., 2000, pp. 133-145. Single or multiple copies of this article are available for a fee from The Haworth Document Delivery Service [1-800-342-9678, 9:00 a.m. - 5:00 p.m. (EST). E-mail address: getinfo@haworthpressinc.com].

 

dard, *Frye v. United States* (legal case), *Daubert v. Merrell Dow Pharmaceuticals, Inc.* (legal case), "gatekeeper" role of trial courts, relevance of scientific testimony to delayed memory litigation

The current controversy caused by the efforts of some to question the existence, validity and reliability of "repressed memory" has a complex relationship to the evolving standards for the admission of expert testimony at trial generally, and to delayed memory sexual abuse cases in particular. This chapter will examine the jurisprudence regarding expert and scientific evidence preceding the recent, important finding in *Daubert v. Merrell Dow Pharmaceuticals,*[1] paying particular attention to *Frye v. United States.* After then analyzing the *Daubert* decision, the chapter turns to interpretation and application of *Daubert* in the context of the "repressed memory" controversy.

An examination of the history of the controversy over expert and scientific evidence beginning with *Frye* is useful for a number of reasons. First, knowledge of the past is always a helpful tool for understanding the present. Second, many states have modeled their rules of evidence on the federal rules, and so will consider federal interpretation of these rules persuasive. Finally, some states have either not addressed the applicability of *Daubert* to their jurisprudence, or have rejected it outright, leaving *Frye* as the law of the state. This chapter argues for a rejection of *Frye,* and a proper application of *Daubert* with due regard for the values embodied in our adversarial system.

## *FRYE AND THE FEDERAL COMMON LAW OF EVIDENCE*

*Frye v. United States*[2] is, as the case name might suggest, a criminal appeal. James Frye was convicted of murder in the second degree. During trial he sought to offer the testimony of an expert witness. The witness would have testified as to the results of a deception or "lie detector" test performed on the defendant with a crude device.

The witness was skilled in the administration of a test described as a "systolic blood pressure deception test." It was this expert's theory that telling the truth is a natural act and does not engender internal conflict in the speaker. According to the expert, conscious deception and its accompanying fear of detection produces internal conflict that manifests itself in a rise in the systolic blood pressure.

The test consisted of measuring and recording the systolic blood pressure of the subject while interrogating him. If a subject was answering truthfully, the systolic readings would steadily decrease during the test as the anxiety of the test environment was replaced by acclimation and comfort in the subject. The readings would exhibit a pattern independent of the questions and answers given. If, on the other hand, the subject was untruthful, the deceptive answer would be signaled by a "spike" or sudden increase in the systolic blood pressure. Thus, a pattern in the results would emerge showing the truthful and untruthful responses.

When examined, the results obtained with Mr. Frye were consistent with someone who was telling the truth. He was, of course, examined as to the facts and occurrences making up the crime in question. His answers indicated that he had not committed the murder.

The proffer of the testimony based on this test was rejected by the trial court upon objection by the prosecutor. The counsel for the defendant then offered to have the witness perform the test in the presence of the jury. This also was objected to and rejected.

In its affirmation of the conviction, the court stated the then-existing rule for the use of expert witnesses:

> The rule is that the opinions of experts or skilled witnesses are admissible in evidence in those cases in which the matter of inquiry is such that inexperienced persons are unlikely to prove capable of forming a correct judgment upon it, for the reason that the subject-matter so far partakes of a science, art, or trade as to require a previous habit or experience or study in it, in order to acquire a knowledge of it. When the question involved does not lie within the range of common experience or common knowledge, but requires special experience or special knowledge, then the opinions of witnesses skilled in that particular science, art, or trade to which the question relates are admissible in evidence.[3]

The court then affirmed the exclusion of the witness's testimony, saying:

> [W]hile courts will go a long way in admitting expert testimony deduced from a well-recognized scientific principle or discovery,

> the thing from which the deduction is made must be sufficiently established to have gained general acceptance in the particular field in which it belongs. We think the systolic blood pressure deception test has not yet gained such standing and scientific recognition among physiological and psychological authorities as would justify the courts in admitting expert testimony deduced from the discovery, development, and experiments thus far made.[4]

A number of observations suggest themselves about the language of this decision and its subsequent application by courts. First, although this decision predates the adoption of the Federal Rules of Evidence, it recognized the liberality that was embodied in those rules. The court acknowledged that courts "will go a long way in admitting expert testimony." This is quite a distinction from the pronouncement of the Fifth Circuit during the pre-*Daubert* fervor over "junk science." Judge Higginbotham expressed the court's philosophy: "[o]ur message to our able trial colleagues: it is time to take hold of expert testimony in federal trials."[5]

Second, the "general acceptance" test seems to have been plucked out of *Frye* with little regard for its origins. *Frye* was decided in 1923, before the advent of much of the scientific information and knowledge that pervades modern life.

Third, the expert witness in *Frye* was asked to testify regarding the veracity of the defendant. The trustworthiness and credibility of witnesses is perhaps the area most jealously reserved in our law to the finder of fact. This is a far cry from evidence presented regarding the existence of traumatic memory loss with later recall. These experts testify about a mechanism of memory formation, retention, and recall. Their expertise lies not in gauging the truthfulness of the sexual abuse survivor, but in explaining the physiological and psychological underpinnings of traumatic amnesia, or repressed memory. Contrast this with the type of expert opinion regularly offered by defendants in these matters. The crux of these opinions is usually that the sexual abuse survivor is imagining things or deliberately fabricating memories. In short, the "false memory" testimony in opposition to plaintiffs in these matters generally focuses on the veracity of the plaintiff.

Finally, the test, as applied in *Frye,* related to the scientific acceptance of a device, and the results from that device, not a methodology or theory as has been the case in later years. It is difficult to determine the accuracy of a machine by observation of the results of its operation alone. However, theories and methodologies as mental constructs can be described and explained to a jury so as to allow the members of the panel to test for themselves the credibility of the theory and weight to be accorded its results.

During the years preceding the enactment of the Federal Rules of Evidence, *Frye* was criticized with increasing frequency because of its restrictive nature.[6]

## *THE MOVE FOR CODIFICATION AND THE EVOLUTION OF THE CURRENT RULES*

*Frye's* continued authority is questionable, not only because of its logical infirmity, but also because of the history of the Federal Rules themselves. In the 1930s, scholars and policy makers developed an increased interest in codification and standardization of the rules of evidence.[7]

Effort was first undertaken by the American Law Institute. The Institute formed its committee, and began drafting in 1938. This effort was not adopted anywhere in the United States.[8] The later effort by the National Conference of Commissioners on Uniform State Laws had considerably more success. Their 1953 effort was approved by the American Bar Association and received limited acceptance in the states. In 1961 an Advisory Committee on Rules of Evidence was appointed by the Judicial Conference of the United States.[9] After numerous drafts and comment periods, the rules were promulgated by the Supreme Court in 1972.[10] The Court acted pursuant to its authority under the Rules Enabling Act of 1934, 28 U.S.C. 2072 (1976). The rules that the Court presented to Congress did not contain a "general acceptance" test for expert testimony. Rather than enacting what the Court had produced with little comment or fanfare, Congress reacted strongly to the new rules. It was most concerned about the 500 series of rules governing privilege. The Congress felt that the rules provided inadequate protection of personal privacy.[11] It reacted with legislation curtailing the Supreme Court's power to promulgate rules, and making it easier for Congress to override the Court's proposals.[12] After scrutiny of the totality of the rules and substantial revision of the 500 series (essentially eliminating it and leaving privilege to state common law), Congress enacted the rules in 1975.[13]

It is important to note that Federal Rules of Evidence 702 and 703 were enacted by Congress without change from the version promulgated by the drafters and approved by the Supreme Court. It should not be assumed that a panel of experts and scholars such as was assembled by the Court to draft the rules would have been unaware of *Frye* and the "general acceptance" test that it posits. That *Frye* was neither included in the rules promulgated by the Supreme Court, nor added to the rules drafted by Congress, is persuasive that *Frye* was not intended to be part of the statutory enactment of the rules. Further, the one area of the rules that received significant attention, privilege, was expressly left to the common law by Congress. Therefore, Congress was well aware that its actions in the rules were supplanting the common law of evidence[14] and chose to avoid that occurrence in privileges.[15] The fact that the rules are a statutory construction which has displaced the pre-existing common law has been recognized by the Supreme Court in *U.S. v. Abel*: "In principle, under the Federal Rules no common law of evidence remains."[16]

Also, the Supreme Court has recognized that the Federal Rules of Evidence are statutory and must be interpreted accordingly. "Because the Federal Rules of Evidence are a legislative enactment, we turn to the 'traditional tools of statutory construction' [cite omitted] in order to construe their provisions." On this issue, see *Beech Aircraft Corp. v. Rainey*,[17] cited with approval, *Daubert v. Merrell Dow Pharmaceuticals, Inc.*[18] *Daubert*, of course, rejected the *Frye* test as unduly restrictive.

For cases exemplifying the pre-*Daubert* split in the circuits, see *In Re: Paoli R. R. Yard PCB Litigation*[19] (expressing a properly liberal standard for admissibility) and *Christophersen v. Allied-Signal Corp.*[20] (improperly grafting *Frye* onto the Federal Rules).

*Daubert v. Merrell Dow Pharmaceuticals, Inc.*[21] was the vehicle the Court chose to use for announcing its opinion on this controversy.

## *THE DAUBERT DECISION*

The *Daubert* case[22] arose out of a controversy over the drug Bendectin. The plaintiff's mother had taken Bendectin during her pregnancy. The plaintiff alleged that his limb reduction defects were due to that drug. The trial court granted summary judgment for defendant after finding that, under the *Frye* test, none of the plaintiff's causation experts' opinions would be admissible at trial. On appeal, this decision was affirmed. The Supreme Court rejected the *Frye* standard, articulated a new multi-factor test, and remanded for further consideration. On remand, the trial court applied the new test and again found plaintiff's experts' opinions inadmissible. The Court of Appeals again affirmed, ending the Dauberts' saga.

The Supreme Court enunciated a test that differed substantially from those in use by the Circuits at the time. This was a multi-part approach to resolution of the controversy regarding the admission of expert witness testimony. First, the court must consider the qualifications of the expert. *Daubert* does not change the liberal standards for qualification of experts.

Next, the court must be satisfied that the expert has an opinion to express regarding "'scientific knowledge' [that] will assist the trier of fact to understand the evidence or to determine a fact in issue."[23] The Court emphasized that "scientific" knowledge is that knowledge gained by the use of the scientific method.[24]

The Court then examined the "assist" language of the rule.[25] The Court characterized this as primarily a question of "relevance."[26] The questions to be answered here are (1) Does the proffered evidence "fit" with the issues in the case so as to bear on a contested fact or issue?[27] and (2) Does the evidence provide some assistance to the trier of fact?

The Court enumerated a non-exclusive list of factors to be considered in evaluating the expert's methodology: (1) Can the methodology employed be tested,[28] and (2) Is the hypothesis refutable? In sciences such as chemistry, this generally connotes replication or refutation by repetition of experiments.

In the context of traumatic amnesia, or repressed memory, experimentation to induce the phenomenon is morally and ethically prohibited. However, the theory is testable, in that many patients who report the recovery or re-emergence of memory can examine the concrete historical record to determine the veracity of this memory. In addition, therapists can examine the reports of numbers of such patients to test hypotheses regarding this phenomenon. Finally, the work of investigators like Bessel van der Kolk on the physiological processes which may underlie this phenomenon offers concrete results similar to those of other "hard sciences" which are testable.[29]

The court also opined that "[a]nother pertinent consideration is whether the theory or technique has been subjected to peer review and publication."[30] The Court cautioned, however, that publication is only one element of peer review, and that it

> is not a *sine qua non* of admissibility; It does not necessarily correlate with reliability, *See,* S. Jasanoff, *The Fifth Branch: Science Advisors as Policymakers* 61-76 (1990), and in some instances well-grounded but innovative theories will not have been published, see Horrobin, *The Philosophical Basis of Peer Review and the Suppression of Innovation,* 263 J. Am. Med. Assn. 1438 (1990).[31]

Thus, while publication of studies by the expert in question, or studies which espouse the same methodology employed by the expert is helpful, counsel need not despair if the particular methodology at issue in the case has not been published or peer reviewed.

Trial courts are also directed to consider the known or potential rate of error of a technique.[32] Thus, the various techniques employed by therapists to aid patients to recover, or to explore recovered memories will be more likely to be admitted if counsel can show that the known or potential rate of error is low or acceptable by the standards of the profession.

The final factor announced by the court is whether the methodology or technique has achieved "general acceptance" in the relevant scientific community.[33] Thus, the *Frye* test has been relegated to one factor among many. As applied to the controversy over repressed memory, it is clear that the position advocated by defendants has not achieved "general acceptance," while that which supports plaintiff's has indeed been "generally accepted" for quite some time. The Court cautioned that trial courts should be dubious in admitting evidence which relates to "a known technique that has been able to attract only minimal support within the community."[34] The use of "memory implantation" experiments such as those conducted by Elizabeth Loftus and others to disprove the veracity of recovered memories can be attacked on this basis.[35]

The court held that

> [t]he inquiry envisioned by Rule 702 is, we emphasize, a flexible one [footnote omitted]. Its overarching subject is the scientific

> validity–and thus the evidentiary relevance and reliability–of the principles that underlie a proposed submission. The focus, of course, must be solely on principles and methodology, not on the conclusions that they generate.[36]

The court also expressed its faith in "the capabilities of the jury," and in "[v]igorous cross-examination, presentation of contrary evidence and careful instruction on the burden of proof" as the "traditional and appropriate means of attacking shaky but admissible evidence."[37]

The controversy generated by the opinion, however, has not yet subsided. While it seems clear that the court adopted a more liberal standard when it rejected the harsh rule of *Frye*, many defense oriented authors have attempted to "spin" the opinion as a defense victory.[38] They focus not on the court's discussion of the liberality embodied in the Federal Rules, but on the court's statements regarding the "gatekeeper" function of the trial courts.

## *APPLICATION OF DAUBERT TO DELAYED MEMORY CASES*

To date, only a handful of decisions have been reported which deal with the admissibility of expert testimony regarding repressed memory. Two of the more significant are discussed herein.

*State v. Hungerford*[39] contains a thorough application of *Daubert* to this controversy. In this criminal matter, the court found evidence of the existence of repressed memory to be inadmissible because the prosecution failed to meet the *Daubert* test as to its expert witnesses. The court found that the theory was not generally accepted, that the published studies that supported it were flawed (and thus that the theory had not truly been peer reviewed), that there was a significant chance for falsification of the phenomenon, and that the theory might well be untestable.

*Hungerford* points up the danger of allowing the opposition to frame the terms of the debate and controversy. Because there is a large body of work and literature discussing traumatic amnesia and recovered memory, counsel must be prepared to show the court how the proffered expert opinion fits nicely into this decades-old line of scientific investigation. If the debate is framed in terms of repression and recovery of memories of sexual abuse, the field of scholarship available to support plaintiffs is dramatically reduced. If, however, the debate is correctly couched in terms of the effect of severe trauma on the ability to consciously recall traumatic events, of which sexual abuse is but one type, then the entire field of research into PTSD on survivors of wartime combat and other traumas becomes clearly related to the controversy at hand.

Such a strategy was successful in another case with related issues. *Isely v. Capuchin Province*[40] involved allegations of sexual abuse of a novitiate at a seminary. Plaintiff alleged that due to this abuse he suffered from Post-Traumatic Stress Disorder (PTSD) and had repressed memories of the events. Defendants filed motions in limine to exclude evidence of plaintiff's experts, insofar as their testimony touched on repressed memory. The court initially noted that where the exclusion of an expert's testimony may be dispositive of certain issues in the case, the preferred practice is to file the motions as long before trial as practical.[41]

The court first examined the qualifications of the expert witnesses. It found that Dr. Carol Hartman, one of the plaintiff's experts, held a doctorate in psychiatric nursing, was a professor of psychiatric nursing at Boston College, and had published 80-90 articles and several book chapters dealing with the subjects of her proffered testimony. The court then examined each of the factors identified in *Daubert,* concluded that Dr. Hartman was qualified, and deemed her testimony regarding the nature and existence of traumatic amnesia and PTSD admissible.

## *APPLICATION OF DAUBERT IN THE FUTURE*

The success of the *Isely* case demonstrates how the factors in the *Daubert* opinion provide a road map for discovery[42] and examination as to the opposing party's expert witnesses, as well as selection and retention of experts on behalf of counsel's own client. Before retaining an expert, examine the theoretical framework of the expert's approach to "delayed" or "repressed" memory. Does it comport with that expressed in published papers? Has the expert published anything herself? Are there any studies or tests which have validated this methodology? How voluminous and credible is the literature which criticizes this methodology? Counsel should examine the potential expert's methodologies with an eye toward their "fit" within the body of work published regarding PTSD, traumatic amnesia and recovered memory.

Before trying a case involving delayed memory, counsel must become thoroughly conversant in the competing theories regarding this phenomenon, and the strengths and weaknesses of these theories. This means that a complete review of the literature and lengthy consultation with experts is in order.

In contrast to its support of experts who affirm the existence of the phenomenon, *Daubert* provides a framework for attack and ultimate exclusion of the "science" espoused by defense-oriented experts. One of the most fertile grounds for attack of experts relying upon experiments similar to Elizabeth Loftus's "implanted memory" experiments is to argue that the proffered evidence does not "fit" with the issues of the case, as required by *Daubert*. Counsel, and counsel's experts, should be prepared to show that implantation of an innocuous or mildly distressing memory into the psyche of an otherwise healthy individual has no bearing on the psychological and physiological processes which occur during formation of memory in an overwhelmingly traumatic experience.

As mentioned above, another useful avenue is to contrast the long lineage of traumatic amnesia in the body of psychological research with the recent fabrication of the theories espoused by defendants. Also, counsel should point out how issue specific these theories are. There is little if any literature suggesting that World War II, Korean War and Vietnam War veterans did not, in fact, suffer traumatic amnesia. It is only when the underlying trauma is sexual abuse that some theoreticians become uneasy. If the phenomenon exists, as we know it does, then it can be caused by any sufficiently traumatic experience. If it does not, then the war veterans were "faking" just as much as sex abuse survivors are alleged to be.

Finally, counsel must contact others who represent survivors of sex abuse and obtain as many transcripts of testimony by the defense oriented experts. Can a pattern be discerned where the expert's testimony is the same, regardless of the underlying facts of the case? Has the expert contradicted himself in previous testimony?

## *CONCLUSION*

Despite much of the "spin" in legal scholarship, *Daubert* should be read as reaffirming the liberality of the Federal Rules of Evidence.

*Daubert* has codified the approach taken by courts in cases such as *In re: Paoli R. R. PCB Litigation, supra*. Counsel has a tool in *Daubert* to properly gain admission of the expert testimony which supports the existence of traumatic amnesia, and to more importantly seek exclusion of the junk science proffered by the theorists whose ideological biases causes them to attempt to deny the existence of traumatic amnesia.

## NOTES

1. *Daubert v. Merrell Dow Pharmaceuticals, Inc.*, 113 S.Ct. 2786, 2793 (1993).
2. *Frye v. United States*, 293 F. 1013 (C.A.D.C. 1923).
3. *Id* at 1014.
4. *Id.*
5. See *In Re Air Crash Disaster at New Orleans*, 795 F.2d 1230, 1234 (5th Cir. 1986).
6. See *Christophersen v. Allied-Signal Corp.*, 939 F.2d 1106, 1132 (5th Cir. 1991).
7. For a description of the progenitors of the modern rules, see, 21 C.A. Wright & K.W. Graham, FEDERAL PRACTICE AND PROCEDURE, Section 5005 (Saint Paul: West Publishing Company, 1977).
8. See, Robert Morgan, *The Future of the Law of Evidence,* 29 TEX. L. REV. 587 (1951).
9. 30 F. R. D. 73 (1962).
10. 51 F.R.D. 315 (1971).
11. See, JOHN H. WIGMORE WIGMORE ON EVIDENCE (Gaithersburg: Aspen Publishers, 1988), Section 6.3, 418 note 22.
12. Act of March 30, 1973, Pub. L. No. 93-12, 87 Stat. 9 (1973).
13. Act of Jan. 2, 1975, Pub. L. No. 93-595, 88 State. 1926 (1975).
14. Of which the *Frye* "general acceptance" test was a part.
15. JACK B. WEINSTEIN & MARGARET A. BERGER, WEINSTEIN'S EVIDENCE, Section 703-5.
16. *U.S. v. Abel*, 469 U.S. 45, 51 (1984).
17. 488 U.S. 153, 163 (1988).
18. 113 S.Ct. 2786, 2793 (1993).
19. 916 F.2d 829 (3rd Cir. 1990), cert. den., 111 S.Ct. 1584 (1991).
20. 939 F.2d 1106 (5th Cir. 1990), cert. den., 112 S.Ct. 1280 (1992).
21. 727 F. Supp. 570; 951 F.2d 1128 (9th Cir.); 113 S.Ct. 2786 (1993).
22. As an aside, Barry J. Nace, counsel for the plaintiffs in Daubert reports that the correct pronunciation of the plaintiff's name is "Daw-bert," not "Dow-bear" as pronounced by most commentators and analysts.
23. Fed. R. Evid. 702.
24. *Daubert, supra* at 2795, "The adjective 'scientific' implies a grounding in the methods and procedures of science. Similarly, the word 'knowledge' connotes more than subjective belief or unsupported speculation." For discussion of the scientific methods, see generally, CARL G. C. HEMPLE, PHILOSOPHY OF NATURAL

SCIENCE (Paramus: Prentice Hall, 1966) and KARL K. POPPER, CONJECTURES AND REFUTATIONS: THE GROWTH OF SCIENTIFIC KNOWLEDGE 5th Ed. (New York: Routledge, 1992).

25. "If scientific, technical or other specialized knowledge will assist the trier of fact to understand the evidence or to determine a fact in issue . . . " Fed. R. Evid. 702.

26. *Daubert, supra* at 2795, "Expert testimony which does not relate to any issue in the case is not relevant and, ergo, [is] non-helpful." 3 Weinstein & Berger 702-18 (702). See also, *United States v. Downing*, 753 F.2d 1224 (CA 1985) ("An additional consideration under Rule 702–and another aspect of relevancy–is whether expert testimony proffered in the case is sufficiently tied to the facts of the case that it will aid the jury in resolving a factual dispute.") The consideration has been aptly described by Judge Becker as one of "fit."

27. Downing, *supra*, James E. Starrs, *Frye v. United States Restructured and Revitalized: A Proposal to Amend Federal Evidence Rule 702,* 26 JURIMETRICS J. 249, 258 (1986).

28. *Daubert, supra* at 2797.

29. *See, e.g.*, Bessel van der Kolk, *The Body Keeps the Score: Memory and the Evolving Psychobiology of Posttraumatic Stress,* HARV. REV. PSYCH., 1:253-65 (1994).

30. *Daubert, supra* at 2797.

31. *Id.* For a discussion of the differences between reliability, accuracy and validity as these concepts are used in the sciences, see, Bert Black, *A Unified Theory of Scientific Evidence,* 56 FORD. L. REV. 595, 599 (1988).

32. *Id.*

33. *Id.*

34. *Id.*

35. *Id.*

36. *Id.* at 2798.

37. *See,* [Name of author], *Controversial Science in the Courtroom: Daubert and the Law's Hubris,* 43 EMORY L. J. 913 (1994).

38. NE2d, TC # 94-s-045 to 94-s-047, 93-s-1734 to 93-s-1936 (N.H. Superior Ct. May 23, 1995)

39. 877 F. Supp. 1055 (E.D. Mi. 1995).

40. *See,* discussion of practical considerations *infra.*

41. Assuming the jurisdiction, unlike Oregon, permits discovery of expert witnesses.

# The Needle in the Haystack: Uncovering Insurance Coverage for the Sexual Abuse Victim

Julian J. Hubbard

**SUMMARY.** Despite the significant damages in sexual abuse cases, the plaintiff's ability to collect the money awarded in settlement or judgment is often precluded by the limited financial resources of the defendant(s). In this chapter, practicing attorney Julian Hubbard introduces the basics of individual and corporate insurance coverage and reviews the development of very limited coverage in sexual abuse cases in statutory and case law. While direct coverage for sexual abuse injuries is as rare as a "needle in a haystack," indirect coverage can be found in some cases, especially those in which the acts of negligent individuals other than the perpetrator facilitated the abuse and thus the plaintiff's injuries. After an overview of relevant insurance issues and law, Mr. Hubbard delineates a practical model for research and legal strategies to ensure reaching any available insurance coverage, and explores the benefits and drawbacks of drawing on administrative resources to help pay for survivors' medical and mental health care. *[Article copies available for a fee from The Haworth Document Delivery Service: 1-800-342-9678. E-mail address: <getinfo@haworthpressinc.com> Website: <http://www.haworthpressinc.com>]*

**KEYWORDS.** Standards for determining intent to harm and insurance coverage (inferred intent, subjective intent, objective intent), vicarious

---

Address correspondence to: Julian J. Hubbard, JD, Attorney at Law, Law Office of Julian Hubbard, 120 North El Camino Real, San Mateo, CA 94401.

[Haworth co-indexing entry note]: "The Needle in the Haystack: Uncovering Insurance Coverage for the Sexual Abuse Victim." Hubbard, Julian J. Co-published simultaneously in *Journal of Aggression, Maltreatment & Trauma* (The Haworth Maltreatment & Trauma Press, an imprint of The Haworth Press, Inc.) Vol. 3, No. 2 (#6), 2000, pp. 147-192; and: *Sexual Abuse Litigation: A Practical Resource for Attorneys, Clinicians, and Advocates* (ed: Rebecca Rix) The Haworth Maltreatment & Trauma Press, an imprint of The Haworth Press, Inc., 2000, pp. 147-192. Single or multiple copies of this article are available for a fee from The Haworth Document Delivery Service [1-800-342-9678, 9:00 a.m. - 5:00 p.m. (EST). E-mail address: getinfo@haworthpressinc.com].

 

liability, "injury," personal or bodily, defined, "accident," importance of in reaching insurance coverage, professional liability, homeowner's insurance, administrative resources for survivors (victim's assistance), liability, exclusions, duty to defend, duty to indemnify, negligence

Obtaining a financial recovery in sexual abuse litigation provides the survivor much-needed resources for rebuilding her life through treatment and compensation for injuries. Yet the prospect of seeking justice through the civil courts can be bleak. In sexual abuse litigation, even successful litigants often find it impossible to obtain funds awarded in civil judgments. The reason is simple: many sexual abuse defendants lack the financial resources to provide such a recovery. In the absence of such resources, financial recovery depends on applicable insurance coverage for the sexual abuse injuries and other theories of recovery against the defendant. To complicate matters, judicial precedent has barred most insurance coverage for injuries and acts associated with sexual abuse under nearly every form of potentially applicable insurance. However, while direct coverage for sexual abuse injuries is as rare as the proverbial "needle in a haystack," indirect coverage may be found in some cases, especially those in which the acts of negligent individuals other than the perpetrator facilitated the abuse or those in which the perpetrator negligently caused other injuries.

The purpose of this article[1] is to acquaint abuse survivors and attorneys who represents abuse survivors with a broad overview of current insurance coverage law related to sexual abuse claims and to review the possibility of alternative means, consistent with the facts in the underlying matter, of triggering and obtaining the financial resources for rebuilding a life.[2] The possibility of insurance coverage is inextricably bound in complex issues of the history and nature of the abuse, the persons and entities involved, and the relationships between the plaintiff and the defendant(s). To assist both the attorney and the client in negotiating these complexities and in assessing the potential for coverage based on well-accepted criteria, I offer "Practice Tips" throughout this chapter, and conclude by offering a step-by-step model for analyzing coverage issues.

## INSURANCE COVERAGE OVERVIEW

In childhood sexual abuse litigation, the relevant insurance policies are those in which a defendant is an insured. The defendant's policies provide coverage for attorneys' fees and costs in defending certain covered claims and provide "indemnity" (money payment for a covered loss) for those claims, if the insured/defendant is found to be liable. Typically, the insurance policies provide that the insurance company retains the right to control the defense and to settle the claims.

### *Distinguishing First and Third Party Claims*

Within the context of insurance, a claim under a policy is considered either a "first-party" or a "third-party" claim. A "first-party" claim is a claim made by the policyholder for compensation under his own insurance policy for damage or loss to himself or to his property. A "third-party" claim is a claim made against the policyholder by a "third-party" (a person demanding compensation for an injury allegedly caused by the policyholder, such as a sexual abuse survivor). A typical liability policy may contain coverage for both first-party and third-party liability claims under different policy provisions. Any claim made by a victim of sexual abuse will always relate to the third party liability provisions only. These policies can often be found in the possession of the defendants, their attorneys, or the agents and brokers of the defendants.

> *Practice Tip: Identify all forms of coverage available to any defendant by means of written interrogatory. Ask specifically for the location and the nature of any policies issued to the defendant. Consider requesting or subpoenaing all insurance records related to any defendant from their insurance agent or broker.*

### *Forms of Coverage, Policy Limits, General Liability, and Professional Liability Policies*

The extent and amount of insurance coverage available in any liability case depends on the nature and the forms of the insurance policies. Different policy forms contain different monetary policy limits and deductibles that must be paid first by the defendant/insured before any coverage or obligation arises on the part of the insurer. In the context of sexual abuse claims, the policies will either be general liability or professional liability polices, each of which has a number of different forms.

The policy forms relate to one or more roles that a defendant played in the context of the victim's life at the time the injuries were suffered. For example, relatives and individuals acting outside the work environment will generally be protected by homeowner's or renter's insurance, while persons working within the scope of their employment will be covered under educational, day care, landlord-tenant/owner's policies, and professional and business general liability policies. The allegations of your complaint will determine which policies are triggered. The most common policies triggered in sexual abuse litigation include:

1. Homeowner's insurance and personal liability umbrella,
2. Educational institution liability insurance,
3. Day care liability insurance,
4. Landlord-tenant or owner's policies,
5. Professional liability policies: for the doctor, lawyer, accountant, dentist, or other professionals,
6. Business general liability policies and business excess or umbrella coverage, and/or
7. A new insurance product for a specialized form of business liability provides coverage for employment practices liability, including coverage for sexual harassment, discrimination and, in some cases, for sexual abuse.[3]

### *The Timing of the Trigger of Coverage: Occurrence and Claims-Made Policies*

Typically, homeowner's, educational, day care, landlord-tenant or owner's and general liability policies are "occurrence" based. The "occurrence" is the event that triggers liability coverage and is defined in most policies as an accident, neither expected nor intended from the standpoint of the insured, which results in bodily injury or property damage. An occurrence has been defined as the time when the damage occurs, not when the wrongful conduct takes place.[4]

Professional liability policies are often "claims" based. In these policies, coverage is triggered under the policies in effect during the year in which the claim is asserted. A single claim can include a series of interrelated acts, errors or omissions, or an act or a series of continuous, repeated, or interrelated wrongful acts. Thus, claims are limited by the coverage available when the client asserts the claim.

The language of liability policies is often opaque and vague; it is the vagary, however, that provides a potential site of interpretation in favor of coverage. Thus, it is important to carefully review the policy language, paying attention to how that language fits with the language of statutory law and case law in your jurisdiction to see if you can make a cogent argument for coverage under the facts, policy, and law in each case.

### *Policy Periods*

More than one policy period may be involved in a claim in the case of a lengthy period of abuse or different causes of injury. Insurance policies tend to run in annual increments and are renewed on a set date each year. Several policy periods may be involved if the injuries inflicted occur over several years. Multiple policies may also be triggered through various policy periods if there are multiple injuries caused by separate and distinct causes. In this event, there may be multiple limits that are applicable to each injury. Multiple limits can vastly increase the amount of coverage and, therefore, the amount of money available for the injured party.

In claims taking place over a long period of time and running through several successive policies, an "occurrence"-based liability insurer will argue that multiple injuries by one perpetrator were the result of a single cause and thus, represent only a single occurrence. The single occurrence then will be limited by the amount of "per occurrence" coverage available even under multiple policies.[5]

Under "claims made" coverage, multiple policy periods cannot typically be triggered unless there were successive claims made during each policy period.

> *Practice Tip: Determine the number of separate and distinct injuries that occurred and identify the period(s) of time in which those injuries took place. Identify whether the injuries all relate to one accident or were the result of multiple causes which varied over different times and places.*

### *Monetary Limits and Deductibles*

Monetary limits are usually denoted as "per occurrence," "per claim," or "aggregate" within a particular policy period. A "per occurrence" monetary limit sets forth the maximum amount an insurer will pay for the injuries relating to a single injury-producing event, error, or omission, regardless of the number of injured parties. For example, if there is a "per occurrence" or "per claim" limit of $300,000.00 under a policy and 15 persons are injured at the same time by the same conduct of the policyholder, those 15 persons will obtain their compensation by dividing the $300,000.00 limit between them. The division of the limited coverage will depend on the relative degree of harm suffered by each claimant, or on other criteria deemed fair by the parties and the court. The "aggregate" monetary limit sets forth the total amount payable under the policy in a given year, regardless of the number of injury-producing events or insureds.

Policies will identify one or more of the defendants as either "insureds" or "additional named insureds" in the declaration pages attached to the policy. Normally, the insurer has equivalent obligations to the "insured" and the "additional named insureds." However, even if there are multiple insureds who have liability in the context of a particular claim, the amounts payable under the policy may be limited by "per occurrence," "per claim," or "aggregate" limits.

Furthermore, some forms of coverage condition any obligation under the policy to the payment of a deductible by the insured. The deductible may apply to expenses related to resolving the claim (through its defense, payment, settlement, judgment, or some combination of these elements). Generally, the higher the deductible, the greater the demands placed on the defendant's personal resources.

> *Practice Tip: The attorney for the injured party will want to investigate the underlying facts to determine if multiple, successive injuries have occurred as a result of different forms of conduct by the defendant(s). If so, the attorney can then argue that the facts indicate several successive courses of independently motivated and caused conduct resulting in differing injuries occurring over time, which trigger the maximum number of potential policies and policy limits.*

### *Typical Liability Coverage Terms*

Insurance policies are contracts which undertake to indemnify the insured against damage arising from a "contingent or unknown event."[6] Liability coverage is usually set forth in insurance policies in the following kind of language:

> We shall pay all sums for which you may become legally obligated to pay as damages caused by 1. Bodily injury, personal injury; 2. Advertising Injury . . . ; 3. Property damage.
>
> We shall defend any suit against you claiming these damages, even if the allegations of the suit are false or groundless.[7]

The terms "damages," "bodily injury," "personal injury," and "advertising injury" are all terms specifically defined by the policy. "Damages" are frequently defined as "the cost of compensating those who suffer bodily injury, personal injury, advertising injury or property damage caused by an occurrence."[8] An "occurrence" is defined as "an accident, including continuous or repeated exposure to conditions which result in bodily injury or property damage neither expected nor intended from the standpoint of the insured."[9] "Bodily injury" is frequently defined as "physical injury."[10] "Personal injury" is defined as an injury arising from a listed "offense," including "discrimination or humiliation not intentionally committed by or at the direction of the insured."[11]

In these provisions, the insurance contract provides that, for covered claims, the policyholder can expect both a defense of the claims and the money to pay them (up to the limits of coverage) if the insured becomes legally obligated to do so. However, for a claim to be covered, it must meet the criteria established by terms defined in the policy. In the next section, I will examine how these policy terms must be understood within the larger context of coverage law, which often excludes coverage for injuries explicitly related to sexual abuse.

## *THE CURRENT STATE OF THE COVERAGE LAW REGARDING CLAIMS FOR SEXUAL ABUSE*

Sexual molestation of a child or an adult is a crime. In reviewing civil claims for injuries arising from molestation, most state courts have adopted public policy arguments that maintain that since molestation of a child is reprehensible and intrinsically harmful, it is a clear case of *intentional* and criminal wrongdoing. The logic of such public policy rejects any excuse that might pardon the perpetrator or require another to shoulder the economic consequences of his conduct, particularly when it comes to insurance coverage.

Furthermore, insurance policies are generally written to provide insurance coverage for accidents and injuries arising from *accidental* conduct by the person or entity insured. Policies contain specific exclusions for damages arising from the criminal misconduct or intentional wrongdoing of the policyholder.

Civil claims for damage arising from sexual molestation are usually found to be uninsured and uninsurable because of this combination of these judicial public policy arguments and the built-in insurance policy exclusions. Accordingly, when a defendant is served with a civil lawsuit alleging sexual misconduct, his request that the insurance company defend and indemnify him in the case will usually be denied. If the plaintiff's attorney has limited the allegations only to claims of sexual misconduct, the insurer's refusal to provide coverage will be upheld by most state courts. Thus, the facts alleged in the complaint that relate to claims of *non-sexual* misconduct become the initial focal point for triggering insurance coverage. The following sections explore these issues.

### *The Duty to Defend Claims of Sexual Molestation*

Liability insurers have two basic obligations to their insureds: an obligation to defend the insured if a covered or potentially covered claim is made against the insured, and an obligation to indemnify (or pay on behalf of) the insured for any covered claim under the policy.

The liability insurer owes a broad duty to defend its insureds against claims that create a potential for indemnity.[12] Accordingly, the insurance carrier must defend any lawsuit that does or may seek damages within the coverage of the policy.[13] Implicit in this rule is the principle that the duty to defend is broader than the duty to indemnify. Thus, an insurer may owe a duty to defend its insured in an action in which no damages ultimately are awarded.[14]

Assessing the insurer's duty to defend involves comparing the allegations of the complaint with the terms of the policy. Facts extrinsic to the complaint may also give rise to a duty to defend if they reveal a possibility that the claim may be covered by the policy.[15] Such extrinsic facts might include materials or matters not referenced in the complaint but which define or identify different elements of the allegations (e.g., letters by one of the parties, medical records relating to dates of injuries, etc.). Thus, the development of facts which create both the potential for a defense and for indemnification is the highest priority for the practitioner.[16]

> *Practice Tip: Include accurate and truthful allegations in the complaint pertaining to any facts that may create a potential for coverage under an existing policy.*

To establish the duty to defend, the insured must prove the existence of a potential for coverage against the insurer's attempt to prove the absence of any such potential. The insured need only show that the underlying claim *may* fall within the policy coverage; the insurer must prove it cannot. Facts merely tending to show that a claim is not covered or may not be covered are insufficient to eliminate the possibility that the damages alleged fall within the scope of coverage.[17] A complaint is to be liberally construed in favor of potential coverage. Theories of recovery or causes of action are often changed or amended by a party after the original complaint is filed. Therefore, courts tend to focus on the allegations least alterable as the underlying facts supporting the complaint.[18] Any doubt as to whether the facts give rise to a duty to defend is resolved in the insured's favor.[19]

Once the defense duty is triggered, the insurer is obligated to defend against all of the claims involved in the action, both covered and non-covered. However, if the insurer can demonstrate that some defense costs are the result of defending a non-covered claim, it may be able to recover those costs from its insured. In order to recover some defense costs, the insurer must provide undeniable evidence supporting the allocation of a specific portion of the defense costs to a non-covered claim.[20]

The duty to defend is limited by the nature and kind of risk covered by the policy.[21] The duty is derived from the insurer's coverage obligations in the insurance contract. Where there is no potential for coverage, courts have repeatedly held that the insurer has no duty to defend.[22]

If there are facts that trigger a duty to defend under one or more existing policies, the victim and her attorney face both good and bad news. The good news is that the insurer is implicitly admitting that the allegations of the complaint have created a potential for coverage under the policy. The claimant's attorney must identify where that potential lies and insure that the claim is fully developed.

The creation of a duty to defend also enhances the possibility of a settlement offer from the insurer. Liability insurers seek to control the costs and expenses associated with the defense of a claim just as managed care organizations seek to control health care costs. Insurers, like other litigants, often look at the economics of litigation as a motivating factor for claim resolution. So, for example, if the costs of defending a claim through trial and appeal may amount to costs and expenses in excess of $50,000.00, and there is a potential for coverage, the insurer may decide that it makes economic sense to make a settlement offer to the victim at that amount.

On the other hand, even prior to settlement, insurers (through their selected defense counsel) will seek to limit the scope of their liability and the amount of damages claimed. Where the liability of the policyholder/defendant is clear, the defense will focus on the damages claim, using independent medical examinations to establish that the victim's psychological damages are attributable mainly to her personal history, or that she has fully recovered from the abuse. Depositions will be taken of the victim and others, and there may be an independent medical examination of the victim by a defense psychiatrist, medical doctor, psychologist, or all three. Accordingly, the risks increase as an insurer-funded defense sets out to eliminate, diminish, or dismiss the victim's claims.

Once the defense is undertaken by the insurer, the insurer will monitor the evidence developed in the ongoing case for any basis for denying its duty to continue the defense and its duty to indemnify. An insurer can withdraw its defense once it proves that is not obligated to make payment of a settlement or judgment on a claim.[23] The insurer can accomplish this by establishing that the facts do not support the possibility of coverage under the policy due to an exclusion in the policy or a legal or statutory bar to coverage, the subjects of the next section.

### *Policy Exclusions and Statutory Bars to Coverage*

Coverage may be barred by policy provisions or by legislatively enacted statutes. Every state has laws that regulate the forms of injury that may be covered by insurance policies, and these laws are often interpreted by courts to clarify the implicit provisions of insurance policies. Many insurance policies contain exclusions that by their stated or implied terms exclude coverage for sexual abuse injuries.

The insurer has the burden to prove the applicability of the exclusion.[24]

The first coverage hurdle for the plaintiff is establishing that an occurrence or an accident has taken place. As explained previously, liability policies only provide coverage for defined events such as "accidents" and the damages that flow from those events in the forms of "bodily injury" and "personal injury." Where insurance provisions define an accident as an "occurrence" neither "expected or intended from the standpoint of the insured," an insurer may argue that sexual abuse is the legal equivalent of intentional misconduct and is not an accident (thereby avoiding the potential of coverage). An intentional act is not an accident within the plain meaning of the word.[25] This roadblock at the definition of "accident" may halt any further inquiry into the nature of the insured's intent and result in a coverage denial.[26] This is because the term "accident" refers to the nature of the conduct by the policyholder, not to his state of mind.[27]

In addition to arguing that there is no accidental conduct involved, an insurer may also focus on the nature of the damage as a means of avoiding coverage. Where covered "injuries" are defined in an insurance policy as "bodily injury" or "physical injury," an insurer may contend that psychological injury and emotional damage arising from sexual molestation is not a covered injury to the body, but rather psychiatric in nature.

In addition to policy exclusions, many state codes contain specific statutes that exclude insurance coverage for the violation of a criminal statute, sexual misconduct, and/or intentional harm. In California, for example, statutes specifically bar insurance companies from providing insurance coverage for intentional misconduct. California Insurance Code §533 precludes coverage as follows: "An insurer is not liable for a loss caused by the willful act of the insured: but is not exonerated by the negligence of the insured or of the insured's agents or others." The statute focuses on losses willfully imposed, on harm intentionally created, as distinguished from losses created by an accident. This preclusion of coverage ostensibly reflects Californian public policy against insurance coverage for injuries caused by intentional, criminal acts, and the statute has, by operation of law, been read into all insurance policies in the state as an equivalent to a policy exclusion.[28] In *J.C. Penney Casualty Insurance Company v. M.K.*,[29] for example, the California Supreme Court applied §533 to preclude coverage for a man who had admitted to willfully and lewdly molesting a minor. Further, California Code §1668 provides:

> All contracts which have for their object, directly or indirectly, to exempt anyone from responsibility for his own fraud or willful injury to the person or property of another, or violation of law, whether willful or negligent, are against the policy of the law.

This statute is implied in every insurance contract in California and excludes coverage in sexual molestation cases.[30,31]

Defendants/insureds have attempted in some cases to circumvent the policy requirement of an accident and the statutory bars on harm caused by intentional or willful misconduct with two principal arguments: first, that the sexual misconduct was negligent, and second, that while the act may have been intended, the harm was not. Some courts have held that the insurer may not escape coverage in cases where the insured did not intend the harm, even if he intended the act.[32] Early cases interpreting these issues in context of criminal misconduct tended to favor an interpretation protective of the policyholder and a finding of a potential for coverage. In *City of Johnstown v. Barrot Standard Insurance Company,* the Second Circuit held that the insurer must prove that the policyholder subjectively intended the resulting injury to deny coverage.[33] In *Clemmer v. Hartford Insurance Company,* the California Supreme Court held that an act which is intentional or willful within the meaning of traditional tort principles will not necessarily exonerate an insurer from liability under Insurance Code §533 unless it is done with a preconceived design to inflict injury.[34]

However, in the context of sexual offenses and the civil injury claims that arise from them, many courts have linked the act of sexual molestation with conduct that cannot be accidental and is always willful. Courts have held that the *Clemmer* approach injects a malice factor into the term "intentional" when that term arises in the intentional act insurance exclusion context, thereby distorting the clarity of the language and the law.[35] For example, in *State Farm Fire & Casualty Company v. Ezrin,* the Northern District court, applying California law, held that the act of nonconsensual sexual assault involving two adults was willful and concluded that insurance coverage was unavailable as a matter of law.[36] In *Merced Mutual Ins. Co. v. Mendez,* the court held that the allegations of a sexual assault of an adult woman could not be construed as accidental:

> All of the acts, the manner in which they were done, and the objective accomplished occurred exactly as appellant intended. No additional, independent or unforeseen act occurred. Whatever the motivation, because Mendez's conduct was "calculated and deliberate," [citation omitted] it was not an "accident" and thus not an "occurrence" within the meaning of the policy.[37]

More recently, in *Quan v. Truck Insurance Exchange,* a court held that an insurance policy's "bodily injury" coverage imposed no duty to defend an insured accused of intentional but negligent sexual assault against a minor, irrespective of any issue of intent to harm.[38] In *Quan,* the court first focused on whether the alleged claim was "accidental," since the relevant Truck policy only provided coverage for "accidents."

The problem was that at the heart of plaintiff's complaint were allegations of intentional, not accidental, conduct. The plaintiff asserted four causes of action in the complaint: assault and battery, intentional infliction of emotional distress, negligence, and negligent infliction of emotional distress. The plaintiff wove the facts of the intentional theories into the negligence theories, alleging in a negligence claim that the insured "[w]ith force and against the consent of Plaintiff, assaulted Plaintiff and raped, ravished, and carnally knew her." Under the intentional theories, the plaintiff stated these same facts were "wrongful and malicious," i.e., intentional. Thus, when he sought coverage under the Truck policies, it appeared to the court that the defendant/insured was simply recasting intentional and noncovered conduct in negligence claims. Describing the basic controversy and its resolution, the court found that:

> The insured's argument attempted to draw a distinction between the intentional tort causes of action and the "negligence-based" causes of action, the insured argues that there will be covered liability if he is found to have been "negligent" in serving alcohol to, touching, kissing, embracing, fondling or having sex with the claimant. The court found that such arguments misconstrue the "accident" requirement in standard general liability policies. "Under California law, the term refers to the nature of the in-

> sured's conduct, not his state of mind." [Citation omitted]. "Negligent" or not, in this case the insured's conduct alleged to have given rise to claimant's injuries is necessarily non-accidental, not because any "harm" was intended, but simply because the conduct could not be engaged in by "accident."[39]

The *Quan* court held that even if liability could be imposed without a finding of any intent to "harm," the lack of such intent would not convert volitional physical acts into "accidents" within the meaning of that term in the policy under California law. In other words, injurious physical contact caused by sexual molestation may have been a "mistake," but it cannot have been an "accident."[40] However, the court left an opening: "An accident can flow from an intentional act only if 'some additional, unexpected, independent, and unforeseen happening'" (i.e., an accident) occurs that produces the injuries.[41] Thus, the *Quan* court suggests that coverage may exist if a victim is injured even after the sexual misconduct by an additional, accidental happening that produces the injury.

> *Practice Tip: In order to trigger insurance coverage, the victim and her counsel must allege any and all facts related to accidental conduct, separate and distinct from that related to the molestation, that unexpectedly resulted in a covered form of bodily, physical, or personal injury. In most cases, there will be no defense or indemnity obligation arising solely from the sexual misconduct. For these non-sexual claims, the question will become whether the non-sexual or the sexual claims caused the victim's alleged injuries.*

In addition to the bar for coverage for intentional acts created by the policy definitions of "occurrence" and "accident" and by state statutes, many policies contain additional, specific exclusions. Some of the most commonly encountered exclusions follow.

*The Intentional Acts Exclusion.* Most policies contain a specific intentional acts exclusion. That exclusion specifically prohibits coverage for "bodily injury . . . intentionally caused by an insured person" or "which is expected or intended by the insured."[42] Some courts require that for this exclusion to be operative, the insurer must establish both the intent of the insured to act and the intent to harm.[43]

*The Criminal Acts Exclusion.* This exclusion typically provides that damages that may reasonably be expected to result from the "criminal acts of an insured person" are excluded from coverage.[44] The applicability of this exclusion depends not on whether the insured intended the damages, but on the type of criminal conduct and what damages would reasonably flow from that conduct.[45] Where the defendant in the civil action has already been convicted or pled *nolo contendre* to violating a penal code, the insurer will easily meet its burden of proving the applicability of this provision.

*Malpractice and Professional Services Exclusion.* In most homeowner and general liability policies, there are exclusions for "bodily injury" arising from "the rendering or failure to render" "any service or treatment conducive to health or of a professional nature." This exclusion has been interpreted broadly to bar coverage.[46]

A careful review of the policy language is, then, essential to locating potential insurance coverage. However, exclusions may not prevent coverage for nonintentional conduct.

> *Practice Tip: If the matter involves an individual rendering professional services to the victim and the only coverage available may be a homeowner or general liability policy, it is important to include allegations pertaining to nonintentional humiliation or discrimination separate and apart from any sexual misconduct, assuming the facts support it.*

*The Athletic Exclusion.* In some policies, there are "athletic exclusion" provisions that prohibit coverage for "bodily injury" to a person practicing for or participating in an athletic/sports contest or exhibition sponsored by the insured. However, the athletic exclusion does not prohibit coverage for "personal injury" (coverage for damages arising from humiliation, wrongful imprisonment, wrongful eviction and defamation) in the same events sponsored by the named insured, nor for "bodily injury" resulting from practicing for and participating in contests and exhibitions not sponsored by the named insured.

> *Practice Tip: In any situation involving school athletes who have been molested by coaches, the practitioner should investigate whether there are facts indicative of negligent coaching resulting in bodily injury (shin splints, stress fractures, etc.) which may have arisen or first become known at*

> *exhibitions not sponsored by the athlete's school and probe for incidents of humiliation and other forms of defined "personal injury."*

*The Exclusion for Sexual, Emotional, and Physical Abuse.* Based on findings of coverage for non-sexual claims in sexual abuse complaints, insurance companies have acted quickly to reduce their coverage risk. Newer policies often contain exclusions for claims of "sexual molestation, corporeal punishment, and infliction of physical or emotional abuse."[47] These exclusions could affect coverage for non-sexual claims made by the victim. For example, "emotional abuse" can be very broadly defined. As the scope of the exclusions tends to expand, the need to identify injuries separate and distinct from abuse is becoming more critical.

### *The Insurer's Duty to Indemnify Claims of Sexual Molestation*

Many courts have addressed the issue of whether a liability insurer owes a duty to indemnify an action for damages arising out of child molestation. Despite the broad duty to defend, most courts have answered in the negative with respect to indemnity.[48] In *J. C. Penney Casualty Insurance Company v. M. K.*, the liability insurer sought a declaratory judgment clarifying that it was not required to indemnify its insured in the child victim's action seeking damages for sexual molestation.[49] The insured had previously pled guilty in a criminal proceeding to a violation of Penal Code §288 (a) for the sexual molestation of a child. The Supreme Court emphasized in *Penney* the narrowness of their holding, stressing that it was only addressing child molestation and no other type of wrongdoing.

In *Horace Mann v. Barbara B.*, the California Supreme Court faced the same issues concerning a molestation claim, which included other tortious misconduct.[50] The insurer, Horace Mann, argued that the other alleged misconduct was directly related to the uninsurable molestation and therefore, it had no duty to defend or indemnify. However, in this case, the Supreme Court found that the insurer had an unwarranted assumption that the other alleged misconduct was necessarily part of the molestation. The holding in *Gray* taught that when facts extrinsic to or outside the allegations of complaint, gathered from the insured or other sources, suggest that the claim may be covered under its policy, the insurer has a duty to defend the action. There are differing views on the question of whether an insurer must defend when the facts of a complaint show a potential for coverage but "extrinsic" facts (facts developed through investigation for trial use) are to the contrary. In *Horace Mann,* the insurer did not escape the duty to defend, as the court found there were unresolved issues pertaining to a potential for non-sexual liability that might involve covered acts. However, the trial court stated, "Our decision is no license to 'plead around' *J.C. Penney* [the inferred intent rule]. . . . We do not sanction relabelling child molestation as negligence in order to secure insurance coverage for plaintiff's injuries."

In 1998, the California Supreme Court reviewed *Horace Mann* and discovered that the non-sexual claims were actually part of the sexual claims, and were therefore excluded from coverage. The evidence developed at trial could not be pigeonholed into separate sexual and non-sexual categories. Despite efforts by the victim's counsel to focus only on the non-sexual torts, the Supreme Court upheld the trial court's decision denying coverage to the victim on the basis that the other acts of public misconduct "facilitated the sexual molestation [by] providing . . . [the molester] with an isolated, alienated, more compliant victim."[51]

In considering both the allegations and extrinsic facts, courts have utilized three standards in determining if the acts or harm alleged were either expected or intended from the standpoint of the insured for purposes of applying the intentional acts statutory bar or policy exclusion: the inferred intent standard, the subjective intent standard, and the objective intent standard.

### *The Three Historic Standards for Determining Intent to Harm and Insurance Coverage*

Some courts have found a duty to defend and indemnify claims where the misconduct admittedly involved an intent to engage in the molestation but not an intent to harm the victim.[52] The standards or tests used to evaluate such duties include the *inferred intent* standard (which holds sexual abuse as conduct so egregious that an intent to harm is inferred as a matter of law),[53] the *subjective* standard (which investigates whether the insured subjectively intended to cause injury), and the *objective,* "reasonable person" standard (which is concerned with whether a "reasonable person" would expect injury to result from the act committed, or whether the natural and ordinary consequences of the act are bodily harm).

*The Inferred Intent Standards Excludes Coverage in a Majority of Jurisdictions.* In cases of adult molestation of a child victim, the majority of courts infer the intent to harm as a matter of law from the act of molestation. In *State Farm Fire and Casualty Co. v. Smith,* the insured admitted that he sexually molested his adopted eleven-year-old daughter on several occasions.[54] Although the insured admitted that the acts were intentional, he denied any intent to harm his daughter. He claimed he was "trying to do her a favor."[55] In the suit brought by the daughter and the mother, the complaint alleged that the conduct was "grossly negligent" and negligent. When the father's insurer brought suit to declare a lack of coverage, the district court rejected the attempt to plead around the intentional acts exclusion contained in the policy. Quoting the language of the lower court's decision, the Ninth Circuit upheld their finding as well: "[T] he vast majority of jurisdictions that have considered this issue have concluded that the intent to harm may be inferred from sexual contact with a minor as a matter of law."[56] In a similar case, *Altena v. United Fire & Casualty Co.*, the Supreme Court of Iowa reasoned similarly:

> The insured admitted the sex acts but denied intending to injure [the victim]. Nevertheless, the nature of the acts, their repetition, the force used in carrying them out, and [the victim's] admitted sexual naiveté convince us to infer intent to injure as a matter of law. The circumstances make it foreseeable that [the victim] would suffer at least mental trauma, if not physical injury.[57, 58]

Most courts considering molestation claims have presumed that this inferred intent of the defendant precludes the possibility of "negligence" on the part of the defendant.

Since child molestation is obviously inherently harmful, according to this logic, it is clear that the defendant must intend the harm. These "inferred intent" courts have relied on social science literature supporting the certainty of injury from the victim's standpoint: "Recent studies on the trauma of rape reinforce the criminal law's recognition of injury inherent in the commission of this offense."[59] As a Wisconsin court argued,

> sexual misconduct with a minor is objectively so certain to result in harm to the minor victim, that the perpetrator cannot be al-

> lowed to escape society's determination that he or she is expected to know that.[60]

This inferred intent of harm, of course, precludes the finding of insurance coverage for "accidents" as well as exclusions for intentional or criminal misconduct. The criminalization of sexual abuse of children puts all policyholders on notice of the "societal understanding that the harm from such conduct is inseparable from its performance."[61]

The inferred intent standard has been applied by a majority of courts to cases involving sexual misconduct not involving violence or penetration (hugging, kissing, rubbing of breasts, rubbing buttocks),[62] where the victim is an adult who suffers from a disability,[63] and those in which the molester allegedly lacked the mental capacity to form any intent.[64]

The argument that the insured was mentally ill, a sexual addict, pedophile, alcoholic, or suffering from a provable psychological disorder has failed to deter the applicability of the inferred intent rule. The courts have analyzed the issue from the standpoint of the nature of the act or the nature of the event (not an accident) irrespective of whether incapacity was a raised and repeatedly excluded coverage.[65]

In cases involving minors molesting minors, depending on jurisdiction, the inferred intent rule may not always be applied. In Florida, Alaska, California, Texas, and Minnesota, it has been held immaterial that the perpetrator was a minor and inferred intent precluded coverage.[66] However, courts in Michigan, Ohio, and Nevada have refused to apply the rule in unusual cases: where a 14-year-old girl molested a three-year-old boy,[67] where a molester was 16 years old,[68] where a young boy sexually assaulted a girl twice (once when he was seven years old and she was four or five years old, and again when he was nine and she was six).[69]

*Analysis and Critique of the Inferred Intent Standard.* The idea that criminalizing child molestation alerts would-be perpetrators that damage caused by their behavior will not be covered under their insurance policies is distinct from ideas held about similar relationships between intentionality, law, and insurance. The same logic could be applied with equal force to environmental torts, running red lights, using excessive speed in traffic, invasion of property interests, appropriation of trade names, employee dishonesty, wrongful imprisonment, and other torts where coverage has been recognized. Making child molestation an exception to the more common type of judicial reasoning appears to be not only a judicial rejection of the theory that the molester's mental illness renders him effectively negligent (incapable of controlling his behavior and/or understanding the effect and consequence of his conduct), but also a refusal to adhere to strict readings of policy language (where an accident is often described as an occurrence "neither expected nor intended from the standpoint of the insured"). The effect of this exceptional treatment of sexual molestation is a *de facto*, judicially wrought pubic policy against coverage for sexual molestation.

*The Objective Intent Standard.* Some courts have held that an insured's coverage for any alleged wrongdoing must be determined by an objective standard.[70] The object standard employs the perspective of a "reasonable person" to determine whether the policyholder intended the harm. One court has set forth the standard in the following manner:

> The test is what a plain ordinary person would expect and intend to result from a mature man's deliberately debauching his six year old stepdaughter and continuing to do so for years. We agree . . . that for a stepfather in such a situation to claim that he did not expect or intend to cause injury flies in the face of all reason, common sense and experience.[71]

Many insurance policies reflect the objective standard in an exclusion for "any bodily injury or property damage which may reasonably be expected to result from the intentional or criminal acts of an insured person or which is in fact intended by an insured person."[72]

The objective intent standard is used in a minority of jurisdictions.[73] In *Allstate v. Freeman,* the court held that some acts are so nearly certain to produce injury that intent or expectation to injure should be inferred as a matter of law.[74]

*Analysis and Critique of the Objective Intent Standard.* Like the inferred intent standard, the objective intent standard ignores the actual language of the policy. The policy language references whether the conduct was accidental from the standpoint of the insured, not a hypothetical reasonable person. This normative standard fails to account for differences in human psychology, standardizing all people under a single rubric. Criminal law has rejected such a standard in the prosecution of crimes involving specific intent burdens of proof. In criminal cases, specific intent can be refuted by evidence of intoxication, cognitive deficit, coercion, duress, and insanity. The objective standard also lacks the directness and honesty of the inferred intent rule by suggesting that there will be some consideration of extrinsic facts, while it ignores the actual intent and psychopathology of the insured. It creates a circular inquiry by posing the question "would the reasonable person expect that harm would come to a child as a result of sexual molestation?" The answer to that question, is clearly "Of course." This answer, then, is compelled by the manner in which the question is asked, and may well disagree with the actual evidence in a particular case if it tends to demonstrate the insureds' inability to anticipate causing harm.

*The Subjective Intent Standard.* Courts that have upheld the subjective intent standard criticize the other standards by noting that they tend to ignore the clear, plain language of the insurance policies involved. Any exclusion that refers to injury "expected or intended by the insured" is referring only to the subjective intent of that policyholder or the actual expectation or intention in the mind of the insured.[75] New Hampshire still adheres to the subjective standard in sexual abuse cases, and it may still be applied to other forms of injurious conduct in other states. The subjective standard has been overruled in most states by public policy flowing from state criminal laws that hold sexual abuse to be so inherently harmful that the sexual abuser must intend the harm. As one court noted, "Cases inferring an intent to harm in sexual abuse cases involving an adult defendant and a minor child do not completely reject the subjective intent; rather, they actually overrule the insured's actual intention in [these] limited circumstances."[76]

*Analysis and Critique of the Subjective Intent Standard.* The subjective standard is vulnerable to manipulation by perpetrators who seek to charge others with their responsibilities and to have an insurer pay for their willful and oppressive misconduct. It may also place too much reliance on a self-serving inquiry for the policyholder and on unscientific retrospective psychological and psychiatric analysis. Further, this standard neglects the reasonable expectations of the other party to the insurance contract: the insurer. An insurer will argue that it never expected to provide insurance coverage for criminal activity.[77] The universal deployment of this standard could open up a Pandora's box of claims for every kind of violent, predatory crime from rape to assault and battery. Finally, the standard's inquiry could require a nearly endless form of inquiry as to whether the insured intended the particular harm or symptom, among a myriad number of injuries: did the policyholder intend the dissociation that resulted from the molestation, the depression, the anhedonia, the panic attacks, the guilt, the low self-esteem, *et cetera?*

> *Practice Tip: The subjective intent standard is, for all practical purposes, useless to practitioners handling cases other than those in New Hampshire. Nonetheless, the practitioner may want to include allegations in the complaint that the perpetrator neither expected nor intended the act nor the harm related to the molestation. Such allegations might shift the moral blame to a third party that could be held liable for failure to control the conduct of the perpetuator, e.g., in the employment context.*

### *Negligence Claims Against Those Who Molest*

As discussed previously in connection with the *Quan* case, claims for negligent sexual molestation will not generally trigger insurance coverage, except perhaps in those states that still use the subjective standard. However, negligence claims against a molester *can* trigger coverage if the negligent acts alleged are not "inseparably intertwined" and in such close temporal and spatial proximity to compel the conclusion that they are inseparable from the molestation itself. The negligence or non-sexual claims need to be linked to an interest of the policyholder/defendant different in purpose and context from the injury resulting from molestation.

On the one hand, potentially covered acts which are in close proximity to non-covered acts of molestation will be excluded from coverage because they are bound together in achieving the non-covered conduct. In *Jane D. v. Ordinary Mutual,* a pastor counseled a fifteen-year-old parishioner for a twenty-year period.[78] The complaint alleged that the pastor engaged in non-sexual misconduct by deploying counseling techniques and using information obtained during the counseling to create transference in order to control and manipulate the plaintiff's behavior into having sex with him. The pastor's policy contained an exclusion for "licentious, immoral or sexual behavior intended or culminating in any sexual act." Because the non-sexual conduct was so close in time and space to the sexual misconduct, and because the victim had alleged that these techniques were utilized to create an inducement for her to engage in and did result in sexual relations with the insured, the court held that there was no coverage and no duty to defend.[79]

Further, non-covered acts intertwined with the molestation are not confined to pre-molestation inducement or a "facilitative nexus" in the commission of the crime. Such acts may also include behaviors designed to conceal the conduct or avoid prosecution. In *Fire Insurance Exchange v. Superior Court (Jennifer O.)*, the defendant molester claimed that separate acts related to his attempts to "dissuade and entice" the victim from cooperating with authorities were severable from the non-covered acts of molestation and entitled to coverage.[80] The court disagreed, holding that the post-molestation acts were "inseparably intertwined" with the molestation. Similarly, in *State Farm v. Century Indemnity*, the molesting teacher's failure to report his own misconduct and his initial denials were part of the cover-up of his misconduct and therefore, not covered.

On the other hand, conviction for criminal sexual misconduct has not barred all potential coverage for other allegations of misconduct not amounting to molestation if they are separable and independent negligent acts and involve a different interest. As discussed above, in *Horace Mann v. Barbara B.*, the insurer offered proof of the defendant/insured's criminal conviction. The court found the sexual misconduct was outside the coverage of the policy. However, the conviction did not eliminate the insurer's duty to defend against the other allegations of misconduct that did not amount to criminal molestation and involved instead claims of public embarrassment and humiliation. Further, the acts that publicly embarrassed and humiliated the minor plaintiff were not so closely linked in time and space to the actual molestation to compel the conclusion that they were inseparable.[81] The court noted that the insurer had not, despite voluminous additional pleadings, proved that the plaintiff's allegations were related only to the molestation or that the other alleged misconduct was outside the course of the defendant's educational employment activities. Indeed, they concluded that

> A teacher's educational roles require close interaction with students; it is not always easy for a court to draw the line between appropriate and inappropriate interaction. Neither precedent nor

> logic dictates that a molester cannot be held liable for torts of negligence against the victim which are apart from and not integral to the molestation.[82]

In a similar fashion, the court in *Waters v. Bourhis* found that claims under a physician's malpractice policy that included both theories of sexual misconduct and medical malpractice triggered the insurer's duty to defend the physician. The court noted:

> The complaint alleges separate and distinct acts of medical malpractice. The factfinder could determine that [the physician] committed separate and independent acts in addition to the sexual abuse that would bring his claim within the coverage of the policy and outside the scope of any exclusion.[83]

> *Practice Tip: As noted above, the attorney should make sure that the complaint alleges all forms of tortious activity and that any misconduct separate from the sexual misconduct be specifically alleged so as to make it distinct in time and place from the non-covered activity.*

In developing coverage by establishing the existence of other torts, the practitioner must look to the law of his or her state to determine if it prohibits the insurer from denying coverage for a covered risk because an excluded act caused additional harm. The court in *State Farm v. Partridge* noted that the "crucial question" was "whether a liability insurance policy provides coverage for an accident caused jointly by an insured risk" and an excluded risk.[84] "The insured could correctly contend," they argued, "that when two such risks constitute concurrent proximate cause of an accident, the insurer is liable so long as one of the causes is covered by the policy."

Under professional liability policies, a limitation on coverage commonly called the "sex cap" provision generally limits coverage to a certain amount (e.g., $25,000.00) when there are allegations of sexual misconduct against the professional. Typically, insurers interpret these provisions to limit coverage for all the allegations, both sexual and non-sexual; that is, if a professional is alleged to have engaged in sexual abuse and negligent mistreatment, the insurer may assert that all damage is limited to the amount of the "sex cap." Courts that have examined these provisions are split on how to interpret them in the case of both sexual and non-sexual allegations of misconduct and injury. Some courts have declared the situation ambiguous, others argue that it violates public policy,[85] and still others find it unambiguous and apply the "sex cap" as a general limitation on coverage for all allegations when sexual misconduct is alleged.

> *Practice Tip: The attorney should advise his client that sexual abuse allegations may actually limit recovery under insurance policies when there are other theories of recovery. If the other claims have a high potential value, both the attorney and client should seriously consider whether they want to press sexual abuse claims.*

Concurrent causation provides another potential theory upon which courts may find coverage under professional liability policies with a sexual misconduct cap. Concurrent causation triggers coverage for non-sexual conduct where that conduct causes, contributes to, or exacerbates the injuries alleged in the plaintiff's complaint. Several courts have found that in general, liability insurance policies should cover claims where more than one cause contributed to the resultant injury, even where there is an exclusion which applies to one or more of the other sources of causation. As the court opined in *Garvey v. State Farm*:

> If committed by separate individuals both actors would be joint tortfeasors fully liable for the resulting injuries. . . . The fact that both acts were committed by a single individual does not alter their nature as concurrent proximate causes. . . . We believe that coverage under a liability insurance policy is equally available to an insured whenever an insured risk constitutes a concurrent proximate cause of the injuries. . . . Once the insured shows that an event falls within the scope of basic coverage under the policy, the burden is on the insurer to prove a claim is specifically excluded. Moreover, exclusionary clauses are interpreted narrowly, whereas clauses identifying coverage are interpreted broadly.[86]

Other courts, reviewing sex cap provisions, have found the potential for coverage based on theories related to the liability of third parties involved in a professional relationship with the main defendant. For example, coverage has been found where the liability is based on partnership liability, breach of fiduciary duty, or some form of negligence.[87]

Finally, at least one court has determined that even in the context of intentional sexual misconduct, there may be a question of fact concerning the negligent or intentional transmission of sexual diseases, such as genital herpes. In *State Farm Fire & Cas. Co. v. Irene S.*,[88] the court reversed a summary judgment for an insurer despite allegations in the complaint that the insured raped and assaulted the plaintiff with the intent of transmitting herpes, based on a question of fact arising from the intentionality of the transmission. For victims of sexual abuse, the transmission of venereal disease can be argued to be outside the known or expected harm which is typically inferred as a matter of law.

### Coverage for Personal Injury

In addition to coverage for "bodily injury," many homeowner and general liability policies provide coverage for "personal injury" where personal injury relates to injuries not bodily but nonetheless personal. "Personal injury" is defined in most insurance policies as damage arising out of a specified list of "offenses" which may include discrimination or humiliation, invasion of privacy, false arrest, detention and imprisonment, and publication of defamatory material or material which invades a person's right of privacy.[89] In addition, excess policies may provide coverage for other "offenses."[90] Allegations of non-intentional infliction of humiliation or discrimination not inseparably intertwined with the sexual abuse may trigger coverage.

### Fellow Travelers and Co-Insureds: Another Potential Source of Coverage

The most direct route to potential coverage may be found in negligence claims against another party insured by the same policy that names the perpetrator (e.g., a spouse, supervisor, co-employee, partner or employer). However, when the primary defendant and another insured both make claims for a defense and indemnification under their policy, a policy exclusion that prevents coverage to the primary defendant may operate to bar coverage to all insureds under all theories, even when there are separate causes of action against each. For example, under homeowner's policies, if the applicable exclusion bars all coverage for the excluded intentional acts or misconduct of "an insured," then the exclusion will typically operate to bar coverage to all insureds, regardless of the number of insureds seeking coverage under the policy.[91]

> *Practice tip: If the policy in question prohibits coverage for the intentional act of any insured, look for independent actions by the co-insured which may create negligence or personal injury liability: defamation, conduct resulting in humiliation or embarrassment, discrimination, and/or invasion of privacy.*

On the other hand, if the exclusion refers only to the conduct of "the insured," the negligent insureds may have coverage based on the theory that the obligations of the policy are separable among the policyholders.[92]

In the employment context, coverage often depends on the theory alleged against the employing agency and co-employees. Nearly every court in the country has held that sexual molestation of an individual cannot be within the normal scope of duties of any employee. In academic and therapeutic environments, for example, sexual misconduct with a student or counselee is not considered activity within the scope of the employee's activities.[93] As stated by the court in *John R. v. Oakland Unified School District*:

> The connection between the authority conferred on teachers to carry out their instructional duties and the abuse of that authority to indulge in personal, sexual misconduct is simply too attenuated to deem a sexual assault as falling within the range of risks allocable to a teacher's employer.[94]

Such vicarious liability does not depend on the independent negligence of the employer but on that of the individual employee who committed the molestation. As a result, coverage is usually denied.[95]

> *Practice Tip: If the lawyer asserts vicarious liability against an employer, he should be sure to include all potential, applicable non-sexual torts in that cause of action in order*

*to avoid the sexual and non-sexual claims being swept out together on a motion by the defense.*

Courts are split on the issue of whether there is insurance coverage for the negligent conduct of an employer or co-employee for acts of sexual molestation committed by the employee on the basis of negligent hiring and retention, or negligent supervision. The imposition of liability and the availability of coverage are both dependent on proof that the employer had knowledge of similar, pre-existing conduct of sexual abuse and failed to undertake adequate precautions or supervision to prevent the injury at issue.

## *UNDER THE RIGHT FACTS, WITH THE RIGHT POLICY, AND IN THE RIGHT JURISDICTION, IT IS STILL POSSIBLE FOR A COURT TO FIND COVERAGE FOR SEXUAL ABUSE*

The unusual case finds the needle in the haystack, insurance coverage for sexual abuse. In *St. Paul Fire and Marine v. F.H., K.W.,*[96] the Ninth Circuit held that some criminal acts may be covered where the policy is marketed as a special package designed for particular organizations and marketed in such a way that an employee might reasonably expect coverage for criminal acts. This case demonstrates how on the right facts, with the right policy, and in the right jurisdiction, all of the prevailing theories negating coverage in other jurisdictions can be turned in favor of coverage and for compensation for the victim. Accordingly, I examine this case in some detail.

Under a policy issued to the Big Brothers/Big Sisters Organization, there was no exclusion for liability arising from intentional acts. Further, a marketing memo sent to the organization by the insurer's agent promised that the special package was the "only certain method of insuring against child molesting claims."

Kenneth McQuade was the executive director of Big Brother/Big Sister of Alaska between 1979 to 1984. He sexually molested two minors, F.H. and K.W. during that time. McQuade was arrested in 1986 and the minors sued. McQuade tendered his defense of the lawsuit and request for indemnification to St. Paul. St. Paul denied McQuade's tender, but accepted the tender of the defense from the Big Brothers Organization. The plaintiffs and McQuade stipulated to a judgment against McQuade with an agreement not to execute against

McQuade's personal assets. St. Paul then filed a declaratory relief action seeking a declaration that McQuade was not entitled to a defense or indemnification of the judgment. Motions for summary judgment were filed and initially granted in favor of St. Paul, denying McQuade coverage. The Ninth Circuit reversed and remanded.

In responding to the insurer's contention that finding coverage for sexual molestation would violate Alaska public policy, the Ninth Circuit wrote:

> It is true, as St. Paul argues, that Alaska recognizes a general public policy against insuring a person against liability for his or her intentional acts. [citations omitted] To this principle, however, there is an exception that the Alaska courts have not yet addressed. Several courts have held that, when liability insurance is designed to compensate innocent third parties for injuries caused by the intentional misconduct of insureds, it may indemnify without violating public policy. This exception is particularly applicable where it is unlikely that insurance coverage induced the insured to engage in misconduct.
>
> . . . A number of courts . . . have held that public policy permits innocent victims of insureds' intentional misconduct to be compensated by the insureds' professional liability policies. [citations omitted]
>
> [Here] St. Paul's policy was clearly designed to compensate victims of sexual abuse, and to indemnify for such liability. It is unlikely that the availability of insurance coverage induced McQuade sexually to abuse K.W. He faced disgrace and severe criminal penalties as illustrated by his conviction and substantial prison sentence. It is equally unlikely that other professionals will be induced to commit sexual abuse if we allow coverage for sexual abuse here. Public policy concerns against allowing McQuade to avoid civil liability by reason of insurance coverage are outweighed by the advantages of assuring that his victim, K.W., will be compensated for the injuries McQuade caused. While no Alaska case addresses compensation of innocent third parties in this specific situation, the Alaska Supreme Court in a different context has permitted insurance to compensate an innocent victim for an injury intentionally caused by an insured.

> [citation omitted] We conclude that the Alaska Court would similarly permit compensation of the victim here. Alaska public policy, therefore, does not prohibit K.W. and F.H. from being compensated under the St. Paul policy for injuries caused by McQuade's sexual abuse of K.W.[97]

Nor was the Ninth Circuit persuaded that sexual abuse could not be within the scope of the employee's occupational duties:

> We do not view the scope of duties that narrowly, however. The phrase is not further defined in the policy, and a reasonable insured could expect it to cover him for liability arising out of the functions of his employment, even though the ultimate acts causing injury were personal. Several activities of McQuade led to the injury. He met K.W. in the course of his duties, and the relationship clearly began as a result of McQuade's exercise of his duties as executive director of BB/BS. He interviewed K.W. and was responsible for placing him in a Big Brother-Little Brother relationship. McQuade certainly had a duty within the scope of his employment to place K.W. with someone other than a pedophile. He also had a duty to screen potential Big Brothers. The fact that McQuade placed K.W. with himself was a cause of the abuse that followed. Indeed, even acting as a Big Brother easily fits within the scope of McQuade's duties. One of his explicit functions as executive director was to interpret the BB/BS program to the community. It hardly exceeds the scope of that duty for McQuade to be an example and serve as a Big Brother himself. And his duty in that Big Brother relationship is to guide and nurture K.W., not to abuse him. Thus, there were several failures of McQuade, committed in the scope of his employment, that acted as cause of the abuse of K.W.
>
> St. Paul argues that the third amended complaint of F.H. and K.W. is a transparent attempt to allege negligent failure of employment duties when the real damage was intentional. But this fact does not alter the analysis. There is no exclusion for criminal acts, but employees like McQuade are explicitly excepted from that exclusion. One reasonable gloss that an insured may put on that exception for employees is that there must be some criminal acts committed in the scope of their employment duties for which

> the employees are covered. Thus the fact that McQuade's failures properly to place K.W., to supervise that placement, to screen K.W.'s Big Brother, and to guide K.W. as a Little Brother, were intentional does not operate to exclude them from coverage.
>
> We conclude, therefore, that McQuade committed several acts within the scope of his employment that caused the ultimate abuse of K.W. Those acts fell within the coverage specified by the policy for employees of BB/BS, and were not excluded by the clause relating to criminal acts.[98]

Where public policy favors compensation to the victim, and when the facts underlying the sale of the insurance policy indicate that the insurer represented that the policy contained coverage for sexual misconduct, some courts may be persuaded to follow the Ninth Circuit's reasoning and holding. The case demonstrates the importance of a careful review of the underlying insurance policy provisions and a willingness to work with the opposing party's counsel in identifying the potential coverages, including background information on circumstances surrounding the purchase of those policies.

> *Practice Tip: Where there is a potential for coverage under any combination of facts and theories, and the insurer has declined a defense and indemnification for the defendant, consider undertaking a stipulated judgment with and against that defendant in order to eliminate the emotional and financial expense of a trial on the molestation. Thereafter, if coverage is found, the insurer may be bound by the amount of damages identified in the stipulated judgment.*

## *PREPARING FOR LITIGATION*

Given the difficulties in finding insurance coverage for sexual misconduct, both the client and the practitioner need to fully investigate and develop appropriate strategies for securing a financial recovery in litigation. This section provides a model for the key aspects of optimizing the chances of a financial recovery: investigating insurance-related issues, identifying non-insurance resources, and drafting a complaint to trigger any applicable insurance coverage.

### Investigating Coverage-Related Issues

In determining whether insurance coverage is available for victims of sexual abuse, the client and the attorney must work together to determine the factual background related to the abuse through several means:

*The Initial Interview.* The attorney begins by taking a careful and detailed history of the course of the abusive contact from the client. Special attention should be paid to the dates and locations the injury or injuries occurred, as well as to persons and witnesses who may have had supervisory responsibility over the defendant molester, who observed harmful conduct, and who can verify medical injuries. The names, addresses, and phone numbers of physicians, therapists, former teachers, and other potential witnesses should be obtained.

*Background Investigation.* The perpetrator must be identified and located. An asset search should be conducted. Investigation then should include a check of (1) court records and judgments to determine the number of other suits in which the potential defendant has been involved; (2) recorded liens, including tax liens; (3) real property interests; (4) bankruptcies; and (5) the identification of all potentially involved witnesses.

*Interviewing Witnesses.* It is recommended that witnesses be interviewed and their recollections summarized in a statement signed by the witness. In this regard, it is absolutely essential that the interviewing attorney or investigator refrain from any suggestive or leading questioning which can be criticized later. Leading and suggestive interviews do more harm than good, as they may contaminate the potential testimony of the subject interviewee. The attorney should pay particular attention to witnesses who observed any form of injurious behavior by the defendant or others.

*Medical Treatment, Educational and Police Records.* Objective evidence of criminal conduct, notice to a supervising individual with caretaking responsibility for the minor victim, revelations in therapy, and the treatment of physical injuries and complaints are critical forms of evidence. The very nature, as well as objective substantiation, of actual physical injury or trauma is a key factor in determining the potential for coverage. Many policies only provide coverage for "bodily injury," meaning an actual injury to the body exhibited by a physical wound or illness. Other policies may provide coverage for "personal injury," which may include humiliation, wrongful imprisonment, invasion of privacy, and even defamation. An injury to the body is more likely to trigger coverage than a psychological injury. Further, medical treatment records may contain the only objective evidence of molestation claims and are, therefore, of the first order of importance, particularly when the client is vulnerable to credibility attack due to age or degree of mental disability or illness.

*Developing a Timeline.* An insurance policy is often triggered by injury-producing conduct occurring during a particular policy period. Therefore, one of the attorney's most critical tools in assessing the application of insurance coverage is a timeline of significant events. The timeline should include reference to the dates of all significant traumatic events, including those which may trigger coverage and those which involve non-covered conduct.

*Identifying the Parties, Their Roles, and the Relationship Dynamics.* The context in which the defendant caused the plaintiff's injuries is another important factor in determining which insurance policy may apply to a particular loss. What is the relationship between the victim and the perpetrator? Is the perpetrator a member of the extended family or does he exist in some professional capacity to the victim, or both? The relationship dynamics can become a focal point for identifying the insureds under existing policies.

*Identifying Non-Sexual Injuries.* Because sexual abuse in any form is not covered in nearly every jurisdiction as a matter of law, the attorney and client must identify other forms of liability on the part of the perpetrator. Often, the defendant has injured the victim in a number of ways; these may be distinguishable and separate injuries from the sexual abuse itself. For example, the perpetrator may have defamed, invaded the plaintiff's privacy through humiliation or embarrassment, or have committed some other form of non-sexual injury. Also, the perpetrator may have negligently caused non-sexual injury by some form of negligence or malpractice that may trigger coverage for those non-sexual claims (e.g., professional malpractice).

Often, injurious non-sexual behaviors are a means of controlling the victim so that the sexual abuse can continue or remain undiscovered. Such behaviors are unlikely to be covered, as they are nearly indivisible from the sexual abuse itself. However, if a perpetrator is outrageously insensitive, negligently careless, or sadistic, such that their behavior leads to severe emotional injury and even bodily injury, this type of non-sexual behavior may well be covered under insurance policies. For example, a daycare worker who sexually abuses a child under his care may also show consistent disregard for the child's well-being, resulting in a medical history of infections or physical injuries of various kinds, including skin rashes, vaginal infections, migraine headaches, sleeplessness, bone bruising, and bloody noses. These forms of injury may be covered (unless linked directly to the molestation) and therefore should be carefully researched and documented.

*Identifying Alternative Explanations for Claims of Abuse.* It goes without saying that the attorney should never take all allegations of sexual abuse as gospel truth without seeking objective corroboration. In fact, concerns over false reporting have become a media *cause celebre.* Recently, therapists, social workers, marriage, family and child counselors, and other mental health care providers have come under increasing attack for allegedly implanting memories of abuse through hypnosis, the use of drug therapy, suggestion, and inappropriate questioning.[99] There are concerted efforts in various sectors of society to attack anyone who supports or advocates on behalf of a child or an adult claiming to be a victim of child sexual abuse. A small number of claims of abuse asserted against parents and others are simply false or confabulated. The attorney must carefully evaluate all claims of sexual abuse derived solely from memory recovered in therapy, under hypnosis, or in the context of child custody disputes. As indicated above, medical records of childhood treatment, police reports, and educational transcripts should be carefully evaluated. The attorney should also consider his client's current diagnosis to evaluate whether the potential exists for fabrication, malingering, deception, or fantasy as an alternative explanation for molestation claims. In this connection, the attorney should obtain as much objective corroboration as possible before undertaking the litigation. Anyone who pursues a claim of sexual abuse in a "she said/he said" controversy faces nearly insurmountable challenges in the courtroom.

*Reviewing Cost Issues with the Client.* As can be seen from the foregoing, the effort and expense of undertaking any sexual abuse action is considerable. Many clients believe that their claim is meritorious and want their day in court. Although this desire is understandable, it may be impractical. First, a trial court is a court of law, not a court of justice. Legal technicalities and fine points such as statutes of limitations can terminate an otherwise meritorious case. Second, all clients should understand from the beginning that most attorneys cannot represent clients for whom litigation costs and time expenditures exceed the potential financial recovery. Sexual abuse litigation often includes the complication of requiring additional legal work on related insurance coverage actions brought by the insurance carriers and in bankruptcy filings by the defendants. In some cases, in order to prevail in such actions, attorneys may be required to retain several experts. Unless the facts suggest a high likelihood of recovery, undertaking such efforts may not yield any return on a substantial emotional and financial investment by both the client and the attorney.

### *Identifying Administrative Resources*

For many survivors, litigation may not provide a financial recovery through insurance or the defendant's personal assets, but there are other means by which they can obtain resources for their medical and psychological care needs. Many states have Victim's Assistance or Victim's Witness Programs designed to provide compensation for medical and therapeutic expenses for victims of crime. Often the medical expense coverage afforded by the programs are "triggered" by the victim filing a report or complaint with the local police. After a determination that a criminal molestation or sexual assault has occurred, no matter how long ago, the victim and her attorney should discuss the filing of a police report and contact with state agencies to determine the possibility of compensation for treatment. The effect of making such claims can be both beneficial and harmful, and thus require careful consideration.

The victim and her attorney must keep in mind that in making police reports and claims for Victim's Assistance, they are going "on the record." Discovery in any civil action may result in the report being produced and used to support legal and technical defenses to the action. The victim should be counseled on issues related to discussing any events that could implicate statutes of limitation or other defenses. If the victim is fragile psychologically, the benefit of proceeding with a police interview may be outweighed by the harm or complications it could bring to the civil action. However, the social value of reporting a crime and preventing further harm, in addition to triggering victim's remedies for medical expenses, may be of paramount importance to the client.

Administrative remedies often require extensive administrative hearings and representation, and may take on a life of their own. The practitioner should be careful to identify and clearly communicate to the client the aspects of this work that are included within the terms of the fee agreement, and which are not. State boards may reject claims in which a long passage of time has elapsed between the injurious acts and the filing for benefits. The victim may be forced to undertake further administrative appeals and review and marshal her resources, including her therapists, to provide further support for her claim. Therefore, the victim may find herself in a situation where she and her counsel are in conflict with the state, with those defendants who participated in or facilitated the molestation and later, with the defendant's insurance company. The continuous nature of these conflicts may become overwhelming for both the victim and her counsel.

Finally, if the victim is successful in obtaining state funding for her medical and therapeutic expenses, the state agency involved may end up filing a lien in the state court action to recover benefits paid. Thus, with this form of "coverage" for medical expenses resulting from the defendant's criminal acts, reimbursement may be required from the settlement or verdict in the civil action.

### *Drafting the Complaint*

In drafting the complaint, the victim's attorney should fully consider the potential existence of insurance coverages that may be involved in the claim, given the particular defendant individual(s) and entities involved in the abuse and its facilitation. The complaint must allege all the facts that will assist in triggering those coverages. Toward that end, the attorney should develop a careful timeline of events and look for evidence of injury-causing behaviors (1) by the primary defendant which are not directly related to the sexual molestation or abuse (invasion of privacy, defamation, humiliation, negligent infliction of emotional distress, false imprisonment), and (2) by third-party defendants who were and are responsible for permitting the primary defendant to gain access to the victim and perpetuate continuing injury. Third-party defendants may include employers, spouses, contracting agencies, and those in a supervisory capacity.

The attorney must also determine the situations or locations where each injury occurred. For example, if a victim was injured at a child care center, a residence, a place of employment, and an educational institution, several different insurance policies with different insureds may be triggered by appropriate allegations in the complaint.

The timing of the traumatic events and the psychological injuries and symptoms which may occur over time may also trigger multiple, successive, and annually renewed insurance policies for each defendant/insured. Under insurance policies, the trigger of coverage may happen not only when the traumatic event takes place but also when the symptoms of the ongoing psychological injury become manifest and known to the victim during a continuing course of misconduct by the perpetrator. For example, a victim is injured both physically and psychologically at the time of a molestation, but additional forms of harm may only become apparent when the child reaches maturity, such as in early adolescence. Furthermore, the defendant may be engaging in continuing conduct over time that humiliates and embarrasses the victim, reminding them of the molestation or continuing a pattern of emotional domination. Arguably, each non-sexual form of injury as it manifests triggers coverage. The attorney must carefully evaluate whether the timing issues present statute of limitations problems and whether a particular jurisdiction's delayed discovery or tolling rules may be applicable.[100]

Against individual defendants, the complaint typically alleges causes of action for negligent and intentional infliction of emotional distress, invasion of privacy, defamation, negligence, negligence *per se,* wrongful imprisonment, sexual battery and assault, and malpractice. As is discussed more thoroughly below, the attorney should look for evidence of non-sexual and nonintentional forms of injury occasioned by the defendant's conduct, forms of injury separate and distinct from the manipulations involved in securing or secreting the sexual misconduct. For example, as discussed above, even causes of action for negligence *per se* based on the violation of state Penal Code sections pertaining to the sexual abuse of minors will not trigger insurance coverage.[101] Further, intentional infliction of emotional or physical injury involves an intentional act and the greater weight of precedent holds that there will be no coverage. Typically, claims for emotional distress will not trigger coverage unless bodily injury is also involved, unless that emotional distress arises from a form of "personal injury" as defined in most policies to include invasion of privacy, humiliation, and defamation.[102]

Against corporate or entity defendants, the plaintiff's attorney will usually plead *respondeat superior*, negligence, negligent infliction of emotional distress, negligent supervision and negligent hiring. Vicarious liability and *respondeat superior* are forms of strict liability, or the imposition of liability without fault on the part of the employer. In many states, the courts refuse to find vicarious liability for sexual misconduct alone. As noted earlier, *John R. v. Oakland Unified School District* denied the connection between educational duties and the authority to sexually abuse children, finding the link "simply too attenuated to deem a sexual assault as falling within the range of risks allocable to a teacher's employer."[103] However, it is important to remember that employers may be held liable for sexual injuries to a child if there is evidence of their independent fault or negligence which resulted in the injury, e.g., they negligently hired or negligently supervised an individual with a background or history of engaging in sexual misconduct.

### *Working with Opposing Counsel*

If the defendant has already been involved in a criminal trial or pled to a charge of molestation, his defense counsel is likely to want to resolve any civil claims as quickly and as reasonably as possible. Under such circumstances, there is nothing for the defendant to gain from going to trial in the civil case, as his culpability has already been adjudicated in the criminal matter.

The plaintiff is likely to be vulnerable in the high stress environment of litigation. She may want to achieve some justice against the individual who caused her harm, but she may not be emotionally able to cope with the strain of extensive cross-examination. Often, therefore, a fair resolution of a civil claim is in the interests of both the parties.

The attorney for the plaintiff should most likely meet as soon as possible with defense counsel and attempt to identify the defendant's resources and insurance policies involved, the limitations on coverage, and the potential for a mediated settlement. Sometimes, the attorney and his client may even decide to permit a face-to-face meeting with the defense attorney so the opposing attorney can evaluate the plaintiff's integrity, honesty, and appeal as a witness. Additionally, in the same informal manner, it may be helpful for the defense to hear from and speak with the plaintiff's therapist or expert witness to assess the degree of plaintiff's psychological, physical, and emotional injury.

Plaintiff's counsel should also assess whether the defendant's attorney is familiar with the nature and extent of coverage issues and is capable of pursuing coverage for the protection of his client. If not, the plaintiff's attorney needs to consider educating the opposing attorneys on the coverage implications of the case's factual background.

Thereafter, if problems persist in obtaining insurance coverage, the attorneys for both parties may want to consider a stipulated judgment. A stipulated judgment would, upon the agreement of the parties, provide that the defendant is agreeing to a stipulated judgment against himself to be entered in the case with a specified amount of damages in exchange for a promise or covenant that the plaintiff will not execute the judgment against the defendant's personal assets and will instead pursue the insurer under state statutes permitting "direct action" against an insurer for judgments involving covered claims.

In many states, a stipulated judgment may be enforced against the defendant's insurer under "direct action statutes."[104] When insurance coverage applies for specific claims and the parties stipulate (or agree) to the facts underlying those claims, the plaintiff may recover money from the insurers by a direct action against them.

## *CONCLUSION*

In cases involving claims for insurance coverage for sexual molestation, one could argue that the courts have deployed logical reductionism with judicial activism. Many courts have, in effect, pronounced that it is obvious that the very act of molestation always intends the harm that follows. However, psychiatric evidence may demonstrate that the perpetrator did not intend an injury due to mental illness or incapacity. Under the plain insurance policy language, coverage is most often triggered if the harm is not intended or expected from the standpoint of the insured. Adopting a subjective intent standard reflects both the emerging scientific research and the language of the insurance policy. Although no current studies exist on the topic, it could be argued that the holdings in most coverage cases involving sexual abuse have a disparate, negative impact on women (the most common plaintiffs in adult survivor abuse cases) and children. Like Alice in Wonderland, the practitioner must accept what she may feel is the current state of illogic in most forums and proceed accordingly.

Direct coverage under insurance policies held by the defendant for sexual abuse is, *St. Paul Fire and Marine v. F.H., K.W.* notwithstanding, rare. To maximize compensation, the practitioner and the client must carefully identify the nonintentional conduct which caused injuries in addition to those caused by the molestation, as well as clarifying the participation of parties other than the perpetrator in the development and evolution of all the injuries. Non-sexual injuries may include professional malpractice, negligence resulting in non sexual bodily injury, non-sexual personal injury as that term is defined in the insurance policy (e.g., humiliation or defamation), and the negligent hiring, supervision, and retention of the perpetrator by third persons. This requires careful, efficient, and timely evaluation of the facts and a working knowledge of the precise details of the plaintiff's relationship with the perpetrator and others in the temporal, relational, and geographic contexts of the abuse.

In addition, both the practitioner and the client must look to the available forms of government aid for victims of crime. In developing the information that is consistent with truth for both civil litigation and for government claims, the victim and her counsel may secure sufficient financial means to begin the process of rebuilding a life.

## NOTES

1. This chapter does not intend to represent an exhaustive exploration of the legal evolution of coverages for sexual abuse claims. For careful and scholarly analysis on the topic from which many ideas and references for this article were obtained, the interested reader is referred to JERRET E. SALE & LINDA BOLDUAN, *Insurance Coverage for Sexual Molestation*, in LAW OF LIABILITY INSURANCE II C-4-11C-87, (Mathew Bender: San Francisco, 1998); DAVID S. FLORING, *Insurance Coverage for Sexual Abuse or Molestation*, 30 TORT AND INSURANCE L.J. 699 (1995); JAMES K. KLOSS & CARL F. MARIANO, *Insurance Coverage in Sexual Misconduct Cases*, INSURANCE LITIGATION REPORTER (January 1991).

2. The creation of any pleading based on sham allegations is to be strictly avoided. Not only is such pleading clearly unethical for the attorney, the dismissal of such claims can undermine the credibility of any remaining claims.

3. In order to provide this new form of coverage, adjustments were required to existing case law. In *Moore v. Continental Insurance Company* (44 Cal.App.4th 10; 1996 Cal.App. LEXIS 274; 51 Cal.Rptr.2d 176; 70 Fair Empl. Prac. Cas. (BNA) 833 (March 28, 1996)), the Fourth District held that a business general liability policy could not provide coverage for wrongful termination claims. The complaint alleged that Weston was forced to leave her employment ("constructive termination") because of sexual harassment. The court specifically noted that California Insurance Code §533 precludes coverage for willful misconduct claims of this nature. Before

the issuance of the new employment practices liability policies, the case was decertified. Some practitioners have indicated a belief that *Moore* was decertified to pave the way for these new policies which arguably cover intentional misconduct.

4. *Remmer v. Glen Falls* (Cal.Ap. 1956) 142 Cal.Ap2 84, 295 P.2d 19. *See also, Montrose Chemical Corporation of California v. Admiral Insurance Co.*, 10 Cal.4th 645, 669-670, 42 C.R.2d 324, 336 (1995).

5. *See Interstate Fire & Cas. v. Portland Archdiocese* (D. Or. 1990) 747 F.Supp. 618, 624-625 (sexual molestation over a period of years constituted one occurrence under employer's liability policy).

6. *See* California Insurance Code §22, *Fraser-Yamor Inc. v. Del Norte County* 68 Cal.App.3rd 201, 137 Cal.Rptr. 118 (1977).

7. *Gray v. Zurich Insurance Company* (1966) 65 Cal.2d 263, 274; 54 Cal.Rptr. 104, 111; 419 P.2d 168. *See also, M. D. Sass Investors Services v. Reliant Ins. Co.*, (N.D. C.A. 1992) 810 F.Supp. 1082, 1084.

8. H. WALTER CROSKEY and MARCUS M. KAUFMAN, CALIFORNIA PRACTICE GUIDE: INSURANCE LITIGATION (Rutter: Encino, 1995), 7a-7.

9. *Id.*, 7a-12, 7:42.

10. *Id.*, 7a-30, 7:122. *See also, Abellon v. Hartford Ins. Co.* (1985), 167 CA3rd 21, 26; 212 C.R. 852, 855. The issue of when or whether the emotional distress constitutes bodily injury is a question of fact and may involve medical and psychological proof.

11. *Fibreboard v. Hartford Acc. and Indem. Co.* (1993), 16 C.4th 492, 511; 20 C.R. 376, 388.

12. *See Gray v. Zurich Insurance Company* (1966) 65 Cal.2d 263; 54 Cal. Rptr. 104, 419 P.2d 168.

13. *Id.*, 275.

14. *See Gray* at 278; *Signal Cos. v. Harbor Insurance Company* (1980) 27 Cal.3d 359, 367, 165 Cal.Rptr. 799, 612 P.2d 889; *Saylain v. California Insurance Guaranty Association* (1986) 179 Cal.App.3d 256, 263, 224 Cal.Rptr. 493.

15. *Gray, supra*, 65 Cal.2d at 276.

16. Courts are often divided on whether extrinsic evidence can be used to defeat a duty to defend. Compare *Waller v. Truck Insurance* 36 Cal.App. 4th 936; 1994 Cal.App. LEXIS 836; 32 Cal.Rptr. 2d 692 (1994), *State Farm Mutual Auto Insurance Company v. Flynn* (1971) 17 Cal.App.3d 538, 548; 195 Cal.Rptr. 2 (holding extrinsic evidence justified denial of defense); *Saylain v. California Insurance Guaranty Association*, 179 Cal.App.3d 256, 264 (same; questionable precedent) and *Fire & Insurance Exchange v. Jiminez* (1986) 181 Cal.App.3d 437, 442 (229 Cal.Rptr. 83) (same), with *CNA Casualty of California v. Seaboard Surety Company* 176 Cal.App.3d 598, 606 (holding extrinsic evidence may create but not eliminate duty to defend); *Jerkins v. Insurance Company of North America* (1990) 220 Cal.App.3d 1481, 1489 (272 Cal.Rptr. 7) (citing CNA with approval); *California Insurance Guaranty Association v. Wood* (1990) 217 Cal.App.3d 944, 948 (266 Cal.Rptr. 250) (same).

17. *Montrose Chem. Corp. v. Superior Court* (1993) 6 Cal.4th 287, 300.

18. *Michaelian v. State Comp. Ins. Fund* (1996) 50 Cal.App.4th 1093, 1106.

19. *CNA Casualty of California v. Seaboard Surely Company* (1986) 176 Cal.App.3d 598, 607 (222 Cal.Rptr. 276).

20. *Hogan v. Midland National Insurance Company* (1973) 3 Cal.3d 553, 564 (91 Cal.Rptr. 153, 476 P.2d 825); *California Union Insurance Co. v. Club Aquarius* (1980) 113 Cal.App.3d 248 (169 Cal.Rptr. 685).

21. *La Jolla Beach & Tennis Club, Inc. v. Industrial Indemnity Co.* (1994) 9 Cal.4th 27, 39.

22. *Id.*, at 40.

23. *California Union Ins. Co. v. Club Aquarius* (1980) 113 Cal.App.3rd 243, 248.

24. *Allstate v. Talbot* 690 F. Supp.886, 889 (N.D. Cal.1998).

25. *Royal Globe Insurance Company v. Whitaker* (1986) 181 Cal.App.3d 532, 537.

26. *Id.*, at 537.

27. *Collin v. American Empire Ins. Co.* (1994) 21 Cal.App.4th 787, 804.

28. *Evans v. Pacific Indemnity Co.* (1975) 49 Cal.App.3d 537, 122 Cal. Rptr. 680.

29. 52 Cal.3d 1009, 804 P.2d 689, 278 CR 64, cert. denied, 502 U.S. 902, 112 S.Ct. 280, 116 L.Ed. 2d 232 (1991).

30. *See e.g.*, *State Farm Fire & Casualty Company v. Huje* (N.D. Cal. 1987) 666 F.Supp. 1402, 1404, as well as in other contexts, *see, e.g.*, *United States Fidelity Guarantee Company v. American Employer's Insurance Company* (1984) 159 Cal.App.3d 277, 283 (arson): *Allstate Insurance Company v. Tankovich* (N.D. Cal. 1991) 776 F.Supp. 1394 (racial harassment).

31. A survey of similar provisions prohibiting insurance coverage or indemnification for willful or criminal injuries for all fifty states is beyond the scope of this chapter; however, the explicit nature of California law in this respect makes it a useful model for analyzing many central issues of coverage law in this area.

32. *California Shoppers Inc. v. Royal Globe Ins. Co.* 175 Cal.App.3d 1, 32, 221 Cal.Rptr. 171 (1985).

33. 877 F.2d 1146 (2d Cir. 1989).

34. 22 Cal.3d 865, 887, 151 Cal.Rptr. 285.

35. *Allstate v. Talbot*, *supra*, 690 F.Supp. at 890.

36. 674 F.Supp. (N.D. Cal. 1991) 153, 156.

37. 213 Cal. App. 3d 41,50 (1989); *see also Morton by Morton v. Safeco Insurance Co.* (9th Cir. 1990) 905 F.2d 1208, 1211.

38. 98 C.D.O.S. 8098 (1998). 67 Cal.App.4th 583, 79 Cal.Rept.2d 134.

39. 67 Cal.App.4th, 595-596.

40. *Id.*, 598. This is particularly true where the allegations solely refer to rape and other forms of deliberate physical contact.

41. *Id.*, 598. *See also*, *Merced Mutual Ins. Co. v. Mendez* (1989) 213 Cal.App.3d 41, 47, 50.

42. *See* SALE and BOLDUAN, IIC-8, *Allstate v. Steinemer*, 723 F.2d 873, 875 (11th Cir. 1984) (intentional acts exclusion inapplicable even where insured intentionally does the act but has no intent to commit the harm).

43. *Id.*

44. *State Farm Fire and Casualty Co.* (N.D. C.A. 1990), 745, F.Supp. 595, 598.

45. *Allstate Ins. Co. v. Talbot, supra*, 690 F.Supp at 889.

46. *Hollingsworth v. Commercial Union Ins. Co.* (1989) 208 Cal.App.3d 800.

47. CROSKEY and KAUFMAN, 7I-18, 7:2244.

48. But see discussion below related to an important exception to this rule–*St. Paul Fire & Marine Ins. Co. v. F.H.*, 55 F.3d 1420, 1995 U.S.App LEXIS 12698 (1995), 133 L.Ed.2d 523, US cert denied.

49. 52 Cal.3d 1009.

50. 4 Cal.4th 1076 (1993), 1082; 846 P.2d 792, 796.

51. *Horace Mann v. Barbara B.* 61 Cal.App.4th 158, 163 (1998). *See also, Fire Insurance Exchange v. Superior Court (Jennifer O.)* 16 Cal.App.4th 1477, 20 Cal.Rptr.2d 750 (no coverage and no duty to defend for a child molester who willfully attempts to thwart his own prosecution by contacting the victim in direct violation of a court order releasing the molester from custody as the conduct was inseparably intertwined with the molestation).

52. *See Sentry Insurance Co. v. Miller* 914 F.Supp. 496, 502 (M.D. Ala.1996) (negligent and reckless misconduct resulting in small girl's touching defendant's penis not barred by exclusion for sexual molestation); *Allstate v. Steamer* 723 F.2d 873, 875 (II Cir. 1984) (intentional acts exclusion not applicable where insured intentionally does act has no intent to commit the harm).

53. *See Allstate v. Roelfs* 698 F.Supp. 815, 819, 820, notes 2, 3, and 4.

54. *State Farm Fire and Casualty v. Smith*, 907 F.2d 900 (9th Cir. 1990).

55. *State Farm v. Smith, supra*, 907 F.2d at 900, 90I.

56. *Id.*

57. 422 N.W.2d 485, 490.

58. *See also, Continental Insurance Company v. McDaniel* (160 Ariz. 183, 772 P.2d 6 (app. 1988) (insured's intent to injure inferred as a matter of law in the sexual harassment of a former employee, despite insured's claim that he intended to provide pleasure and satisfaction).

59. *Altena v. United Fire & Cas. Co.* 422 N.W.2d 485, 490 (Iowa 1988).

60. *Whitt v. DeLea* 707 F. Supp. 1011, 1016 (W.D.Wis. 1989).

61. *Wiley v. State Farm Fire & Cas. Co.*, 995 F.2d 457, 464 (3d Cir. 1993).

62. *Whitt v. DeLea, supra*, at 10, 12 (fondling of a minor's genitals); *Scudder v. Hanover Ins. Co.* 201 Ill.App. 3d 921, 923, 928, 559 N.E.2d 559, 560, 563, 147 Ill.Dec. 386, 387, 390 (1990).

63. *Doe v. State, Dept. of Health and Human Resources*, 623 So.2d 72, 73-74 (La.Ct. App.) writ denied, 627 So. 2d 653 (La. 1993) (victim retarded).

64. *Allstate v. Hampton* 173 Mich.App. 65, 67, 433 N.W.2d 334, 336 (1988).

65. *Wiley v. State Farm* 995 F.2d 457, 465 (3d Cir. 1993); but see the occasional exception: *U. S. F. & G. Ins. Co. v. Brannan* 22 Wash.App. 341, 589 P.2d 817 (1979) (defense of intoxication negated intent required by the intentional acts exclusion).

66. E.g., *State Farm v. Robin R.* (1989) 227 Cal.App. 190, 264 CR 326 (coverage excluded for minor age 14 to 15 who admitted to repeated acts of molestation) but see also, *Heather F. v. Topa Insurance* II CA4th 54; 13 Cal.Rptr.2d 783 (1992) (triable issues of fact remained as to whether a 12 year old intended harm to infant he molested, "We cannot equate Matthew's behavior with the criminal sexual molesta-

tion performed by an adult which formed the basis of the opinion in *J.C. Penney.*" "Public policy does not prohibit insurance coverage for negligence liability which arises even out of criminal or wrongful behavior.") II CA4th at 64, 66.

67. *Allstate v. Jack* 709 F.Supp. 963, 966 (D.Nev. 1989).

68. *Cuervo v. Cincinnati Ins. Co.* No. 93APE12-1715, 1994 WL 521161 (Ohio Ct. App. Sept. 22, 1994) (unpublished opinion) (motion to certify appeal allowed, 71 Ohio St. 3d 1466, 644 N.E.2D L388 (1995)).

69. *Fire Ins. Exch. v. Diehl* 206 Mich. App. 108; 520 N.W.2d 675 (1974).

70. *Allstate v. Freeman* 60 Mich. App. 349, 408 N.W.2d 53 (1987).

71. *CNA v. McGinnis* 282 Ark. 90, 666 S.W.2d 689 (1984); cited in SALE and BOLDUAN, IIC, 9-10.

72. *Id.*

73. *See Allstate v. Roelfs* 698 F. Supp. 815, 819 (D.Alaska 1987).

74. *Allstate v. Freeman* 60 Mich. App. 349, 408 N.W.2d 53 (1987).

75. *MacKinnon v. Hanove Ins. Co.* 124 N.H. 456, 459; 471 A.2d 1166 (1984). *See also Rodriguez v. Williams*, 107 Wash.2d 381, 729 P.2d 627 (1986) ("While doubtlessly the average purchaser of insurance would believe that incest would harm a child, the policy specifically states that the insured must expect or intend harm. Thus, the policy language itself is inconsistent with a blanket objective person standard, and the policy language must control. Moreover, if an objective standard is used, virtually no intentional act would ever be covered. Intentional acts that result in injury generally are expected, from the standpoint of the insured, to result in injury. An objective standard, especially provided after the fact, would seem to render meaningless the plain language providing for coverage for certain intentional acts." *Id.* at 386.) The *Rodriguez* court went on to adopt the inferred intent standard.

76. *Rodriguez v. Williams* 107 Wash.2d 381, 386; 729 P.2d 627, 630 (1986). *See also Linebaugh v. Berdish* 144 Mich. App. 750, 376 N.W.2d 400, 1985.

77. However, it should be noted that there is often coverage for other forms of criminal activity where it is undertaken by third parties or agents of the policyholder: e.g., employee dishonesty, fire, and burglary coverage.

78. 32 Cal.App.4th 643, 653, 38 Cal.Rptr.2d 131 (1995).

79. 32 Cal.App.4th 643, 652; *see also, Houg v. State Farm* (Minn.Ct.App. 1992) 481 N.W.2d 393 (Houg, a pastor sought coverage for a complaint which alleged that the pastor had set out on a course of conduct designed to entice and seduce the victim into sexual relations and which resulted in sexual relations; the pastor's attempt to reframe this conduct as negligent counseling because "any negligent counseling [was] . . . so intertwined with Houg's sexual exploitation of a psychologically dependent person as to be inseparable." *Id.* at 397); *State Farm v. Century Indemnity* 59 Cal.App.4th 648, 69 Cal.Rptr.2d 403 (1997) (non-sexual conduct urged to create coverage was inseparably intertwined with molestation where it involved a teacher's failure to report his own acts of molestation, an integral part of the "shroud of secrecy" that typically cloaks such acts) *Id.* at 79 Cal.App.4th 648, 662.

80. 17 Cal.App.4th 90l, 909, 22 Cal.Rptr.2d 299, 303.

81. In *Horace Mann Insurance Co. v. Barbara B.* 61 Cal.App.4th 158; 71 Cal.Rptr.2d 350 (1998), the Fourth District held that after a full trial there was no

evidence presented that did actually separate the sexual and non-sexual misconduct and therefore, a denial of coverage was proper.

82. 4 Cal.4th at 1083.

83. *Waters v. Bourhis* (1985) 40 Cal.4th 424, 433-436.

84. (1973) 10 Cal.3d 94, 102.

85. In *American Home Assur. Co. v. Cohen*, 881 P.2d 1001 (Wash. 1994) a Washington court in American Home found that the following insurance policy language was void as a matter of public policy: "in the event any [erotic contact is] alleged at any time, either in a complaint, during discovery, at trial or otherwise, any and all causes of action alleged and arising out of the same or related courses of professional treatment and/or relationships shall be subject to the aforesaid $25,000.00 aggregate limit of liability and to all other provisions of this clause."

86. *Garvey v. State Farm Fire and Casualty Company* (1989) 48 Cal.3d 395 (earth movement case where one cause excluded from coverage, another not, held that event was covered). Another case which found full coverage under a concurrent proximate cause theory had instructive language: *Cranford Ins. Co. v. Allwest Ins. Co.*, 645 F.Supp. 1440 (N.D. Cal. 1986). Court found that the therapist's "abuse of the transference process by having sex with his patient and his abandonment [of his patient] were each potential proximate causes of [the patient's] psychological injuries." "According to [the plaintiff's expert], Dr. R. [the therapist] terminated his treatment at a time when his patient [Ms. G.] had continuing psychiatric problems requiring therapy. Dr. R. failed to take necessary steps to see that Ms. G. consulted with another psychiatrist. This abandonment in and of itself may have contributed to Ms. G.'s injuries. The malpractice the doctor committed in abandoning his patient was wholly independent of his sexual intimacy with her, and consisted only of his failure to see that she continued treatment."

87. *See, e.g., Doe v. Hutchinson, No.* 107636 (California-Ventura Cty. Sup. Ct., Aug. 11, 1994) (dentist and his partnership were found liable for dentist's sexual assault of patient because (1) partnership did not have a policy regarding dentists working alone with patients, and (2) dentist's assistant had negligently failed to act when she found the dentist's door locked. *See also, D.D. v. Ins. Co. of North America*, 1995 WL 694591 (Alaska 1995) (in which physician/building owner referred patient to another physician in Physician A's building; Physician B sexually assaulted patient; patient sued Physician A on the theory that as a building owner he had a duty to protect her from a colleague whom he had reason to know might sexually assault the patient. Alaska Supreme Court held that as patient's injury was not caused by Physician A's treatment (which was excluded from building owner's policy), building owner's insurance company (INA) had a duty to defend Physician A and that the "'medical treatment' coverage exclusion contained in [Physician A's] policy is inapplicable since [patient's] injuries caused by [Physician B's] assault did not 'arise out of' medical treatment").

88. 138 A.D.2d 589, 526 N.Y.S.2d 171, 173 (1988) (memorandum, decision).

89. CROSKEY and KAUFMAN, 7C-18-19.

90. Excess policies are obtained by an insured in the event that the primary policy coverage monetary limits have been exhausted through payment, or in the event that coverage does not apply to all the facts of the underlying case.

91. *See Allstate Ins. Co. v. Freeman*, 432 Mich. 656, 443 N.W.2d 734 (1989) (no coverage for husband sued on negligence theory that he provided guns to wife who shot the plaintiff); *Allstate v. Gilbert* 852 F.2d 449 (9th Cir. 1988) (wife prohibited from coverage on negligence theories for husband's molestation under policy which precluded coverage for the intentional acts of any insured).

92. *See American States v. Borbor* (husband and wife owners of a nursery school had policy precluding coverage for intentional acts of "the insured;" the court construed the clause against the insurer and wife was covered).

93. *See Horace Mann Insurance Company v. Analisa N.* (1989) 214 Cal.App. 850, 853 "The fundamental question Analisa poses is whether a reasonable teacher could interpret the phrase 'in the course of the insured's education employment activities' to include sex acts performed at school and shortly after school hours . . . Contrary to Analisa's argument, in our view the plain language of the policy requires, at the very least, that an insured event occur while the teacher is engaged in activity, which is reasonably related to the goal of educating children."

94. (1989) 48 Cal.3d 438, 447, 452.

95. *See Horace Mann v. Independent School Dist.* No. 656, 355 N.W.2d 413 (Minn. 1984) (policy would provide coverage for negligent hiring and supervision but not vicarious liability).

96. 55 F.3d 1420 (9th Cir., Alaska) (1995), 133 L.Ed. 2d 523 cert. denied.

97. 55 F.3d at 1422-1424.

98. *Id.*, 1424.

99. *See, e.g.*, Elizabeth F. Loftus, *Researchers are showing how suggestion and imagination can create memories of events that did not occur*, SCIENTIFIC AMERICAN, September, 1997; Tracy Thompson, *Delayed Lawsuits of Sexual Abuse on the Rise; Alleged Victims Base Legal Actions on Memories Critics Say May Be Implanted in Therapy*, WASHINGTON POST, AUGUST 14, 1991, final ed. at B1.

100. Some states, such as California, have legislatively endorsed and embraced the concept of delayed discovery by enacting statutes specifically authorizing extended time periods for bringing legal actions based on childhood sexual abuse. *See* Ca. Code of Civil Procedure §340.1. Other states, such as Florida, have gone so far as to deny recovery and time bar a complaint based on allegations that the plaintiff suffered sexual abuse during childhood and completely repressed all memory of the abuse until she obtained psychological counseling as an adult. *Lindabury v. Lindabury* (Fla. App. 3 Dist. 1989) 552 So.2d 1117, 1117-1118 (cause dismissed), 560 So.2d 233 (Fla. Sup. Ct.). *See also* Mary Williams' chapter on statutes of limitations in this volume for an exploration of these issues.

101. See discussion below.

102. In *Servants of Paraclete, Inc. v. Great Am. Ins. Co.*, 857 F.Supp. 822, opinion amended in part and clarified in part on other grounds, 866 F.Supp. 1560 (D.N.M. 1994), the court held that psychological and emotional injuries suffered by adult survivors of sexual abuse such as depression, anxiety, poor self-esteem, and self-destructive behavior, "may be sickness" within the definition of "bodily injury." 857 F.Supp. at 834. However, bodily injury is held in most states to mean actual physical injury.

103. (1989) 48 Cal.3d 438, 447, 452.

104. *See* Cal. Insurance Code §II580.

# *RESOURCE APPENDICES*

# Appendix A: State by State Analysis of Reported Decisions and Statutes of Limitations Governing Childhood Sexual Abuse Actions

Mary R. Williams

### *ALABAMA*

No CSA statute. Code of Alabama, Title 6, Civil Procedure, section 6-2-38(l) provides 2 years for personal injury, and section 6-2-8(a) tolls until age 19 and for insanity.

#### *Reported Decisions*

*Travis v. Ziter*, 681 So.2d 1348 (Ala. 1996). Plaintiff sued priest and Diocese alleging repressed memory until one year of filing. *Held*: Tolling for insanity not invoked by claim of repressed memory. Theory of repressed memory not supported by consensus in relevant scientific community. Discovery rule in Alabama is statutorily prescribed for certain actions and not applied otherwise.

---

[Haworth co-indexing entry note]: "Appendix A: State by State Analysis of Reported Decisions and Statutes of Limitations Governing Childhood Sexual Abuse Actions." Williams, Mary R. Co-published simultaneously in *Journal of Aggression, Maltreatment & Trauma* (The Haworth Maltreatment & Trauma Press, an imprint of The Haworth Press, Inc.) Vol. 3, No. 2 (#6), 2000, pp. 193-282; and: *Sexual Abuse Litigation: A Practical Resource for Attorneys, Clinicians, and Advocates* (ed: Rebecca Rix) The Haworth Maltreatment & Trauma Press, an imprint of The Haworth Press, Inc., 2000, pp. 193-282. Single or multiple copies of this article are available for a fee from The Haworth Document Delivery Service [1-800-342-9678, 9:00 a.m. - 5:00 p.m. (EST). E-mail address: getinfo@haworthpressinc.com].

 

*Analysis*

No CSA statute.

Judicial discovery rule not applicable unless statutorily prescribed. Tolling for insanity not invoked by claim of repressed memory caused by the abuse.

## *ALASKA*

Alaska Statutes, Title 9, Code of Civil Procedure:

**Section 09.10.060: Actions against peace officers or coroners, for certain statutory penalties, or for sexual abuse to be brought in three years.**

> (c) A person who was the victim of sexual abuse may not maintain an action for recovery of damages against the perpetrator of the act or acts of sexual abuse based on the perpetrator's intentional conduct for an injury or condition suffered as a result of the sexual abuse unless the action is commenced within three years. In this subsection, "sexual abuse" means an act committed by the defendant against the plaintiff maintaining the cause of action if the defendant's conduct would have violated a provision of AS 11.41.440 or 11.41.450-11.41.455 at the time it was committed.

**Section 09.10.140: Disabilities of minority and incompetency.**

> (b) An action based on a claim of sexual abuse under AS 09.55.650 may be brought more than three years after the plaintiff reaches the age of majority if it is brought under the following circumstances:
>
> (1) if the claim asserts that the defendant committed one act of sexual abuse on the plaintiff, the plaintiff shall commence the action within three years after the plaintiff discovered or through use of reasonable diligence should have discovered that the act caused the injury or condition;
>
> (2) if the claim asserts that the defendant committed more than one act of sexual abuse on the plaintiff, the plaintiff shall commence the action within three years after the plaintiff discovered or through use of reasonable diligence should have discovered the effect of the injury or condition attributable to the series of acts; a claim based on an assertion of more than one act of sexual abuse is not limited to plaintiff's first discovery of the relationship between any one of those acts and the injury or condition, but may be based on plaintiff's discovery of the effect of the series of acts.

**Section 09.55.650: Claim based on sexual abuse to a minor under 16 years of age.**

(a) A person who, as a minor under 16 years of age, was the victim of sexual abuse may maintain an action for recovery of damages against the perpetrator of the act or acts of sexual abuse based on the perpetrator's intentional conduct for an injury or condition suffered as a result of the sexual abuse.

(b) If the defendant committed more than one act of sexual abuse on the plaintiff, the plaintiff is not required to prove which specific act caused the injury.

(c) In this section "sexual abuse" means an act committed by the defendant against the plaintiff maintaining the cause of action if the defendant's conduct would have violated a provision of AS 11.41.410-11.41.440 or 11.41.450-11.41.455, former AS 11.15.120, 11.15.134, or 11.15.160, or former AS 11.40.110 at the time is was committed.

Note: Added by sections 1, 2, 3, and 4, ch. 4, SLA 1990, effective February 2, 1990. Section 11 of the enacting legislation provides that the 1990 amendments apply to "all actions commenced on or after February 2, 1990, regardless of when the cause of action may have arisen."

***Reported Decisions***

None re CSA actions by adults.

***Analysis***

CSA statute provides three years from date plaintiff discovered or through use of reasonable diligence should have discovered that CSA caused the injury. Appears to apply to Type 1, but issue has not been interpreted.

Statute has language of revival, but issue has not been interpreted.

Statute expressly applies only to actions against the perpetrator. Issue has not been interpreted.

## *ARIZONA*

No CSA statute. Arizona Rev. Stat. Ann., Title 12, Courts and Civil Proceedings, sections 12-542 and 12-502, provide two years for personal injury actions and toll for minority.

***Reported Decisions***

*Florez v. Sargeant,* 185 Ariz. 521, 917 P.2d 250 (Ariz.1996). Two actions consolidated for review in Supreme Court. One plaintiff age 30 sued priest, one plaintiff age 39 sued father, both alleging that PTSD (but not repression) rendered them of sufficiently "unsound mind" to toll the running of the two-year statute, or invoked delayed accrual. *Held*: Alleged PTSD would not invoke exception for unsound mind, which requires that plaintiff have been unable to manage his or her affairs. Discovery rule not applicable because plaintiffs were always aware of the identity and conduct of the tortfeasor.

*Floyd v. Donahue,* 186 Ariz.App. 409, 923 P.2d 875 (Ariz.App.1996). Plaintiff sued father approximately nine years after first having sought counseling for the abuse. Alleged she had not fully realized her injuries until she began treatment with a counselor who specialized in working with sexual abuse victims, within two years of filing action. *Held*: Judicial discovery rule delays accrual until plaintiff knows identity of wrongdoer, what they had done, and that it had caused them harm. In instant case the action had accrued at latest when plaintiff first disclosed the abuse to a counselor. Fact that plaintiff did not appreciate full extent of injuries until later would not further delay accrual. Nature of abuse did not invoke estoppel. Emotional injuries that prevented her full recognition of injury did not invoke tolling for insanity.

*Doe v. Roe*, 187 Ariz. 605, 931 P.2d 1115 (Ariz.App.1996), rev.grtd. Plaintiff sued parents alleging she had repressed memories of CSA, had begun having flashbacks several years before filing suit, but had not been able to believe that the flashbacks were valid until discussions with family members which occurred within two years of filing suit. *Held*: Tolling for unsound mind not invoked by repressed memory and emotional injuries caused by the abuse. Estoppel not invoked unless defendant did some positive act in addition to the abuse, to conceal it or induce plaintiff to forebear from filing suit. Judicial discovery rule is invoked by repressed memory. Under rule, accrual delayed until date plaintiff knew or reasonably should have known that defendant harmed her. In repressed memory case, accrual would occur upon plaintiff's first recovery of memory, and would not be delayed further by plaintiff's subjective uncertainty as to the validity of the memories.

*Logerquist v. Danforth*, 188 Ariz. 16, 932 P.2d 281 (Ariz.App.1997). Plaintiff sued former pediatrician for medical malpractice and sexual abuse based on repressed memories. *Held*: Allegations of repressed memory of CSA do not invoke tolling for unsound mind, but do invoke application of judicial discovery rule. Under rule, action does not accrue until date plaintiff knew or by exercise of reasonable diligence should have known of defendant's wrongful conduct. Allegations of repressed memory raise triable issue of material fact precluding summary judgment on the issue.

*Nolde v. Frankie,* 190 Ariz. 422, 949 P.2d 511 (Ariz.App.1997), rev. grtd. Plaintiffs sued former coach and school district alleging that psychological effects of the abuse had prevented them from being able to understand the causal connection between their emotional problems and the earlier abuse until within two years of filing (Type

1 discovery). *Held*: Under *Florez,* with which the court expressly and lengthily disagrees, neither tolling for unsound mind, nor equitable estoppel for inherent fraud and duress, nor delayed accrual for delayed discovery of the essential elements of the cause of action, are invoked by allegations that psychological effects of the abuse prevented plaintiffs from understanding its causal connection to their psychological injuries until later. Court openly urges Supreme Court to change its course and apply discovery rule to Type 1 discovery of CSA.

*Doe v. Roe,* 955 P.2d 951 (*Doe v. Roe II*) (Ariz.1998). Review of appellate court's decision holding that although discovery rule would apply to Type 2 discovery of CSA, accrual would not be further delayed by plaintiff's inability to accept or believe the memories until later. *Held*: Allegations that the psychological effects of the abuse also caused plaintiff to be unable, until some time after first recovering the memories, to believe them and accept them as true, raised triable issues of material fact regarding whether plaintiff was reasonably delayed in discovering the essential elements of her cause of action. The requirement that plaintiff use due diligence to discover her cause of action should not be applied without taking into consideration the psychological effects of recovering repressed memories of CSA. Also, allegations that the trauma of recovering memories of CSA rendered plaintiff psychologically disabled in such a way as to be unable to connect and articulate events in a manner that would enable her to pursue her legal rights, raised triable issue of material fact regarding whether plaintiff was of "unsound mind" for purposes of tolling the statute. Tolling for unsound mind may be invoked not only by an inability to manage one's affairs, but also by an inability to comprehend one's legal rights. Thus, an ability to manage some or most of one's affairs does not necessarily negate tolling for unsound mind.

***Analysis***

No CSA statute. Judicial discovery rule may be invoked by allegations of Type 1 as well as Type 2 discovery. Tolling for unsound mind may also be invoked by allegations that psychological effects of CSA caused inability to comprehend legal rights.

## *ARKANSAS*

Arkansas Code Ann., Title 16, Practice, Procedure & Courts:

**Section 16-56-130: Civil actions based on sexual abuse.**

(a) Notwithstanding any other statute of limitations or any other provision of law that can be construed to reduce the statutory period set forth in this section, any civil action based on sexual abuse which occurred when the injured person was a minor, but is not discovered until after the injured person reaches the age of majority, shall be brought within three (3) years from the time of discovery of the sexual abuse by the injured party.

(b)(1) A claim based on an assertion of more than one (1) act of sexual abuse is not limited to the injured party's first discovery of the relationship between any one (1) of those acts and the injury or condition, but may be based on the injured party's discovery of the effect of the series of acts.

(2) It is not necessary for the injured party to establish which act in a series of acts of childhood sexual abuse caused the injury or condition that is the subject of the lawsuit.

(c) For the purposes of this section:

(1) "Childhood sexual abuse" means sexual abuse which occurred when the injured person was a minor;

(2) "Minor" means a person of less than eighteen (18) years of age; and

(3) "Time of discovery" means when the injured party discovers the effect of the injury or condition attributable to the childhood sexual abuse.

Note: Added by Acts 1993, No. 370, sec. 1. Section 2 provides that the act "is applicable to all actions filed on or after the effective date of the act /August 13, 1993/."

### *Reported Decisions*

None re CSA actions by adults.

### *Analysis*

CSA statute provides three years from discovery, defined as "when the injured party discovers the effect of the injury or condition attributable to the childhood sexual abuse." Appears to apply to Type 1 discovery, but issue has not been interpreted. Also, the statute ties accrual to the date of actual discovery, without providing in the alternative that the action accrues when plaintiff reasonably should have discovered the effect.

Statute does not have express language of revival; issue has not been interpreted.

Statute applies to actions "based on" CSA; issue has not been interpreted.

## *CALIFORNIA*

California Codes Ann., Code of Civil Procedure:

**Section 340.1: Childhood sexual abuse: time of commencing action.**

(a) In any civil action for recovery of damages suffered as a result of childhood sexual abuse, the time for commencement of the action shall be within eight years of the date the plaintiff attains the age of majority or within three years of the date the plaintiff discovers or reasonably should have discovered that psychological injury or illness occurring after the age of majority was caused by the sexual abuse, whichever period expires later.

(b) "Childhood sexual abuse" as used in this section includes any act committed by the defendant against the plaintiff that occurred when the plaintiff was under the age of 18 years and that would have been proscribed by Section 266j of the Penal Code; Section 285 of the Penal Code; paragraph (1) or (2) of subdivision (b), or of subdivision (c), of Section 286 of the Penal Code; subdivision (a) or (b) of Section 288 of the Penal Code; paragraph (1) or (2) of subdivision (b), or of subdivision (c), of Section 288a of the Penal Code; subdivision (h), (i), or (j) of Section 289 of the Penal Code; Section 647.6 of the Penal Code; or any prior laws of this state of similar effect at the time the act was committed.

(c) Nothing in this section shall be construed to alter the otherwise applicable burden of proof, as defined in Section 115 of the Evidence Code, that a plaintiff has in a civil action subject to this section.

(d) Every plaintiff 26 years of age or older at the time the action is filed shall file certificates of merit as specified in subdivision (e).

(e) Certificates of merit shall be executed by the attorney for the plaintiff and by a licensed mental health practitioner selected by the plaintiff declaring, respectively, as follows, setting forth the facts which support the declaration:

(1) That the attorney has reviewed the facts of the case, that the attorney has consulted with at least one mental health practitioner who is licensed to practice and practices in this state and who the attorney reasonably believes is knowledgeable of the relevant facts and issues involved in the particular action, and that the attorney has concluded on the basis of that review and consultation that there is reasonable and meritorious cause for the filing of the action. The person consulted may not be a party to the litigation.

(2) That the mental health practitioner consulted is licensed to practice and practices in this state and is not a party to the action, that the practitioner is not treating and has not treated the plaintiff, and that the practitioner has interviewed the plaintiff and is knowledgeable of the relevant facts and issues involved in the particular action, and has concluded, on the basis of his or her knowledge of the facts and issues, that in his or

her professional opinion there is a reasonable basis to believe that the plaintiff had been subject to childhood sexual abuse.

(3) That the attorney was unable to obtain the consultation required by paragraph (1) because a statute of limitations would impair the action and that the certificates required by paragraphs (1) and (2) could not be obtained before the impairment of the action. If a certificate is executed pursuant to this paragraph, the certificates required by paragraphs (1) and (2) shall be filed within 60 days after filing the complaint.

(f) Where certificates are required pursuant to subdivision (d), separate certificates shall be filed for each defendant named in the complaint.

(g) A complaint subject to subdivision (d) may not be served upon the defendant or defendants until the court has reviewed the certificates of merit filed pursuant to subdivision (e) and has found, in camera, based solely on those certificates of merit, that there is reasonable and meritorious cause for the filing of the action. At that time, the complaint may be served upon the defendant or defendants. The duty to serve the defendant or defendants with process shall not attach until that time.

(h) A violation of this section may constitute unprofessional conduct and may be the grounds for discipline against the attorney.

(i) The failure to file certificates in accordance with this section shall be grounds for a demurrer pursuant to Section 430.10 or a motion to strike pursuant to Section 435.

(j) In any action subject to subdivision (d), the defendant or defendants may not be named except by "Doe" designation in any pleadings or papers filed in the action until there has been a showing of corroborative fact as to the charging allegations against any defendant alleged to have committed an act or acts of childhood sexual abuse against the plaintiff.

(k) At any time after the action is filed, plaintiff may apply to the court for permission to amend the complaint to substitute the name of the defendant or defendants for the fictitious designation, as follows:

(1) The application shall be accompanied by a certificate of corroborative fact executed by the attorney for the plaintiff. The certificate shall declare that the attorney has discovered one or more facts corroborative of one or more of the charging allegations against a defendant or defendants, and shall set forth in clear and concise terms the nature and substance of the corroborative fact. If the corroborative fact is evidenced by the testimony of a witness or the contents of a document, the identity and location of the witness or document shall be included in the certificate. For purposes of this section, a fact is corroborative of an allegation

if it confirms or supports the allegation. The opinion of any mental health practitioner concerning the plaintiff shall not constitute a corroborative fact for purposes of this section.

(2) Where the application to name a defendant is made prior to that defendant's appearance in the action, neither the application nor the certificate of corroborative fact by the attorney shall be served on the defendant or defendants, nor on any other party or their counsel of record.

(3) Where the application to name a defendant is made after that defendant's appearance in the action, the application shall be served on all parties and proof of service thereof provided to the court, but the certificate of corroborative fact by the attorney shall not be served on any party or their counsel of record.

(l) The court shall review the application and the certificate of corroborative fact in camera and, based solely on the certificate and any reasonable inferences to be drawn therefrom, shall, if one or more facts corroborative of one or more of the charging allegations against a defendant have been shown, order that the complaint may be amended to substitute the name of the defendant or defendants.

(m) The court shall keep under seal and confidential from the public and parties to the litigation other than the plaintiff any and all certificates of corroborative fact filed pursuant to subdivision (k).

(n) Upon the favorable conclusion of the litigation with respect to any defendant for whom a certificate of merit was filed or for whom a certificate of merit should have been filed pursuant to this section, the court may, upon the motion of a party or upon the court's own motion, verify compliance with the section by requiring the attorney for the plaintiff who was required by subdivision (e) to execute the certificate to reveal the name, address, and telephone number of the person or persons consulted with pursuant to subdivision (e) that were relied upon by the attorney in preparation of the certificate of merit. The name, address, and telephone number shall be disclosed to the trial judge in camera and in the absence of the moving party. If the court finds there has been a failure to comply with this section, the court may order a party, a party's attorney, or both, to pay any reasonable expenses, including attorney's fees, incurred by the defendant for whom a certificate of merit should have been filed.

(o) The amendments to this section enacted at the 1990 portion of the 1989-90 Regular Session shall apply to any action commenced on or after January 1, 1991, including any action otherwise barred by the period of limitations in effect prior to January 1, 1991, thereby reviving those causes of action which had lapsed or technically expired under the law existing prior to January 1, 1991.

(p) The Legislature declares that it is the intent of the Legislature, in enacting the amendments to this section enacted at the 1994 portion of the 1993-94 Regular Session, that the express language of revival added to this section by those amendments shall apply to any action commenced on or after January 1, 1991.

Note: Added by Stats. 1986, ch. 914, s. 1. Amended by Stats. 1990, ch. 1578 (SB 108), s. 1; Stats. 1994, ch. 288 (A.B. 2846), s. 1. The section originally provided three years from majority for CSA actions against a family or household member, with no provision for discovery accrual. The 1990 amendments dropped the restriction to actions against a family or household member; changed the limitations period to eight years from majority or three years from discovery that psychological injury or illness occurring after majority was caused by the sexual abuse, whichever period expires later; and added certificates of merit procedure. The 1994 amendments added express language of revival; declared the language of revival applicable to all actions filed since January 1991; and added the certificate of corroborative fact procedure.

***Reported Decisions***

*DeRose v. Carswell,* 196 Cal. App.3d 1011, 242 Cal.Rptr. 368 (Cal.App.1987), rev. den. Action filed prior to CSA statute by 24-year-old plaintiff alleging Type 1 discovery. *Held*: Judicial discovery rule not applicable to plaintiff who knew the incidents had occurred but claimed delayed discovery that it had caused her adult psychological injuries (Type 1 discovery). Facts alleged also did not invoke tolling for equitable estoppel.

*Snyder v. Boy Scouts of America,* 205 Cal.App.3d 1318, 253 Cal.Rptr. 156 (Cal.App.1988). Action filed prior to CSA statute against former scout leader and organization by 19-year-old plaintiff alleging Type 1 discovery. *Held*: Facts of abuse did not invoke estoppel for fraud and misrepresentation by scout leader. Plaintiff's awareness of appreciable harm at the time negated application of judicial discovery rule. Three-year CSA statute did not apply to actions against persons other than a family or household member.

*Colleen L. v. Howard M.,* 209 Cal.App.3d 542, 257 Cal.Rptr. 263 (Cal.App.1989). Action filed after first CSA statute by 20-year-old plaintiff. *Held*: Statutory tolling for minority applies to CSA statute, which starts to run upon plaintiff's majority.

*Liebig v. Superior Court,* 209 Cal.App.3d 828, 257 Cal.Rptr. 574 (Cal.App.1989), rev. den. Action filed after first CSA statute by 20-year-old plaintiff. *Held*: CSA statute expressly revives actions filed after its effective date which had technically lapsed prior to its effective date. Legislature has power to do so in the case of a civil action.

*Evans v. Eckelman*, 216 Cal.App.3d 1609, 265 Cal.Rptr. 605 (Cal.App.1990). Action filed after first CSA statute by plaintiffs ages 28 to 31 alleging Type 1 discovery. *Held*: Although judicial discovery accrual is not invoked by allegation that the psychological effects of the abuse caused delayed discovery of the causal connection between long-term psychological injuries and the earlier abuse, the discovery rule may be invoked by allegations that such abuse caused plaintiffs reasonably to be unable to discover the wrongfulness of the defendant's conduct until later. Dismissal reversed and remanded with directions to grant leave to amend to plead delayed discovery of wrongfulness in more detail.

*Marsha V. v. Gardner*, 231 Cal.App.3d 265, 281 Cal.Rptr. 473 (Cal.App.1991). Action filed prior to 1991 statute by plaintiff alleging Type 1 discovery. *Held*: Judicial discovery rule not invoked by Type 1 discovery. The 1991 statute did not apply to the action. Court stated in dicta that even if it did it might not change the result.

*David A. v. Superior Court*, 20 Cal.App.4th 281, 24 Cal.Rptr.2d 537 (Cal.App.1993), rev. den. Action filed after 1991 statute by plaintiff under the age of 26 whose action had expired under the law in effect prior to 1991. *Held*: 1990 amendments lacked express language of revival and thus did not revive actions that had lapsed under prior law.

*Debbie Reynolds Studios v. Superior Court*, 25 Cal.App.4th 222, 30 Cal.Rptr.2d 514 (Cal.App.1994), rev. den. Action filed after 1991 against former dance teacher and teacher's employer. *Held*: CSA statute not applicable to action sounding in negligence against persons other than the perpetrator. Dance studio not subject to *respondeat superior* liability for instructor's sexual abuse. Court declined to decide whether the CSA statute would apply to *respondeat superior* liability were it to exist.

*Chaney v. Superior Court*, 39 Cal.App.4th 152, 46 Cal.Rptr.2d 73 (Cal.App.1995). Action filed after 1991 statute by 22-year-old plaintiff, against former neighbor for CSA and wife for negligence. *Held*: CSA statute not applicable to action against non-perpetrator for negligence.

*Lent v. Doe*, 40 Cal. App.4th 1177, 47 Cal.Rptr. 2d 389 (Cal.App.1995), rev. den. Action filed after 1991 by Type 1 plaintiff. Demurrer granted on grounds that under *DeRose* the judicial discovery rule is not invoked by Type 1 facts, and under *David A.* the 1991 statute did not revive actions that had lapsed under the law in effect prior to 1991. During pendency of appeal the 1994 amendments became effective, adding express language of revival to the statute, and making the language of revival applicable to all actions filed since January 1991. *Held*: Express language of revival is constitutionally valid and applies to actions pending on appeal. The discovery accrual provision of the 1991 statute applies to Type 1 discovery of the causal connection between psychological injuries occurring after majority and the earlier abuse. It does not require that plaintiff allege repressed memory of the abuse.

*Sellery v. Cressey,* 48 Cal.App.4th 538, 55 Cal.Rptr.2d 706 (Cal.App.1996). Action filed after 1991 by Type 1 plaintiff. Summary judgment granted on grounds plaintiff had always had conscious memory of some of the abuse and thus did not qualify for discovery accrual under *DeRose.* During pendency of appeal the 1994 amendments became effective. *Held*: CSA statute does not require repression of the abuse; whether plaintiff's delay in making the connection between the abuse and her adult psychological injuries was reasonable is a question of fact not determinable as a matter of law upon motion for summary judgment.

*Tietge v. Western Province of the Servites, Inc.*, 55 Cal.App.4th 382, 64 Cal.Rptr.2d 53 (Cal.App.1997). Action filed after 1991 against religious brother and his order. Several plaintiffs, alleging both Type 1 and Type 2 discovery. Demurrer granted on grounds the actions had lapsed under law in effect prior to 1991 and were not revived by the 1991 statute. During pendency of appeal the 1994 amendments adding express language of revival became effective. *Held*: 1994 amendments expressly revive actions that had lapsed under the law in effect prior to 1991. However, in agreement with *Debbie Reynolds,* the CSA statute does not apply to actions sounding in negligence against persons other than the perpetrator of the abuse.

### *Analysis*

Amended CSA statute provides eight years from plaintiff's majority or three years from date plaintiff discovers or reasonably should have discovered that psychological injury occurring after the age of majority was caused by the abuse, whichever period expires later. Statutory language has been held to apply to Type 1 discovery.

Amendments effective January 1995 added express language of revival, applicable to all actions filed since January 1991. Revival provision has been held constitutional.

Statute applies to actions "for recovery of damages suffered as a result of childhood sexual abuse." Has been held not to apply to actions for negligence against non-perpetrators.

## *COLORADO*

Colorado Rev. Stat. Ann., Title 13, Courts and Court Procedure:

**Section 13-80-103.7: General limitation of actions–sexual assault or sexual offense against a child–six years.**

(1) Notwithstanding any other statute of limitations specified in this article, or any other provision of law that can be construed to reduce the statutory period set forth in this section, any civil action based on a sexual assault or sexual offense against a child shall be commenced within six years after a disability has been removed for a person under disability, as such term is defined in subsection (3.5) of this section, or within six years after a cause of action accrues, whichever occurs later, and not thereafter. Nothing in this section shall be construed to extend the statutory period with respect to vicarious liability.
(2) For the purpose of this section, "sexual assault" means subjecting another person of any age to sexual contact, as defined in section 18-3-401(4), C.R.S.; sexual intrusion, as defined in section 18-3-401(5), C.R.S.; or sexual penetration, as defined in section 18-3-401(6), C.R.S.
(3) For the purpose of this section, "sexual offense against a child" shall include all offenses listed in section 18-3-411, C.R.S.
(3.5)(a) For the purpose of this section, "person under disability" means any person who is a minor under eighteen years of age, a mental incompetent, or a person under other legal disability and who does not have a legal guardian. "Person under disability" also includes a victim of a sexual assault when the victim is in a special relationship with the perpetrator of the assault or is a victim of a sexual offense against a child or is a victim who is residing in an institutional facility, such as a nursing home, regional center, or residential facility for the treatment and care of persons with mental illness or for the care of persons with developmental disabilities and where the victim is psychologically or emotionally unable to acknowledge the assault or offense and the harm resulting therefrom. For the purpose of this subsection (3.5), "special relationship" means a relationship between the victim and the perpetrator of the sexual assault which is a confidential, trust-based relationship, such as attorney-client, doctor-patient, psychotherapist-patient, minister-parishioner, teacher-student, or familial relationship. It is the intent of the general assembly to leave in place the six-year limitation for adults subjected to a sexual assault except in the situations described in this paragraph (a) in which the victim is in a special relationship with the perpetrator of the assault. In the circumstances in which a victim is in a special relationship with the perpetrator of the assault or is a victim of a sexual offense against a child or a victim who is residing in an institutional facility, such as a nursing home, regional center, or residential facility for the treatment and care of persons with mental illness or for the care of persons with developmental disabilities and where the victim is psychologically or emotionally unable to acknowledge the assault or offense and the harm resulting therefrom, the six-year limitation shall be tolled until the disability is removed. For the purpose

of this section, where the plaintiff is a victim of a series of sexual assaults or sexual offenses against a child, the plaintiff need not establish which act of a series of acts caused the plaintiff's injury, and the statute of limitations set forth in this section shall commence with the last in the series of acts, subject to the provisions of this section regarding disability. However, as elements of the cause of action, a person under disability who is psychologically or emotionally unable to acknowledge the assault or offense and the harm resulting therefrom shall have the burden of proving that the assault or offense occurred and that such person was actually psychologically or emotionally unable to acknowledge the assault or offense and the harm result in therefrom.

(b) Notwithstanding the provisions of section 13-90-107, the filing of a claim pursuant to this subsection (3.5) is deemed to be a limited waiver of the doctor-patient privilege or the psychotherapist-patient privilege to persons who are necessary to resolve the claim, and a doctor or psychologist who provided medical care and treatment or counseling and treatment to the plaintiff for injuries upon which an action under this subsection (3.5) is based may be examined as a witness. All medical records pertaining to any relevant medical care and treatment or counseling and treatment of the plaintiff are admissible into evidence in an action brought pursuant to this subsection (3.5) and shall be available for inspection upon request by the parties to the action.

(c) If the plaintiff brings a civil action under this subsection (3.5) fifteen years or more after the plaintiff attains the age of eighteen, the plaintiff may only recover damages for medical and counseling treatment and expenses, plus costs and attorney fees.

(d) It is the intent of the general assembly in enacting this subsection (3.5) to extend the statute of limitations as to civil actions based on offenses described in subsection (1) of this section as amended on July 1, 1993, for which the applicable statute of limitations in effect prior to July 1, 1993, has not yet run on July 1, 1993.

(3.7) An action may not be brought pursuant to subsection (3.5) of this section if the defendant is deceased or is incapacitated to the extent that the defendant is incapable of rendering a defense to the action.

(4) It is the intent of the general assembly in enacting this section to extend the statute of limitations as to civil actions based on offenses described in subsection (1) of this section for which the applicable statute of limitations in effect prior to July 1, 1990, has not yet run on July 1, 1990.

(5) The provisions of this section shall not be construed to extend or suspend the statute of limitations or statute of repose applicable to a claim alleging negligence in the course of providing professional services in the practice of medicine. This

subsection (5) shall not be construed to preclude pursuing a civil action pursuant to this section alleging a sexual offense based on a legal theory other than negligence in the course of providing professional services in the practice of medicine, unless the sexual assault forms the basis for the claim of such negligence.

Note: Added by Laws 1990, H.B. 90-1085, s. 1, effective April 16, 1990. Amended by Laws 1993, H.B 93-1259, s. 1, effective July 1, 1993. The 1993 amendment added subsections (3.5) and (3.7) and made related clerical changes.

***Reported Decisions***

*Cassidy v. Smith*, 817 P.2d 555 (Colo.App.1991). Action filed prior to CSA statute by plaintiffs ages 33 and 30, alleging Type 1 discovery. *Held*: Under judicial discovery rule, plaintiffs' alleged unawareness of the wrongfulness of defendant's conduct and its causal connection to their psychological injuries would not delay accrual where plaintiffs admittedly knew they suffered appreciable psychological injuries at and after the abuse.

*Bohrer v. DeHart*, 943 P.2d 1220 (Colo.App.1996). Action for CSA against youth counselor and for negligence against church, filed after CSA statute by adult plaintiff. On appeal from judgment for plaintiff after trial, the decision does not discuss the statute of limitations.

*Analysis*

CSA statute provides six years from the removal of a psychological disability to sue, defined as being "psychologically or emotionally unable to acknowledge the assault or offense and the harm resulting therefrom." Definition appears to apply to Type 1 discovery, but issue has not been interpreted in any published appellate decision.

Statute expressly applies only to actions filed after its effective date that had not expired under the prior law. Issue has not been interpreted. Under prior caselaw, Type 1 discovery was held not to invoke the judicial discovery rule.

Statute applies to actions "based on" CSA, and expressly excludes actions based on vicarious liability. Issue has not been interpreted.

## *CONNECTICUT*

Conn. Gen. Stat. Ann., Title 52, Civil Actions:

**Section 52-577d: Limitation of action for damages to minor caused by sexual abuse, exploitation or assault.**

Notwithstanding the provisions of section 52-577, no action to recover damages for personal injury to a minor, including emotional distress, caused by sexual abuse, sexual exploitation or sexual assault may be brought by such person later than seventeen years from the date such person attains the age of majority.

Note: Added by amendment in 1991, P.A. 91-240.

### *Reported Decisions*

*Roberts v. Caton*, 224 Conn. 483, 619 A.2d 844 (Conn.1993). *Held*: Following general rule in Connecticut, CSA statute applies retroactively to revive actions that had lapsed under prior law.

*Almonte v. New York Medical College*, 851 F.Supp. 34 (D.Conn.1994). *Held*: CSA statute applies to actions against persons or entities other than perpetrator.

*Henderson v. Wooley*, 230 Conn. 472, 644 A.2d 1303 (Conn.1994). Supreme Court answered question certified by federal district court. *Held*: Parental immunity doctrine does not bar action by minor child against parent for injuries arising out of sexual abuse.

*Giordano v. Giordano*, 59 Conn.App. 183, 664 A.2d 1136 (Conn.App.1995). *Held*: 17-year statute for CSA not unconstitutional but rationally related to legitimate government interest. Action not barred by laches.

*Todd M. v. Richard L.*, 44 Conn.Sup. 527, 696 A.2d 1063 (Conn.Super. 1995). Minor sued school bus driver and board of education in negligence for injuries caused by sexual abuse by fellow students on bus. *Held*: All causes of action for injuries caused by sexual abuse are governed by the CSA statute, including those against non-perpetrators for negligence.

### *Analysis*

CSA statute provides 17 years from majority, with no requirement of nor further exception for delayed discovery.

Statute has been held to revive lapsed actions.

Statute has been held to apply to actions against persons other than the perpetrator.

## *DELAWARE*

No CSA statute. Delaware Code Ann., Title 10, Courts and Judicial Procedure, section 8119, provides that actions for personal injury must be commenced within 2 years from the date the injury is sustained. The tolling provision, section 8116, does not apply to actions governed by section 8119.

***Reported Decisions***

None re CSA actions by adults.

## *DISTRICT OF COLUMBIA*

No CSA statute. District of Columbia Code, Title 12, Right to Remedy, section 12-301, provides one year from accrual for willful torts including battery, three years for an independent action for intentional infliction of emotional distress, and three years for actions otherwise unspecified.

***Reported Decisions***

*Farris v. Compton*, 802 F.Supp. 487 (D.D.C.1992). Plaintiffs ages 44 and 47 sued older brother alleging Type 2 discovery. *Held*: Judicial discovery rule applies only where the injury-causing event itself is objectively verifiable. CSA is not objectively verifiable and thus discovery rule is not applicable.

*Farris v. Compton*, 652 A.2d 49 (*Compton II*) (D.C.App.1994). On appeal from district court's dismissal, federal circuit court certified question to District of Columbia Court of Appeals. *Held*: Judicial discovery rule applicable to CSA actions alleging Type 2 discovery of the abuse.

*Cevenini v. Archbishop of Washington*, 707 A.2d 768 (D.C.App.1998). Three former altar boys sued church for negligent hiring and supervision of priest who allegedly sexually molested them when they were teenagers. Actions were filed in 1995. One plaintiff alleged he had repressed memory of the abuse until 1991, and had been unable to realize its impact until 1993. Other plaintiffs did not allege memory repression. All plaintiffs alleged they had no knowledge or notice of church's liability for negligence until a series of articles appeared in the *Washington Post* in 1995, establishing the church's prior knowledge of the priest's pedophilia. *Held*: Three year statute of limitations applies. Accrual occurs on inquiry notice. Accrual of action for sexual abuse may be delayed only for repressed memory of the abuse, not for delayed understanding of the impact. Knowledge of the abuse constitutes inquiry notice commencing the statutory period. Because plaintiffs always knew the church was responsible for the hiring and supervision of the molesting priest, accrual of their action against church for negligence occurred simultaneously with accrual of action against priest for the abuse.

*Analysis*

No CSA statute. Three-year statute for personal injury applies. Judicial discovery rule has been held applicable to Type 2 but not Type 1 discovery.

## *FLORIDA*

Florida Stat. Ann., Title VIII, Limitations:

**Section 95.11: Limitations other than for recovery of real property.**

> (7) **For intentional torts based on abuse.** An action founded on alleged abuse, as defined in s. 39.01 or s. 415.102, or incest, as defined in s. 826.04, may be commenced at any time within 7 years after the age of majority, or within 4 years after the injured person leaves the dependency of the abuser, or within 4 years from the time of discovery by the injured party of both the injury and the causal relationship between the injury and the abuse, whichever occurs later.

Note: Added by Laws 1992, ch. 92-102, s. 1, effective April 8, 1992. Section 2 provides that a plaintiff whose claim had lapsed under the prior period of limitations has 4 years from April 8, 1992, in which to commence suit.

***Reported Decisions***

*Lindabury v. Lindabury*, 552 So.2d 1117 (Fla.App.1989). Action filed and decided prior to CSA statute, by 31-year-old plaintiff alleging Type 2 discovery. *Held*: Judicial discovery rule not applicable to repressed memory of CSA on policy grounds.

*Roof v. Wiley*, 622 So.2d 1018 (Fla.App.1993). Action filed prior to but decided after CSA statute, by 33-year-old plaintiff, against grandfather for CSA and other relatives for negligence. *Held*: Section 4 of CSA statute, permitting revival of actions filed within four years of statute's effective date, is valid. Statute applies only to actions against the perpetrator.

*Salinas v. Mason*, 627 So.2d 525 (Fla.App.1993). CSA statute's revival provision upheld per *Roof v. Wiley*.

*Wiley v. Roof*, 641 So.2d 66 (Fla.1994). On review of decision by court of appeal. *Held*: CSA statute's window provision for revival is an unconstitutional violation of defendant's due process right to a vested interest in repose.

*Mason v. Salinas*, 643 So.2d 1077 (Fla.1994). Revival provision held unconstitutional per *Wiley v. Roof*.

*Boyce v. Cluett*, 672 So.2d 858 (Fla.App.1996). Revival provision invalid per *Wiley*; no cause of action stated for continuing tort based on allegations of parents' continuing financial and emotional control over plaintiff.

*Zlotogura v. Geller*, 681 So.2d 778 (Fla.App.1996). Per *Wiley,* CSA statute did not revive action that had lapsed under prior law.

*Doe v. Dorsey,* 683 So.2d 614 (Fla.App.1996). 17-year-old former altar boy sued priest and church alleging Type 1 discovery. Trial court dismissed on limitations grounds; plaintiff appealed as against church only. *Held*: Action against church for negligence governed by four-year statute of limitations for negligence, not by CSA statute. Delayed discovery not invoked by claimed inability to become aware of the wrongfulness or injuriousness of the abuse until later.

### *Analysis*

CSA statute provides seven years from majority or four years from discovery of the causal relationship between the injury and the abuse, whichever occurs later. Appears to apply to Type 1 but issue has not been interpreted.

Provision for revival of lapsed actions has been held unconstitutional. Under prior case law, judicial discovery accrual had been held inapplicable, even to Type 2 discovery.

Statute applies to actions "founded on" CSA, and has been held not to apply to actions against non-perpetrators.

## *GEORGIA*

Code of Georgia Ann. (1994 Rev.), Title 9, Civil Practice:

### Section 9-3-33.1: Childhood sexual abuse.

(a) As used in this Code section, the term "childhood sexual abuse" means any act committed by the defendant against the plaintiff which act occurred when the plaintiff was under the age of 18 years and which act would have been proscribed by Code Section 16-6-1, relating to rape; Code Section 16-6-2, relating to sodomy and aggravated sodomy; Code Section 16-6-3, relating to statutory rape; Code Section 16-6-4, relating to child molestation and aggravated child molestation; Code Section 16-6-5, relating to enticing a child for indecent purposes; Code Section 16-6-12, relating to pandering; Code Section 16-6-14, relating to pandering by compulsion; Code Section 16-6-15, relating to solicitation of sodomy; Code Section 16-6-22, relating to incest; Code Section 16-6-22.1, relating to sexual battery; or

> Code Section 16-6-22.2, relating to aggravated sexual battery, or any prior laws of the state of similar effect which were in effect at the time the act was committed.
> (b) Any civil action for recovery of damages suffered as a result of childhood sexual abuse shall be commenced within five years of the date the plaintiff attains the age of majority.

Note: Added by Acts 1992, p. 2473, effective July 1, 1992.

***Reported Decisions***

None re CSA actions by adults.

***Analysis***

CSA statute provides five years from majority, with no requirement of or exception for discovery accrual. (Original proposed bill had a discovery accrual provision which was dropped. See, 9 Ga.St.U.L.Rev. 154 (1992).

Statute has no language of revival; issue has not been interpreted.

Statute applies to actions "for recovery of damages suffered as a result of" CSA; issue has not been interpreted.

## *HAWAII*

No CSA statute. Hawaii Rev. Stat., Title 36, Civil Remedies and Defenses, Chapter 657, Limitations of Actions, section 657-7, provides two years for action for personal injury. Section 657-13 tolls for minority.

***Reported Decisions***

*Dunlea v. Dappen,* 83 Haw. 28, 924 P.2d 196 (Haw.1996). 45-year-old plaintiff sued father alleging Type 1 discovery. *Held*: Judicial discovery rule applies to actions based on CSA. Under rule, action accrues when plaintiff discovered or reasonably should have discovered causal connection between her psychological injuries and the earlier abuse. Question of reasonableness of alleged delay is question of fact for jury, precluding summary dismissal.

***Analysis***

No CSA statute. Judicial discovery rule applicable to Type 1 discovery.

## *IDAHO*

Idaho Code, Title 6, Proceedings in Special Actions:

**Section 6-1701: Tort actions in child abuse cases.** An action may be brought by or on behalf of any child against any person who has:

(1) Wilfully and lewdly committed any lewd or lascivious act or acts upon or with the body or any part or member of a child under the age of sixteen (16) years as defined in section 18-1508, Idaho Code; or
(2) Sexually abused any child as defined in section 18-1506, Idaho Code; or
(3) Sexually exploited any child for a commercial purpose as defined in section 18-1507, Idaho Code; or
(4) Injured a child as defined in section 18-1501, Idaho Code.

This civil cause of action exists independently of any criminal action commenced pursuant to chapter 15, title 18, Idaho Code. A civil action may be pursued under the provisions of this chapter even if a criminal prosecution is not pursued.

**6-1702: Who may bring action.** A child abuse tort action under the provisions of this chapter may be brought by the child or on the child's behalf by a parent or the child's legal representative.

**6-1703: Damages-Attorney's fees.** Damages in an action brought pursuant to the provisions of this chapter shall consist of compensation for past and future damages and may consist of emotional and physical pain and suffering, mental anguish, disability, loss of society and companionship, expenses for past and future therapy, and punitive damages where the claimant proves malicious or outrageous conduct by the party against whom the claim for punitive damages is asserted.

The prevailing party in a child abuse tort action shall be entitled to costs and reasonable attorney's fees.

**6-1704: Statute of limitations.** Notwithstanding any limitation contained in chapter 2, title 5, Idaho Code, an action under the provisions of this chapter must be commenced within five (5) years from the date that an aggrieved child reaches the age of eighteen (18) years.

**6-1705: Effective date**. This act shall be in full force and effect on and after July 1, 1989. Provided, that an action may be brought under this chapter only if the cause of action accrued on or after July 1, 1989. Provided further, that nothing in this chapter is intended to affect or limit causes of action for damages or other relief recognized by common law or statutory provisions for events that occurred before July 1, 1989.

Note: Added by S.L. 1989, chapter 47.

***Reported Decisions***

*Bonner v. Roman Catholic Diocese of Boise,* 128 Idaho 351, 913 P.2d 567 (Id.1996). Two adult brothers sue priest and Church alleging Type 2 discovery. *Held*: Idaho does not apply the judicial discovery rule to CSA actions. Action accrues when there is some objectively ascertainable damage, and inability of plaintiff to ascertain it due to repression of memory does not delay accrual.

***Analysis***

CSA statute provides five years from majority, with no requirement of or exception for discovery accrual. Court has held the judicial discovery rule does not apply, even to Type 2 discovery.

Statute expressly applies only to actions that accrued on or after July 1, 1989, thereby not applying retroactively to revive actions that had lapsed prior to that date, nor even to govern actions that had accrued prior to that date. Issue has not been interpreted.

Statute expressly applies only to actions against the perpetrator. Issue has not been interpreted.

## *ILLINOIS*

Illinois Compiled Stat. Ann., Act 5, Code of Civil Procedure, Article 13, Limitations:

**Section 5/13-202.2: Childhood sexual abuse.**

(a) In this Section: "Childhood sexual abuse" means an act of sexual abuse that occurs when the person is under 18 years of age. "Sexual abuse" includes but is not limited to sexual conduct and sexual penetration as defined in Section 12-12 of the Criminal Code of 1961.
(b) An action for damages for personal injury based on childhood sexual abuse must be commenced within 2 years of the date the person abused discovers or through the use of reasonable diligence should discover that the act of childhood sexual abuse occurred and that the injury was caused by the childhood sexual abuse.
(c) If the injury is caused by 2 or more acts of childhood sexual abuse that are part of a continuing series of acts of childhood sexual abuse by the same abuser, then the discovery period under subsection (b) shall be computed from the

date the person abused discovers or through the use of reasonable diligence should discover (i) that the last act of childhood sexual abuse in the continuing series occurred and (ii) that the injury was caused by any act of childhood sexual abuse in the continuing series.

(d) The limitation periods under subsection (b) do not begin to run before the person abused attains the age of 18 years; and, if at the time the person abused attains the age of 18 years he or she is under other legal disability, the limitation periods under subsection (b) do not begin to run until the removal of the disability.

(e) This Section applies to actions pending on the effective date of this amendatory Act of 1990 as well as to actions commenced on or after that date. The changes made by this amendatory Act of 1993 shall apply only to actions commenced on or after the effective date of this amendatory Act of 1993.

Note: Added by P.A. 86-1346, s. 1, effective January 1, 1991; amended by P.A. 88-127, s. 5, effective January 1, 1994. The 1990 legislation provided that no cause of action could be filed more than 12 years from the date of plaintiff's majority. The 1993 amendment dropped this provision.

### *Reported Decisions*

*Johnson v. Johnson*, 701 F.Supp. 1363 (*Johnson I*) (N.D.Ill.1988). 32-year-old plaintiff alleging Type 2 discovery. *Held*: Illinois would apply judicial discovery rule to repressed memory of CSA.

*Franke v. Geyer*, 209 Ill.App.3d 1009, 568 N.E.2d 931 (Ill.App.1991). Decided after effective date of 1991 CSA statute. 31-year-old plaintiff alleging Type 1 discovery. *Held*: Judicial doctrine of discovery accrual requires knowledge of the connection between the wrongful act and the injury. However, because plaintiff suffered emotional distress at the time, she had sufficient information about her injury and its cause to put her on inquiry notice as to her cause of action. Equitable estoppel is not applicable absent affirmative conduct by defendant preventing plaintiff from acting.

*Johnson v. Johnson*, 766 F.Supp. 662 (*Johnson II*) (N.D.Ill.1991). After 1991 CSA statute became effective, defendant moved for summary judgment based on plaintiff having filed the action more than 12 years after reaching the age of majority. *Held*: The 12-year statute of repose applies to bar the action.

*Phillips v. Johnson*, 231 Ill.App.3d 890, 599 N.E.2d 4 (Ill.App.1992). 35-year-old plaintiff alleging Type 2 discovery. *Held*: The 12-year statute of repose may not constitutionally be applied retroactively to an action that was pending on its effective date, and cannot be applied to shorten a limitations period unless the plaintiff affected by it has a reasonable time within which to file after its effective date. Discovery rule is applicable to Type 2 discovery, despite absence of any extrinsic verifiable evidence of the abuse.

*Doe v. Board of Education*, 833 F.Supp. 1366 (N.D.Ill.1993). Civil rights action under 42 U.S.C. section 1983, based on school district's negligence in employing a teacher who molested plaintiff and other students. No cause of action brought for CSA. *Held*: Judicial discovery rule applies; accrual occurred when plaintiff knew or had reason to know her constitutional rights had been violated. Allegations that school personnel took action to cover up teacher's sexual misconduct established question of fact as to reasonableness of plaintiff's delay.

*Boggs v. Adams*, 838 F.Supp. 1293 (N.D.Ill.1993). Type 2 plaintiff, over 30, filed after effective date of 1991 statute. *Held*: The 12-year statute of repose applies to an action filed after its effective date.

*Boggs v. Adams*, 45 F.3d 1056 (7th Cir.1995). On appeal from District court decision. *Held*: An action filed after effective date of statute of repose may not be barred by it if the plaintiff did not, on the facts, have a "reasonable period of time" after the effective date of the statute in which to file.

*Hawley v. Kenley*, 261 Ill.App.3d 307, 634 N.E.2d 20 (Ill.App.1994). 26-year-old plaintiff sued grandfather for CSA and grandmother for negligence. Plaintiff testified that she had always known the "general fact" that the defendant had molested her, but had only recently begun to remember specifically what he had done. Letters established that plaintiff had complained of it to her mother at least seven years before filing. Plaintiff had been in psychotherapy four years before filing. *Held*: Applying discovery rule under 1991 CSA statute, the facts establish that plaintiff had as a matter of law discovered, or reasonably should have discovered, her action more than two years before filing. CSA statute does not apply to actions against non-perpetrators for negligence.

*D.P. v. M.J.O.*, 266 Ill.App.3d 1029, 640 N.E.2d 1323 (Ill.App.1994). Plaintiffs ages 26 and 28, alleging Type 1 discovery. *Held*: 1991 CSA statute does not expressly, and could not constitutionally, revive actions that had lapsed under prior law. However, under prior law the judicial discovery rule is applicable to CSA actions, and delays accrual until plaintiff knows or reasonably should have discovered not only that the abuse occurred but also the causal connection between the abuse and the injury. Knowledge that the abuse occurred does not, in and of itself, establish notice of the causal connection to injury.

*M.E.H. and D.M.H. v. L.H. and G.H.*, 283 Ill.App.3d 241, 669 N.E.2d 1228 (Ill.App.1996). Plaintiffs in 40's sued father for CSA and mother for intentional infliction and negligence, alleging Type 2 discovery. Complaint filed in 1994, after effective date of 1993 amendments repealing the statute of repose. *Held*: Statute of repose effective January 1991 extinguished plaintiffs' causes of action at that time, regardless of whether or not the causes had yet "accrued." Legislature did not, in repealing the statute of repose, express an intention to retroactively revive causes of action that had been extinguished by it. Plaintiffs had had a reasonable period of time after enactment of the statute of repose in which to bring their claims, and thus were not entitled to the "reasonable period of time" exception.

*Benton v. Vonnahman*, 288 Ill.App.3d 199, 679 N.E.2d 1270 (Ill.App.1997). 31-year old plaintiff alleging Type 1 discovery sued priest for CSA and Church for vicarious liability and negligence. Complaint filed in 1994, after repeal of statute of repose. *Held*: Statute of repose extinguished the causes of action when plaintiff turned 30 in 1992. Plaintiff had had 22 months after enactment of statute of repose before he turned 30, thus had had reasonable time period in which to file before his right was extinguished. Even if not barred by statute of repose, plaintiff did not file within two years of discovery accrual, as facts established that he had known that the sexual relationship with the priest had been wrong and illegal for many years before filing.

*M.E.H. and D.M.H. v. L.H. and G.H.*, 177 Ill.2d 207, 685 N.E.2d 335 (Ill.1997). On review of appellate court decision, Supreme Court affirmed. *Held*: Repeal of statute of repose could not revive actions that had been extinguished; plaintiffs had had reasonable period of time after enactment of statute to file.

*Pedigo v. Pedigo,* 292 Ill.App.3d 831, 686 N.E.2d 1180 (Ill.App.1997). 34-year-old plaintiff alleging Type 2 discovery filed action in 1990, before effective date of 1991 CSA statute. *Held*: Statute of repose does not apply retroactively to extinguish causes of action filed before its effective date. Judicial discovery rule applies to Type 2 discovery.

### *Analysis*

CSA statute provides 2 years from plaintiff discovers or through reasonable diligence should have discovered that the injury was caused by CSA. Has been held applicable to Type 1 and Type 2 discovery.

Statute does not have language of revival and has been held not to revive lapsed actions, but has been held to be a codification of the pre-existing judicial discovery rule.

Original statute effective 1991 contained 12-year statute of repose, which was repealed effective 1994. Statute of repose extinguished the causes of action of those over 30 during the time it was effective, unless the actions had been filed prior to its effective date, or the plaintiff did not have a reasonable time period after its effective date in which to file before being extinguished.

Statute applies to actions "based on" CSA; has been held not to apply to causes of action against non-perpetrators.

## *INDIANA*

No CSA statute. Indiana Stat. Ann., Title 34, Civil Procedure, section 34-1-2-2, provides 2 years for personal injury actions, and section 34-1-2-5 tolls the period during minority or other legal disability.

### *Reported Decisions*

*Hildebrand v. Hildebrand*, 736 F.Supp. 1512 (S.D.Ind.1990). Action filed by 26-year-old plaintiff alleging Type 1 discovery. Plaintiff alleged that her father, a physician, fraudulently concealed her action by diagnosing her injuries as caused by a chemical imbalance. *Held*: Judicial discovery rule delays accrual until both injury and probable cause are ascertained or reasonably ascertainable. Although facts of CSA lend themselves to discovery rule, Indiana court probably would not apply it to CSA actions as it has been reluctant to extend it beyond situations in which the damage is inherently unascertainable. However, the allegations of fraudulent concealment by defendant raise a question of material fact as to when her injuries themselves were ascertainable.

*Fager v. Hundt*, 610 N.E.2d 246 (Ind.1993). Action filed by 37-year-old plaintiff alleging Type 2 discovery. *Held*: Parental immunity doctrine not applicable to CSA action. Discovery rule not generally applicable to actions based upon CSA, as responsibility to learn of child's injuries is on the parent and sound public policy assumes the parent will notice an injury and take action. This rule is subject to an equitable exception for fraudulent concealment where the injury is alleged to have been committed by the parent. The equitable exception ceases when the plaintiff discovers or reasonably should have discovered that a childhood injury was caused by defendant's conduct. Repression of memory, caused by the CSA, may raise question of material fact as to reasonableness of delay.

*Ernstes v. Warner*, 860 F.Supp. 1338 (S.D.Ind.1994). Action against teacher for CSA and school for negligence under 42 USC section 1983, by plaintiff alleging Type 2 discovery. *Held*: Under *Fager*, Indiana would not delay accrual of CSA action against non-parent for repressed memory, as knowledge of the injury would be imputed to the parents as a matter of law. Although discovery rule applies to federal civil rights claims, no reasonable finder of fact could find that a boy molested repeatedly by his teacher at ages 13 to 16, would not have known what was occurring at the time.

*Doe v. Roe*, 52 F.3d 151 (7th Cir.1995). Action by 34-year-old plaintiff alleging Type 2 discovery of abuse by brother and negligence by mother. *Held*: *Fager* exception for fraudulent concealment applies only to causes of action for abuse by the parent. The fact that the parent knew of the abuse but did not protect would not change the rule.

*A.M. v. Roman Catholic Church,* 669 N.E.2d 1034 (Ind.App.1996). 35-year-old plaintiff sued priest and Church alleging Type 2 discovery within two years of filing. Plaintiff's mother had discovered the abuse when plaintiff was a child, had gone to Church about it, and had been persuaded to go along with Church's strategy of keeping it a secret to protect everyone from embarrassing publicity. *Held*: Discovery of CSA by parent is imputed to the child. Exception for fraudulent concealment by parent applies only where parent was abuser. Fact that parent colluded with the abuser to keep it secret does not trigger the exception.

*Konkle v. Henson,* 672 N.E.2d 450 (Ind.App.1996). 22-year-old plaintiff sued minister and Church for vicarious liability and negligence. Plaintiff alleged continuing tort including acts occurring within two years of filing. *Held*: CSA was not continuing tort for purposes of delaying accrual for the whole course of conduct until the last act. Rather, a limitations period for CSA began to run upon the occurrence of each act, and expired within two years of the act. Statute of limitations for negligent hiring began to run when plaintiff knew the acts were occurring and were wrong, and was not delayed by continuing acts of abuse.

*Doe v. United Methodist Church*, 673 N.E.2d 839 (Ind.App.1996). 25-year-old plaintiff sued minister and Church alleging minister had seduced her when she was 16, relationship had continued until she was 20, and despite telling professional counselors about it in early 20's she did not believe that it was abuse until she disclosed to her parents within two years of filing the action. *Held*: Under discovery rule, accrual occurs when an objectively reasonable person would have discovered the cause of action and is not delayed by the plaintiff's subjective inability to do so until later. No tolling for fraudulent concealment where plaintiff's continued reliance on defendant's fraudulent misrepresentations was not objectively reasonable. Court rejects what it terms "very slim minority" position that the objectively reasonable person standard takes into account the psychological effects on such a person of the wrongful conduct to which the plaintiff had been subjected.

*Gilp v. Neville,* 681 N.E.2d 1173 (Ind.App.1997). Sisters sued former neighbor for CSA, alleging Type 2 discovery within two years of filing. *Held*: Alleged fact that plaintiffs had repressed the abuse, and thus parents also could not discover it during plaintiffs' childhoods, would not change the rule that knowledge of harm to the child will be imputed to the parents as a matter of law.

*Analysis*

No CSA statute. Court has held judicial discovery rule is not applicable to CSA actions, because knowledge of harm to the child is imputed to the parent as a matter of law. Court has fashioned equitable tolling exception for fraudulent concealment where the CSA was committed by plaintiff's parent. The tolling ceases when plaintiff discovers or reasonably should have discovered that a childhood injury was caused by the parent's CSA. Court has held that allegations of Type 2 discovery raise questions of fact on issue of reasonableness of delay. Has not addressed Type 1 discovery.

## *IOWA*

Iowa Code Ann., Title XXXI, Civil Practice and Procedure, Chapter 614, Limitation of Actions:

**Section 614.8A: Damages for child sexual abuse-time limitation.**

An action for damages for injury suffered as a result of sexual abuse which occurred when the injured person was a child, but not discovered until after the injured person is of the age of majority, shall be brought within four years from the time of discovery by the injured party of both the injury and the causal relationship between the injury and the sexual abuse.

Note: Added by Acts 1990 (73 G.A.), chapter 1241, s. 2, effective July 1, 1990. Section 3 provides that the Act "is applicable to all actions filed on or after the effective date of the Act."

***Reported Decisions***

*Callahan v. State*, 464 N.W.2d 268 (Iowa 1990). Action by minor's parents under State Tort Claims Act and 42 USC section 1983. Although CSA statute not involved, court noted it as evidence of public policy in favor of allowing belated pursuit of CSA claims. *Held*: Judicial discovery rule applicable and parent's discovery, not child's knowledge of abuse, triggers accrual.

*Doe v. Cherwitz*, 518 N.W.2d 362 (Iowa 1994). Action against physician for sexual abuse of plaintiff at age 18, filed in federal district court, prior to CSA statute. District court certified questions to Iowa Supreme Court. *Held*: The term "child" in CSA statute means person under 14, hence CSA statute does not govern action filed by person who was abused at age 18. Therefore, it is unnecessary to address whether the statute would revive an action that had lapsed under prior law. However, plaintiff's causes of action are subject to judicial discovery rule, and did not accrue until she discovered both her injury and its cause.

*Claus v. Whyle*, 526 N.W.2d 519 (Iowa 1994). Action filed after CSA statute by plaintiff alleging Type 2 discovery. *Held*: CSA statute governs. Discovery accrual occurred at time plaintiff first remembered the abuse in a flashback. (Court did not address question of statutory revival of lapsed claim.)

*Frideres v. Schiltz*, 540 N.W.2d 261 (Iowa 1995). Action in federal district court by plaintiff alleging Type 1 discovery. District court certified questions to Iowa Supreme Court. *Held*: Lacking express language of revival, CSA statute does not revive actions which had lapsed under prior law. However, under prior law, discovery rule applied and would permit Type 1 discovery. CSA statute does apply to actions for recovery of damages resulting from CSA regardless of the legal theory of recovery, including claims for negligence against non-perpetrator.

*Woodroffe v. Hasenclever*, 540 N.W.2d 45 (Iowa 1995). Action filed after CSA statute by 40-year-old plaintiff alleging Type 1 discovery. Plaintiff had disclosed the abuse to a therapist more than four years before filing. *Held*: CSA statute not retroactive to revive lapsed claims. Judicial discovery rule applicable to Type 1, but would not delay accrual past time of inquiry notice, which occurred when plaintiff began remembering some of the abuse and disclosed it in treatment.

*Frideres v. Schlitz*, 113 F.3d 897 (8th Cir.1997). After Iowa Supreme Court answered certified questions, district court denied motion for summary judgment and defendant appealed. *Held*: Mere knowledge of the abuse will not necessarily start the limitations period running. But where the plaintiff is aware of facts that would prompt a reasonably prudent person to begin seeking information as to the problem and its cause, the plaintiff will be deemed to be on inquiry notice and the limitations period will start.

### *Analysis*

CSA statute provides four years from discovery accrual, defined as discovery by the injured person of both the injury and the causal relationship between the injury and the sexual abuse. Has been held applicable to Type 1 and Type 2 discovery.

Statute has no language of revival; has been held not to revive lapsed actions. However, judicial discovery rule has been held applicable to Type 1 and Type 2 discovery.

Statute applies to actions "for damages suffered as a result of" CSA; has been held to apply to causes of action for negligence against non-perpetrators.

## *KANSAS*

Kansas Stat. Ann., Chapter 60, Procedure, Civil:

**Section 60-523: Limitations on actions for recovery of damages suffered as a result of childhood sexual abuse.**

(a) No action for recovery of damages suffered as a result of childhood sexual abuse shall be commenced more than three years after the date the person attains 18 years of age or more than three years from the date the person discovers or reasonably should have discovered that the injury or illness was caused by the sexual abuse, whichever occurs later.

(b) As used in this section:

(1) "Injury or illness" includes psychological injury or illness, whether or not accompanied by physical injury or illness.

(2) "Childhood sexual abuse" includes any act committed against the person which act occurred when the person was under the age of 18 years and which act would have been a violation of any of the following:

(A) Indecent liberties with a child as defined in K.S.A. 21-3503 and amendments thereto; (B) aggravated indecent liberties with a child as defined in K.S.A. 21-3504 and amendments thereto; (C) aggravated criminal sodomy as defined in K.S.A. 21-3506 and amendments thereto; (D) enticement of a child as defined in K.S.A. 21-3509 and amendments thereto; (E) indecent solicitation of a child as defined in K.S.A. 21-3510 and amendments thereto; (F) aggravated indecent solicitation of a child as defined in K.S.A. 21-3511 and amendments thereto; (G) sexual exploitation of a child as defined in K.S.A. 21-3516 and amendments thereto; or (H) aggravated incest as defined in K.S.A. 21-3603 and amendments thereto; or any prior laws of this state of similar effect at the time the act was committed.

(c) Discovery that the injury or illness was caused by childhood sexual abuse shall not be deemed to have occurred solely by virtue of the person's awareness, knowledge or memory of the acts of abuse. The person need not establish which act in a series of continuing sexual abuse incidents caused the injury or illness complained of, but may compute the date of discovery from the date of discovery of the last act by the same perpetrator which is a part of a common scheme or plan of sexual abuse.

(d) This section shall be applicable to:

(1) Any action commenced on or after July 1, 1992, including any action which would be barred by application of the period of limitation applicable prior to July 1, 1992;

(2) Any action commenced prior to July 1, 1992, and pending on July 1, 1992.

Note: Added by Laws 1992, chapter 307, section 1.

### *Reported Decisions*

*Swartz v. Swartz,* 20 Kan.App.2d 704, 894 P.2d 209 (Kan.App.1995). Action filed after effective date of CSA statute by Type 1 plaintiff. *Held*: Although CSA statute expressly provided for revival of actions that had lapsed under prior law, it did not and could not operate to revive actions that had been extinguished by operation of Kansas's 8-year statute of repose on actions arising during plaintiff's minority (K.S.A. 60-515(a)). Although when the CSA statute was enacted the Legislature also amended the statute of repose to except CSA actions from its operation, this could not revive an action that had already been extinguished by operation of the statute of repose.

*Ripley v. Tolbert,* 260 Kan. 491, 921 P.2d 1210 (Kan.1996). 50-year-old plaintiff sued father for CSA and mother for failure to protect. Plaintiff alleged Type 2 discovery and argued that the statute of repose had not extinguished her action because the action had not accrued until her discovery of the abuse in 1991, and the statute of repose had been repealed in 1992. *Held*: The eight year statute of repose started to run at time of injury and by operation of law extinguished plaintiff's cause of action after eight years, regardless of whether or not the action had accrued under discovery principles.

*Shirley v. Reif,* 260 Kan. 514, 920 P.2d 405 (Kan.1996). Brothers ages 25 and 22 sued former priest for CSA and church for negligence and vicarious liability, alleging Type 1 discovery within one year of filing the action. *Held*: The actions had not been extinguished by the eight-year statute of repose before it was repealed for CSA actions in 1992. Therefore, the CSA statute's language of revival revived the actions as of 1992. Plaintiffs' allegations that they did not discover the causal connection between their psychological injuries and the earlier abuse until within one year of filing, raised questions of fact precluding summary judgment on the limitations issue. Issue of whether the CSA statute applies to causes of action against non-perpetrator not raised or addressed.

### *Analysis*

CSA statute provides three years from majority or three years from discovery that the injury was caused by the sexual abuse, whichever occurs later. Provides that knowledge or memory of the abuse shall not be deemed to constitute discovery that the injury was caused by the sexual abuse. Has been held to apply to Type 1 discovery.

Statute has express language of revival which has been held constitutional and effective to revive action that had lapsed under law in effect prior to CSA statute. But the revival provision has been held constitutionally unable to revive an action that had been extinguished by operation of the previously existing 8-year statute of repose for actions arising during the plaintiff's minority.

Statute applies to actions for injuries "suffered as a result of CSA." Issue has not been interpreted.

## *KENTUCKY*

No CSA statute. Kentucky Rev. Stat. Ann., section 413.140, provides one year from accrual for personal injury actions, and section 413.170 tolls the period during minority or other legal disability.

### *Reported Decisions*

*Rigazio v. Archdiocese of Louisville,* 853 S.W.2d 295 (Ky.App.1993). Action against former teacher for CSA and church/school for negligence, by 24-year-old male plaintiff alleging Type 2 discovery. Evidence established that plaintiff's alleged repression did not occur until some time after the abuse had stopped, and even sometime after he had reached the age of majority. *Held*: One-year statute for personal injury actions applies. Tolling exception for disability of unsound mind is not invoked by repression of memory of the abuse. And, even if repression were to be held sufficient to invoke the discovery rule (which Court does not decide), because in the instant case plaintiff's alleged repression did not occur until sometime after he had reached the age of majority, it would not in any case have prevented accrual of the action or the running of the one-year statute.

*Roman Catholic Diocese of Covington v. Secter,* 966 S.W.2d 286 (Ky.App.1998). Action against former teacher for CSA and church/school for negligence, by 34-year-old male plaintiff alleging Type 1 discovery of the injuries caused by the CSA and delayed discovery of the Church's negligence. Trial court dismissed action against teacher on limitations grounds, but held there were triable issues of fact as to whether plaintiff could reasonably have discovered the Diocese's negligence earlier and whether the Diocese obstructed plaintiff from obtaining information material to his discovery of the case. Trial judge gave limitations issue against Church to the jury, which returned verdict for plaintiff. Church appealed. *Held*: Under Rigazio plaintiff's Type 1 discovery of his injuries does not invoke the discovery rule. Although there is precedent in other states for extending the discovery rule to plaintiff's delayed discovery of the Church's negligence, Court declines to do so as a general principle. However, the evidence that the Church actively concealed information regarding its knowledge of the teacher's pedophilia invokes KRS 413.190(2) which provides that a statute of limitations may be tolled during the period in which the defendant conceals himself or obstructs the prosecution of the action.

*Analysis*

No CSA statute. Discovery rule is not invoked by Type 1 discovery. Court has not directly held that it is not invoked by Type 2, but has indicated a disinclination to extend discovery rule.

## *LOUISIANA*

Louisiana Stat. Ann. Rev., Title 9, Civil Code Ancillaries:

**Section 2800.9 Action against a person for abuse of a minor.**

(a) An action against a person for sexual abuse of a minor, or for physical abuse of a minor resulting in permanent impairment or permanent physical injury or scarring, is subject to a liberative prescriptive period of ten years. This prescription commences to run from the day the minor attains majority, and this prescription shall be suspended for all purposes until the minor reaches the age of majority. Abuse has the same meaning as provided in Louisiana Children's Code Article 603(1)(c). This prescriptive period shall be subject to any exception of peremption provided by law.

(b) Every plaintiff twenty-one years of age or older at the time the action is filed shall file certificates of merit executed by the attorney for the plaintiff and by a licensed mental health practitioner selected by the plaintiff declaring, respectively, as follows:

(1) That the attorney has reviewed the facts of the case, that the attorney has consulted with at least one licensed mental health practitioner who is licensed to practice and practices in this state and whom the attorney reasonably believes is knowledgeable of the relevant facts and issues involved in the particular action, and that the attorney has concluded on the basis of that review and consultation that there is reasonable and meritorious cause for the filing of the petition. The person consulted may not be a party to the litigation.

(2) That the mental health practitioner consulted is licensed to practice and practices in this state and is not a party to the action, has interviewed the plaintiff and is knowledgeable of the relevant facts and issues involved in the particular action, and has concluded, on the basis of his knowledge of the facts and issues, that in his professional opinion there is a reasonable basis to believe that the plaintiff has been subject to criminal sexual activity during his childhood as defined in this Section.

(3) That the attorney was unable to obtain the consultation required by Paragraph (1) because a statute of limitations would impair the action

and that the certificates required by Paragraphs (1) and (2) could not be obtained before the impairment of the action. If a certificate is executed pursuant to this Paragraph, the certificates required by Paragraphs (1) and (2) shall be filed within sixty days after filing the petition.

(c) Where certificates are required pursuant to Subsection B of this Section, separate certificates shall be filed for each defendant named in the complaint.

(d) A petition filed pursuant to Subsection B of this Section may not name the defendant or defendants until the court has reviewed the certificates or merit and has determined, in camera, based solely on those certificates of merit, that there is reasonable and meritorious cause for filing of the action. At that time, the petition may be amended to name the defendant or defendants. The duty to give notice to the defendant or defendants shall not attach until that time.

(e) A violation of Subsection B of this Section may constitute unprofessional conduct and may be the grounds for discipline against the attorney.

Note: Added by Acts 1993, No. 694, section 1; amended by Acts 1995, No. 503, section 1. The 1995 amendment added actions for severe physical abuse of minor to the causes of action governed by the statute.

***Reported Decisions***

*Bock v. Harmon,* 526 So.2d 292 (La.App.1988). Action filed by 20-year-old plaintiffs alleging Type 1 discovery, decided prior to CSA statute. *Held*: Psychological mechanisms caused by the CSA that inhibited plaintiff's ability to sue do not invoke the equitable doctrine of "contra non valentum" (the prescriptive period does not run against one unable to act).

*Doe v. Ainsworth,* 540 So.2d 425 (La.App.1989), writ den. Action filed by 26-year-old plaintiff alleging Type 1 discovery, decided prior to CSA statute. *Held*: "Contra non valentum" not invoked by psychological effects of CSA. Although plaintiff alleged defendant had used his position as minister to exercise psychic and spiritual control over plaintiff and prevent him from being able to act, the doctrine requires evidence that defendant took some affirmative action to prevent plaintiff from suing.

*Crosby v. Keys,* 590 So.2d 601 (La.App.1991), writ den. Action decided prior to CSA statute. *Held*: "Contra non valentum" not invoked by psychological effects of CSA.

*Held v. State Farm Ins. Co.,* 610 So.2d 1017 (La.App.1992), writ den. Action filed by 20-year-old plaintiff alleging Type 1 discovery, decided prior to CSA statute. *Held*: Diagnosis of PTSD plus evidence that parents had refused to pay for plaintiff's therapy, were sufficient to invoke the third type of situation to which the doctrine of "contra non valentum" may be applied, in which the plaintiff is unable to act due to defendant's having done some affirmative act to prevent plaintiff from suing. Court distinguished *Bock* and *Doe* as lacking evidence of any affirmative act by defendant to prevent plaintiff from suing.

*Wimberly v. Gatch*, 621 So.2d 633 (La.App.1993), writ grtd. Action filed prior to but decided after CSA statute, by parents on behalf of minor child, for CSA by neighbor. *Held*: Under prior law, one year prescriptive for personal injury actions was not suspended during plaintiff's minority. Although legislation effective 1993 provided for suspension of the prescriptive period during minority in actions for CSA, the legislation was not and could not be retroactive, as the right to be free of the claim had vested once the prior prescriptive period had expired. Therefore, the action is governed by the law in effect prior to the CSA statute. Under prior law, the doctrine of "contra non valentum" is not invoked by the psychological effects of the abuse, without defendant having taken some other action to prevent plaintiff from suing.

*Fontaine v. Roman Catholic Church,* 625 So.2d 548 (La.App.1993), writ den. Action filed prior to CSA statute but decided after, against priest for CSA and church-related defendants, by plaintiff alleging Type 1 discovery. *Held*: "Contra non valentum" is not applicable where there is no evidence that defendants took any action to prevent plaintiff from filing suit, or that plaintiff suffered from diagnosed PTSD or other disorder.

*Wimberly v. Gatch,* 635 So.2d 206 (La.1994). On appeal from decision of intermediate appellate court. *Held*: Judicial doctrine of "contra non valentum" is invoked by the normal reactions of a child to sexual abuse (the Child Sexual Abuse Accommodation Syndrome), and would suspend the prescriptive period during plaintiff's minority until the parents discovered the abuse.

*Wagoner v. Dyson*, 647 So.2d 493 (La.App.1994). Action filed prior to CSA statute by parents of minor victim of CSA, against special deputy sheriff (perpetrator) and parish sheriff (employer). *Held*: Judicial doctrine of "contra non valentum" suspended prescriptive period for parents until they knew of the child's abuse.

*Doe v. Roman Catholic Church,* 656 So.2d 5 (La.App.1995), writ den. Action filed prior to CSA statute by 43-year-old plaintiff alleging Type 2 discovery. Evidence established she had not totally repressed the abuse, and had begun to remember some of it more than a year before filing. *Held*: Judicial doctrine of "contra non valentum" can by invoked by plaintiff's repressed memory of the abuse. Doctrine not applicable in the present case because plaintiff discussed the abuse with her therapist and some family members more than one year before filing, and was not prevented from pursuing claim by any act of defendant.

*Harrison v. Gore*, 660 So.2d 563 (La.App.1995), writ. den. Action filed prior to CSA statute by 25-year-old plaintiff alleging Type 1 discovery. *Held*: CSA statute not retroactive to revive previously barred action. Under prior law, judicial doctrine of "contra non valentum" is not invoked for delayed discovery where there is no evidence of a diagnosed psychological dysfunction sufficient to toll the statute.

*Doe v. Doe*, 671 So.2d 466 (La.App.1995), writ.den. Action filed prior to CSA statute by Type 1 plaintiff. *Held*: CSA statute not retroactive to revive previously barred action. "Contra non valentum" not invoked for delayed discovery based on plaintiff's personal, subjective disability. Plaintiff's alleged inability to make the connection between the abuse and his injuries was subjective in nature.

*Landreneau v. Fruge*, 676 So.2d 701 (La.App.1996). Action by teenager and her mother against teacher for CSA and others for negligence in permitting and encouraging it. *Held*: Action based on CSA had prescribed and was not subject to delayed accrual for plaintiff's emotional problems.

*G.B.F. v. Keys*, 687 So.2d 632 (La.App.1997). 20-year-old plaintiff sued former Boy Scout leader for CSA and organization for negligence. *Held*: CSA statute permitting 10-year prescriptive period for CSA cannot be applied retroactively to revive an action that had already lapsed under the prior law. Under judicial doctrine of "contra non valentum" the psychological effects of the abuse, without more, do not suspend the running of prescriptive period once plaintiff had become an adult (distinguishing *Wimberly v. Gatch* where prescriptive period was suspended by the CSA Accommodation Syndrome during the plaintiff's minority).

### *Analysis*

CSA statute provides ten years from majority, without exception for or requirement of discovery accrual.

Under prior law, the judicial doctrine of "contra non valentum" has been held unable to suspend the running of limitations period past the plaintiff's minority for Type 1 discovery, unless the defendant had done some other affirmative act to prevent the plaintiff from being able to sue. Court has indicated that the prescriptive period might be suspended for Type 2 discovery.

Statute has no express language of revival and has been held not constitutionally able to revive lapsed actions.

Statute applies to actions "against a person for sexual abuse of a minor." Issue has not been interpreted.

## *MAINE*

Maine Rev. Stat. Ann., Title 14, Court Procedure-Civil:

**Section 752-C: Sexual acts towards minors.**

Actions based upon sexual intercourse, as defined in Title 17-A, section 556, subsection 1-B, or a sexual act, as defined in Title 17-A, chapter 11, with a person under the age of majority must be commenced within 12 years after the cause of action accrues, or within 6 years of the time the person discovers or reasonably should have discovered the harm, whichever occurs later.

Note: Added Laws 1985, ch. 343, s. 1. Amended 1989, ch. 292; 1991, ch. 551, s. 1; 1993, ch. 176, s. 1. Original statute provided 6 years from accrual; 1989 amendment added 3 years from discovery; 1991 amendment extended time to 12 years from accrual or 6 years from discovery, and expressly provided the amendment would apply prospectively only; 1993 amendment provided the definition of sexual intercourse in Title 17-A, section 556, subsection 1-B would be applicable.

***Reported Decisions***

*Archibald v. Archibald*, 826 F.Supp. 26 (D.Me.1993). Action filed in state court and removed to federal by defendant, dismissed for lack of in personam jurisdiction without addressing limitations issue.

*Carlson v. Rice,* 832 F.Supp. 17 (D.Me.1993). Action filed after CSA statute, by plaintiff alleging Type 2 discovery. *Held*: Allegations of repressed memory and an inability to engage in usual activities are sufficient to raise triable issue of material fact regarding tolling for mental illness. Court did not rely upon repression alone, but stated that all the allegations taken together indicated the effects of the abuse itself had rendered plaintiff unable to comprehend and exercise her legal rights. Court declined to address whether the discovery provision in the CSA statute would apply.

*McAfee v. Cole*, 637 A.2d 463 (Me.1994). Action filed after CSA statute by plaintiff alleging Type 2 discovery. *Held*: CSA statute as amended in 1989 and 1991 to provide for discovery accrual, expressly applies only to actions for which the claim has not yet been barred by the previous statute of limitations, and thus does not revive actions that had previously lapsed. Court declines to fashion a judicial discovery rule applicable to CSA actions. Plaintiff did not preserve the issue of tolling for mental illness.

*Nuccio v. Nuccio* (1st Cir.1995) 62 F.3d 14. Federal circuit court certified question to Maine Supreme Court: Whether court would apply equitable estoppel to toll statute where plaintiff alleged defendant's conduct had caused her to repress memory of the abuse.

*Harkness v. Fitzgerald*, 701 A.2d 370 (Me.1997). 34-year-old plaintiff sued parents for CSA and intentional and negligent infliction of emotional distress alleging that although she had always known her parents had physically and emotionally abused her she had not remembered the sexual abuse until within six years of filing her action. *Held*: CSA statute being prospective only, it did not apply to plaintiff's actions which had lapsed before it had become effective. Facts did not come within the 6-year statute for actions that have been fraudulently concealed.

### *Analysis*

CSA statute provides twelve years from accrual or six years from the time plaintiff discovers or reasonably should have discovered the harm, whichever occurs later. Unclear whether statutory language applies to Type 1 discovery, and issue has not been interpreted.

Statute expressly prospective only. Court has declined to apply judicial discovery rule or other equitable exception applicable to CSA.

Statute applies to actions "based on" CSA. Issue has not been interpreted.

## *MARYLAND*

No CSA statute. Ann. Code Maryland, Courts & Judicial Proceedings, Title 5, Limitations, section 5-105 provides one year for assault. Section 5-101 provides three years for anything not covered by other sections. Section 5-201 tolls for minority and mental incompetency. Section 5-203 provides discovery accrual where knowledge of the cause of action is kept from plaintiff by the fraud of an adverse party.

### *Reported Decisions*

*Doe v. Maskell*, 342 Md. 684, 679 A.2d 1087 (Md.1996). Action by Type 2 plaintiffs against Catholic priest and school. *Held*: The applicable statute is 5-101 providing three years from accrual. Alleged repression of memory is insufficient to invoke the discovery rule or tolling for mental incompetence, because there is insufficient scientific evidence to support the theory that a special psychological mechanism of repression, separate and apart from ordinary forgetting, can be caused by CSA.

*Doe v. Archdiocese of Washington*, 114 Md.App. 169, 689 A.2d 634 (Md.App.1997). 35-year-old former altar boy sued priests and Church for CSA, intentional and negligent infliction of emotional distress, and fraudulent concealment, alleging Type 1 discovery. *Held*: Judicial discovery rule not applicable to Type 1 discovery of the wrongfulness of the acts or their long-term damaging effects.

*Murphy v. Merzbacher*, 346 Md. 525, 697 A.2d 861 (Md.1997). Former students of Catholic middle school, in their thirties, sued for CSA that had occurred in the 1970s.

Plaintiffs alleged that death threats and similar duress by offending priest should equitably estop the limitations defense. *Held*: Although threats as described could create an estoppel, the estoppel would only last until the cessation of the intimidating conduct, and the plaintiff must then bring the action within three years.

### *Analysis*

No CSA statute. Court has refused to apply discovery rule or tolling for mental disability to either Type 2 or Type 1 discovery. No tolling for duress past the cessation of the intimidating conduct.

## *MASSACHUSETTS*

Ann. Laws of Massachusetts, Part 3, Courts and Proceedings, Title V, Statutes of Frauds and Limitations, Chapter 260, Limitations of Actions:

**Section 4C: Sexual abuse of minors.**

Actions for assault and battery alleging the defendant sexually abused a minor shall be commenced within three years of the acts alleged to have caused an injury or condition or within three years of the time the victim discovered or reasonably should have discovered that an emotional or psychological injury or condition was caused by said act, whichever period expires later; provided, however, that the time limit for commencement of an action under this section is tolled for a child until the child reaches eighteen years of age.

For purposes of this section, "sexual abuse" shall mean the commission of any act against a minor as set forth in section thirteen B, thirteen H, twenty-two, twenty-two A, twenty-three, twenty-four or twenty-four B of chapter two hundred and sixty-five or section two, three, four, fourA, fourB, seven, eight, thirteen, seventeen, twenty-nine A, thirty-four, thirty-five or thirty-five A of chapter two hundred and seventy-two.

Note: Added by St. 1993, c. 307.

### *Reported Decisions*

*Hoult v. Hoult*, 792 F.Supp. 143 (D.Mass.1992). Action decided prior to CSA statute by plaintiff alleging Type 2 discovery. *Held*: Massachusetts would apply discovery accrual to Type 2 case.

*Phinney v. Morgan*, 39 Mass.App. 202, 654 N.E.2d 77 (Mass.App.1995). Action against mother for negligence in permitting CSA to occur, filed prior to but decided after CSA statute, alleging Type 1 discovery of the abuse and the negligence. *Held*: CSA statute applicable only to claims against perpetrator. Actions against non-perpetrator governed by 3-year statute for tort actions, subject to judicial discovery rule. Facts establish that plaintiffs discovered or should have discovered their claims more than three years before filing.

*Flanagan v. Grant*, 897 F.Supp. 637 (D.Mass.1995). Action filed prior to effective date of CSA statute but decided after, by plaintiff alleging Type 1 discovery. *Held*: Three-year statute for tort claims applies, subject to judicial discovery rule. Whether Type 1 or Type 2 discovery alleged, Under discovery rule the question is whether the delay was reasonable. In Type 1, the question is whether plaintiff was actually and reasonably delayed in making the connection between the abuse and some injury. In instant case plaintiff had been "intellectually aware" of the connection more than three years before filing. Alleged inability to connect the two "emotionally" until later would not further delay statute.

### *Analysis*

CSA statute provides three years from time plaintiff discovers or reasonably should have discovered that an emotional or psychological injury or condition was caused by the CSA. Has been held to be a codification of judicial discovery rule. Has been held applicable theoretically to both Type 1 and Type 2 discovery, but an emotional inability to connect the injury to the abuse has been held unable to delay accrual if plaintiff had knowledge of the abuse.

Statute has no language of revival, but the court has held the judicial discovery rule applicable.

Statute applies to actions "for assault and battery alleging the defendant sexually abused a minor," and has been held not to apply to actions against non-perpetrators. However, actions against non-perpetrators for negligence are also governed by a three-year statute, subject to the judicial discovery rule.

## *MICHIGAN*

No CSA statute. Michigan Stat. Ann., Title 27A, Judicial System and Procedure, section 27A.5805, provides two years for battery and three years for all other actions to recover damages for injury to a person. Section 27A.5851 tolls for minority or insanity, and provides that an action must be brought within one year of removal of the disability.

***Reported Decisions***

*Meiers-Post v. Schafer*, 170 Mich.App. 174, 427 N.W.2d 606 (Mich.App.1988). 30-year-old plaintiff sued former high school teacher, alleging facts that could constitute either Type 1 or Type 2 discovery. Teacher's confession was in evidence. *Held*: Three-year statute applies, and is tolled where there is evidence that plaintiff repressed memory of the facts upon which the claim is based, and objective corroboration that the abuse occurred.

*Nicolette v. Carey,* 751 F.Supp. 695 (W.D.Mich.1990). 31-year-old plaintiff sued father alleging Type 2 discovery. Plaintiff had remembered one incident more than three years before filing, but claimed that she did not remember more until within one year of filing, and that she had been mentally disabled by depression and PTSD. Plaintiff also submitted a letter from defendant containing admissions to some incidents. *Held*: Evidence of repression of most incidents until within three years, plus mental disability, plus some corroboration, fulfilled *Meiers-Post* and precluded summary judgment.

*Lemmerman v. Fealk,* 201 Mich.App. 544, 507 N.W.2d 226 (Mich.App.1993), writ grtd. 54-year-old plaintiff sued father's estate, mother and aunt, alleging Type 2 discovery, without corroboration. *Held*: Discovery rule applies to actions for CSA and does not require corroborating evidence. Evidence of PTSD and other mental disability caused by the abuse raises triable issue of material fact regarding tolling of statute for insanity.

*Lemmerman v. Fealk,* 449 Mich. 56, 534 N.W.2d 695 (Mich.1995). Supreme Court reversed appellate court's decision. *Held*: Neither disability exception nor discovery rule will delay the limitations period for CSA actions, even with corroborative evidence. Although court appears to have overruled prior decisions, by holding that the period would not be tolled "even upon presentation of allegedly 'objective and verifiable evidence' of a plaintiff's claim," the court also stated in a footnote that it did not address *Meiers-Post* and *Nicolette,* where "express and unequivocal admissions" took the cases "outside the arena of stale, unverifiable claims with which we are concerned in the present cases." Court stated that the Legislature was a more appropriate forum for resolving the competing concerns relating to delayed suits for CSA.

*Guerra v. Garratt,* 222 Mich.App. 285, 564 N.W.2d 121 (Mich.App.1997). 32-year-old plaintiff sued former teacher and teacher's housemate for CSA and infliction of emotional distress, alleging Type 2 discovery. *Held*: Following *Lemmerman,* neither discovery rule nor exception for insanity based on alleged repression will delay running of limitations period for CSA. The reference in *Lemmerman* to former cases where there were express admissions addressed the issue of the retroactivity of the ruling, and did not carve out a general exception for such cases.

*Analysis*

No CSA statute. Under *Lemmerman* (1995) neither discovery rule nor tolling for mental disability are applicable to Type 1 or Type 2 actions.

## MINNESOTA

Minnesota Stat. Ann., Part IV, Redress of Civil Injuries, Chapter 541, Limitation of Time:

**Section 541.073: Actions for damages due to sexual abuse; special provisions.**

Subd. 1. Definition. As used in this section, "sexual abuse" means conduct described in sections 609.342 to 609.345.

Subd. 2. Limitations period.

(a) An action for damages based on personal injury caused by sexual abuse must be commenced within six years of the time the plaintiff knew or had reason to know that the injury was caused by the sexual abuse.

(b) The plaintiff need not establish which act in a continuous series of sexual abuse acts by the defendant caused the injury.

(c) The knowledge of a parent or guardian may not be imputed to a minor.

(d) This section does not affect the suspension of the statute of limitations during a period of disability under section 541.15.

Subd. 3. Applicability. This section applies to an action for damages commenced against a person who caused the plaintiff's personal injury either by (1) committing the sexual abuse against the plaintiff, or (2) negligently permitting sexual abuse against the plaintiff to occur.

Note: Added by Laws 1989, ch. 190, s. 2. Amended Laws 1991, ch. 232, s. 1; Laws 1992, ch. 571, art. 12, s. 2. 1989 statute expressly applied to actions pending on or commenced on or after May 20, 1989, but required plaintiffs whose claims had expired under prior law to file before August 1990 and to establish that they had consulted with an attorney within two years of discovery. The 1991 amendment added the "applicability" subsection expressly referring to actions against persons negligently permitting the abuse to occur. The 1991 amendment provided that a plaintiff whose action would have been time-barred under the 1989 statute had until August 1992 to file suit.

***Reported Decisions***

*K.E. v. Hoffmann* (Minn.App.1990) 452 N.W.2d 509, rev. den. Action filed prior to but decided after 1989 statute, by 22-year-old plaintiff alleging Type 2 discovery of CSA by former elementary school teacher, and asserting causes of action against teacher and against school for negligence. *Held*: Express language in 1989 statute, that it applies to "all cases pending" as well as those filed after its effective date, shows Legislature's intent to revive actions that had lapsed under prior law, and such revival is not unconstitutional. Issue of whether statute applies to causes of action against non-perpetrator was apparently not raised.

*H.D. v. White* (Minn.App.1992) 483 N.W.2d 501. Action filed prior to 1989 statute, decided after 1991 amendment. *Held*: One-year window period enacted in 1991 applied only to actions that would not be barred under the six-year limitations period enacted by the same legislation.

*ABC v. Archdiocese of St. Paul* (Minn.App.1994) 513 N.W.2d 482. Action filed in 1991 alleging Type 1 discovery. Priest had allegedly begun sexual relationship with plaintiff when she was 15 and had continued into her early adulthood. Plaintiff claimed she had not realized it was abuse and caused her injuries until later. *Held*: The "reason-to-know" language in the discovery provision of the CSA statute requires that discovery of the causal connection between the CSA and the abuse must be deemed to have occurred when a reasonable person would have been able to make such discovery, applying an objective reasonable person standard rather than the subjective standard of plaintiff's own mental or emotional state. Evidence that plaintiff had disclosed the abuse and its effects to family and friends more than six years before filing defeated claim of reasonable delay.

*Roe v. Archdiocese of St. Paul* (Minn.App.1994) 518 N.W.2d 629, rev.den. Action filed in 1992 by plaintiff alleging Type 2 discovery. Evidence showed plaintiff had been aware of the abuse and had realized it was wrong, but had subsequently suppressed or repressed her memory. *Held*: Under objective reasonable person standard, plaintiff who had awareness of abuse and injury for many years after the abuse had ended, but subsequently repressed memory of the abuse, was barred.

*Park v. Gravett* (Minn.App.1994) 521 N.W.2d 376. Action filed in 1992 under window provision of 1991 amendment. *Held*: Window provision applied to revive action which was less than six years old as of the effective date of the 1989 statute.

*Blackowiak v. Kemp* (Mich.App.1995) 528 N.W.2d 247, rev.grtd. Action filed in 1992. Plaintiff did not claim complete repression of awareness of the abuse, but that he did not think about it nor disclose it to anyone until 1991, when a former classmate's disclosure that he had been abused by the same teacher triggered plaintiff's awareness that the abuse had probably caused many of his own behavioral problems. *Held*: Distinguishing *ABC* and *Roe,* there is no evidence establishing as a matter of law that plaintiff was or reasonably should have been aware of some injury caused by the abuse more than six years before filing. Question of material fact exists precluding summary judgment.

*Oelschlager v. Magnuson* (Minn.App.1995) 528 N.W.2d 895, rev.den. Action filed in 1991, against pastor for CSA and Church for negligence and vicarious liability. *Held*: CSA statute expressly applies to actions against persons who cause injury either by committing abuse or negligently permitting abuse to occur, and thus by implication does not apply to actions premised on mere vicarious liability.

*Green v. Sawdey* (Minn.App.1995) 529 N.W.2d 520, rev.den. Action filed in 1993 by Type 1 plaintiff who had disclosed the abuse to a fiancé and to her husband more than six years before filing suit. *Held*: As matter of law plaintiff reasonably should have known of her injury at the time of her earlier disclosures.

*M.L. v. Magnuson* (Minn.App.1995) 531 N.W.2d 849, rev.den. Action against pastor for CSA and Church for negligence and vicarious liability. *Held*: CSA statute does not apply to actions against employer for vicarious liability. Evidence supported jury's finding that plaintiff did not have "reason to know" his injuries were the result of sexual abuse until within the statutory period, in that plaintiff testified his memories of abuse did not surface until he saw a news report about others complaining of abuse by the same priest, and there was expert testimony that he had not been able to appreciate the connection until then.

*Doe v. Redeemer Lutheran Church* (Minn.App.1995) 531 N.W.2d 897, rev.grtd. Action filed in 1991 against pastor for CSA and Church for negligence and vicarious liability, alleging Type 1 discovery. *Held*: Two-part inquiry to determine accrual: (1) when reasonable person in plaintiff's position would be aware that the sexual contact was abusive, and (2) when reasonable person in plaintiff's position would be aware that the abuse caused his or her injuries. Issue is normally one of fact. Evidence supported jury's finding that plaintiff, who was abused as teenager but suffered relatively "intangible" injuries such as alcoholism, social phobia, panic attacks and depression, and did not disclose the abuse to others until within limitations period, had been reasonably delayed in recognizing that the abuse had caused his injuries.

*S.E. v. Shattuck-St. Mary's School* (Minn.App.1995) 533 N.W.2d 628, rev.den. Action filed in 1993 against former teacher for CSA and school for vicarious liability, alleging Type 1 discovery. *Held*: Evidence that plaintiff avoided defendant after the abuse, knew that it had hurt him emotionally, thought of it when bad things happened to him, and engaged in abusive behavior himself as a result of it, plus lack of expert testimony indicating plaintiff was unable to make the connection until later, established that plaintiff objectively had "reason to know" that the abuse had caused him injury. Summary judgment for defendants affirmed.

*K.B. v. Evangelical Lutheran Church* (Minn.App.1995) 538 N.W.2d 152. 40-year-old plaintiff sued pastor and Church alleging Type 1 discovery. Priest initiated sexual contact when plaintiff was 12. Relationship had continued until plaintiff was age 18, when priest was transferred. Plaintiff had disclosed the relationship to others in her twenties, and in her thirties disclosed it to therapist during psychological treatment, more than six years before filing. *Held*: Plaintiff's disclosures demonstrate that she had awareness that what had happened was abuse, and had enough information to have reasonably been aware that she had been injured by the abuse, more than six years before filing.

*Winkler v. Magnuson* (Minn.App.1995) 539 N.W.2d 821. 38-year-old male plaintiff sued pastor and Church alleging Type 1 discovery. Abuse began when plaintiff was 13 and ended when he ran away from his foster home at age 16. Plaintiff did not disclose it to anyone until, within three years of filing, he disclosed it to his brother and learned that his brother had also been molested by the priest. *Held*: Plaintiff's claim that he had not reasonably been able to connect the abuse to his injuries until later, supported by undisputed evidence that he had not disclosed the abuse to anyone until within three years of filing and evidence that the abuse had caused him to believe he was homosexual, raises question of fact that precludes summary judgment on cause of action for CSA. CSA statute does not apply to actions based on vicarious liability. Claims of negligence against Church are governed by the statute, but summary judgment upheld on grounds plaintiff had produced no evidence of negligence.

*Blackowiak v. Kemp* (Minn.1996) 546 N.W.2d 1 (*Blackowiak II*). Supreme court reversed appellate court decision that had held that plaintiff's claim of Type 1 discovery raised a question of fact precluding summary judgment. *Held*: Because the nature of criminal sexual conduct is such that an intent to injure can be inferred as a matter of law, the concepts of sexual abuse and injury are one and the same in the law. Statutory period begins to run when plaintiff knows or "has reason to know" that he was injured by the abuse. Objective reasonable person standard required. Knowledge that one was sexually abused is reason to know that one was injured. Dissent says majority decision is semantic and ignores both the literal meaning of the statute and its apparent intent to permit Type 1 discovery.

*Sarafolean v. Kauffman* (Minn.App.1996) 547 N.W.2d 417, rev.den. Action against adoptive father for CSA, adoptive mother and county for negligence. *Held*: Claim for CSA time-barred because not filed within window period provided in CSA statute. Claims against county based on vicarious liability not subject to delayed discovery. Insufficient evidence to support claims of negligence against social worker and mother.

*Scheffler v. Archdiocese of St. Paul and Minneapolis* (Minn.App.1997) 563 N.W.2d 767. 27-year-old male plaintiff sued priest and Church alleging priest abused him at age 14 and that he had not understood it as abuse or connected it to his adult psychological problems until within six years of filing. *Held*: Under *Blackowiak II,* as a matter of law a reasonable person in plaintiff's situation would have known that he was injured by the abuse.

*W.J.L. v. Bugge* (Minn.1998) 573 N.W.2d 677. Female plaintiff in mid-thirties sued former female high school teacher for CSA, alleging Type 1 discovery of the causal connection between the abuse and psychological problems in her adult life. *Held*: Following *Blackowiak II,* because CSA involves both physical and emotional injury at the time, under the "knew or had reason to know" language of the CSA statute an objectively reasonable person would have had reason to know of the injury and its cause at the time of the CSA, and thus accrual cannot be delayed by the psychological effects of the CSA unless these include a mental disability such as repressed memory. As in *Blackowiak II,* Justice Gardebring strongly dissents that this interpretation goes against the intent of the CSA statute. Justice Gardebring's dissent is joined by Justice Blatz.

*J.J. v. Luckow* (Minn.App.1998) 578 N.W.2d 17. Action by 24-year-old plaintiff alleging Type 1 discovery. *Held*: Per *Blackowiak II* and *W.J.L.*, emotional and psychological injuries or conditions caused by the abuse but falling short of repression do not delay accrual, as knowledge of the abuse is knowledge of injury as a matter of law.

### *Analysis*

CSA statute provides six years from discovery accrual, defined as knowing or "having reason to know" that the injury was caused by the abuse. Under *Blackowiak II* (1996), the "reason to know" language in the CSA statute requires application of an objective reasonable person standard, pursuant to which knowledge of the abuse constitutes knowledge of resulting injury as a matter of law. This reasoning effectively negates the possibility of delayed accrual for Type 1 discovery.

Statute expressly revived lapsed actions commenced before August 1992. Court has held actions filed after 1992 not subject to revival.

Statute expressly applies to actions for negligently permitting the abuse to occur. Has been held not to apply to vicarious liability.

## *MISSISSIPPI*

No CSA statute. Mississippi Code Ann., Title 15, Limitations of Actions, section 15-1-35 provides one-year for assault and battery and other personal injury.

### *Reported Decisions*

*Tichenor v. Roman Catholic Church* (5th Cir.1994) 32 F.3d 953. Plaintiff alleging Type 1 discovery. *Held*: Under Mississippi law discovery rule does not apply to actions for which a limitations period is prescribed unless the action involves latent injury or disease. Plaintiff's inability to recognize the injury caused by the sexual abuse was insufficient to constitute the kind of "inherently unknowable" harm that would trigger application of the discovery rule.

### *Analysis*

No CSA statute. Judicial discovery rule has been held not applicable to Type 1. Applicability to Type 2 has not been addressed.

## *MISSOURI*

Ann. Missouri Stat., Chapter 516, Statutes of Limitations, and Chapter 537, Statutory Actions and Torts:

**Section 516.371: Limitation on action for sexual contact by certain persons.**

Notwithstanding any provision of law to the contrary, there shall be a ten-year statute of limitations on any action for damages for personal injury caused to an individual by a person within the third degree of affinity or consanguinity who subjects such individual to sexual contact, as defined in section 566.010, RSMo.

Note: Added by Laws 1989, S.B. No. 420, sec. A, Sec. 1.

**Section 537.046: Childhood sexual abuse, injuries or illness defined - action for damages may be brought when.**

(1) As used in this section, the following terms mean:

(a) "Childhood sexual abuse," any act committed by the defendant against the plaintiff which act occurred when the plaintiff was under the age of eighteen years and which act would have been a violation of section 566.030, 566.040, 566.050, 566.060, 566.070, 566.080, 566.090, 566.100, 566.110, or 566.120, RSMo.

(b) "Injury or illness," either a physical injury or illness or a psychological injury or illness. A psychological injury or illness need not be accompanied by a physical injury or illness.

(2) In any civil action for recovery of damages suffered as a result of childhood sexual abuse, the time for commencement of the action shall be within five years of the date the plaintiff attains the age of majority or within three years of the date the plaintiff discovers or reasonably should have discovered that the injury or illness was caused by the sexual abuse, whichever later occurs.

(3) This section shall apply to any action commenced on or after August 28, 1990, including any action which would have been barred by the application of the statute of limitation applicable prior to that date.

Note: Added by Laws 1990, H.B. No. 1370, 1037 & 1084, section A, section 3.

***Reported Decisions***

*J.D. v. M.F.* (Mo.App.1988) 758 S.W.2d 177. Action filed and decided prior to CSA statute. *Held*: CSA action is governed either by two-year statute for assault and battery or five-year statute for torts not specifically provided for by name. Delayed accrual or tolling not addressed.

*Doe v. Roman Catholic Diocese of Jefferson City* (Mo.1993) 862 S.W.2d 338. Action filed after CSA statute. *Held*: CSA statute's provision for revival is unconstitutional violation of due process. Expiration of former limitations periods created vested right to repose.

*Vandenheuvel v. Sowell* (Mo.App.1994) 886 S.W.2d 100, rev. den. Action filed after CSA statute by 48-year-old Type 2 plaintiff against deceased father's estate. *Held*: Action had become barred under two-year statute for assault and battery prior to CSA statute's enactment, and under *Doe* was not revived. Accrual of action is not delayed by repressed memory of the abuse, as section 516.100 provides that an action accrues when resulting damage is sustained and "capable of ascertainment," regardless of whether plaintiff is subjectively able to ascertain it.

*Swartz v. Swartz* (Mo.App.1994) 887 S.W.2d 644, rev. den. Action filed after CSA statutes by 24-year-old Type 1 plaintiff. Plaintiff attempted to bring action within five-year statute for tort actions not otherwise provided for by alleging that defendant negligently permitted himself to be in her presence when he knew of his propensities, and that mother negligently permitted the abuse to occur. *Held*: Action is timely as filed within five years of majority. Although section 516.371, enacted in 1989, shortened this period by enacting a 10-year outer time limit on actions for injuries caused by a relative who subjects a child to sexual abuse, a statute which shortens a limitations period may not be applied retroactively unless it permits those affected by it a reasonable period of time within which to file suit.

*Sheehan v. Sheehan* (Mo.1995) 901 S.W.2d 57. Action filed after CSA statute by 28-year-old plaintiff alleging Type 2 discovery. *Held*: CSA statute is prospective only. The action is therefore governed by the two-year statute for assault and battery. However, section 516.100 provides that the limitations period for a civil wrong does not necessarily begin to run when the wrong is done, but begins to run when the resulting injury is sustained or objectively ascertainable. The pleading as to repressed memory of the abuse raises a triable issue regarding when the injuries were sustained or objectively ascertainable. Therefore, judgment on the pleadings must be reversed. The court distinguishes *Vandenheuvel* as involving a motion for summary judgment, in which the court could consider evidence outside the pleadings on the issue of objective ascertainability. The dissent argues that the majority is implicitly departing from an objective standard regarding ascertainability of damage.

*L.M.S. v. N.M. and V.P.* (Mo.App.1995) 911 S.W.2d 703. 29-year-old plaintiff sued parents alleging Type 2 discovery within one year of filing. *Held*: Following *Sheehan,* there is a question of fact as to whether the injuries were objectively ascertainable before the plaintiff recovered her memories. Therefore, dismissal on the pleadings must be reversed.

*H.R.B. v. J.L.G. et al.* (Mo.App.1995) 913 S.W.2d 92. 44-year-old man sues priest and Church alleging facts which could be construed as including Type 2 discovery. *Held*: Pursuant to *Sheehan,* dismissal on pleadings as to priest must be reversed, as pleaded allegations create a triable issue as to when the injuries were objectively ascertainable.

*Hehner v. Hehner* (Mo.App.1996) 918 S.W.2d 283. 38-year-old man sued parents for CSA and infliction of emotional distress, alleging Type 2 discovery approximately 4 years before filing the action. Plaintiff had filed an action earlier, within three years of alleged discovery, and had dismissed it voluntarily without prejudice to refiling. *Held*: Provision allowing tolling if action refiled within one year applies only to specific statutes of limitations, not including the one involved here.

*K.G. v. R.T.R.* (Mo.1996) 918 S.W.2d 795. 28-year-old female sued father alleging Type 2 discovery. *Held*: Because plaintiff alleged repression until 1993, it is possible that her cause of action for assault and battery did not accrue, and thus did not expire, until after enactment of CSA statute, thereby enabling the CSA statute to apply. Even so, the action is barred by the 10-year statute of repose and by the three-years-from-discovery provision of the CSA statute.

*Analysis*

CSA statutes provide five years from majority or three years from reasonable discovery that the injury was caused by the sexual abuse, with a ten year statute of repose on actions against a relative. Statutory discovery language appears to apply to Type 1, but issue has not been interpreted.

Express language of revival has been held unconstitutional, hence CSA statute not applicable to actions that had expired under prior law. Prior to 1990, CSA actions were governed by two-year statute for assault and battery. Accrual of assault and battery action occurs when injury is sustained or is objectively ascertainable. Appellate decisions have been split on whether repressed memory can delay objective ascertainability.

Statute of repose on actions against relative is subject to requirement that plaintiffs have a reasonable window period in which to file.

Statute applies to actions "for recovery of damages suffered as a result of" CSA; applicability issue has not been interpreted.

## *MONTANA*

Montana Code Ann., Title 27, Civil Liability, Remedies and Limitations, Chapter 2, Statutes of Limitations:

**Section 27-2-216: Tort actions-childhood sexual abuse.**

(1) An action based on intentional conduct brought by a person for recovery of damages for injury suffered as a result of childhood sexual abuse must be commenced not later than:

(a) 3 years after the act of childhood sexual abuse that is alleged to have caused the injury; or

(b) 3 years after the plaintiff discovers or reasonably should have discovered that the injury was caused by the act of childhood sexual abuse.

(2) It is not necessary for a plaintiff to establish which act, in a series of acts of childhood sexual abuse, caused the injury that is the subject of the suit. The plaintiff may compute the period referred to in subsection (1)(a) from the date of the last act by the same perpetrator.

(3) As used in this section, "childhood sexual abuse" means any act committed against a plaintiff who was less than 18 years of age at the time the act occurred and that would have been a violation of 45-5-502, 45-5-503, 45-5-504, 45-5-505, 45-5-507, 45-5-625, or prior similar laws in effect at the time the act occurred.

(4) The provisions of 27-2-401 apply to this section.

Note: Enacted Laws 1989, ch. 158, s. 2. Section 5 provided the act applied to all actions commenced on or after October 1, 1989, regardless of when the cause of action arose, and was to this extent retroactive.

***Reported Decisions***

*E.W. v. D.C.H.* (Mont.1988) 754 P.2d 817. Action by 34-year-old plaintiff alleging Type 1 discovery, filed and decided prior to CSA statute. *Held*: Judicial discovery accrual not applicable where plaintiff always knew the abuse had occurred.

*Cosgriffe v. Cosgriffe* (Mont.1993) 864 P.2d 776. Action filed after CSA statute by 41-year-old plaintiff alleging Type 1 discovery. *Held*: Express language of revival is valid, does not violate due process. Statutory discovery accrual provision applies to Type 1 discovery.

*Were v. David* (Mont.1996) 913 P.2d 635. Adult daughter in forties sued stepfather's estate for CSA and mother for negligence in failure to protect her from it, alleging Type 1 discovery of the causal connection between the abuse and her adult psychological injuries within three years of filing the action. Verdict for plaintiff after trial. Defendant appealed on limitations and other grounds. *Held*: (1) CSA statute applies to Type 1 discovery. Under CSA statute plaintiff's action is timely if filed within three years of the time she discovered or reasonably should have discovered the connection between the abuse and her mental disorders. Evidence in record, that she disclosed to therapist and others more than three years before filing, but was only diagnosed with PTSD within three years of filing, could give rise to conflicting inferences regarding whether plaintiff reasonably should have discovered her action more than three years before she filed. It was within the province of the jury as trier of fact to find for plaintiff on this issue. (2) CSA statute governs causes of action for third-party negligence that are based on the CSA. CSA statute governs actions "based on" intentional conduct. This does not preclude its applicability to actions against third-parties for negligence that contributed to the occurrence of the abuse. Such an action may be said to be "based on" the intentional CSA in the sense of founded upon or resting upon, as the action for negligence would not come into existence without the occurrence of the CSA.

***Analysis***

CSA statute provides three years from time plaintiff discovers or reasonably should have discovered that the injury was caused by the CSA. Has been held to apply to Type 1 discovery.

Statute has language of revival which has been upheld.

Statute applies to actions "based on" intentional conduct. Court has held that actions against third parties for negligence that contributed to the occurrence of the CSA are "based on" the CSA and thus governed by the statute.

## *NEBRASKA*

No CSA statute. Rev. Stat. Nebraska, Chapter 25, Civil Procedure, section 25-208 provides one year for assault and battery, and section 25-213 tolls for minority (under age 20) or mental disability.

### *Reported Decisions*

*Teater v. State of Nebraska* (Neb.1997) 252 Neb. 20, 559 N.W.2d 758. 36-year-old plaintiff sued State for damages resulting from negligence of DSS in permitting her to be sexually abused while in foster care. Plaintiff had complained and been removed from the foster placement at age 14. She claimed not to have been able to discover her cause of action until she discovered that, contrary to what her foster father had told her, his early petition to adopt her had not been granted, thus making the State liable for her continued placement in his care. Also that she had been prevented by a mental disorder from being able to understand her right to maintain the action. *Held*: Discovery rule does not delay accrual until one has discovered the identity of the legally responsible party, but runs when one has knowledge of one's injury. Evidence insufficient to establish plaintiff had been prevented by a mental disorder.

### *Analysis*

No CSA statute. Whether judicial discovery rule would be applied to Type 1 or Type 2 discovery of CSA has not yet been addressed.

## *NEVADA*

Nevada Rev. Stat. Ann., Title 2, Civil Practice, Chapter 11, Limitation of Actions:

**Section 11.215: Actions for damages for injury arising from sexual abuse of minor.**

(1) Except as otherwise provided in NRS 217.007, an action to recover damages for an injury to a person arising from the sexual abuse of the plaintiff

which occurred when the plaintiff was less than 18 years of age must be commenced within 10 years after the plaintiff:

(a) Reaches 18 years of age; or

(b) Discovers or reasonably should have discovered that his injury was caused by the sexual abuse, whichever occurs later.

(2) As used in this section, "sexual abuse" has the meaning ascribed to it in NRS 432B.100.

Note: Enacted 1991, ch. 58, s. 1, p. 117. Amended 1993, ch. 143, s. 1, p. 254; 1993, ch. 212, ss. 4 & 5, pp. 455, 456. The 1993 amendments changed the limitations period from three years to ten years.

### *Reported Decisions*

*Petersen v. Bruen* (Nev.1990) 106 Nev. 271, 792 P.2d 18. Action by plaintiff in early 20s, alleging Type 1 discovery, filed and decided prior to CSA statute. *Held*: No existing statute of limitations would bar action for CSA where plaintiff submits clear and convincing evidence that the abuse had occurred. Opinion suggested the Legislature act on the issue.

### *Analysis*

CSA statute provides ten years from majority or ten years from date plaintiff discovers or reasonably should have discovered that his injury was caused by the abuse, whichever occurs later. Appears to apply to Type 1 discovery but issue has not been interpreted.

Statute has no language of revival; issue has not been interpreted.

Statute applies to actions "for recovery of damages arising from" CSA; issue has not been interpreted.

## *NEW HAMPSHIRE*

No CSA statute. New Hampshire Rev. Stat. Ann., Title 52, Actions, Chapter 508, Limitation of Actions, section 508.4, as amended in 1986 provides, for any personal injury action, three years from the injury or, where the causal connection between the injury and the wrongful act could not reasonably have been discovered at the time of the injury, three years from the time the plaintiff discovers or reasonably should have discovered the injury and its causal connection to the act or omission complained of. The 1986 amendment applies to any action arising on or after July 1986. Prior to 1986, the statute provided six years from the time the cause of action accrued.

***Reported Decisions***

*McLean v. Gaudet* (D.N.Hamp.1990) 769 F.Supp. 30. Action based on abuse occurring between 1970 and 1982, by plaintiff apparently alleging Type 1 discovery. *Held*: Pre-1986 statute, permitting six years from accrual, applies to actions based on abuse occurring before 1986, and is subject to judicial discovery rule, whereby action accrues when plaintiff discovers or reasonably should have discovered that the injury may have been caused by the defendant's conduct. Reasonableness of delay is usually a question of fact not determinable upon a motion to dismiss on the pleadings.

*Sinclair v. Brill* (D.N.Hamp.1993) 815 F.Supp. 44. Action filed in 1991 by plaintiff alleging that parents physically abused her, concealed from her the nature and cause of her injuries, and, as a result, she did not remember the injury-causing incident until 1988. *Held*: The action is governed by the 6-year statute, subject to discovery accrual. Motion for judgment on pleadings denied.

*Sinclair v. Brill* (D.N.Hamp.1994) 857 F.Supp. 132. Trial court granted defendant's motion for summary judgment on grounds the evidence established that plaintiff had always known about the injury-causing incident of abuse. *Held*: Plaintiff's alleged inability to discover the connection between the incident of abuse and her long-term injuries would delay accrual if reasonable, and evidence presents triable question of fact on the issue.

*McCollum v. D'Arcy* (N.Hamp.1994) 638 A.2d 797. Action filed in 1991 by 50-year-old plaintiff alleging repressed memory of abuse. *Held*: Judicial discovery rule applies to CSA actions and is invoked by repressed memory of the incidents. Court will not impose a requirement of corroboration.

*Conrad v. Hazen* (N.Hamp.1995) 665 A.2d 372. Action filed in 1993 against former "minister" in cult religion, by plaintiff alleging Type 1 discovery. Plaintiff always knew the abuse had occurred, experienced numerous emotional difficulties afterward, began counseling more than six years before filing, and first disclosed the abuse in counseling five years before filing. Trial court granted summary judgment on limitations grounds, applying the three-year statute. *Held*: The incidents of abuse having occurred prior to 1986, the action is governed by the six-year statute. The six-year statute is subject to the common law discovery rule, which delays accrual until plaintiff discovers or in the exercise of reasonable diligence should have discovered both the fact and cause of the injury. Under New Hampshire caselaw, if the original injury was "sufficiently serious to apprise the plaintiff that a possible violation of her rights had taken place," the common law discovery rule will not apply. Although plaintiff admits that she suffered physical and emotional pain and injuries at the time of the abuse, and these injuries would appear to be sufficiently serious to have apprised her that a possible violation of her rights had taken place, that question is a factual issue that should be determined by the trial court in the first instance. The trial court did not make such a determination in its ruling on the motion for summary judgment below. Judgment reversed and matter remanded to trial court.

*Taylor v. Litteer* (N.D.Hamp.1996) 925 F.Supp. 898, motion for reconsideration denied, 930 F.Supp. 691. 20-year-old former Boy Scout sued former troop leader for CSA and Boy Scouts for negligence, alleging Type 1 discovery of causal connection between the abuse and psychological injuries. *Held*: Defendant's alleged conduct having occurred prior to 1986, the action is governed by six-year statute, subject to common law discovery rule. Referring to an unpublished order of the New Hampshire Supreme Court in the appeal of two consolidated cases (referenced as *Grover v. Roman Catholic Bishop of Manchester* and *Carnevale v. MacRae,* Case No. 94-550, New Hampshire Supreme Court, Order dated September 28, 1995), the federal District Court holds that the New Hampshire Supreme Court would not apply the discovery rule to Type 1 discovery under the circumstances of this case, because the acts of abuse were of a "sufficiently serious nature" as to have apprised the plaintiff at the time of the incidents that a violation of his rights had probably taken place. Plaintiff's on-going awareness of the acts that had occurred was sufficient to trigger accrual of the action at the time of the abuse.

### *Analysis*

No CSA statute. Six-year statute applicable to actions based on conduct that occurred prior to 1986; three-year statute to actions based on conduct that occurred thereafter. Judicial discovery rule is applicable to six-year statute, and codified into three-year statute. Discovery rule has been held applicable to Type 2 discovery. State Supreme Court has indicated that it would probably hold the discovery rule inapplicable to Type 1 discovery of an action for CSA, because CSA is generally of a "sufficiently serious nature" as to apprise the plaintiff that a violation of his or her rights had taken place.

## *NEW JERSEY*

New Jersey Stat. Ann., Title 2A: Administration of Criminal and Civil Justice:

**Chapter 61B-Sexual Abuse.**

**2A:61B-1: Definitions; civil remedy; period of limitations; evidence; closed circuit testimony; confidentiality; in camera proceedings; damages.**

(a) As used in this act:

(1) "Sexual abuse" means an act of sexual contact or sexual penetration between a child under the age of 18 years and an adult. A parent, foster parent, guardian or other person standing in loco parentis within the household who knowingly permits or acquiesces in sexual abuse by any other person also commits sexual abuse, except that it is an affirmative defense if the parent, foster parent, guardian or other person standing in loco parentis was subjected to, or placed in, reasonable fear of physical or sexual abuse by the other person so as to undermine the person's ability to protect the child.
(2) "Sexual contact" means an intentional touching by the victim or actor, either directly or through clothing, of the victim's or actor's intimate parts for the purpose of sexually arousing or sexually gratifying the actor. Sexual contact of the adult with himself must be in view of the victim whom the adult knows to be present.
(3) "Sexual penetration" means vaginal intercourse, cunnilingus, fellatio or anal intercourse between persons or insertion of the hand, finger or object into the anus or vagina either by the adult or upon the adult's instruction.
(4) "Intimate parts" means the following body parts: sexual organs, genital area, anal area, inner thigh, groin, buttock or breast of a person.
(5) "Injury or illness" includes psychological injury or illness, whether or not accompanied by physical injury or illness.
(b) In any civil action for injury or illness based on sexual abuse, the cause of action shall accrue at the time of reasonable discovery of the injury and its causal relationship to the act of sexual abuse. Any such action shall be brought within two years after reasonable discovery.
(c) Nothing in this act is intended to preclude the court from finding that the statute of limitations was tolled in a case because of the plaintiff's mental state, duress by the defendant, or any other equitable grounds. Such a finding shall be made after a plenary hearing, conducted in the presence of the jury. At the plenary hearing the court shall hear all credible evidence and the Rules of Evidence shall not apply, except for Rule 4 or a valid claim of privilege. The court may order an independent psychiatric evaluation of the plaintiff in order to assist in the determination as to whether the statute of limitations was tolled.
(d)(1) Evidence of the victim's previous sexual conduct shall not be admitted nor reference made to it in the presence of a jury except as provided in this subsection. When the defendant seeks to admit such evidence for any purpose, the defendant must apply for an order of the

court before the trial or preliminary hearing, except that the court may allow the motion to be made during trial if the court determines that the evidence is newly discovered and could not have been obtained earlier through the exercise of due diligence. After the application is made, the court shall conduct a hearing in camera to determine the admissibility of the evidence. If the court finds that evidence offered by the defendant regarding the sexual conduct of the victim is relevant and that the probative value of the evidence offered is not outweighed by its collateral nature or by the probability that its admission will create undue prejudice, confusion of the issues, or unwarranted invasion of the privacy of the victim, the court shall enter an order setting forth with specificity what evidence may be introduced and the nature of the questions which shall be permitted, and the reasons why the court finds that such evidence satisfies the standards contained in this section. The defendant may then offer evidence under the order of the court.

(2) In the absence of clear and convincing proof to the contrary, evidence of the victim's sexual conduct occurring more than one year before the date of the offense charged is presumed to be inadmissible under this section.

(3) Evidence of the victim's previous sexual conduct shall not be considered relevant unless it is material to proving that the source of semen, pregnancy or disease is a person other than the defendant. For the purposes of this subsection, "sexual conduct" shall mean any conduct or behavior relating to sexual activities of the victim, including but not limited to previous or subsequent experience of sexual penetration or sexual contact, use of contraceptives, living arrangement and life style.

(e) (1) The court may, on motion and after conducting a hearing in camera, order the taking of the testimony of a victim on closed ciruit television at the trial, out of the view of the jury, defendant, or spectators upon making findings as provided in paragraph (2) of this subsection.

(2) An order under this section may be made only if the court finds that the victim is 16 years of age or younger and that there is a substantial likelihood that the victim would suffer severe emotional or mental distress if required to testify in open court. The order shall be specific as to whether the victim will testify outside the presence of spectators, the defendant, the jury, or all of them and shall be based on specific findings relating to the impact of the presence of each.

(3) A motion seeking closed circuit testimony under paragraph (1) of this subsection may be filed by:

(a) The victim or the victim's attorney, parent or legal guardian;
(b) The defendant or the defendant's counsel; or
(c) The trial judge on the judge's own motion.

(4) The defendant's counsel shall be present at the taking of testimony in camera. If the defendant is not present, he and his attorney shall be able to confer privately with each other during the testimony by a separate audio system.

(5) If testimony is taken on closed circuit television pursuant to the provisions of this act, a stenographic recording of that testimony shall also be required. A typewritten transcript of that testimony shall be included in the record on appeal. The closed circuit testimony itself shall not constitute part of the record on appeal except on motion for good cause shown.

(f) (1) The name, address, and identity of a victim or a defendant shall not appear on the complaint or any other public record as defined in P.L.1963, c. 73 (C. 47:1A-1 et seq.). In their place initials or a fictitious name shall appear.

(2) Any report, statement, photograph, court document, complaint or any other public record which states the name, address and identity of a victim shall be confidential and unavailable to the public.

(3) The information described in this subsection shall remain confidential and unavailable to the public unless the victim consents to the disclosure or if the court, after a hearing, determines that good cause exists for the disclosure. The hearing shall be held after notice has been made to the victim and to the defendant and the defendant's counsel.

(4) Nothing contained herein shall prohibit the court from imposing further restrictions with regard to the disclosure of the name, address, and identity of the victim when it deems it necessary to prevent trauma or stigma to the victim.

(g) In accordance with R. 5:3-2 of the Rules Governing the Courts of the State of New Jersey, the court may, on its own or a party's motion, direct that any proceeding or portion of a proceeding involving a victim sixteen years of age or younger be conducted in camera.

(h) A plaintiff who prevails in a civil action pursuant to this act shall be awarded damages in the amount of $10,000, plus reasonable attorney's fees, or actual damages, whichever is greater. Actual damages shall consist of compensatory and punitive damages and costs of suit, including reasonable attorney's fees. Compensatory damages may include, but are not limited to, damages for pain and suffering, medical expenses, emotional trauma, diminished childhood, diminished enjoyment of life, costs of counseling, and lost wages.

Note: Enacted Laws 1992, ch. 109, s. 1. Section 2 provided that the act would take effect immediately but not apply to any action commenced before its effective date.

### *Reported Decisions*

*Jones v. Jones* (N.J.App.1990), 242 N.J.Super. 195, 576 A.2d 316. Action by plaintiff alleging Type 1 discovery due to mental impairment and duress resulting from the CSA. Action filed and decided prior to CSA statute. *Held*: Mental trauma resulting from incest may invoke tolling for insanity. Plaintiff's allegations of mental impairment raise issue of material fact whether she was prevented by the effects of the abuse from being able to pursue her rights, and whether the statute should be tolled for duress.

*Dattoli v. Yanelli* (D.C.N.J.1995) 911 F.Supp. 143. Action filed after effective date of CSA statute, by 35-year-old plaintiff alleging mixture of Type 2 and Type 1 discovery. *Held*: Under the terms of the CSA statute, plaintiff's claim that defendant's conduct had caused him to repress and deny the existence and impact of the abuse entitles him to a plenary hearing on the issue of when he discovered the causal connection between the abuse and his psychological injuries. At the hearing the plaintiff must sustain his burden of proof "that his discovery of the causal relationship between the sexual abuse and his injuries did not occur until" a date within two years of filing. His own assertions that this was the case will not be enough. Expert testimony explaining the inability to discover will be needed.

### *Analysis*

CSA statute provides two years from "reasonable discovery of the injury and its causal relationship to the act of sexual abuse." Appears to apply to Type 1 but has not been interpreted. Also does not preclude exceptions for mental disability and duress.

Statute provides it shall not apply to any action commenced before its effective date. Issue of whether it revives actions filed after its effective date which had lapsed under prior law has not been addressed.

Statute applies to actions against any person "standing in loco parentis" within the household who knowingly permits or acquiesces in the abuse. Issue has not been interpreted.

## *NEW MEXICO*

New Mexico Stat. 1978 Ann., Chapter 37: Limitation of Actions.

**Section 37-1-30: Action for damages due to childhood sexual abuse; limitation on damages.**

(A) An action for damages based on personal injury by childhood sexual abuse shall be commenced by a person, before the latest of the following dates:

(1) the first instant of the person's twenty-fourth birthday;

(2) three years from the date of the time that a person knew or had reason to know of the childhood sexual abuse and that the childhood sexual abuse resulted in an injury to the person, as established by competent medical or psychological testimony.

(B) As used in this section, "childhood sexual abuse" means behavior that, if prosecuted in a criminal manner, would constitute a violation of:

(1) Section 30-9-11 NMSA 1978, regarding criminal sexual penetration of a minor;

(2) Section 30-9-13 NMSA 1978, regarding criminal sexual contact of a minor; or

(3) the Sexual Exploitation of Children Act /30-6A-1 to 30-6A-4 NMSA 1978/.

Note: Enacted, Laws 1993, ch. 136, s. 1; s. 2 provides the Act is effective July 1, 1993. Amended effective June 16, 1995, revising the definition of accrual in subparagraph A(2) and dropping former A(3), which had provided for accrual within three years of plaintiff's beginning treatment for a "dissociated, repressed or forgotten" act of CSA.

***Reported Decisions***

*Martinez-Sandoval v. Kirsch* (N.Mex.App.1994) 118 N.M. 616, 884 P.2d 507, rev.den. Action against former parish priest by plaintiff alleging Type 1 discovery, filed prior to but decided after CSA statute. Plaintiff did not rely upon CSA statute during appeal. *Held*: Judicial discovery accrual applies to Type 1 discovery. Test of reasonableness is what a reasonable person who had been subjected to the alleged sexual abuse would have been able to know or discover. That plaintiff knew she suffered physical pain and emotional distress at the time did not necessarily trigger accrual. But that plaintiff knew at the time that she had acquired venereal disease and had become pregnant as a result of the CSA did trigger accrual, as these injuries were substantial and accrual could not be further delayed by failure to appreciate causal connection between the abuse and adult psychological injuries.

***Analysis***

CSA statute permits filing before plaintiff's twenty-fourth birthday or three years from discovery accrual, whichever occurs later, and defines discovery accrual as date plaintiff "knew or had reason to know" of both the CSA and that the CSA resulted in an injury, as established by competent medical/psychological opinion. Statutory discovery accrual language has not yet been interpreted.

Judicial discovery rule has been held to apply to Type 1 discovery, subject to an objective reasonable person standard. Court has held that awareness of physical pain and emotional injury at the time of the abuse would not necessarily trigger accrual, but awareness of substantial injury would.

Statute has no language of revival; issue has not been interpreted.

Statute applies to actions "for damages based on personal injury by childhood sexual abuse;" issue has not been interpreted.

## *NEW YORK*

No CSA statute. Con. Laws of New York Ann., Civil Practice Laws and Rules, Section 215(3) provides one year for assault and battery; section 214(5) provides three years for negligence; section 208 tolls for minority and insanity. Section 201 states, "No court shall extend the time limited by law for the commencement of an action," and has been interpreted as prohibiting the courts from applying judicial discovery accrual unless legislatively mandated.

### *Reported Decisions*

*Smith v. Smith* (2nd Cir.1987) 830 F.2d 11. Action filed by Type 2 plaintiff. *Held*: PTSD caused by CSA does not invoke tolling for insanity, which requires overall inability to function in society. Alleged conduct of defendant does not give rise to equitable estoppel, so long as plaintiff was, as she concedes, aware that she had been abused and that it had caused her harm.

*Hoffmann v. Hoffmann* (N.Y.App.1990) 162 A.D.2d 249, 556 N.Y.S.2d 608. Action filed by Type 2 plaintiff. *Held*: No equitable estoppel based on gravity of defendant's acts per se, and plaintiff did not bring action within reasonable time of removal of any estoppel. PTSD insufficient to invoke tolling for insanity.

*Bassile v. Covenant House* (N.Y.Sup.1991) 152 Misc.2d 88, 575 N.Y.S.2d 233. Action filed by Type 1 plaintiff, alleging negligent sexual abuse by priest and negligence by church. *Held*: Discovery rule cannot be applied to CSA (or any other tort action) absent legislative direction to do so.

*Burpee v. Burpee* (N.Y.Sup.1991) 152 Misc.2d 466, 578 N.Y.S.2d 359. Action by

Type 2 plaintiff. *Held*: Psychological trauma and resulting repression of memory cannot invoke tolling for insanity in absence of overall incapacity to function. Equitable estoppel cannot be invoked for gravity of tortious conduct itself, but only if defendant subsequently affirmatively acts to prevent plaintiff from pursuing action. Defendant's admission of CSA was not grounds to avoid statute.

*Schmidt v. Bishop* (S.D.N.Y.1991) 779 F.Supp. 321. Type 1 plaintiff alleging CSA by priest. *Held*: CSA is intentional tort and cannot be cast as negligence. Clergy malpractice is not actionable tort as this would require setting standards for clergy conduct in violation of First Amendment. No judicial discovery rule in New York. No equitable estoppel based on the CSA itself.

*Anonymous v. Anonymous* (N.Y.Sup.1992) 154 Misc.2d 46, 584 N.Y.S.2d 713. Type 2 plaintiff. *Held*: While repression not in itself sufficient to invoke tolling for insanity, evidence of repression plus additional PTSD symptoms were sufficient to raise triable issue of material fact regarding whether plaintiff was unable to function in society and thus entitled to tolling for insanity, and fact-finding hearing was required. Allegations regarding defendant's fraud and misrepresentation regarding nature of his conduct raised triable issue of material fact regarding whether plaintiff was entitled to equitable estoppel exception.

*Bassile v. Covenant House* (N.Y.App.1993) 191 A.D.2d 188, 594 N.Y.S.2d 192. Appellate Division affirmed lower court's decision finding no discovery rule applicable absent legislative direction.

*Doe v. Roe* (N.Y.App.1993) 192 A.D.2d 1089, 596 N.Y.S.2d 620. Action for CSA framed as for fraud. *Held*: Action for CSA is action for intentional tort, may not be recast as for fraud to obtain longer statute of limitations. CSA does not in itself invoke equitable estoppel.

*Overall v. Klotz* (S.D.N.Y.1994) 846 F.Supp. 297. Type 2 plaintiff. *Held*: Tolling for duress not invoked by repression, even if repression allegedly caused by duress inherent in the CSA.

*Zoe G. v. Frederick F.G.* (N.Y.App.1994) 208 A.D.2d 675, 617 N.Y.S.2d 370. *Held*: Tolling for duress and/or equitable estoppel invoked only by affirmative conduct additional to underlying tort.

*Overall v. Klotz* (2nd Cir.1995) 52 F.3d 398. On appeal from district court's decision granting summary judgment. *Held*: No tolling for duress inherent in CSA, even if it caused repression of memory of the abuse.

### *Analysis*

No CSA statute. Code section limits power of courts to apply judicially created exceptions to statutes of limitations. Courts have consequently refused multiple attempts to apply discovery accrual or tolling for insanity, equitable estoppel, or fraud and duress. Numerous reported decisions suggest the Legislature should address the issue.

## *NORTH CAROLINA*

No CSA statute. Gen. Stat. North Carolina Ann., Chapter 1: Civil Procedure, section 1-54(3) provides one year for assault and battery, and 1-52(5) provides three years for a personal injury action not otherwise provided for. Section 1-52(16) provides that except for professional malpractice, personal injury actions shall not accrue until bodily harm is or reasonably ought to be apparent to plaintiff, provided that no cause of action shall accrue more than 10 years from the last act giving rise to it. Section 1-17(a) tolls for minority and for adult incompetency, and provides three years from removal of the disability.

### *Reported Decisions*

*Doe v. Doe* (4th Cir.1992) 973 F.2d 237. Action by 37-year-old plaintiff alleging Type 1 discovery. *Held*: Emotional distress governed by three-year statute in section 1-52(5). North Carolina court probably would not apply the section 1-52(16) discovery accrual provision to actions for emotional distress, but even if it did this action would be barred by the 10-year repose provision contained in the same section.

*Leonard v. England* (N.C.App. 1994) 115 N.C.App. 103, 445 S.E.2d 50. Defendant's petition for review granted; plaintiff's subsequent petition to dismiss action granted. Action by 39-year-old plaintiff alleging Type 2 discovery. Psychologist testified plaintiff had recovered repressed memory in therapy, and that the abuse had rendered her psychologically unable to discover it or to act on her rights earlier. *Held*: Expert testimony sufficient to raise question of material fact regarding tolling for mental incompetency.

### *Analysis*

No CSA statute. Personal injury other than malpractice governed by three-year statute with express provision for discovery accrual and provision that no action shall accrue more than ten years from the last act giving rise to it. State appellate court has held expert evidence of repressed memory is sufficient to invoke tolling for mental incompetency. Defendant's petition for review was granted in 1994, and plaintiff's petition to dismiss the action was granted in 1995.

## *NORTH DAKOTA*

No CSA statute. North Dakota Century Code, Title 28, Judicial Procedure, Civil, section 28-01-18 provides two years from accrual for assault and battery. Section 28-01-25 tolls for minority.

### *Reported Decisions*

*Osland v. Osland* (N.D.1989) 442 N.W.2d 907. Action by 22-year-old plaintiff alleging Type 1 discovery. *Held*: Action for CSA governed by two year statute for assault and battery; judicial discovery rule applies to Type 1 discovery of connection between the abuse and the injury.

*Peterson v. Huso* (N.D.1996) 552 N.W.2d 83. Action by 27-year-old plaintiff alleging Type 2 discovery. *Held*: Plaintiff alleging repression of CSA entitled to two years from recovery of memory to bring suit. Repression is not a mental disability tolling an accrued cause of action (after the removal of which one would have one year to sue under North Dakota law), but delays the accrual of the cause of action.

### *Analysis*

CSA actions governed by two-year assault and battery statute, subject to judicial discovery rule, which has been held applicable to Type 1 and 2 discovery.

## *OHIO*

No CSA statute. Ohio Rev. Code Ann., Title 23, Courts and Common Pleas, Chapter 2305, Limitation of Actions, section 2305.111 provides one year for assault and battery, section 2305.10 provides two years for bodily injury, and section 2305.09(D) provides four years for intentional infliction of emotional distress. Section 2305.16 tolls for minority and unsound mind.

### *Reported Decisions*

*McKay v. Cutlip* (Ohio App.1992) 80 Ohio App.3d 487, 609 N.E.2d 1272. 35-year-old plaintiff alleging Type 1 discovery of action based on father's ongoing sexual and physical abuse from childhood until less than a year before filing action, and arguing that alcoholism, drug abuse and PTSD caused by CSA invoked tolling for unsound mind. *Held*: Although there was expert evidence as to her conditions and that they were caused by CSA, the psychologist did not express an opinion as to plaintiff's inability to have initiated legal proceedings earlier, and thus evidence did not raise question of material fact re tolling for unsound mind. Court declined to apply discovery rule to civil CSA actions.

*Benge v. Jones* (Ohio App.1992) 80 Ohio App.3d 420, 609 N.E.2d 581. 40-year-old plaintiff sued mother's estate alleging Type 1 discovery. *Held*: Allegations of abuse are subject to one-year and two-year statutes. Discovery rule may be applicable, but evidence established that plaintiff knew all necessary facts many years before filing suit.

*Bechtel v. England* (Ohio App.1993) 87 Ohio App.3d 348, 622 N.E.2d 374. 34-year-old plaintiff sued father for assault, negligence and mental anguish, alleging Type 1 discovery and tolling for unsound mind. *Held*: Evidence did not raise question of material fact re tolling for unsound mind. Although plaintiff's expert declared CSA had rendered plaintiff unable to bring suit earlier, expert was only a licensed social worker and was not competent to testify regarding psychological diagnoses as required by Ohio law.

*Prebble v. Hinson* (S.D.Ohio 1993) 825 F.Supp. 185. 24-year-old plaintiff alleging Type 2 discovery. *Held*: Ohio court would not apply discovery accrual or tolling for unsound mind to alleged repression of memory of CSA.

*Kotyk v. Rebovich* (Ohio App.1993) 87 Ohio App.3d 116, 621 N.E.2d 897. 25-year-old plaintiff sued priest and church for battery, clergy malpractice, fraud and misrepresentation, negligence, and vicarious liability, alleging Type 1 discovery. Evidence that plaintiff had disclosed to counselor at age 18 and had told church officials at age 19. *Held*: Discovery accrual of all causes of action occurred no later than upon disclosure to counselor, and evidence failed to establish tolling for unsound mind.

*Doe v. First United Methodist Church* (Ohio 1994) 68 Ohio St.3d 531, 629 N.E.2d 402. 27-year-old plaintiff sued teacher, school and church for multiple causes of action premised on teacher's CSA, alleging Type 1 discovery through counseling. *Held*: Actions premised on CSA are subject to one-year statute. Actions for negligent failure to protect are subject to two-year statute. Even if the court were to adopt a rule of discovery accrual for CSA actions, it would not avail this plaintiff, who knew at the time of reaching majority that the abuse had occurred and the identity of the perpetrator. Plaintiff's failure to appreciate full extent of psychological injuries until later would not delay accrual.

*Ault v. Jasko* (Ohio 1994) 70 Ohio St.3d 114, 637 N.E.2d 870. 29-year-old plaintiff sued father for CSA alleging Type 2 discovery. *Held*: One-year statute applicable to CSA actions may be delayed where victim has repressed memory of abuse. Discovery accrual occurs when plaintiff recalls or otherwise discovers the abuse, or through reasonable diligence should have discovered it. Concurring and dissenting opinions express caution about applying discovery accrual on basis of repressed memory, especially if memories were "retrieved" as a result of psychotherapy, due to uncertain scientific reliability.

*Smith v. Rudler* (Ohio 1994) 70 Ohio St.3d 397, 639 N.E.2d 66. Summary judgment reversed and case remanded per *Ault.*

*Herald v. Hood* (Ohio 1994) 70 Ohio St.3d 1210, 639 N.E.2d 109. Appeal from trial verdict for plaintiff; appeal dismissed per *Ault.*

*Doe v. Doe* (Ohio 1994) 70 Ohio St.3d 469, 639 N.E.2d 432. Judgment reversed and case remanded per *Ault.*

*Stewart v. Kennedy* (Ohio 1994) 70 Ohio St.3d 536, 639 N.E.2d 790. Judgment reversed and case remanded per *Ault.*

*O'Connor v. Zimmer* (Ohio App.1995) 104 Ohio App.3d 143, 661 N.E.2d 248. Action filed more than one year after plaintiff first remembered the abuse. Dismissal upheld per *Ault.*

*Scott v. Borelli* (Ohio App.1995) 106 Ohio App.3d 449, 666 N.E.2d 322. Action against psychologist for sexual abuse during patient's minority. Plaintiff first remembered some of the abuse more than one year before filing. *Held*: Actions for sexual assault and for psychological malpractice are both subject to one-year statutes. Awareness of the abuse triggers accrual, which does not wait until plaintiff becomes aware of full extent of the abuse or injury. Plaintiff's emotional problems preventing earlier suit did not constitute mental disability sufficient to toll statute.

*Casey v. Casey* (Ohio App.1996) 109 Ohio App.3d 830, 673 N.E.2d 210. Plaintiff sued father and mother alleging Type 2 discovery. Facts established that she discussed the abuse with a therapist about six years before filing. *Held*: Action for CSA governed by one-year statute, action for negligence governed by two-year statute, both subject to delayed accrual for repression of memory of the abuse. Plaintiff presented no facts entitling her to further tolling for "unsound mind."

*Moore v. Schiano* (Ohio App.1997) 117 Ohio App.3d 326, 690 N.E.2d 597. 33-year-old plaintiff sued former neighbor claiming that the abuse had rendered her psychologically unable to act on her rights earlier. *Held*: Plaintiff's lay testimony as to her psychological condition not sufficient to invoke tolling for unsound mind. Affidavit of psychologist who did not examine plaintiff until after the action was filed and therefore had no personal knowledge of her earlier psychological condition was also insufficient to invoke tolling for unsound mind.

*Analysis*

No CSA statute. Actions for CSA governed by one-year statute, actions for negligent failure to protect governed by two-year statute. One-year statute subject to delayed accrual for repressed memory of the abuse.

## *OKLAHOMA*

Oklahoma Stat. Ann., Title 12, Civil Procedure, Chapter 3, Limitation of Actions:

**Section 95, subsection 6:**

Civil actions other than for the recovery of real property can only be brought within the following periods, after the cause of action shall have accrued, and not afterwards:

(6) . . . An action based on intentional conduct brought by any person for recovery of damages for injury suffered as a result of childhood sexual abuse incidents or exploitation as defined by Section 845 of Title 21 of the Oklahoma Statutes or incest can only be brought within the latter of the following periods:

(a) within two (2) years of the act alleged to have caused the injury or condition, or

(b) within two (2) years of the time the victim discovered or reasonably should have discovered that the injury or condition was caused by said act or that the act caused the injury for which the claim is brought.

Provided, however, that the time limit for commencement of an action pursuant to this paragraph is tolled for a child until the child reaches the age of eighteen (18) years. No action may be brought against the alleged perpetrator or the estate of the alleged perpetrator after the death of such alleged perpetrator. An action pursuant to this paragraph must be based upon objective verifiable evidence in order for the victim to recover damages for injuries suffered by reason of such sexual abuse, exploitation or incest. The evidence should include both proof that the victim had psychologically repressed the memory of the facts upon which the claim was predicated and that there was corroborating evidence that the sexual abuse, exploitation or incest actually occurred. The victim need not establish which act in a series of continuing sexual abuse incidents, exploitation incidents or incest caused the injury complained of, but may compute the date of discovery from the date of discovery of the last act by the same perpetrator which is part of a common scheme or plan of sexual abuse, exploitation or incest. Provided further, any action based on intentional conduct specified in paragraph 6 of this section must be commenced within twenty (20) years of the victim reaching the age of eighteen (18).

Note: Laws 1992, ch. 344, s. 1, effective Sept. 1, 1992. Amended, Laws 1994, ch. 356, s. 11, effective Sept. 1, 1994.

***Reported Decisions***

*Lovelace v. Keohane* (Okla.1992) 831 P.2d 624. Decided prior to CSA statute. Plaintiff sued priest and Church for sexual abuse by priest at ages 19-22, alleging repression and Type 2 discovery. Court answered questions certified by federal circuit court: (1) whether "MPD" constitutes legal disability tolling personal injury statute, and (2) whether discovery rule is invoked by allegations of repressed memory. *Held*: MPD and repressed memory do not invoke tolling for mental disability or discovery accrual, as plaintiff was chargeable with knowledge of her injury and its probable cause.

*Analysis*

CSA statute provides two years from date plaintiff discovered or reasonably should have discovered that the injury or condition was caused by the abuse, and requires objective verifiable evidence corroborating both the abuse and that it had been repressed. The latter requirement appears to limit delayed accrual to Type 2 discovery.

Statute has no language of revival, and issue has not been interpreted. Under prior law court had refused to apply discovery accrual to repressed memory, or to toll for mental disability.

Statute applies to actions "based on intentional conduct;" issue has not been interpreted.

Note: Statute also provides outer time limit of 20 years from majority.

## *OREGON*

Oregon Rev. Stat., Title 2, Procedure in Civil Actions, Chapter 12, Limitations of Actions:

**Section 12.117: Actions based on child abuse.**

(1) Notwithstanding ORS 12.110, 12.115 or 12.160, an action based on conduct that constitutes child abuse or conduct knowingly allowing, permitting or encouraging child abuse accruing while the person who is entitled to bring the action is under 18 years of age shall be commenced not more than six years after that person attains 18 years of age, or if the injured person has not discov-

ered the injury or the causal connection between the injury and the child abuse, nor in the exercise of reasonable care should have discovered the injury or the causal connection between the injury and the child abuse, not more than three years from the date the injured person discovers or in the exercise of reasonable diligence should have discovered the injury or the causal connection between the child abuse and the injury, whichever period is longer.

(2) As used in subsection (1) of this section, "child abuse" means any of the following:

(a) Intentional conduct by an adult that results in:

(i) Any physical injury to a child; or

(ii) Any mental injury to a child which results in any observable and substantial impairment of the child's mental or psychological ability to function caused by cruelty to the child, with due regard to the culture of the child;

(b) Rape of a child, which includes but is not limited to rape, sodomy, unlawful sexual penetration and incest, as those acts are defined in ORS ch. 163;

(c) Sexual abuse, as defined in ORS ch. 163, when the victim is a child; or

(d) Sexual exploitation of a child, including but not limited to:

(i) Conduct constituting violation of ORS 163.435 and any other conduct which allows, employs, authorizes, permits, induces or encourages a child to engage in the performing for people to observe or the photographing, filming, tape recording or other exhibition which, in whole or in part, depicts sexual conduct or contact; and

(ii) Allowing, permitting, encouraging or hiring a child to engage in prostitution, as defined in ORS ch. 167.

(3) Nothing in this section creates a new cause of action or enlarges any existing cause of action.

Note: Enacted 1989, ch. 643, ss. 2 & 3. Amended 1991, ch. 386, s. 4; 1991, ch. 932, s. 1; 1993, ch. 18, s. 5; 1993, ch. 296, s. 1; 1993, ch. 622, s. 2. Original legislation provided five years from majority, did not provide for discovery accrual, and did not expressly provide for retroactivity. 1991 amendments provided six-years from majority or three years from discovery accrual, an outer time limit of plaintiff's 40th birthday, and express language of revival applicable to all actions filed since October 1989. 1993 amendments repealed the outer time limit and expressly made this change applicable to all actions filed since 1989, including actions that had been dismissed based upon the outer time limit, which could be refiled within one year of the 1993 amendment.

***Reported Decisions***

*A.K.H. v. R.C.T.* (Or.1991) 312 Or. 497, 822 P.2d 135. Action filed in 1990 by plaintiff alleging Type 1 discovery accrual. Federal court certified question to Supreme Court, whether 1989 legislation was retroactive to revive lapsed action. While certification was pending the 1991 amendments to the CSA statute were enacted, which added express language of revival. *Held*: CSA statute as amended in 1991 expressly revives lapsed actions. Revival provision is not unconstitutional and revives an action still pending on appeal on its effective date.

*Cooksey v. Portland Public School District* (Or.App.1996) 143 Or.App.527, 923 P.2d 1328. Action on behalf of minor against teacher for molestation and school for negligence, filed more than two years after the molestation. *Held*: Oregon Tort Claims Act requires claim be filed within two years of the alleged injury notwithstanding any other provision of law. Concurring opinion notes that this absolute time limit thwarts the CSA statute's extension of time in actions involving public entities, but only the Legislature could change that.

*Flaningam v. Flaningam* (Or.App.1996) 145 Or.App. 432, 929 P.2d 1084. Sister sued brother for CSA, alleging Type 1 discovery. Trial court granted summary judgment on grounds of evidence that plaintiff had known of the sexual abuse and had discussed it with others more than six years before filing. On appeal plaintiff argued PTSD had reasonably prevented her from acting sooner, and submitted psychological literature on PTSD and similar effects of abuse. *Held*: Summary judgment affirmed because plaintiff did not submit evidence to the trial court that she had been diagnosed with PTSD or any other condition that would delay accrual.

*Lourim v. Swensen* (Or.App.1997) 147 Or.App. 425, 936 P.2d 1011. Former Boy Scout sued former volunteer for CSA and BSA for vicarious liability and negligence. *Held*: No vicarious liability of BSA for sexual abuse by employee/volunteer as acts of abuse not within scope of employment. As to causes of action for negligence in hiring or employment, CSA statute governs such causes only if there is an element of actual knowledge on the part of the negligent third party. Legislature could have used the common phrase "knew or should have known" if it had wished to include situations involving constructive knowledge or notice. Dismissal of negligence causes of action upheld because there were no allegations or evidence of such actual knowledge on the part of the Boy Scouts.

*Fearing v. Bucher* (Or.App.1997) 147 Or.App. 446, 936 P.2d 1023. Plaintiff sued former priest for CSA and Archdiocese for vicarious liability and negligence. *Held*: Dismissal of vicarious liability claim and negligence claims affirmed under *Lourim*. Allegations that the Archdiocese knew enough about pedophilia that it should have known that the priest presented a risk to children do not rise to level of actual knowledge required by the CSA statute.

*Sipes v. Sipes* (Or.App.1997) 147 Or.App. 462, 936 P.2d 1027. Son sued father for abuse and mother for negligence. Bankruptcy court asked for ruling as to whether negligence cause of action was timely under the statute. *Held*: Plaintiff's allegations that mother had actual knowledge of the abuse but took no action to prevent it bring the negligence action within the CSA statute.

*Walthers v. Gossett* (Or.App.1997) 148 Or.App. 548, 941 P.2d 575. Plaintiff sued dentist and his professional corporation, of which he was the sole officer and shareholder, alleging he sexually molested her during treatment when she was a teenager, and that the corporation was negligent in failing to protect her. Action against professional corporation dismissed on limitations grounds. *Held*: Allegation that the corporation knew that the dentist had an intent to molest and failed to act to protect plaintiff state a cause of action for negligently permitting the abuse to occur, coming within the CSA statute. Reversed and remanded.

### *Analysis*

CSA statute provides either six years from majority or three years from date plaintiff discovers or in exercise of reasonable diligence should have discovered that the injury was causally connected to the abuse, whichever occurs later.

Statute expressly revives lapsed actions; revival has been upheld.

Statute expressly applies to persons who knowingly permit the abuse to occur. Has been held to require that defendant have had actual knowledge of the abuse, not constructive. Knowledge of facts that would cause a reasonable person to suspect abuse is not sufficient.

## *PENNSYLVANIA*

No CSA statute. Pennsylvania Con. Stat. Ann., Title 42, Judiciary and Judicial Procedure, Part VI, Actions and Proceedings, Chapter 55, Limitation of Actions, section 5524 provides two years for assault, battery, and negligent personal injury. Section 5533 tolls for minority but not for insanity.

### *Reported Decisions*

*Bowser v. Guttendorf* (Pa.Super.1988) 373 Pa.Super. 402, 541 A.2d 377. 22-year-old plaintiff sued former foster father for CSA and foster mother for failing to protect. *Held*: Action governed by two-year statute. Allegations of mental inability to pursue claim, and of fraud or concealment, are not sufficient to invoke equitable tolling. Discovery accrual can only apply if a reasonable person would have been unaware of the salient facts.

*Bailey v. Lewis* (E.D.Pa.1991) 763 F.Supp. 802, aff'd 950 F.2d 721 (3rd Cir.1991). 32-year-old male plaintiff alleging Type 2 discovery of CSA by family friend during his teenage years. *Held*: Pennsylvania would not apply discovery accrual to Type 2 CSA action. Pennsylvania applies discovery rule only where reasonable person exercising due diligence could not have discovered the injury or its cause earlier. Where plaintiff is aware of facts that would cause an objectively reasonable person to know or suspect the injury and its cause, plaintiff's subjective inability to discover action sooner is irrelevant. Pennsylvania also does not permit tolling for mental incapacity of plaintiff, as is allowed in many states which have permitted discovery accrual in CSA actions.

*Hewczuk v. Sambor* (E.D.Pa.1992) 803 F.Supp. 1063. Female plaintiff alleging Type 2 discovery of CSA by her foster parents when she was ages five to six. *Held*: Pennsylvania would apply discovery rule to alleged repression of CSA where the delay is not objectively unreasonable. *Bailey* distinguished as turning on facts that made plaintiff's alleged delay objectively unreasonable as a matter of law: i.e., a reasonable teenage boy would know the sexual contact by an adult male friend of the family was wrong, whereas reasonable five or six year old girl would not necessarily know sexual contact by foster parent was wrong.

*Messina v. Bonner* (E.D.Pa.1993) 813 F.Supp. 346. Sisters ages 29 and 32 sued stepfather for CSA and mother for negligence, alleging Type 1 discovery. *Held*: Pennsylvania would not apply discovery accrual to Type 1 or Type 2 discovery of CSA.

*E.J.M. v. Archdiocese of Philadelphia* (Pa.Super.1993) 424 Pa.Super. 449, 622 A.2d 1388. 27-year-old male plaintiff sued priest for CSA and clergy malpractice and church for negligence and vicarious liability, alleging Type 1 discovery of CSA occurring during teenage years. *Held*: Discovery accrual not applicable to Type 1 discovery of CSA because the injury is not objectively unknowable to a reasonable person with due diligence. Court did not decide whether discovery accrual could apply to Type 2, but strongly agreed with legal analysis in *Bailey*.

*Seto v. Willits* (Pa.Super.1994) 432 Pa.Super. 346, 638 A.2d 258. 42-year-old female plaintiff alleging Type 2 discovery of CSA by father, which allegedly caused her to develop MPD and repressed memory. *Held*: Discovery accrual does not apply to

Type 2 discovery of CSA, because Pennsylvania applies objective reasonable person standard and does not toll limitations periods for insanity.

*Pearce v. Salvation Army* (Pa.Super.1996) 449 Pa.Super. 654, 674 A.2d 1123. Plaintiff alleged repressed memory. *Held*: Following *Seto,* alleged repressed memory caused by the abuse does not meet the requirement that the injury have been objectively undiscoverable.

*Dalrymple v. Brown* (Pa.1997) 701 A.2d 164. Plaintiff in mid-thirties sued for assault, battery, infliction of emotional distress, alleging repressed memory until within two years of filing. *Held*: Line of decisions by lower appellate court is correct. Although plaintiff argues that her repressed memory is not a subjective incapacity but an objectively reasonable response to the abuse, and is part of the injury itself, this does not meet the standard of objectivity that is required. The injury must be such that "no amount of reasonable diligence" would have enabled the injured party to ascertain the injury. Court acknowledges that this strict interpretation of the objectively reasonable requirement is a minority position.

### *Analysis*

No CSA statute and no statutory tolling for insanity. Courts have declined to apply discovery accrual even to Type 2 discovery of CSA, on grounds that repression is a subjective response to the abuse and does not satisfy objective reasonable person standard.

## *RHODE ISLAND*

General Laws of Rhode Island, Title 9, Courts and Civil Procedure:

**Section 9-1-51: Limitation on actions based on sexual abuse or exploitation of a child.**

> (a) All claims or causes of action based on intentional conduct brought by any person for recovery of damages for injury suffered as a result of childhood sexual abuse shall be commenced within seven (7) years of the act alleged to have caused the injury or condition, or seven (7) years of the time the victim discovered or reasonably should have discovered that the injury or condition was caused by said act, whichever period expires later.
> (b) The victim need not establish which act in a series of continuing sexual abuse or exploitation incidents cause the injury complained of, but may compute the date of discovery from the date of the last act by the same perpetrator which is part of a common scheme or plan of sexual abuse or exploitation.

(c) The knowledge of a custodial parent or guardian shall not be imputed to a person under the age of eighteen (18) years.

(d) For purposes of this section, "childhood sexual abuse" means any act committed by the defendant against a complainant who was less than eighteen (18) years of age at the time of the act and which act would have been a criminal violation of chapter 37 of title 11.

Note: P.L. 1992, ch. 84, s. 1; P.L. 993, ch. 274, s. 1. Section 2 of P.L. 1992 ch. 84 provides that 9-1-51 shall apply to all causes of action pending on the date of passage (6-17-92) or filed thereafter.

***Reported Decisions***

*Doe v. LaBrosse* (R.I.1991) 588 A.2d 605 (*LaBrosse I*). Action decided prior to CSA statute. Sisters ages 34 and 35 sued father alleging Type 1 discovery. Trial court denied defendant's motion for summary judgment, holding discovery accrual applicable. *Held*: Trial court should have made factual determination as to the date upon which plaintiffs discovered or reasonably should have discovered the causal connection between their injuries and the CSA. Remanded for evidentiary hearing on discovery accrual.

*Doe v. LaBrosse* (R.I.1993) 625 A.2d 222 (*LaBrosse II*). After evidentiary hearing on date of discovery, matter had returned to Supreme Court. CSA statute became effective during pendency of review. *Held*: Review dismissed and matter remanded to trial court with directions to apply the newly enacted statute to the findings of fact.

*Kelly v. Marcantonio* (R.I.1996) 678 A.2d 873. Answering questions certified from federal district courts in actions against priests and church. *Held*: CSA statute does not revive previously lapsed actions as to do so is unconstitutional violation of due process. CSA statute does not govern actions against persons other than perpetrator, which are governed by three-year statute for personal injury. Court will not judicially apply a discovery rule to CSA actions against non-perpetrators. Whether repression of memory would toll the statute for mental disability requires a trial court hearing on whether repressed recollection constitutes a scientifically accepted and valid theory and if so whether the alleged repression qualifies as "unsound mind."

***Analysis***

CSA statute provides seven years from time plaintiff discovered or reasonably should have discovered that the injury or condition was caused by the abuse. Whether statute applies to Type 1 discovery has not been interpreted.

Statute expressly applies to actions pending on its effective date, but court has held revival of lapsed claims unconstitutional.

Statute applies to actions "based on intentional conduct" and has been held inapplicable to actions against non-perpetrators. Court has declined to apply judicial discovery rule to actions against non-perpetrators.

## *SOUTH CAROLINA*

No CSA statute. Code of Laws of South Carolina, Title 15, Civil Remedies and Procedures, section 15-3-535, provides three years from accrual for personal injury actions. Section 15-3-40 tolls for minority and insanity, but provides that the action must be brought within one year of removal of either disability, and that the limitations period cannot be extended more than five years for insanity.

### *Reported Decisions*

*Doe v. R.D.* (S.C.1992) 308 S.C. 139, 417 S.E.2d 541. 39-year-old male plaintiff sued father for CSA and mother for negligence, alleging Type 1 discovery. *Held*: Judicial discovery rule not applicable to Type 1 discovery of CSA action, in absence of legislative mandate.

*Roe v. Doe* (4th Cir.1994) 28 F.3d 404. 45-year-old female plaintiff sued cousin for CSA and aunt for negligence, alleging Type 2 discovery. Evidence established she had knowledge of enough facts to suspect the abuse more than three years before filing, although she alleged she had not recovered specific memories until later. *Held*: South Carolina's discovery rule applies an objective standard of when the facts known to the plaintiff would put a person of common knowledge and experience on notice that a claim might exist. Fact that victims of CSA who have suffered repressed memory may commonly begin to suspect abuse before having specific recollections of it does not justify application of different standard to such plaintiffs.

### *Analysis*

No CSA statute. Court has declined to apply discovery accrual to Type 1 or Type 2 actions absent legislation.

## *SOUTH DAKOTA*

South Dakota Codified Laws, Title 26, Minors, Chapter 26-10, Offenses By and Against Minors:

**Section 26-10-25: Time limit on civil action arising out of sexual abuse of**

**child.** Any civil action based on intentional conduct brought by any person for recovery of damages for injury suffered as a result of childhood sexual abuse shall be commenced within three years of the act alleged to have caused the injury or condition, or three years of the time the victim discovered or reasonably should have discovered that the injury or condition was caused by the act, whichever period expires later.

**Section 26-10-26: Date of discovery in child sexual abuse action.** The victim need not establish which act in a series of continuing sexual abuse or exploitation incidents caused the injury complained of, but may compute the date of discovery from the date of discovery of the last act by the same perpetrator which is part of a common course of conduct of sexual abuse or exploitation.

**Section 26-10-27: Knowledge of parent or guardian.** The knowledge of a custodial parent or guardian may not be imputed to a person under the age of eighteen years for the purposes of sections 26-10-25 to 26-10-29, inclusive.

**Section 26-10-28: "Child" defined.** For the purposes of sections 26-10-25 to 26-10-29, inclusive, a child is any person under the age of eighteen years.

**Section 26-10-29: "Childhood sexual abuse" defined.** As used in sections 26-10-25 to 26-10-19, inclusive, childhood sexual abuse is any act committed by the defendant against the complainant who was less than eighteen years of age at the time of the act and which act would have been a violation of chapter 22-22 or prior laws of similar effect at the time the act was committed which act would have constituted a felony.

Note: S.L. 1991, ch. 219, ss. 1-5.

***Reported Decisions***

*Shippen v. Parrott* (S.D.1993) 506 N.W.2d 82. Action filed prior to CSA statute by 25-year-old male plaintiff alleging Type 1 discovery. *Held*: South Dakota has legislatively adopted an "occurrence" rule rather than a "discovery" rule of accrual for personal injury actions, thus courts are not free to adopt a discovery rule. Majority opinion does not discuss CSA statute. Dissent refers to statute, noting it is not applicable to this action, filed before it was enacted.

*Koenig v. Lambert* (S.D. 1995) 527 N.W.2d 903. Action filed after CSA statute, by 44-year-old male plaintiff. *Held*: CSA statute is not expressly retroactive, and in any case would be powerless to revive a lapsed action. Under prior law, judicial discovery rule is not applicable to CSA.

*Stratmeyer v. Stratmeyer* (S.D.1997) 567 N.W.2d 220. Several plaintiffs in their late twenties and early thirties sued their uncle for CSA alleging Type 1 discovery within one year of filing. *Held*: CSA statute was intended to and does apply retroactively to "all acts of intentional sexual abuse of children." *Koenig* overturned.

### *Analysis*

CSA statute provides three years from time plaintiff discovered or reasonably should have discovered that the injury or condition was caused by the abuse. Has been applied to action involving Type 1 discovery.

Statute has no express language of revival, but has been held to apply retroactively to all acts of intentional sexual abuse of children.

Statute applies to actions based on "intentional conduct." Issue has not been interpreted.

## *TENNESSEE*

No CSA statute. Tennessee Code Ann., Title 28, Limitation of Actions, section 28-3-104(a) provides one year from accrual for personal injury actions. Section 28-1-106 provides tolling for minority and unsound mind.

### *Reported Decisions*

*Doe v. Coffee County Board of Education* (Tenn.App. 1992) 852 S.W.2d 899. 20-year-old plaintiffs sued former teacher for CSA and school for negligent hiring, alleging Type 1 discovery. *Held*: Judicial discovery rule does not apply to Type 1 discovery of CSA, where plaintiff knows that she has been injured (wronged) by the conduct at the time. Tolling for unsound mind not invoked by psychological effects of CSA.

*Jacobs v. Baylor School* (E.D.Tenn.1996) 957 F.Supp. 1002. Former student sued instructor for sexual harassment and school for negligence, seeking tolling for unsound mind. *Held*: Evidence of mental instability of plaintiff during relevant time period does not amount to showing of unsound mind for purposes of the disability exception to the running of the personal injury statute.

*Hunter v. Brown* (Tenn.1997) 955 S.W.2d 49. 25-year-old plaintiff sued former foster father alleging repressed memory until within one year of filing. At age 15, plaintiff had undergone an abortion for a pregnancy that resulted from defendant's rape. She had told social workers and the district attorney about it at that time, but no prosecution had occurred. She claimed to have repressed memory of the rape, pregnancy and abortion until years later when she had another abortion. *Held*: Evidence establishes plaintiff was aware of her injury and its wrongful cause at the time of the earlier abortion, precluding delayed accrual for subsequent repression. Court expressly declined to decide whether under appropriate circumstances alleged repressed memory would invoke delayed discovery accrual.

### *Analysis*

No CSA statute. Court has held that neither judicial discovery rule nor tolling for unsound mind are invoked by Type 1 discovery. Type 2 discovery has not been addressed.

## *TEXAS*

Texas Codes Ann., Civil Practice & Remedies Code:

**Section 16.0045. Five-Year Limitations Period.**

(a) A person must bring suit for personal injury not later than five years after the day the cause of action accrues if the injury arises as a result of conduct that violates:

(1) Section 22.011, Penal Code (sexual assault); or

(2) Section 22.021, Penal Code (aggravated sexual assault).

(b) In an action for injury resulting in death arising as a result of conduct described by subsection (a), the cause of action accrues upon the death of the injured person.

(c) The limitations period under this section is tolled for a suit on the filing of a petition by any person in an appropriate court alleging that the identity of the defendant in the suit is unknown and designating the unknown defendant as "John or Jane Doe." The person filing the petition shall proceed with due diligence to discover the identity of the defendant and amend the petition by substituting the real name of the defendant for "John or Jane Doe" not later than the 30th day after the date that the defendant is identified to the plaintiff. The limitations period begins running again on the date that the petition is amended.

Note: Added by Acts 1995, 74th Leg., ch. 739, sec. 1, eff. June 15, 1995.

### *Reported Decisions*

*Archambault v. Archambault* (Tex.App.1992) 846 S.W.2d 359. Action decided prior to CSA statute. 27-year-old plaintiff sued parents alleging Type 2 discovery. *Held*: Plaintiff having pleaded delayed discovery, summary judgment could not be granted without evidence negating the alleged delay. Defendant's argument that discovery rule should not be applied to CSA actions was not made below and therefore could not be considered on appeal.

*Sanchez v. Archdiocese of San Antonio* (Tex.App.1994) 873 S.W.2d 87. Action decided prior to CSA statute. 57-year-old plaintiff sued church alleging Type 2 discovery. Plaintiff was aware of the CSA at the time and reported it to church authorities but allegedly repressed it before reaching adulthood. *Held*: Judicial discovery rule applies only where the fact of the injury is unknown and inherently unknowable to plaintiff at the time, and does not apply where plaintiff was aware of the incidents and their wrongfulness at the time, even if later repressed. It is not proper to apply discovery rule where the sole evidence of the abuse is the repressed/recovered memory of the plaintiff and there is no objective verification.

*Vesecky v. Vesecky* (Tex.App.1994) 880 S.W.2d 804, writ grtd. (*Vesecky I*). Action decided prior to CSA statute. 20-year-old plaintiff sued father alleging Type 2 discovery. *Held*: Judicial discovery rule applies to CSA actions where psychological defense mechanisms such as repression prevent discovery.

*S.V. v. R.V.* (Tex.1996) 933 S.W.2d 1,(*Vesecky II*). Review and reversal of appellate court decision in *Vesecky I.* Decided after CSA statute. *Held*: CSA statute applies prospectively only. Court will apply judicial discovery rule to CSA actions only where the abuse was "inherently undiscoverable" and "objectively verifiable." Assuming without deciding that repressed memory can satisfy the "inherently undiscoverable" requirement, a repressed memory case still cannot go forward unless there is evidence establishing that the injury is objectively verifiable. The kinds of evidence that would suffice would be a confession by the abuser, a criminal conviction, contemporaneous records or written statements; medical records showing contemporaneous physical injury resulting from the abuse; or an objective eyewitness account.

*Marshall v. First Baptist Church of Houston* (Tex.App.1997) 949 S.W.2d 504. 22-year-old plaintiff sued Church for negligence in connection with sexual abuse at age 12 by youth music director. Plaintiff disclosed to Church officials while still a minor, and the Church failed to respond to his reports and requests for help. Alleged Type 1 discovery. *Held*: Plaintiff's inability to make the connection between the abuse and his psychological problems, even if caused by the abuse, does not fulfill the requirement that the injury have been "inherently undiscoverable." Church's failure to act on his earlier complaints did not constitute a continuing tort nor trigger estoppel. Emotional problems caused by the abuse, even if severe, do not invoke tolling for mental incapacity.

*Analysis*

CSA statute provides five years from majority with no provision for discovery accrual. Judicial discovery rule has been held not applicable to Type 1 discovery. Court has indicated in dicta, without deciding, that discovery rule may apply to Type 2 discovery if the abuse itself is "objectively verifiable."

Statute has no language of revival; has been held not to apply prospectively only.

Statute applies to actions for "personal injury arising as a result of" CSA; issue has not been interpreted.

## *UTAH*

Utah Code Ann., Title 78, Judicial Code, Chapter 12, Limitation of Actions:

**Section 78-12-25.1: Civil actions for sexual abuse of child.**

(1) As used in this section:

(a) "Child" means a person under 18 years of age.

(b) "Discovery" means when a person knows or reasonably should know that the injury or illness was caused by the intentional or negligent sexual abuse.

(c) "Injury or illness" means either a physical injuryor illness or a psychological injury or illness. A psychological injury or illness need not be accompanied by physical injury or illness.

(d) "Molestation" means touching the anus, buttocks, or genitalia of any child, the breast of a female child younger than 14 years of age, or otherwise taking indecent liberties with a child, or causing a child to take indecent liberties with the perpetrator or another, with the intent to arouse or gratify the sexual desire of any person.

(e) "Negligently" means a failure to act to prevent the child sexual abuse from further occurring or to report the child sexual abuse to law enforcement when the adult who could act knows or reasonably should know of the child sexual abuse and is the victim's parent, stepparent, adoptive parent, foster parent, legal guardian, ancestor, descendant, brother, sister, uncle, aunt, first cousin, nephew, niece, grandparent, stepgrandparent, or any person cohabiting in the child's home.

(f) "Person" means an individual who was intentionally or negligently sexually abused. It does not include individuals whose claims are derived through another individual who was sexually abused.

(g) "Sexual abuse" means acts or attempted acts of sexual intercourse, sodomy, or molestation directed towards a child.

(2) A person shall file a civil action for intentional or negligent sexual abuse suffered as a child:

(a) within four years after the person attains the age of 18 years; or

(b) if a person discovers sexual abuse only after attaining the age of 18 years, that person may bring a civil action for such sexual abuse within four years after discovery of the sexual abuse, whichever period expires later.

(3) The victim need not establish which act in a series of continuing sexual abuse incidents caused the injury complained of but may compute the date of discovery from the date of discovery of the last act by the same perpetrator which is part of a common scheme or plan of sexual abuse.

(4) The knowledge of a custodial parent or guardian shall not be imputed to a person under the age of 18 years.

(5) A civil action may be brought only against a living person who intentionally perpetrated the sexual abuse or negligently permitted the sexual abuse to occur.

Note: Laws 1992, ch. 185, s. 1, effective April 27, 1992.

### *Reported Decisions*

*Whatcott v. Whatcott* (Utah 1990) 790 P.2d 578. Decided prior to CSA statute. 23-year-old plaintiff alleging Type 1 discovery. Record showed plaintiff was aware of the abuse at age 18. *Held*: Where plaintiff aware of the abuse at time of reaching majority, inability fully to understand the harm until later does not invoke discovery accrual. Incest-related mental illness not rising to level of general mental incompetence does not toll statute.

*O'Neal v. Division of Family Services* (Utah 1991) 821 P.2d 1139. Decided prior to CSA statute. 26-year-old plaintiff alleging Type 1 discovery. *Held*: Where plaintiff aware of the abuse at time of reaching majority, psychological inability to reveal the abuse to others does not invoke discovery accrual nor toll for mental incompetence.

*Olsen v. Hooley* (Utah 1993) 865 P.2d 1345. Filed prior to but decided after CSA statute. 31-year-old plaintiff alleging Type 2 discovery. *Held*: CSA statute does not apply to action filed before its effective date. Psychological problems caused by CSA, including repressed memory, do not toll for mental incompetence, but repression can invoke judicial discovery rule. Plaintiff must produce evidence establishing that she did in fact repress memory, as well as evidence corroborating the abuse.

*Roard v. Crabtree* (Utah 1995) 893 P.2d 1058. 34-year-old plaintiff filed action after enactment of CSA statute. Plaintiff alleged Type 1 discovery occurred after effective date of the statute. *Held*: CSA statute not expressly retroactive; legislative history shows deletion of a retroactivity provision, indicating intent that statute not operate retroactively.

*Analysis*

CSA statute provides four years from majority or from date plaintiff discovers the sexual abuse. Appears to apply only to Type 2 discovery, but issue has not been interpreted.

Judicial discovery accrual has been held applicable only to Type 2, and only where plaintiff can produce evidence corroborating the allegations of abuse.

Statute has no language of revival and has been held not to apply retroactively to abuse that occurred prior to its effective date.

Statute applies to actions for intentional and negligent CSA, the latter being where a family or household member knows or has reason to know of the abuse and fails to prevent or report it.

## *VERMONT*

Vermont Stat. Ann., Title 12, Court Procedure, Chapter 23, Limitation of Time:

**Section 522: Actions based on childhood sexual abuse.**

(a) A civil action brought by any person for recovery of damages for injury suffered as a result of childhood sexual abuse shall be commenced within six years of the act alleged to have caused the injury or condition, or six years of the time the victim discovered that the injury or condition was caused by the act, whichever period expires later. The victim need not establish which act in a series of continuing sexual abuse or exploitation incidents caused the injury.
(b) If a complaint is filed alleging an act of childhood sexual abuse which occurred more than six years prior to the date the action is commenced, the complaint shall immediately be sealed by the clerk of the court. The complaint shall remain sealed until the answer is served or, if the defendant files a motion to dismiss under Rule 12(b) of the Vermont Rules of Civil Procedure, until the court rules on that motion. If the complaint is dismissed, the complaint and any related papers or pleadings shall remain sealed. Any hearing held in connection with the motion to dismiss shall be in camera.

(c) As used in this section, "childhood sexual abuse" means any act committed by the defendant against a complainant who was less than 18 years of age at the time of the act and which act would have constituted a violation of a statute prohibiting lewd and lascivious conduct, lewd or lascivious conduct with a child, sexual assault or aggravated sexual assault in effect at the time the act was committed.

Note: 1989, No. 292 (Adj.Sess.), s. 2. Section 4(b) provided that section 2 shall apply to all causes of action commenced on or after July 1, 1990, as long as either the act of sexual abuse or the discovery that the injury or condition was caused by the sexual abuse occurred on or after July 1, 1984.

***Reported Decisions***

*Barquin v. Roman Catholic Diocese of Burlington* (D.Vt.1993) 839 F.Supp. 275. Action filed after CSA statute. 40-year-old plaintiff sued nun and church alleging Type 2 discovery. *Held*: Legislature's omission of phrase "or reasonably should have discovered" from the discovery accrual provision in the CSA statute must be construed as intentional. Thus, under the statute, date of discovery accrual is date of plaintiff's actual discovery.

***Analysis***

CSA statute provides six years from the abuse or six years from discovery that the injury or condition was caused by the abuse. Discovery accrual provision refers only to plaintiff's actual discovery and does not require that the delay have been reasonable. Appears to apply to Type 1 discovery, but the issue has not been interpreted.

Statute has language of revival and has been held to revive lapsed actions.

Statute applies to actions "for recovery of damages for injury suffered as a result of" CSA. Issue has not been interpreted, but related actions for negligence have been held subject to judicial discovery rule.

## *VIRGINIA*

Code of Virginia Ann., Title 8.01, Civil Remedies & Procedure:

**Section 8.01-249. When cause of action shall be deemed to accrue in certain personal actions.**

The cause of action in the actions herein listed shall be deemed to accrue as follows:

(6) . . .In actions for injury to the person, whatever the theory of recovery, resulting from sexual abuse occurring during the infancy or incompetency of the person, when the fact of the injury and its causal connection to the sexual abuse is first communicated to the person by a licensed physician, psychologist, or clinical psychologist. As used in this subdivision, "sexual abuse" means sexual abuse as defined in subdivision 6 of section 18.2-67.10 and acts constituting rape, sodomy, object sexual penetration or sexual battery as defined in Article 7 (section 18.2-61 et seq.) of Chapter 4 of Title 18.2.

Note: Enacted Acts 1991, ch. 674. Clause 2 provided that the act "shall apply to all actions filed on or after July 1, 1991, without regard to when the act upon which the claim is based occurred, provided that no such claim which accrued prior to July 1, 1991, shall be barred by application of those provisions if it is filed within one year of the effective date of this act." After the revival provision was declared unconstitutional by the court in Starnes (1992), infra., a constitutional amendment was passed in 1994 specifically permitting the Legislature to define the accrual date for civil actions based on intentional torts and to provide for retroactive application of a change in the accrual date. See, Constitution of Virginia, Article IV, section 14. Acts 1995, ch. 268, deleted an outer time limit of ten years from majority that had been included in the original statute. Acts 1996, ch. 377, declared that the CSA statute, as amended in 1995, shall apply to all actions filed on or after July 1, 1995.

### *Reported Decisions*

*Starnes v. Cayouette* (Va.1992) 419 S.E.2d 669. Action filed in July 1991, immediately after effective date of CSA statute and within its "window period" for revival of lapsed claims, by 27-year-old plaintiff alleging Type 1 discovery. *Held*: CSA statute could not constitutionally revive claim that had lapsed under prior law.

### *Analysis*

CSA statute applies discovery accrual to the 2-year statute for personal injuries, and defines discovery as when the injury as its causal connection to the sexual abuse is communicated to the plaintiff by a licensed physician or psychologist. Appears to apply to Type 1 discovery, but issue has not been interpreted.

By constitutional amendment and subsequent legislation, statute revives lapsed actions filed after July 1995.

Statute applies to actions "for injury to the person, whatever the theory of recovery, resulting from sexual abuse." Issue has not been interpreted.

## *WASHINGTON*

Rev. Code of Washington Ann., Title 4, Civil Procedure:

**Section 4.16.340: Actions based on childhood sexual abuse.**

(1) All claims or causes of action based on intentional conduct brought by any person for recovery of damages for injury suffered as a result of childhood sexual abuse shall be commenced within the later of the following periods:

(a) Within three years of the act alleged to have caused the injury or condition;

(b) Within three years of the time the victim discovered or reasonably should have discovered that the injury or condition was caused by said act; or

(c) Within three years of the time the victim discovered that the act caused the injury for which the claim is brought:

Provided, that the time limit for commencement of an action under this section is tolled for a child until the child reaches the age of eighteen years.

(2) The victim need not establish which act in a series of continuing sexual abuse or exploitation incidents caused the injury complained of, but may compute the date of discovery from the date of discovery of the last act by the same perpetrator which is part of a common scheme or plan of sexual abuse or exploitation.

(3) The knowledge of a custodial parent or guardian shall not be imputed to a person under the age of eighteen years.

(4) For purposes of this section, "child" means a person under the age of eighteen years.

(5) As used in this section, "childhood sexual abuse" means any act committed by the defendant against a complainant who was less than eighteen years of age at the time of the act and which act would have been a violation of chapter 9A.44 RCW or RCW 9.68A.040 or prior laws of similar effect at the time the act was committed.

Note: Laws 1988, ch. 144, s. 1. Amended Laws 1989, ch. 317, s. 2, effective May 11, 1989. Clarified, Laws 1991, ch. 212, s. 2. The 1988 legislation provided that it applied to all actions commenced after its effective date, regardless of when the cause of action may have arisen. The 1989 amendment clarified that the statute was tolled for plaintiff's minority. The 1991 amendment clarified that it was the intent of the Legislature in enacting the CSA statute to reverse *Tyson* as well as the line of decisions holding that plaintiff's knowledge of any injury whatsoever would commence the running of the statute.

***Reported Decisions***

*Tyson v. Tyson* (Wash.1986) 107 Wash.2d 72, 727 P.2d 226. Action by 26-year-old plaintiff alleging Type 2 discovery, filed and decided prior to CSA statute. Federal district court certified question to Supreme Court of Washington: Does the discovery rule apply to intentional torts where the victim has blocked the incident from conscious memory? *Held*: Judicial discovery rule should be utilized only where the risk of stale claims is outweighed by the unfairness of precluding justified causes. Due to inherent lack of evidence and difficulties of proof in actions alleging repressed memory of CSA, discovery accrual should not be applied. Decision was subsequently abrogated by CSA statute.

*Raymond v. Ingram* (Wash.App.1987) 47 Wash.App. 781, 737 P.2d 314. Decided prior to CSA statute. Plaintiff alleging Type 1 discovery sued grandfather for CSA and grandmother for negligently permitting it. *Held*: Inability to discover causal connection between abuse and later psychological injury does not invoke discovery accrual. Subsequently *abrogated* by CSA statute.

*Kaiser v. Milliman* (Wash.App.1988) 50 Wash.App. 235, 747 P.2d 1130. Decided prior to CSA statute. Plaintiff alleging Type 1 discovery sued father. *Held*: Discovery accrual not applicable where plaintiff could not submit objective, verifiable evidence of the abuse. *Abrogated* by CSA statute.

*St. Michelle v. Robinson* (Wash.App.1988) 52 Wash.App. 309, 759 P.2d 467. Decided after enactment of CSA statute but before its effective date. Plaintiff alleging Type 1 discovery sued father. *Held*: Causes of action for outrage and intentional infliction of emotional distress governed by 3-year "catch-all" statute of limitations and thus not barred.

*Jamerson v. Vandiver* (Wash.App.1997) 85 Wash.App. 564, 934 P.2d 1199. Plaintiff sued brother for CSA and parents for negligence. *Held*: CSA statute applies only to actions against the person who committed the abuse, not to actions against third parties for failure to protect.

*Oostra v. Holstine* (Wash.App.1997) 86 Wash.App. 536, 937 P.2d 195. 25-year-old plaintiff sued stepfather alleging Type 1 discovery. *Held*: CSA statute defines discovery accrual as date the plaintiff discovers or should have discovered the nexus between the abuse and her injury. Applicable to Type 1 discovery.

*C.J.C. v. Catholic Bishop of Yakima* (Wash.App.1997) 88 Wash.App. 70, 943 P.2d 1150. 29-year-old plaintiff sued several priests and Diocese alleging priests had fondled his genitals when he was 15. At the time of the incidents the touchings were not proscribed by penal statute unless the victim was under age 14 or force was used.

*Held*: CSA statute expressly limited to acts which would have violated a penal code section in effect at the time the acts were committed. However, the section prescribing "communication with a child for an immoral purpose" could be construed to apply to the priests' conduct, thus bringing the action within the CSA statute.

### *Analysis*

CSA statute provides three years from majority or three years from date plaintiff discovers or reasonably should have discovered that the injury or condition was caused by the sexual abuse. Declaration of legislative intent added in 1991 makes clear the statute is intended to apply to Type 1 as well as Type 2 discovery, and court has so interpreted it.

Statute has express language of revival; issue has not been interpreted.

Statute applies to actions "based on intentional conduct" and has been held not to apply to actions against persons other than the perpetrator.

## *WEST VIRGINIA*

No CSA statute. West Virginia Code Ann., Chapter 55, Actions, Article 2, Limitation of Actions, section 55-2-12 provides two years for personal injuries. Section 55-2-15 tolls for minority and mental disability.

### *Reported Decisions*

None re CSA actions by adults.

## *WISCONSIN*

Wisconsin Stat. Ann., Chapter 893, Limitation of Actions:

**Section 893.587: Incest; limitation.**

An action to recover damages for injury caused by incest shall be commenced within two years after the plaintiff discovers the fact and the probable cause, or with the exercise of reasonable diligence should have discovered the fact and the probable cause, of the injury, whichever occurs first.

Note: 1987 Act 332, section 22m, effective July 1, 1989.

### *Reported Decisions*

*Hammer v. Hammer* (Wis.App.1987) 142 Wis.2d 257, 418 N.W.2d 23. Action decided prior to CSA statute, by 21-year-old plaintiff alleging Type 1 discovery. *Held*: Causes of action premised on incestuous abuse will not accrue until the victim discovers or in the exercise of reasonable diligence should have discovered the fact and cause of the injury.

*Byrne v. Bercker* (Wis.1993) 176 Wis.2d 1037, 501 N.W.2d 402. Action filed after CSA statute by 50-year-old plaintiff who had begun to remember the incidents of abuse more than two years before filing suit and had been informed by her therapist at that time of its probable connection to certain psychological problems, but claimed she had been unable to "shift the blame" from herself to the perpetrator until later. *Held*: Under *Hammer* and its codification in the CSA statute, an action for CSA accrues when the plaintiff discovers or with reasonable diligence should have discovered both the fact and the probable cause of the injury. Inability to "shift the blame" until later is not a basis for further delay.

*Doe v. Paukstat* (E.D.Wis.1994) 863 F.Supp. 884. Civil rights action under 42 USC 1983 against former teacher and school district by 26-year-old plaintiff alleging Type 1 discovery of teacher's CSA. *Held*: Accrual of a section 1983 action based on sexual abuse should be guided by Wisconsin state law as set forth in *Byrne,* wherein action accrues when plaintiff knew, or a reasonable person in plaintiff's circumstances would have known, of the injury and its cause. Issues of fact as to when plaintiff's claim accrued preclude summary judgment.

*Pritzlaff v. Archdiocese of Milwaukee* (Wis.1995) 194 Wis.2d 303, 533 N.W.2d 780. Former parishioner sued priest and Church alleging Type 1 discovery. Trial court dismissed on pleadings as barred by limitations; appellate court reversed, and petition for review by Archdiocese was granted. *Held*: Under judicial discovery rule the action accrues when plaintiff knows all the essential elements including the wrongful act and the fact of some injury; inability to appreciate full extent of injury until later (Type 1 discovery) does not delay accrual. Special discovery rule articulated in *Hammer* and subsequently codified in CSA statute is limited to cases of incest where special factors of trust and intimidation create need to accommodate plaintiff's delayed ability to act on rights.

*Doe v. Archdiocese of Milwaukee* (Wis.1997) 211 Wis.2d 312, 565 N.W.2d 94. Seven plaintiffs sued priests and Archdiocese, some alleging Type 1 and some Type 2 discovery. Trial court dismissed all claims. Supreme court reviewed on consolidated certification from court of appeals. *Held*: All causes of action accrued when the acts of abuse took place. Knowledge of some harm is presumed from awareness of the acts of abuse; suppression of knowledge of full extent of harm until later (Type 1 discovery) does not delay accrual. Repression of knowledge of the acts themselves (Type 2 discovery) will not be permitted to invoke the judicial discovery rule for reasons of public policy, including the potential for fraud or mistake in claims that may be postponed indefinitely and the lack of certainty regarding validity of recovered memory. Legislature decided to limit the extension of time to actions based on incest only, and court should not extend it beyond that.

*Joseph W. v. Catholic Diocese of Madison* (Wis.App.1997) 212 Wis.2d 925, 569 N.W.2d 795. Adult plaintiff alleging Type 1 discovery and his parents sued Diocese for negligence in connection with priest's sexual abuse of plaintiff during childhood. *Held*: Following *Doe v. Archdiocese,* all causes of action accrued when the acts of abuse occurred. Parents' causes of action cannot be delayed indefinitely based on failure of child to tell them of the abuse.

### *Analysis*

CSA statute provides two years from reasonable discovery of the fact and the cause of the injury in actions based on incest. Prior to statute, court had applied judicial discovery rule to Type 1 discovery of CSA in a case involving on father-daughter incest. Court has held that the CSA statute does not apply to actions based on non-incestuous abuse, and has refused to extend the judicial discovery rule to such actions, on grounds the legislature had intentionally limited the extension to actions based on incest.

Statute has no language of revival but has been held to codify the judicial discovery rule with respect to actions based on incest.

Statute applies to actions "to recover damages for injury caused by incest." Whether statute can be applied to third party liability for incest has not been determined.

## *WYOMING*

Wyoming Stat. Ann., Title 1, Civil Procedure, Chapter 3, Limitation of Actions:

**Section 1-3-105(b):**

(b) Notwithstanding subsection (a) of this section, a civil action based upon sexual assault as defined by W.S. 6-2-301(a)(v) against a minor may be brought within the later of:

(i) Eight (8) years after the minor's eighteenth birthday; or

(ii) Three (3) years after the discovery.

Note: Added Laws 1993, ch. 215, s. 1. Accompanying sections state the law shall apply to any action filed on or after its effective date, and shall be effective immediately.

### *Reported Decisions*

None re CSA actions by adults.

***Analysis***

CSA statute provides longer of eight years from majority or three years from discovery, but does not define discovery accrual, and issue has not been interpreted.

Statute has no language of revival; issue has not been interpreted.

Statute applies to actions "based on" CSA; issue has not been interpreted.

# Appendix B: States Without Specific Statutes of Limitations Governing Childhood Sexual Abuse Actions (Summarizing Appendix A)

Mary R. Williams

| *STATE* | *STATUTE* | *CASE LAW* |
|---|---|---|
| Alabama | 2 years | No discovery accrual for CSA |
| Arizona | 2 years | Discovery accrual in Type 1 and 2 |
| Delaware | 2 years[1] | None |
| District of Columbia | 1 year | Discovery accrual in Type 2; not in Type 1 |
| Hawaii | 2 years | Discovery accrual in Type 1 |
| Indiana | 2 years | No discovery accrual; exception for fraudulent concealment in action against parent |
| Kentucky | 1 year | No discovery accrual or tolling |
| Maryland | 3 years | No discovery accrual or tolling |
| Michigan | 3 years | No discovery accrual or tolling |
| Mississippi | 1 year | No discovery accrual in Type 1; Type 2 unaddressed |
| Nebraska | 1 year | Discovery accrual applicable; scope unclear |
| New Hampshire | 3 years | Discovery accrual in Type 2; probably not Type 1 |

[Haworth co-indexing entry note]: "Appendix B: States Without Specific Statutes of Limitations Governing Childhood Sexual Abuse Actions (Summarizing Appendix A)." Williams, Mary R. Co-published simultaneously in *Journal of Aggression, Maltreatment & Trauma* (The Haworth Maltreatment & Trauma Press, an imprint of The Haworth Press, Inc.) Vol. 3, No. 2 (#6), 2000, pp. 283-284; and: *Sexual Abuse Litigation: A Practical Resource for Attorneys, Clinicians, and Advocates* (ed: Rebecca Rix) The Haworth Maltreatment & Trauma Press, an imprint of The Haworth Press, Inc., 2000, pp. 283-284. Single or multiple copies of this article are available for a fee from The Haworth Document Delivery Service [1-800-342-9678, 9:00 a.m. - 5:00 p.m. (EST). E-mail address: getinfo@haworthpressinc.com].

| | | |
|---|---|---|
| New York | 1 year | No discovery accrual or tolling |
| North Carolina | 3 years | Tolling for incompetency may apply in Type 2; Type 1 unaddressed |
| North Dakota | 2 years | Discovery accrual in Type 1 and 2 |
| Ohio | 1 year | Discovery accrual in Type 2 only |
| Pennsylvania | 2 years[2] | No discovery accrual or tolling |
| South Carolina | 3 years | No discovery accrual |
| Tennessee | 1 year | No discovery accrual in Type 1; Type 2 unaddressed |
| West Virginia | 2 years | None |

NOTES

[1] No tolling for minority.
[2] No tolling for insanity.

# Appendix C: States with Specific Statutes of Limitations Governing Childhood Sexual Abuse Actions (Summarizing Appendix A)

Mary R. Williams

Key: The symbols used in this chart are to be read as follows:
- * The statutory language is unclear and the issue has not been judicially interpreted.
- ** It appears from the statutory language, but the issue has not been judicially interpreted.
- *** The issue has been judicially interpreted.

| *STATE* | *STATUTE* | *TYPE 1 DISCOVERY* | *REVIVAL OF LAPSED ACTIONS* | *APPLICABILITY TO NON-PERPETRATOR* |
|---|---|---|---|---|
| Alaska | 3 years from majority or from discovery | yes** | yes** | no** |
| Arkansas | 3 years from discovery | yes** | * | no** |
| California | 8 years from majority or 3 years from discovery | yes*** | yes*** | no*** |

[Haworth co-indexing entry note]: "Appendix C: States with Specific Statutes of Limitations Governing Childhood Sexual Abuse Actions (Summarizing Appendix A)." Williams, Mary R. Co-published simultaneously in *Journal of Aggression, Maltreatment & Trauma* (The Haworth Maltreatment & Trauma Press, an imprint of The Haworth Press, Inc.) Vol. 3, No. 2 (#6), 2000, pp. 285-287; and: *Sexual Abuse Litigation: A Practical Resource for Attorneys, Clinicians, and Advocates* (ed: Rebecca Rix) The Haworth Maltreatment & Trauma Press, an imprint of The Haworth Press, Inc., 2000, pp. 285-287. Single or multiple copies of this article are available for a fee from The Haworth Document Delivery Service [1-800-342-9678, 9:00 a.m. - 5:00 p.m. (EST). E-mail address: getinfo@haworthpressinc.com].

 

| *STATE* | *STATUTE* | *TYPE 1 DISCOVERY* | *REVIVAL OF LAPSED ACTIONS* | *APPLICABILITY TO NON-PERPETRATOR* |
|---|---|---|---|---|
| Colorado | 6 years from removal of psychological disability to sue | yes** | no** | no** |
| Connecticut | 17 years from majority | N/A | yes*** | yes*** |
| Florida | 7 years from majority or 4 years from discovery | yes** | no*** | no*** |
| Georgia | 5 years from majority | N/A | * | yes** |
| Idaho | 5 years from majority | N/A | no** | no** |
| Illinois | 2 years from discovery | yes*** | no*** | no*** |
| Iowa | 4 years from discovery | yes*** | no*** | yes*** |
| Kansas | 3 years from majority or from discovery | yes*** | yes***[1] | yes** |
| Louisiana | 10 years from majority | N/A | no*** | no** |
| Maine | 12 years from accrual or 6 years from discovery | * | no*** | no** |
| Massachusetts | 3 years from discovery | yes*** | no*** | no***[2] |
| Minnesota | 6 years from discovery | no*** | no if filed after August, 1992 | yes***[3] |
| Missouri | 5 years from majority or 3 years from discovery | yes** | no*** | yes** |
| Montana | 3 years from discovery | yes*** | yes*** | yes*** |
| Nevada | 10 years from majority or from discovery | yes** | no** | yes** |
| New Jersey | 2 years from discovery | yes** | yes** | yes**[4] |

| | | | | |
|---|---|---|---|---|
| New Mexico | Until 24th birthday or 3 years from discovery | yes*** | no** | no** |
| Oklahoma | 2 years from discovery | no** | no** | no** |
| Oregon | 6 years from majority or 3 years from discovery | yes*** | yes*** | yes*** |
| Rhode Island | 7 years from discovery | yes** | no*** | no*** |
| South Dakota | 3 years from discovery | yes*** | yes*** | no** |
| Texas | 5 years from majority | N/A | no*** | yes** |
| Utah | 4 years from majority or from discovery | no** | no*** | yes** |
| Vermont | 6 years from discovery | yes** | yes*** | yes** |
| Virginia | 2 years from discovery | yes** | yes**[5] | yes** |
| Washington | 3 years from discovery | yes*** | yes** | no*** |
| Wisconsin | 2 years from discovery (incest only) | yes*** | *[6] | no*** |
| Wyoming | 8 years from majority or 3 years from discovery | * | no** | no** |

## NOTES

[1] However, the language of revival has been held unable to revive actions that had been extinguished by operation of the eight-year statute of repose that was in effect prior to enactment of the CSA statute (which repealed the statute of repose as to CSA actions).

[2] However, a 3-year statute applies to actions for negligence, subject to discovery rule.

[3] For actions in negligence only, not vicarious liability.

[4] Only to persons standing *in loco parentis*.

[5] Express retroactivity initially held unconstitutional by Court; after constitutional amendment to permit it, retroactivity was re-enacted.

[6] CSA statute has been held to be a codification of prior law as set forth in *Hammer*.

# Appendix D: Questions for Plaintiff Forensic Expert: Direct Examination

Barbara Jo Levy

*These questions were used in the trial from which the deposition and court testimony in Appendices F and G were taken. They have been edited for publication, with much of the plaintiff's personal information having been removed. The answers contained after the questions were the anticipated answers to Levy's questions; like any lawyer, Ms. Levy knows the essence of the answer before asking the question. In this context, they are not suggested answers for the reader's expert witness, but to give an idea of the kind of testimony on the direct examination of the expert witness in this particular trial. The questions are open-ended and permit the entry of several exhibits to help the judge and/or jury make sense of the information being provided.*

I. BACKGROUND/CREDENTIALS:

A. Would you please state your name?
B. What is your professional address?
C What is your profession? (e.g., psychologist or psychiatrist)
D. What is your educational background?
E Please describe your professional licensure:
   1. Where
   2. When
   3. What requirements are there for licensure as a (psychologist/ psychiatrist) in (state)?

---

[Haworth co-indexing entry note]: "Appendix D: Questions for Plaintiff Forensic Expert: Direct Examination." Levy, Barbara Jo. Co-published simultaneously in *Journal of Aggression, Maltreatment & Trauma* (The Haworth Maltreatment & Trauma Press, an imprint of The Haworth Press, Inc.) Vol. 3, No. 2 (#6), 2000, pp. 289-295; and: *Sexual Abuse Litigation: A Practical Resource for Attorneys, Clinicians, and Advocates* (ed: Rebecca Rix) The Haworth Maltreatment & Trauma Press, an imprint of The Haworth Press, Inc., 2000, pp. 289-295. Single or multiple copies of this article are available for a fee from The Haworth Document Delivery Service [1-800-342-9678, 9:00 a.m. - 5:00 p.m. (EST). E-mail address: getinfo@haworthpressinc.com].

 

F. What have you done in the field of (psychology/psychiatry) since your licensing?

G. What has your teaching consisted of (if the witness is a professor)?

   1. Do you have a background in social psychology?
   2. Based on your background in social psychology, do you think you are able to give opinions about the work of other social psychologists?

H. Have you published in scientific journals? If yes,

   1. What has been the focus of your research (psychological impact of sexually coercive events on people)?
   2. Where are your articles published?
   3. Are there differences in the quality of scientific journals?
   4. What are those differences?

I. Do you have a private clinical practice? Do you treat trauma victims? Do you diagnose people with psychological disorders?

*Enter Witness's Curriculum Vitae as Exhibit 1*

J. Establishing the previous forensic experience of the witness:

   1. Have you testified in cases other than this one?
   2. What kinds?
   3. Have you testified primarily on one side?

II. SCIENTIFIC LITERATURE ON TRAUMA & MEMORY

A. Is there an identifiable body of scientific literature on the psychological aspects of trauma?

B. Are you familiar with the literature on the psychological and emotional consequences of trauma?

C. Could you briefly tell us about the development of scientific knowledge of the psychological consequences of trauma? (The expert should outline the lengthy body of scientific literature, from nineteenth century studies, to combat veterans and political prisoners, to the codification of dissociative disorders and Post Traumatic Stress Disorder (PTSD) resulting from violent crime and trauma in the American Psychiatric Association's *Diagnostic and Statistical Manual of Mental Disorders, Fourth Edition* (the *DSM IV*).)

D. What is the *DSM IV?*

*Exhibit 2: PTSD Diagnostic Criteria*

E. What is PTSD?

F. What are the criteria? (Trauma, re-experiencing, avoidance and numbing physiological responses.)

G. Is child sexual abuse considered a type of trauma that can result in PTSD? Why?

1. Does trauma produce the same impact for children as it does for adults? (My expert testified that there is probably a great deal of overlap, although outward manifestiations will differ.)
2. Why and how is it different for children? (My expert testified that trauma in children is different than in adults due to developmental impacts and a more limited number and variety of coping mechanisms amongst chilren.)
3. Does this mean that a child who has been traumatized will necessarily show the trauma–say in school, or in her behavior? (No.)
4. Why not? (The child may cope by trying to be "perfect" and excel.)
5. Can you determine that a child has *not* been sexually abused if physical evidence is absent? (For example, if a medical doctor is going to testify for the defense that a girl's hymen was intact, does that mean that she was not sexually abused?)

H. Is there any scientific evidence that people can forget traumatic experience? (Yes.)
   1. Can you please tell us about the scientific literature in this area? (The expert should delineate the history of studies on trauma and memory.)
   2. Is it generally accepted in psychology community that this occurs? (Yes, and people in general have experienced this.)
   3. Are there different words that are used to describe this forgetting process. (Yes.)
   4. What are they? (Repression, suppression, forgetting, amnesia dissociation.)
   5. Do these words mean the same thing (Mental health professionals and the public in general use these words somewhat interchangeably, often using a particular term depending on their school of education.)
   6. What did Sigmund Freud mean by repression as against common usage today?
   7. What are we really talking about when we say "repression" now? (A period of time when a person has no memory of traumatic experience that occurred prior to that time.)

I. Are you aware of the controversy concerning repressed or forgotten memories? (Yes.)

J. Would you describe that controversy? (One extreme side of the controversy holds that the phenomenon of traumatic memory disruption does not occur, that people do not forget traumatic experience.)

K. What is your assessment of this controversy?

(A:) The evidence actually shows that memory impairment and loss is more likely to happen with children, and more with physical and sexual abuse, than amongst adults and other types of trauma. Psychological theory explains this phenomenon.

(a) Children are helpless to get out of abusive situations so they are more likely to encounter long-standing abuse.

(b) Children have few psychological defenses to deal with trauma.

(c) One of children's few defenses is to forget or dissociate and engage in denial (to say that it really did not happen to them).

(d) Children are often threatened by those in an authority position and\ told to keep abuse a "secret."

L. Does it matter if trauma is forgotten between each incident? (No.) Why not?

(A:) Some children think that if they tell, they will not be believed. Some children get better at denying that the abuse occurred with repeated rehearsals of that denial. There is another argument that holds that people are alleging memories that are not memories of actual events, but are really a product of social influence.

M. What do you mean by that? (There are people who think they have been sexually abused who have not.)

N. Is there evidence to support this position? (Yes, there is anecdotal evidence, such as the "shopping mall" and "mousetrap" studies, as well as some retractions of alleged memories of sexual abuse.)

O. Does this evidence persuade you that adults who are in therapy are being made to believe they have been sexually abused? (No.)

P. Why not? (There is not evidence that therapists treating patients are doing the same things that researchers are doing to create "false memories.")

Q. Is there scientific evidence that persuades you that it *could* happen? (Yes.)

R. Why do you believe that? (Social influence evidence shows that people can be made to have erroneous beliefs.)

S. Can this happen under any condition? (No. Certain conditions have to exist.)

T. What conditions?

(A:) Conditions leading to erroneous beliefs ("brainwashing") include:

a. The presence of a trusted authority figure (such as a parent or other relative, priest, teacher, or therapist) who

b. over time can lead a person to have an erroneous belief

c. with repeated exposure

d. and group pressure

e. given that they have control over that person's life (for example, controlling when they're fed, whether they can leave home, go to bathroom, etc.)

f. and can exert psychological control through fear.

U. What is the evidence that a person may experience a period of to recall for a traumatic event and later recall the memory?
(Studies by Judith Herman, John Briere and Jon Conte, Linda Meyer-Williams, Elizabeth Loftus, Shirley Feldman-Summers.)[1]

V. Are these studies perfect? (No, but one can base conclusions on the accumulation of studies.)

W. Are you aware of the criticisms of the studies? (Yes.)

X. Can you tell us what they are and how you respond to them?

(A:) Some critics of studies argue that methodological weak nesses in the studies they reviewed that make it impossible to conclude that individuals can repress memories of sexual abuse. However, there are now at least 25 studies that demonstrate either partial or total abuse-specific amnesia. This is a robust finding across studies that are clinical and non-clinical, random and non-random, retrospective and prospective.[2]

III. EVALUATION OF PLAINTIFF

A. Did I ask you to do a psychological evaluation of plaintiff? (Yes.)

B. Did you reach an assessment? (Yes.)

*Exhibit 3: List of Materials Submitted to the Witness*

C. On what did you base your assessment?

(A:) 1. Clinical Interview Of Plaintiff
2. Interview Of Therapists
3. Interview Of Siblings, Family Members
4. Interview Of Plaintiff
5. Review of Records
   a. Treating Therapist(s)
   b. Interrogatories
   c. List of Memories Written by the Plaintiff
   d. Plaintiff's Journal and Writings
   e. Letter(s) From Plaintiff to Defendant, others
   f. Various Medical Records
   g. Report of Defense Expert Witness or Medical Evaluator
   h. Report of Plaintiff's Treating Therapist
   i. Report of Plaintiff's Medical Doctor
6. Depositions of:
   a. Plaintiff
   b. Defendant(s)

c. Sibling(s)
d. Parent(s)
e. Defense Expert(s)
f. Plaintiff's Treating Therapist (s)
g. Plaintiff's Medical Doctor(s)
h. Other Witness(es)

D. Purpose of Assessment. (To form an opinion of plaintiff's psychological condition and causes thereof.)

E. Did you reach any opinions? (Yes.) What? (Suffering from a variety of psychological symptoms)

F. What are these psychological symptoms? (From forensic evaluation.)

*Exhibit 4: Plaintiff's Psychological Symptoms (listed)*

G. Did you reach a diagnosis?

H. What is your diagnosis? (PTSD.)

I. What is the basis for your diagnosis?

J. Did you come to a conclusion as to the cause or causes for this. (Yes.)

K. What is your opinion? (That on a more probable than not basis, it was primarily the traumatic sexual abuse experiences in childhood at the hands of her father.)

L. Are you certain. (No.)

M. Why not? (I do not believe certainty is possible in cases like this, with no eye witnesses and no admission by the defendant.)

N. You say you're not certain. Can anyone be certain? (No. There is no evidence that can demonstrate with 100% certainty one way or the other that plaintiff was sexually abused by her father.)

O. What has led you to the conclusion that the trauma that produced her symptoms was sexual abuse by her father?

A. Plaintiff self-reports of flashbacks of childhood sexual abuse.

P. You have seen the list of plaintiff's memories. Do you have any general comments about the list?

(A:) 1. The vast majority of items on the list describe sexual abuse of a type that is frequently reported in the literature and in my clinical practice.

2. Nothing reported is impossible, or inconsistent with other evidence.

3. Plaintiff's involvement in litigation has served as an obstacle to working through memories, which is common.

Q. Why? (Because loss of privacy and exposure of therapeutic situation to litigation impacts therapeutic process.)

R. Is it your opinion that plaintiff's memories are accurate in every detail? (Not necessarily.)

S. Does that effect your opinion that plaintiff was sexually abused? (No.)

T. Why not? (I have no way of knowing if details are accurate. Regard less of the details, this issue does not impact my general opinion because of the way memories work.)

U. In your opinion, are traumatic memories distinguishable from non-traumatic memories? (Yes.)

V. What is the basis for that opinion? (Scientific literature and clinical experience.)

W. What do scientific literature and your practice tell you?

1. Traumatic memories are filed differently.
2. When people deal with traumatic memory, they talk about it as if it were current experience.
3. Part of therapy is to help those memories become more like non-traumatic memories.

IV. OTHER

A. Criticism of treating therapist's interview, report, and/or deposition.

B. Criticism of reports from defense witness(es).

C. Did plaintiff need therapy? Does she need future therapy? How much?

D. What is the plaintiff's prognosis?

NOTES

1. *See, e.g.*, JUDITH L. HERMAN and EMILY SCHATZOW, *Recovery and Verification of Memories of Childhood Sexual Abuse Trauma,* 4 PSYCHOANALYTIC PSYCHOLOGY 1, 1 (1987); JOHN BRIERE and JON CONTE, *Self-Reported Amnesia of Childhood Sexual Abuse in Adults Molested as Children,* 6 JOURNAL OF TRAUMATIC STRESS 1, 21 (1993); LINDA MEYER-WILLIAMS, *Recall of Childhood Trauma: A Prospective Study of Women's Memories of Childhood Sexual Abuse,* 62 JOURNAL OF CONSULTING AND CLINICAL PSYCHOLOGY 6, 1167 (1994); ELIZABETH F. LOFTUS, SARA POLONSKY and MINDY THOMPSON FULLILOVE, *Memories of Childhood Sexual Abuse: Remembering and Repressing,* 18 PSYCHOLOGY OF WOMEN QUARTERLY 1, 67 (1994); SHIRLEY FELDMAN-SUMMERS and KENNETH S. POPE, *The Experience of 'Forgetting' Childhood Abuse: A National Survey of Psychologists,* 62 JOURNAL OF CONSULTING AND CLINICAL PSYCHOLOGY, 3, 636 (1994) (*see also,* SHIRLEY FELDMAN-SUMMERS and KENNETH S. POPE, *The Experience of 'Forgetting' Childhood Abuse: A National Survey of Psychologists: Correction,* 62 JOURNAL OF CONSULTING AND CLINICAL PSYCHOLOGY, 4, 800 (1994)).

2. *See, generally,* ALAN W. SHEFLIN and DANIEL BROWN, *Repression, Memory or Dissociative Amnesia,* 24 JOURNAL OF PSYCHIATRY AND THE LAW 2, 143, 174-82 (1996).

# Appendix E: Questions for Plaintiff Forensic Expert: Rebuttal

Barbara Jo Levy

*These questions were used in the trial from which the deposition and court testimony in Appendices F and G were taken. They have been edited for publication, with much of the plaintiff's personal information having been removed. The answers contained after the questions were the anticipated answers to her questions; like any lawyer, Ms. Levy knows the essence of the answer before asking the question. In this context, they are not suggested answers for the reader's expert witness, but to give an idea of the kind of testimony on rebuttal in this particular trial.*

I. SCIENTIFIC EVIDENCE

Q. A. Defense experts have testified that there is no scientific evidence for repression or forgetting multiple traumatic episodes.

1. Do you agree? (No.)
2. Why not?

Answers:

a. Because there are numerous accounts in the scientific literature of adults in treatment having had periods of time in which they have not been able to recall a series of traumatic events.

b. Because in my clinical experience there are adults who had the experience of no recollection of abuse as children and later remember sexual abuse. (The subjects of these studies were not litigants, and thus had no motivation for fabricating memories.)

Q. B. At least one defense expert has testified that global amnesia is very rare.

[Haworth co-indexing entry note]: "Appendix E: Questions for Plaintiff Forensic Expert: Rebuttal." Levy, Barbara Jo. Co-published simultaneously in *Journal of Aggression, Maltreatment & Trauma* (The Haworth Maltreatment & Trauma Press, an imprint of The Haworth Press, Inc.) Vol. 3, No. 2 (#6), 2000, pp. 297-301; and: *Sexual Abuse Litigation: A Practical Resource for Attorneys, Clinicians, and Advocates* (ed: Rebecca Rix) The Haworth Maltreatment & Trauma Press, an imprint of The Haworth Press, Inc., 2000, pp. 297-301. Single or multiple copies of this article are available for a fee from The Haworth Document Delivery Service [1-800-342-9678, 9:00 a.m. - 5:00 p.m. (EST). E-mail address: getinfo@haworthpressinc.com].

 

1. Do you agree with that?

Answer: A substantial minority of adults abused as children have amnesia not only for abuse but also for non-traumatic past. (Examples given from clinical practice.)

2. Do you have the opinion plaintiff has global amnesia? Why or why not?

Q. C. Some of the defense experts have suggested that the evidence you cited regarding multiple episodes of abuse being repressed is not scientific evidence of forgetting of true memories because there has been no corroboration.

1. Do you agree? Why not?

Answers:
a. There is nothing unscientific about self-report.
b. When subjects report recovery of memories of sexual abuse, there often is no independent corroboration available.
c. Such corroboration is often impossible to obtain, since the abuse occurred decades before.
d. It would be scientifically possible to subject children to trauma and follow up on them, but it would be unethical and morally reprehensible.
e. So, if "scientific evidence" means a study where experimenters cause trauma, then we won't be able to have scientific evidence.
f. But where we have study after study supporting the phenomenon, and have cases of offender corroboration, and have a theoretical basis that explains the phenomenon, and have clinical experience that explains the phenomenon, there is scientific evidence.

Q. D. At least one of the defense experts testified that scientific evidence shows that memories are unreliable and subject to influence under certain conditions and concluded from that, that memories without direct corroboration should not be accepted.

1. Do you agree? Why not?

Answers:
a. It is true that peripheral details of memory may be unreliable and that under certain circumstances they can be influenced.
b. Part of how we define ourselves are our memories.
c. But when circumstances constituting undue influence are not present and we are not talking about details, it would be inaccurate to say we cannot pay attention whether memory was at one point forgotten or not.

2. What kinds of circumstances constitute undue influence?

Q. E. Some of the defense experts testified that there are studies which demonstrate that people can be persuaded to believe they have had an experience they have not, in fact, had.

1. Are you familiar with those studies? (Yes.)
2. What conclusions can be drawn from these studies about adults who remember childhood sexual abuse after a period of forgetting?

Answers:
a. Not much. Most of the studies that have been done are

anecdotal accounts in the literature. The most successful experiences involve young children; it is clearly easier to make children believe things than adults.

b. There are alternative explanations for outcomes. Just because subjects say they believe something happened does not mean they believe it. There is something called the experimenter effect where the subject assumes what the experimenter wants and tries to be a good subject.

c. And in vast majority of subjects, the suggestion does not work anyway. So the studies do not enable us to draw conclusions about traumatic memories of abuse.

Q. F. One of the defense experts testified that experts and therapists cannot know whether sexual abuse occurred or whether details of sexual abuse are accurate.

1. Would you agree with that? (Yes.)
2. Does that mean then that an expert or therapist is unable to formulate an opinion on a more-probable-than-not basis as to whether sexual abuse occurred? (No.)
3. Why not?
    a. There is a difference between certainty and having opinions on a more-probable-than-not basis. I was not there when the abuse occurred, so I cannot be certain that it did occur. That, however, does not mean I cannot come to an opinion as to probability based on evidence in this case and my own professional experience.
    b. The issue of causation and determining probability of occurrence and causation is critical part of therapy and is part of the normal course of my practice. (For example, if I don't believe what a client is saying, it affects my therapy. That doesn't mean my working hypothesis won't change. But I make these determinations in the normal course of my practice as a therapist.)

II. PLAINTIFF INFORMATION

A. Plaintiff's mother testified that there was insufficient privacy in the home for sexual abuse to occur–e.g., that the girls shared a bedroom. What is your reaction to that testimony?

Answers: 1. The fact that the girls shared a bedroom wouldn't preclude the possibility of sexual abuse. The girls wouldn't always be together in the bedroom, and abuse could occur outside the girls' bedroom.

2. We know from the scientific literature that many women who are married to abusers do not know the abuse is occurring or are in such denial that they do not see or recognize evidence of abuse when it is in front of them.

B. When plaintiff's mother testified about her memories of plaintiff as a child, she said that the plaintiff always had a restricted range of affect, an exaggerated startle response, sleep problems, and was always melancholy and quiet. She said that when plaintiff was 6, she described plaintiff's sister as daytime and plaintiff as nighttime.

1. If these descriptions were true, Doctor, would that mean plaintiff's symptoms are not related to sexual abuse but arise from genetic temperament? (No.)
2. Why not?

Answer: Although children are born with different temperaments and sensitivities, it is unlikely that those descriptions are simply a result of temperament. If we can trust plaintiff's mother's accounts (given the passage of time and the circumstances of her testimony), it indicates that the plaintiff had some significant problems as a child that could be related to sexual abuse. (The plaintiff's mother could be seeing symptoms of abuse she didn't recognize.)

C. One of the defense experts testified that the list of memories prepared by plaintiff indicated that her abuse instances became progressively weirder which indicated to him they were false and a product of therapist influence.

1. Do you agree? (No.)
2. Why not?

Answer: The memories described were only partially related to sexually abusive experiences, and only a few are unusual. If we look carefully we can see unusual items are dispersed throughout, not concentrated at the end. How ever, even if it were true that abuse memories became more unusual or severe as she progressed in therapy, one couldn't conclude they were false. In fact, we have evidence that the most severe abuse memories take longer to recollect because they are harder to deal with.

D. One of the defense experts testified that because plaintiff sees herself in the memories rather than observing others from the position of the perceiver, that is an indication that the memory is false.

1. Do you agree? (No.)
2. Why not?

Answer: Seeing oneself in memory is common for survivors of sexual abuse and indicates dissociation. (Examples given.)

E. One of the defense experts testified that because plaintiff remembers numerous sexual abuse incidents involving her sisters that her sisters are unable to recall, that it is a demonstration that the memories are false.

1. Do you agree? (No.)
2. Why not?

Answer: First, there are only five memories (in this case), some of which may be of the same incident. Second, the plaintiff is the oldest child. The events she recalls may not be recalled by her siblings because they were too young or for other reasons.

F. One of the defense experts said plaintiff's memory of people standing around a fire is a "full-blown satanic cult visualization" and that it is predictable that there will be a progression to visualizations of cannibalism.

1. Do you agree? (No.)
2. Why not?

Answer: This is a memory fragment that is also mentioned in plaintiff's therapy in which she reports being frightened and believes the people may be wearing masks. It is more likely to be the case that she is remembering a rather common experience of being around a campfire at night as a child and being frightened. Children are often frightened of the dark. The masks could simply be a reflection of faces in front of the fire. There is no mention by plaintiff of satanic cults or cannibalism. The expert is engaged in wild speculation with no basis in fact.

# Appendix F: Selections, Deposition Testimony of Elizabeth Loftus, PhD

Barbara Jo Levy

*Lynn Crook vs. Bruce Murphy and Lucille Murphy*, No. 91-2-01102-5, Superior Court of the State of Washington, County of Benton

Deposition Upon Oral Examination of Elizabeth Loftus, PhD

January 24, 1994

Seattle, Washington[1]

***

4[2]

ELIZABETH LOFTUS: Being first duly sworn by the Notary Public on oath testified as follows:

EXAMINATION BY MS. LEVY:

Q. Would you state your name and business address for the record.

A. Elizabeth Loftus, Psychology Department, University of Washington, Seattle, 98195.

Q. What is your profession?

A. Professor of psychology.

Q. Is there an area in which you specialize in psychology?

****

A. Yes, my specialty is memory.

Q. Is your specialty in memory in general, or specific things about memory?

[Haworth co-indexing entry note]: "Appendix F: Selections, Deposition Testimony of Elizabeth Loftus, PhD." Levy, Barbara Jo. Co-published simultaneously in *Journal of Aggression, Maltreatment & Trauma* (The Haworth Maltreatment & Trauma Press, an imprint of The Haworth Press, Inc.) Vol. 3, No. 2 (#6), 2000, pp. 303-347; and: *Sexual Abuse Litigation: A Practical Resource for Attorneys, Clinicians, and Advocates* (ed: Rebecca Rix) The Haworth Maltreatment & Trauma Press, an imprint of The Haworth Press, Inc., 2000, pp. 303-347. Single or multiple copies of this article are available for a fee from The Haworth Document Delivery Service [1-800-342-9678, 9:00 a.m. - 5:00 p.m. (EST). E-mail address: getinfo@haworthpressinc.com].

 

5

A. I would say in general memory, although even within the area of memory I have been specializing in memory distortion.

***

Q. So the two major areas that you would be working in memory is long-term memory and memory distortion?

A. And eyewitness testimony, just memory in general, but mostly long-term memory.

Q. And you would call yourself an experimental psychologist; is that correct?

A. Yes.

Q. You don't do any clinical work?

A. Correct.

Q. You have never seen a client or a patient for therapy?

A. Correct.

Q. You've never diagnosed someone with a mental disorder?

6

A. Right.

Q. And you've never seen clients for therapy at all; is that correct?

A. Right.

***

Q. Does this inch of papers constitute all of the records you've seen in this case?

A. No.

Q. What else have you seen?

7

***

8

***

Q. So you have reviewed to some extent everything that is on a page called Index of Exhibits, Volume 1, and Index of Exhibits, Volume 2?

A. Yes.

***

Q. In addition to these documents, what else have you reviewed?

***

9

***

Q. Then you have a bill for services to Floyd Ivey dated January 19, 1994, and that amount is for $1,186.70; is that correct?

A. Yes.

Q. And that is for services from 12-10-93 through 1-19-94; is that correct?

A. Yes.
***
Q. Is this all that you have charged so far to him, total?
A. Well, no. There is a retainer in there.
Q. How much is that?
A. A $1,200 retainer that I received.
Q. So this is on top of the $1,200?
A. Right.
Q. So it's $2,400, about, that you have charged him through January 19, 1994?
A. Right.
Q. And your services were $300 an hour in 1993, and you have raised them to $350 an hour in 1994?
A. Correct.

10
Q. It was your testimony, I believe, that Mr. Ivey first contacted you sometime in 1993. Is there any document that would show when you were contacted in this case?
***
Q. You've given me your latest vitae, is that correct?
A. Yes.
***
Q. What have you been asked to do in this case?
A. Testify at trial on the subject of memory and memory distortion and suggestibility.
Q. So are you talking about general memory, or [Plaintiff]'s memory, or both?
A. I'm talking about general memory and suggestibility and the creation of false memories in general, and then specific examples of suggestion that occurred in this case.

11
Q. Have you been asked to give an opinion as to whether or not [Plaintiff]'s memories are accurate or inaccurate?
A. No.
Q. Do you have an opinion as to whether [Plaintiff]'s memories are accurate or are inaccurate?
A. Well, without corroboration there is no way to know one way or the other, at least that's true of the memories that are being dredged up of things that supposedly occurred after the offset of childhood amnesia. As for memories that supposedly occurred at the age of one or two, there is probably good scientific reason to be especially suspicious about them, but even then I wouldn't be saying absolutely they are false.

Q. In terms of memories after age three or four, do you have an opinion as to whether the memories, [Plaintiff]'s memories are accurate or inaccurate?
A. Well, my professional opinion is that there is no way to know without corroboration one way or another.

12

Q. Have you given Mr. Ivey any information that you wanted him to obtain from any witnesses in this case?
A. *** I'm interested in the book *Soul Survivors*, which I don't have a copy of. It seems to be possibly playing a role in this case. ***
Q. Did you ask Mr. Ivey to obtain any information via depositions from any witnesses that would be helpful for your testimony?
A. Well, we have had discussions on the phone in which I've talked about my opinions and my examination of the materials, be they

13

documents or people's testimony to find, if they exist, examples of suggestion so he knows that as a general rule, that's what I'm interested in knowing about.
Q. Is suggestions to [Plaintiff]
A. Yes, if they existed.
Q. We will get into that, and I take it that you have an opinion that there were suggestions to her; is that correct?
A. I do believe there were suggestions in the environment in which she lived; yes.
Q. Do you know how many times you've testified in cases regarding so-called repressed memories, and that's a term that you do use, isn't it?
A. Yes.
Q. What is your definition of repressed memories?
A. Well, there are all kinds of definitions.
Q. Your definition. Do you have a definition?
A. I have many definitions because they are the definitions that many people use.
Q. If we are going to be talking about a term repressed memories, what does that mean to you for purposes of your testimony?
A. Sometimes it means, to some people, that they didn't think about something horrible or awful

14

that happened to them for a long time and then they were reminded of it later. Sometimes it means they actively blocked or banished from their conscious awareness a series of traumatic events and buried those in their unconscious and then they dug them out later and they were reliable. And those are at least two of the ways that repression is used.

Q. Can you tell me how many times you have testified in cases regarding repressed memories?
A. Oh, let me think, maybe fifteen times.
***

15
***

Q. That's fine. Of the fifteen, approximately fifteen times you've testified in trial

16

regarding cases that have repressed memory issues, how many of those have been civil and how many criminal?
A. At least three criminal cases, maybe more.
Q. How many times have you testified in depositions for the plaintiff?
A. At least two, and maybe more.
Q. Can you give me the names of those cases?
A. I know the names by the attorneys. One is [name omitted]'s case in San Francisco where I testified on behalf of the father who is suing the therapist and the hospital for implanting memories. The other is [name omitted] from Dallas, Texas, I testified on behalf of the patient who is suing her former therapist for malpractice.
Q. So in all cases that you've testified in then, Dr. Loftus, you have found, or you've testified on the side of there being suggestive or false memories; is that correct?
A. When there actually has been testimony, yes.
Q. You've never testified in a case regarding repressed memories where you have testified for a plaintiff to the effect that you have the opinion that the memories are true; is that correct?

17

A. Right, I've never done that. I have worked on plaintiff's cases, four of them, as a consultant, but I have not actually testified.
***

18
***

Q. Other than this *Crook vs. Murphy* case, how many other cases are you working on regarding repressed memory at this time?
A. Maybe another fifteen or twenty.
***

19
***

Q. Other than those two cases, are all the other cases you are working on for the defense?

A. No.
Q. Are you working on other cases where someone is suing a therapist or a hospital for implanting false memory?
A. Yes.
Q. Other than those types of cases, are all your cases for the defense?
A. No. Let me think. I think so. I think yes. There are so many variations of these cases, I lost track of who is the plaintiff and who is the defense, but I think the answer is yes.
***

20
Q. So other than the case for [name omitted] and [name omitted], all the cases that you are working on you are on the side of there being a suggestive or false memory, whether it's for the plaintiff or the defendant?
A. I'm exploring the case to see if there is suggestion.
Q. But for someone who is trying to show that there is suggestive or false memory?
A. Yes.
Q. Do you have an estimate of how many hours you plan to spend on this case from now through the time of trial?
A. Well, I have approximately ten more hours into the case since my last bill. I believe that if I get the documents that I've asked for, that might take up another hour.
***
Q. Do you charge for travel time?

21
Q. How much do you charge for that?
A. $350 an hour.
Q. So you charge $350 an hour for everything?
A. I do; yes.
Q. If you fly to the Tri-Cities and have to spend the night there, how do you charge for that?
A. A maximum of twelve hours a day.
***

22
***
23

Q. Can you tell me how much money you earned doing forensic work in the last year?
A. No, because I haven't done my taxes yet, but I could give you the year before that, the year I have data.

Q. Okay, what would that be?

A. It would be

Q. –1992

A. 1992. Well, it's hard to know because the amount includes royalties and forensic work and I don't have it separated.

Q. What would be the amount for the two of those?

A. Maybe $100,000 salary, approximately. That's just approximate, for royalties and–book royalties and forensic work.

Q. My understanding is you have a separate corporation set up for collecting for your forensic work and your royalties; is that correct?

A. Right.

Q. And you take a salary out of that corporation?

A. Right.

Q. So does some money stay within the corporation then that you don't take?

A. No, nothing stays in the corporation, but the money does pay for the travel expenses and the other expenses of doing business.

24

Q. But you take all of the net profits as your salary out of the corporation?

A. Yes.

Q. What is your salary as a professor here at the university?

A. My nine-month salary? Oh, approximately $75,000, maybe, for nine months, roughly.

Q. What are you teaching now?

A. Eyewitness testimony and a seminar on cognitive psychology that I run.

Q. What other

A. You mean right now?

Q. This quarter.

A. Yes, that's this quarter.

Q. What other kinds of courses do you teach?

A. I teach cognitive psychology, a large undergraduate course, I teach a course on repressed memories, last year I did it and I'm going to do it again.

Q. What goes on in your course on repressed memories?

A. We read articles and book chapters and discuss cases.

25

Q. What do you have your class read in that course?

A. Lots of articles.

Q. Can you give me authors of the articles that you have your class read?

***

A. . . . You know, they read Briere and Conte, all the articles that I'm sure you know about, Herman & Schatzow, my *Reality of Repressed Memory,* they read *Making Monsters.* They read one law review article. They read some articles written by clinicians. I'm about to teach it again and there will be a lot of overlap, a lot a new articles now, so I will be changing the syllabus this year.
Q. What new articles are you going to have your class read?

26

A. Well, I don't know yet exactly what will go into this packet, but probably whatever is new and important in this field.
Q. So do you discuss in this class what you think is good research and bad research, or what makes sense out of the articles or what doesn't make sense, or how they might have done a better study or how the study was well done, that kind of thing?
A. Yes.
Q. Have you reached any opinions in this case?
A. Yes.
Q. What are those opinions?
A. Well, my first opinion is that the study of memory and suggestibility and the study of false memories and the creation of false memories and the characteristics of false memories is relevant to understanding what might be happening or might have happened in this case, and it's my opinion that there is suggestion in this case that could be responsible for the creation of some of these memories, if they are false memories.
Q. Do you have an opinion as to whether or not the memories in this case are false memories?

27

A. Without corroboration there is really no way to know whether they are true or false, particularly if they are memories of things that supposedly happened after the age of three or four. For some of the memories that occurred prior to the age of two or three, the literature on childhood amnesia would suggest that these are highly unlikely to be real memories.
Q. So the first opinion you have is that information on memories and false memories and the creation of false memories is relevant to this case?
A. Yes.
Q. Can you tell me in what ways those studies are relevant in this case?
A. There is a lot of literature on false memories, and memory distortion is about how it is that human beings develop false memories and how they can be confident in detail about them, even though they are false. In my opinion that's relevant information for a jury to have to understand and appreciate the ways in which these memories might have developed, if they are false.

28

Q. Can you tell me then what it is that is relevant about those studies and that information to this particular case?

A. It's basic work on the development of false memories.

Q. What is that? What is the work on false memories that is relevant to this case?

A. The literature on the misinformation effect, the literature on reality monitoring or the breakdown of reality monitoring, the literature on hypnotically produced pseudo memories. These are just some sub areas in the memory distortion work that I think are relevant.

Q. What is it in the literature on the misinformation effect that is relevant to this case?

A. That's the literature that shows that when you expose people to suggestive information they can adopt that information and incorporate it into their memories and contaminate, distort or transform the prior recollections.

Q. Do you believe that there is misinformation in this case?

A. I believe there may be.

29

Q. What would that be?

A. I believe there is suggestive information. I don't know if its erroneous information, but there is suggestive information in this case

Q. What is the suggestive information in this case?

A. Well, would you like me to go through and find the various points of concern that I have about what went on?

Q. Sure.

A. I need to review my notes.

Q. You are looking at what's been marked as Exhibit 4; is that correct?

A. Yes. I have not grouped these together in any particular order, but just a few of the things that concern me as potential sources of suggestion, first in the materials from [Plaintiff's Therapist], he expresses a series of beliefs that I believe are, at least in dispute in the scientific literature, sometimes contradicted by the scientific literature, and therefore may be inappropriate information to communicate to a patient.

Q. What are those beliefs?

30

A. Well, first his definition of flashbacks that the claims the plaintiff had as brief memories of past events demonstrates a belief that these things are memories when they may not be. His opinion that the plaintiff was abused from age one to age twelve seems to be completely uncritical about the problem of childhood amnesia. He seems to have uncritically accepted her claims of bestiality, I mean and all the various acts that are listed without ever having bothered to find any supporting evidence. He used hypnosis to–apparently to uncover memories, and there is literature to suggest that that can be a dangerous thing to do to people. He characterizes the confrontation with the father as evidence, or it is evident, he suggests, that the father remembered some of the abuse and communicated this belief. He recommended a book, *Soul Survivors,* which I haven't seen yet, but I would like to examine that for the information it might contain.

31

His belief in repression is also evident in his deposition and his belief that the plaintiff recalled things that were repressed. He recommended *The Courage to Heal* and *The Courage to Heal Workbook,* or at least he recommends that most often to his patients, and these do contain some suggestive information that has worried me and others in terms of their potential for leading people to develop false memories. He seems to believe that eating disorders are related to sexual abuse despite some recent work that suggests that there may be absolutely no relationship between eating disorders and a history of child sex abuse. He seems to believe all the plaintiff's memories without any kind of critical eye whatsoever. The plaintiff then went to see [Plaintiff's Therapist/Group Therapy], and while I have not read her deposition because of the missing pages, it's clear that she has either taken workshops or favors certain books which contain, in my opinion, misinformation about memory. She

32

seems to believe in body memories despite the fact that there is no evidence that I know of whatsoever to suggest that these represent real memories.
Q. Where does it say that she believes in body memories? Was she just asked for her definition of body memories, or what her understanding is?
A. She was asked about body memories on page 43 of her deposition, and I wrote she seems to believe in them, so I forgot the details of her answer.
Q. Do you recall her also saying that she saw [Plaintiff] doing something with her hands and seemed to tighten her hands but that could have just been anxiety, she didn't know which it was? Do you recall that in her deposition?
A. I don't remember that.
Q. So you are saying it just seems that she believes in body memories?
A. Yes. I don't know what it is exactly that made me write that down. She defines flashbacks as an image of something that happened in the past, something real, supposedly. Those are a few of the things that bothered me about this case.

33

Q. Is there anything else other than those few things?
A. Well, just, you know, she is in this group therapy and the memories seem to get more and more and more bizarre and wild. Her various therapists, at least one of

them, seem to be, if anything, encouraging confrontation with the family before bothering to take the time to find out whether these memories are real or not.
Q. How would a therapist bother to find out whether the memories are real or not?
A. Ask her to bring in some evidence.
Q. What kinds of evidence would there be?
A. It's hard to know. Judith Herman apparently asked her patients to bring in evidence, and they brought in corroboration.
Q. What would be corroboration to you?
A. Well, according to Judith Herman there were photographs, contemporaneous diaries and other kinds of information that the patients were able to bring in.
Q. Generally there is not photographs of sexual abuse, though, wouldn't you agree?

34
A. There are cases where there is pornography made. It may not be that common, but it certainly does exist, and that's just one example.
Q. It could be that somebody could have pictures, but it's not real common for there to be–for a victim of sexual abuse to find pictures of it?
A. That was one of the forms of corroboration that was mentioned in the Judith Herman and Schatzow article.
Q. Besides journals and photographs, what else would consist of corroboration to you?
A. A perpetrator confession that clearly wasn't coerced or intimidated might be a form of corroboration.
Q. What else would constitute corroboration to you?
A. Independent other witnesses to the acts being recalled, if they were truly independent, might be corroboration.
Q. What else would constitute corroboration to you?
A. Maybe even having talked to somebody at the time about it, and the record of that

35
contemporaneous conversation might be considered corroboration, depending on the conditions.
Q. Anything else?
A. I can't think of anything else right now.
Q. Do you know under what conditions [Plaintiff's Therapist] tried to use hypnosis with [Plaintiff]?
A. There was just evidence of it in a number of places in her journals, in his deposition, et cetera.

Q. Do you have any reason or any information to contradict a statement that he would make that he tried hypnosis one time to help [Plaintiff] remember happy memories of childhood and was unsuccessful in doing so?
A. I don't recall that.
Q. Do you have any information to contradict that?
A. Well, in the plaintiff's case study there is–we tried hypnosis twice, and I would have to go through various notes to find more. There is hypnosis, also relaxation with suggestion mentioned on page 20 of the deposition of [Plaintiff's Therapist].
Q. Do you know what was involved in that relaxation?

36
A. No, I don't.
Q. It would depend on what was involved in that relaxation and suggestion for you to determine whether or not there was suggestive information about memories of sexual abuse, wouldn't it?
A. Right, and what followed it as well, but right, what was produced during the hypnosis.
Q. What, if anything, was produced during the hypnosis?
A. Right.
Q. And what, if anything, was suggested in a relaxation technique?
A. That would be important too.
Q. So if [Plaintiff's Therapist] said I want you to remember a peaceful place so that you can relax, and that was the end of it, would not necessarily be suggestions of childhood sexual abuse; isn't that correct?
A. Right.
Q. Have you read the book *Courage to Heal?*
A. Yes.
Q. Have you had memories of sexual abuse that were repressed come to you after reading that book?

37
A. No.
Q. What workshops has [Plaintiff's Therapist/Group Therapy?] taken that had misinformation on memory?
A. On page 4 of her deposition she is asked about titles and workshops and she mentions Fredrickson. On her vitae she also lists workshops she has gone to between 1989 and the present. She talks about Fredrickson. The book *Repressed Memories* by Fredrickson has a number of suggestive things that have been heavily criticized recently.
Q. What is in there that has been criticized recently?

A. Just her insinuation of the massive prevalence of repressed memories and kinds of techniques that she recommends and so on.
Q. Who has criticized her work?
A. Steve Ceci at Cornell, Steve Lindsey at Victoria, Don Read at the University of Lethbridge, just for example.
Q. And there are other people who support her work; is that correct?
A. Well, the recovered memory movement does.
Q. So is it that you are on one side or the other side?

38

A. It's just the people who recognize that some of the techniques that she is advocating are dangerous that are worried.
Q. What techniques is she advocating that you believe are dangerous?
A. I believe that she probably is advocating dream work and imagistic work that potentially can lead to the creation of false memories.
Q. Is there any indication in this case that there was any dream work that led to false memories–any dream work, period?
A. It seems to me that I read something about dreams, or maybe the plaintiff bringing dreams in this case, but I don't remember the details of it right now.
Q. Do you remember any interpretation of dreams in this case?
A. No.
Q. Can you point to anything in the records that shows that [Plaintiff] was asked to do imaging work and as part of that imaging work she came up with memories of sexual abuse?
A. Not as I sit here right now; no.
Q. Is there any evidence that shows that reading

39

a book such as *Courage to Heal* can cause a person who was not sexually abused to believe that she was?
A. Well, there are numerous cases of retractors now who were subjected to a regimen of suggestive techniques and came to believe that they were sexually abused and they now, in their mind, realize their memories are false. There is no way to know whether the book did it, whether the other elements of suggestion did it, or whether the combination did it.
Q. Or whether they are wrong in the retractions?
A. They even might be possibly wrong in their retractions, although there was never any other evidence in the first place.
Q. What is the regimen of therapy that you were talking about?

A. It's different for different women, but there are a collection of suggestive things that therapists have done or do, and some various combinations of them existed in these various retractor cases.
Q. Are some of those elements in those retractor cases present in this case?

40

A. Well, I've listed them already, some of them.
Q. Those elements that you said about [Plaintiff's Therapist/Group Therapy] and [Plaintiff's Therapist]?
A. Right, and the books and the other aspects that I've talked about already.
Q. You talked about the therapy and beliefs with [Plaintiff's Therapist] and [Plaintiff's Therapist/Group Therapy] and some books. Is there anything else that you think could have led to a false memory or suggestion of abuse in this case?
A. There were conversations amongst the various people that I think might be responsible for some memories, if they are false.
Q. Conversations with
A. For example, with the plaintiff and her sisters.
Q. Anything else?
A. Well, not that I can be sure of right now.
Q. Have you conducted an experiment to show whether people who read books regarding sexual abuse start having false memories of sexual abuse?
A. No.
Q. Have you read any such study?
A. I have done studies showing that when people

41

read things they can develop false memories, but not with sexual abuse. It would probably not be ethical to actually sit down and do that study, but I have done many studies where people read things and then they develop false memories about what they read.
Q. Can you tell me about those studies?
A. They are just the scores of misinformation studies that I've done where we allow people to read another witness' version of what they have seen, and they then tell us that they saw those various objects or details.
Q. So these would be your studies where someone actually witnessed something, him or herself, and then read someone else's account, and then their version may have been affected by reading someone else's account?
A. Right.
Q. But they had actually been part of the experiment or seen some activity themselves
A. In most of those studies; yes.

Q. And in those cases you are looking at details of information being changed by reading someone else's account?
A. Right. In most of those, yes.

42

Q. Are there any where it was something other than details?
A. Well, I would say for the most part the studies involve changing memory for detail. Sometimes there is adding a whole detail or adding something that wasn't present. In one of the studies, convincing people that they saw a man hit a girl when he didn't even get near her, so is that changing a detail or is that creating something completely new? It's sometimes hard to draw the line.
Q. And it is accepted by you and other memory experts that recalled details can be altered under certain circumstances; correct?
A. Yes.
Q. What are those factors or circumstances that cause people to recall events incorrectly?
A. To be susceptible to misinformation, or just generally to be wrong about things?
Q. Well, to be suggestible and to be wrong, let's do both.
A. There are scores and scores of facts there, so we could be here for three months if you wanted a whole lesson on memory and what makes it accurate and inaccurate.

43

Q. Well, you have some basic ideas of what can cause people to recall details incorrectly.
A. Yes. First of all, if the events supposedly happened a long time ago the memory is more susceptible to suggestion. If the person issuing the suggestion is something of an authority figure a person is more susceptible to the suggestion. If you repeatedly suggest things it looks like you can enhance suggestion as opposed to suggesting just a single time. Those are a few of the factors that enhance, or conversely would make somebody more resistant to suggestibility.
Q. And it's your opinion that post-event information can affect memory; isn't that correct?
A. Yes.
Q. And that leading questions can affect memory?
A. Yes.
Q. I would like to give you a hypothetical situation, okay? I would like you to assume that an OB/GYN had a private practice for 11 years, from 1957 to 1968. I would like you to further assume that he saw 20 patients a day,

44

six days a week, and that approximately 5 to 10 percent of those patients were in the area of 17 years old. I would like you to further assume that he saw a patient one time

in 1960, and this was the only time he ever talked to that patient for any length of time. I would like you to further assume that from 1968 to 1970 he was in school, and then he started teaching, so that he would have started teaching in about 1970. What do you think would be the chances of his having details, remembering details of that gynecological exam in 1970?
A. You mean in 1960, the ones
Q. The one that he had in 1960; yes.
A. He is asked in 70 about something that happened ten years before?
Q. He starts talking about this case in 1970.
A. Well, I'm not sure. Did he have any notes that he took that he refreshed his memory with?
Q. Assume that he had no notes.
A. Well, I would say that there isn't a lot of reason to believe that his memory would be very good for that, under those circumstances.

45
***

46
Q. I would like you to further assume, Dr. Loftus, that 32 to 33 years after this one gynecological exam, so this would be 1993, 1994, maybe it's even 34 years after the gynecological exam, this doctor learned other information from the patient's parents, so you would characterize that as post-event information; right? Would that be a correct characterization of that kind of information?
A. It could be post-event.
Q. Information he didn't know at the time of his examination?
A. Okay.

47
Q. What is the likelihood that this post-event information could affect the details of these memories?
A. It might have. I mean it could.
Q. Would there be an even further likelihood that this post-event information could affect this doctor's memories if he had respect for these parents?
A. It's certainly possible.
Q. I think you testified a few minutes ago that information coming from an authority figure is something that you look at in terms of it being suggestive; correct?
A. Well, to be more precise about it, there are at least three studies of post-event suggestion that do show that the source of the suggestion is important, and that we will more readily accept suggestion from some sources rather than others. That's the basis for my opinion about that.

Q. Are one's parents a source of information that people are more likely to believe than from other sources?
A. It's not the example that is used in the studies, but it depends. If the source of

48
information has some reason to know something, has some basis for the information, then someone might be more willing to be persuaded by it.
Q. And young children are typically persuaded by what their parents tell them; isn't that correct?
A. Well, I don't want to answer that in terms of the suggestibility studies. I can answer about what those studies have shown, that kids are more persuaded by an adult trying to mislead them than they are by another child trying to mislead them.
Q. Would it be your opinion that that would be even more true if the adult was a parent?
A. I haven't seen a study about that. It may be true.
Q. My understanding from going through this with you before is that basically there are three stages in memory; right?
A. Yes.
Q. There is the acquisition stage, the retention stage and the retrieval stage.
A. Yes.
Q. And you look at elements of all three stages in looking at the reliability of memory.

49
A. Yes. In the first phase, the acquisition phase is where an event happened or supposedly happened; correct?
Q. And in this case you don't know whether or not [Plaintiff] was sexually abused by her father?
A. There is no way to know without corroboration.
Q. Since you don't know, is there anything in this particular case about the acquisition phase that is relevant to your testimony?
A. Well, not that I can think of right now.
Q. And you are aware, are you not, that one sister, [Plaintiff's Sister 4], also has memories of her father abusing her?
A. I'm aware of her testimony in her deposition, although these aren't independent memories, nor are they corroboration of the events that the plaintiff is claiming happened to her.
Q. They are memories that she had after [Plaintiff] had memories?
A. Right, and they had numerous discussions, apparently.
Q. Are you aware that [Plaintiff's Sister 3] also stated that there was a sexual abuse episode with her father?

50

MR. IVEY: Object to the form of the question, or statement, it should be put into terms of alleged, that [Plaintiff's Sisters 3 and 4] have alleged that there have been events that have occurred in their past.

Q. Thank you, Mr. Ivey. Now you may answer the question.

A. I'm aware of their making some allegations.

Q. Are you aware that [Plaintiff's Sister 3] has said that she always had the memory of her father asking her to play with his penis which he called his dolly?

A. I vaguely remember something about that being somewhere.

Q. And my understanding is, Dr. Loftus, and you've written about this in a book, that you were sexually abused as a child; correct?

A. Yes.

Q. And you always had the memory of being sexually abused?

A. Right.

Q. Is there any independent corroboration of that abuse?

A. No.

51

Q. Could anyone ever convince you that you were not sexually abused?

A. Well, I sort of doubt it, but it's not impossible.

Q. Are you aware that [Plaintiff's Sister 1]–that [Plaintiff]'s sister [Plaintiff's Sister 1] can't remember whether or not her father gave her a premarital gynecological examination?

A. I don't remember that one way or another.

Q. Did you read [Plaintiff's Sister 2]'s deposition?

A. Yes.

Q. Do you recall her testimony that she was sitting in a corner with her legs apart and her father told her to put her knees together because that position meant she wanted him? Do you recall that?

A. Well, I know there was discussion about a comment the father made. I don't remember exactly that.

Q. Do you recall something along that line?

A. I recall a lot of discussion about how you are supposed to tell someone to put their legs together.

Q. Would I be correct in assuming that the allegations of [Plaintiffs' Four Sisters] the

52

items that I just discussed with you, do not corroborate [Plaintiff]'s allegations, in your opinion?

A. Well, they are not independent corroboration, for obvious reasons.

Q. Why are [Plaintiff's Sister 3]'s allegations not independent?
A. Well, first of all, she is not claiming that she saw anything involving the plaintiff, and there is some dispute about what her testimony really is.
Q. What is the dispute about [Plaintiff's Sister 3]'s testimony?
A. I don't remember where I saw this, but that the whole discussion about dolly, whether it really involved the father or not, at least as it was brought out earlier in the child–in the growing up years.
Q. Do you recall [Plaintiff's Sister 3] saying she always knew it was her father in her testimony?
A. What I'm recalling right now is the ambiguity of that as far as the others who heard that comment as they were growing up.
Q. Is there any testimony that [Plaintiff's Sister 3] talked about this episode with her father as she was growing up?
A. No, it was saying something about it being a joke in the family.

53

Q. One person testified that [Plaintiff's Sister 3] called it a bad joke.
A. Somewhere in there there is something about it being a joke in the family. I just don't remember the details. I didn't really pay that much attention to that particular detail.
Q. I'm trying to find out what your understanding of this memory of [Plaintiff's Sister 3]'s is. Is it a memory that she always had, is it a memory that has changed over time?
A. I think she is now claiming it's a memory she has always had. I would have to go back to my–to her deposition or to Shirley Feldman-Summers' analysis of it or something like that.
Q. I can show you in Shirley's report. This isn't Shirley's report. Do you have Shirley Feldman-Summers' report there? The first paragraph of the last page of the report.
A. Well, in Shirley's report she has–she mentions that [Plaintiff's Sister 3] remembered this, so then the confusion about whether it was a bad family joke or not is somewhere else, not in this report of Shirley's. I would have to go back to the original deposition.

54

Q. Do you recall anyone other than [Plaintiff's Sister 2] calling this a bad joke?
A. No, I don't remember even who called it that.
Q. Have you conducted any studies on the biological differences of encoding of traumatic versus nontraumatic memories?
A. No.
Q. Have you read any studies on that?

A. Yes.
Q. What have you read?
A. I've read a number of papers of Bessel Van der Kolk and others on biological consequences of traumatic experiences.
Q. What is your opinion of Dr. Van der Kolk's writings on this topic?
A. He seems to be demonstrating that there might be some changes in the neurotransmitters and other neurochemical systems when people experience trauma, but he, in my opinion, hasn't demonstrated that this means that somehow memories are deeply repressed and reliably recovered.
Q. But that is nothing that you have found, researched yourself or been part of any

55

research study?
A. Not yet.
Q. Do you intend to do that?
A. I might; yes.
Q. Do you have someone in mind to work with on that particular topic?
A. Well, I have had one initial meeting with some investigators who have access to Vietnam vets and we are contemplating doing something together.
Q. And this would be with medical doctors then?
A. No, but there are people who work in PTSD with vets.
Q. So you just have had one meeting on that topic so far?
A. Right.
Q. Is there anything in the retention phase of this case that is significant?
A. Well, yes, that's where the post-event information in the life of this plaintiff comes in, and you have this long-period of time passing between ages–between the time when the plaintiff would have been one to seventeen years old when she is claiming various abusive things happened to her, and

56

then a series of kinds of information or information situations that might be responsible for the creation of false memories, if these are false.
Q. And what are those elements of post-event information?
A. We have already talked about a lot of them, the therapists, the therapy beliefs, the therapist techniques, the books, the information in those books. In addition, the conversations that the plaintiff had with others, her work with the sexual assault program certainly did expose her to lots and lots and lots of stories of sexual abuse and assault. This is just information that could, according to George Gannaway and others, be responsible for the creation of false memories, if these memories are false.

Q. Are you aware that [Plaintiff] had her first memory of sexual abuse after her fourth therapy session?
A. Well, according to my records she had a flashback on February 24th, 1989, or thereabouts, and that was approximately four months after she started seeing [Plaintiff's Therapist].

57
Q. Do you recall from [Plaintiff's Therapist]'s therapy records and his billings that she had only seen him four times prior to that flashback?
A. I could look at the notes, but I don't have it in my calendar.
Q. Can you assume that for deposition purposes today?
A. Yes.
Q. Prior to that flashback [Plaintiff's Therapist] had not suggested that she read any books on sexual abuse; isn't that correct?
A. I don't remember exactly when he made the book recommendation.
Q. Do you have any information that he made a recommendation prior to February 24, 1989?
A. No, not necessarily; no.
Q. Are you aware that she had a number of memories of sexual abuse prior to his recommending, or he doesn't even say he recommended that book in this case, maybe recommending that book ?
A. I'm sorry, say that again. I missed the question.
Q. Are you aware of the fact that [Plaintiff] had numerous memories of sexual abuse prior to

58
[Plaintiff's Therapist] suggesting that she read any books on sexual abuse, if, indeed, he did make such a recommendation?
A. Well, I assume he made recommendations because in the plaintiff's case study she talked about her therapist recommending *Soul Survivors,* and in his deposition he talks about recommending *Soul Survivors, Courage to Heal, The Courage to Heal workbook,* et cetera.
Q. He says he recommends that generally, he didn't say he did in this case.
A. Right. It at least seems possible that he did recommend these books, although I don't have any notation as to exactly when he did, if he did.
Q. And it's your opinion that [Plaintiff] was surrounded by stories of sexual abuse in her work at the sexual assault center?
A. Well, it's an assumption.
Q. And if she said she only knew a few cases that had any details at all in her work, would that change your opinion at all in this case?

A. Well, that would lessen the possibility that she would get details from that source.
Q. Now, the last time I took your deposition, which was about three years ago,

59

I think, you were just starting this shopping mall study of trying to get people to have a memory of being lost in a shopping mall when they hadn't been.
A. Right.
Q. Can you tell me where you are in this study at this point?
A. Well, first of all, the shopping mall study is taking much longer than I ever expected. To be able to address the same issue of whether you can implant an entire memory into the mind of someone I've focused my efforts in a couple of other directions, and completed a couple of other studies in which we have implanted entire memories as the shopping mall study still progresses.
Q. Can you tell me where you are on the shopping mall study, and where you are on these other studies?
A. Well, I think we have probably completed maybe eight subjects or something in the formal shopping mall study.
Q. Eight subjects in which you have been able to implant a false memory?
A. No, just eight subjects which are completed

60

right now, and we are aiming for about 50. We started over for a number of reasons.
Q. So can you tell me why you started over?
A. The chief investigator left the project and left the paperwork in somewhat of a disrepair and didn't follow through on the phone calls and the final interviews, so I decided to start the study over with some exceedingly trustworthy research assistants, and that's what's happening right now.
Q. So in terms of the study, you have totally thrown out the first part of the study?
A. Well, there were six subjects that finally finished in the first study before the research assistant left, and I don't know that we will merge them with the new subjects or not.
Q. In your discussion of being able to implant false memories in people, are you using those first six subjects as part of your study?
A. No, not the first six. I still do talk about the five published case histories, but adding to that I now add these other studies that I and others have done using this basic kind of paradigm.

61

Q. I want to go to the shopping mall study first, because I know a little bit about that one. How many people did you and your research assistants try to implant false memories into?

A. We are going to do it with 50, and there are various phases of the process right now.
Q. How many have you completed, eight?
A. Something like eight.
Q. Of those eight how many were you able to successfully implant false memories?
A. At least one that I know of, and maybe only one, of these particular eight.
Q. Of the first six, you had six in the first group, how many of those?
A. I don't know that we are going to use those data, because when you change the procedure a little bit you don't merge, but approximately half of those six produced some recollection.
Q. If you are asked to testify about your experiments–
A. Right
Q. –of implanting false memories, would you use those first six?
A. No, I don't think I will use the first six. I will use the five case histories that are

62

already published but not the six that have followed. In about half of those six they produced something that was indicative of some possible memory, but we are not planning to use those anyhow.
Q. Would you use those in testimony?
A. I don't think so; no.
Q. You would not use those in testimony?
A. No. If somebody asked me I will answer, as you are now.
Q. Well, in support of being able to implant false memories.
A. Well, I have these other studies that are completed, and in press where I have a better handle on the data and the studies have been done in a more accomplished way so I don't need to–
Q. You don't need to use that six?
A. I don't need to use those six.
Q. What about the five case histories that are published? What is that about?
A. Those are the first five that you know about that were the five case histories that we did and I presented at the American Psychological Association before we presented the formal

63

study, and those show that it is possible. They are sort of the existent proof.
Q. How many people did you have to test to come up with five case histories?
A. There may have been a couple others that various people tried to implant the same kind of idea and didn't succeed, but those are just five case histories that did succeed, and I don't even pretend to say that that even means that five out of seven of the population will be able to do it.

Q. You just found five of them where it worked?
A. Right.
Q. What is that published in? What are those case histories published in?
A. It's in a book chapter that is going to happen in a NATO volume, North Atlantic Treaty Organization edited by Doug Peters and scheduled for publication sometime this year, 1994.
Q. Do you have a copy of that book chapter?
A. Yes, I do.
Q. Can I get a copy of that?
A. Yes. If you will remind me I will send it to you and you can do what you want with it.

64
Q. Why don't I write it down, because there may be some other things that we will want.
A. Okay. This is the NATO chapter.
Q. It's five case histories?
A. Right.
Q. What are the other two studies that you've done?
A. Well, then in conjunction with Steve Ceci we took the basic idea of using a relative to suggest an event that didn't happen, in this case that you got your finger caught in a mousetrap and had to go to the hospital to get it removed, and put that question repeatedly to some children and looked to see whether they would subsequently remember this as having happened to them, and through repeated questioning over a seven- to ten-week period many of the children did come to remember this. I don't know the exact percentages. I would have to look that up, but a sizable percentage of them.
Q. So if a father suggested over and over to a daughter that a snake was on her he might be able to get her to believe that was, in fact, the case?

65
A. It's possible.
Q. Or if a father suggested over and over to someone, to a young girl, that she put her hand in a horse's anus he might be able to get her to believe that that actually occurred?
A. Well, it's possible, yes.
Q. Is this second study in publication?
A. Well, the one place that it is described, I believe, is in Steve Ceci's, an address he gave last summer at the American Psychological Association, but we are writing this up now for publication.

Q. So it hasn't been written yet.
A. It's in draft for publication.
Q. Is there a copy of that study or a draft of it that I can get?
A. I might be able to get you something on that; yes.
Q. What would I call that?
A. Mousetrap.
Q. What's the third study that you've done?
A. We have recently taken college students and made them believe that they saw a drug bust when they didn't.
Q. Can you tell me

66
A. -how?
Q. What the study consisted of.
A. These young adults saw a series of events, these are police training films, they include, for example, a bank robbery, a liquor store shoot-out, a couple of other events that are police training films, and one week later in one of the studies and two weeks later in the second study we suggest to them that they saw a drug bust scene or scenario when they didn't. In the first of these studies, 29 out of 45–I'm just analyzing these data right now–claim that they saw this drug bust. This does look as if it's going to be an exceedingly interesting study, because when they describe the suspects they are more often than not black or Hispanic, so we may be seeing some
Q. Prejudice?
A. -unfortunate prejudice at work here.
Q. So what they were actually seeing was a bank robbery–
A. A liquor store shooting, and a couple other events.

67
And what they are telling you in these follow-up studies is that they are seeing a drug bust instead of the bank robbery or the liquor store shooting?
A. No, they described the real memories, and they also now describe this non-existent drug bust that we suggested to them through leading questions.
Q. So they are saying in addition they saw a drug bust?
A. Right.
Q. Where are they saying that this drug bust occurred, in the scene at the liquor store?
A. Sometimes they import details from one of the other scenes to create their drug bust and sometimes it's brand-new.
Q. Is this written up somewhere, this study written up?
A. Not yet. I just analyzed the data this weekend.

Q. Is this a study that you are able to testify to? Is there enough information for you to testify on this data at this point?
A. Well, I prefer to wait until I've written it up, and so it depends on whether I'm asked or

68

not. I haven't told you about another study that was presented, this is not my own study, but it uses my lost in a shopping mall paradigm, and this one was already reported at a scientific meeting, so if somebody asks me for examples I would prefer to give examples that are either presented in the scientific meeting or a little more available.
Q. This third study is something that you that still analyzing?
A. Right.
Q. If Mr. Ivey asks you to testify about that particular study would you do so in trial, or would you feel uncomfortable in doing that?
A. If he asked in the same way you are asking, "what are you doing right now," I might say it's very preliminary, I have just analyzed the data. By that time I will have made one presentation about it.
Q. Where are you presenting on that study?
A. In the cognitive seminar tomorrow.
Q. In your class?
A. Well, it's the whole cognitive area. It is every Tuesday afternoon for the cognitive seminar.

69

Q. This isn't a presentation to your colleagues?
A. These are colleagues; yes.
Q. There are other teachers here, professors here?
A. Yes.
Q. And you would tell them that it is a preliminary study?
Q. And you are still analyzing the data?
A. Right.
Q. What's the purpose of your presenting this study tomorrow?
A. This is an opportunity where faculty and graduate students present their ongoing work and get reactions to it, get suggestions for further directions and ways to think about it for purposes of writing it up and so on.
Q. So you could get some criticism of your study too?
A. I could.
Q. Can you tell me about the fourth study that someone else has done?

A. This is Ira Hyman at Western Washington who used a paradigm that basically is modeled

70

after the lost in a shopping mall paradigm and convinced young adults that at the age of five they went to the hospital for a suspected ear infection and had to spend the night. Approximately 20 percent were successfully misled into developing this memory.

Q. Was this study written up?

A. It was presented at the Psychonomic Society, and there is a handout of some sort. He is doing one more study before he writes it up for publication, and it now exists as a poster presentation and handout.

Q. What does that mean?

A. It's the way you present your work in scientific meeting. Sometimes there are speeches that you give and sometimes there are poster presentations. There is a large room full of poster board and you put your–you may have that much space and you put your presentation up and then people wander through for several hours and they read it like on the poster board and talk to you about it.

Q. So the person isn't orally giving the presentation, there are pages of their presentation tacked to a poster and you actually go and read the presentation?

71

A. Right, but it's equivalent to a presentation at a scientific meeting in terms of what it is and the usual quality of the work, the completeness of the work.

Q. Do you have a copy of that study?

A. Well, I once had the handout that he gave. He gave a handout. I'm not sure that I know where it is right now. He is at Western Washington and you can write to him or call him and get his handout.

Q. And its I R A, H Y M A N?

A. M A N, yes.

Q. And this is in Bellingham?

A. Yes.

Q. And he is in the psych department?

A. Yes.

Q. Is there any way for you to tell who will and who won't have a false memory in a study that you do?

A. No.

Q. Is there a study written anywhere to determine who will and who won't have a false memory?

A. There are discussions in the literature about individual differences and suggestibility, so

72

for example, just as an example, there is literature showing that people who are highly hypnotizable are more susceptible to suggestion.
Q. Do you have information in this case that [Plaintiff] is highly hypnotizable?
A. I don't have any information about that.
Q. What other factors are there about who could be suggestive to false memory?
A. That's the one that comes to mind. There are age effects, of course.
Q. If they are really young or really old they tend to be more suggestible to false memory?
A. Right. Good.
Q. I'm a good student. I have a good memory for your class here that I've taken numerous times.
A. It's too bad you have to pay so much to take it each time.
Q. In your shopping mall study you needed some details to be true to help support the false memory; isn't that correct?
A. Well, we hypothesize that that might be a way to get the false memory going, to have a germ that would allow this flower to bloom.
Q. Such as it being a shopping mall where the person actually had been?
A. Right.
Q. And you also used close family members in that case to make the suggestion?
A. Yes.
Q. Would that also be true in your mousetrap study?
A. Yes. The child is told these are some things your mommy or daddy say may have happened to you, and the same thing in Ira Hyman's study.
Q. Are those factors at all pertinent to the police training film study?
A. No. There the suggestion is accomplished through leading questions.
Q. So the studies have shown that leading questions can lead to false memory?
A. Yes.
Q. Or that a relative making suggestions of false information surrounded by some true information can lead to false memories?
A. Yes.
Q. Anything else from these four studies that are relevant in terms of what can lead to false memories, the age of the children, I suppose

74

would be part of it, at least in the mousetrap study?

A. Yes–well, no, the misinformation literature as a whole shows that the younger children and then the elderly are more susceptible to suggestion. Well, we have done studies showing that media exposure can create false memories. I don't know if you would consider that relevant, but it's just another form of post-event information.
Q. Do you consider that relevant in this case?
A. Just for generally showing that exposure to a variety of suggestions can lead to supplementation or a change in memory. It's just one more example. Not that there was some media that affected –
Q. –[Plaintiff]?
A. Right. Although I don't know, I mean she may have–did I see Geraldo or any of these other programs in her information environment? I just don't remember right now.
Q. There are several studies that show that a percentage of sexually abused children repress memories; correct?
A. That depends on what you mean by repression.

75

There are certainly studies that show that a percentage of people who were sexually abused forget.
Q. What are those studies?
A. Well, the studies that are widely cited to supposedly bear on this question of whether people remember or forget or repress or what have you, are Briere and Conte, Herman & Schatzow, and then Linda Meyer-Williams, and then a study that I collaborated on with Mindy Fullilove.
Q. In your own study you found that 18 percent of the subjects had repressed memories of sexual abuse?
A. First of all, the figure is actually 19 percent when you use the proper denominator.
Q. You wrote 18 percent.
A. I know, and that's because I didn't throw out missing data, but if you throw out missing data and then recalculate it goes to 19 percent.
Q. Okay.
A. What those 19 percent do is they claim there is a period of time where they have forgot and then later remembered, or later the memory

76

returned. That's what they claim, they forgot. There was a period, I don't remember the exact wording right now, in which they forgot and then later the memory returned.
Q. Did you do anything in that study to corroborate the memories?
A. No.

Q. Are you aware of any studies where repressed memories have been authenticated?
A. Well, in Linda Meyer-Williams' study, which has been accepted for publication, she found that there is reason to believe that abuse happened, sexual abuse happened, because there is an emergency room report of it, and that 17 years later a sizable percentage of people don't remember that incident.
Q. About 30 percent?
A. 38 percent. We don't know whether those memories were repressed or not, we only know that these 38 percent don't remember.
Q. And sometimes not remembering and repression are used interchangeably, correctly or incorrectly they are used interchangeably; isn't that correct?
A. Yes, but people have said in many places that repression is supposed to be something

77

that is beyond ordinary forgetting, so something special.
Q. So we don't know in this case if they have forgotten and they could easily be made to remember the abuse, or whether it's a deep repression?
A. Right.
Q. Are you aware of any studies showing that a person who states she has PTSD or a dissociative disorder or depression or was a victim of incest sees it as a prestige-enhancing memory?
A. Any studies? No, I don't know of a study like that; no.
Q. My understanding is that you've done studies where people misremembered things and they tend to misremember information in a way that's to their benefit, in other words that they remember that they voted when they didn't vote or that they did more housework than they actually did, and you call that prestige-enhancing memories; correct?
A. Yes. Now, I, myself, have not done all of those studies. I've written about them, but I

78

have done studies on remembering voting when you haven't voted, but remembering you gave more to charity or you took more airplane trips than you really did, your kids walked and talked at an earlier age, those have been done by others.
Q. And people tend to remember in the prestige-enhancing way rather than I gave less charity than I thought I did, my kids talked later than I thought they did; isn't that correct?
A. Right.
Q. So they tend to remember their lives and their kids and their own behavior as being better than it actually was?

A. Right.

Q. Your studies show that there is a percentage of people who will give factually correct information despite your best efforts to make them believe otherwise; correct?

A. Yes.

Q. Typically the smaller the detail the more likely it is you can manipulate the memory, unless it's some really minuscule memory; is that correct?

79

A. Well, I don't know how to think about small. I don't know that we have ever looked at the size.

Q. I don't mean small meaning small, I mean a small detail of the memory, not something that is small in size.

A. You mean a peripheral detail or something?

Q. Right.

A. It's easier to suggest a peripheral detail.

Q. Than a central factor in a memory?

A. Right.

Q. You do believe, don't you, Dr. Loftus, that repression in memory is possible?

A. It's possible.

Q. And you believe

A. Particularly under some of the definitions of it.

Q. And you believe that someone can experience something so painful that they block it from their memory, don't you?

A. I think they can experience something that is so painful that they avoid thinking about it.

Q. And that they block it from their consciousness, do you believe that that is possible?

80

A. I wouldn't put it that way because I don't know if it's blocked from their consciousness or if they aren't thinking about it.

Q. Do you believe that it's possible that someone can experience a very painful experience, and if they are asked if that occurred to them that they wouldn't remember?

A. Yes.

Q. In fact, that's what Linda Meyer-Williams' study shows?

A. Yes. Although her events, it's my understanding, are primarily one-time events, not 61 or 90 horrible things happening between the ages of one and seventeen.

Q. Are you aware that there are some therapists who believe that the more someone experiences a traumatic event the more likely it is that they are to repress the memories?
A. I've seen that claim in the literature, or something along that line; yes.
Q. You would agree, would you not, that sexual abuse by a parent can be a very painful experience?
A. I would; yes.
Q. And that would be especially true if someone

81
were punished when they tried to tell about the sexual abuse?
A. Well, I don't know if that would make it even worse. It's already a pretty bad thing to begin with, or it can be, anyhow.
Q. Do you have an opinion as to the age a child would have to be to realize that being abused by a father was wrong, that there was something wrong about it?
A. No.
Q. Do you have any studies to show that returned repressed memories are inaccurate?
A. Only in case examples.
Q. And those are the studies that you've done, is that what you've talked about?
A. No, no, because those are wholly suggested memories, they are not–
Q. –repressed memories?
A. Repressed memories, they are just created memories. When I have seen memories that are biologically impossible or geographically impossible or physiologically impossible, then I know they are false, or I presume they are false.

82
Q. These are anecdotal episodes that you are talking about?
A. Right.
Q. You don't know of any studies that show the returned repressed memories are inaccurate?
A. No
Q. Without corroboration do you have an opinion as to whether a retrieved repressed memory is inaccurate or accurate?
A. Well, you would need corroboration to know whether the memory happened or didn't happen.
Q. So without corroboration you don't know whether it happened or didn't happen; right?
A. Right.
***

83

Q. Do you have an opinion here as to whether [Plaintiff] has deliberately fabricated any memories?

A. I don't know one way or another. I assume that she is sincere in these beliefs.

Q. Do you agree that children who are sexually molested are likely to suffer emotional or psychological injuries?

A. There is evidence to that effect; yes.

Q. You are not going to testify in this case that memories cannot be repressed, are you, Doctor?

A. No.

Q. And you are not going to testify that memories of childhood sexual abuse cannot be repressed, are you?

A. No.

***

84

***

Q. Dr. Loftus, looking at your *vitae,* you have an article, "The Reality of Repressed Memory" that was published in 1993 in *The American Psychologist.*

A. Yes.

***

Q. Are there any other articles that you have written or books that you have written that are on your *vitae* that deal specifically with repressed memory? I see one called "Let Sleeping Memories Lie," that deals with repressed memories.

A. Yes. That came out in the *Journal of Criminal Law and Criminology.*

Q. And then you have an article, "Sleeping Memories on Trial." Does that have to do with repressed memories?

A. Yes.

Q. Reactions of memories that were previously repressed?

85

A. Yes.

Q. *International Digest of Human Behavior, Science and Law?*

A. *Expert Evidence,* doesn't it say?

Q. Yes. That's the name of the entire journal, *Expert Evidence?*

A. The short title is *Expert Evidence,* and then there is a subtitle to the journal. I put both of them on the *vitae.*

Q. And then you wrote an invited editorial in *The Washington Post* called "You Must Remember This, Oh, Do You, How Real Are Repressed Memories?"

A. Yes.

Q. Then you wrote an article in *USA Today Magazine,* and you write on there, you put in parentheses that "It is an academic magazine, not the newspaper, an article in press called "Repressed Memories of Childhood Trauma, Could Some of Them Be Suggestive?"
A. Yes.
Q. Do you have a copy of that article?
A. Yes. As a matter of fact it just came out.
Q. How would I ask you for a copy of that article in this list?

86
A. *USA Today Magazine* article.
Q. Under 1994 and in press you have Loftus & Yapco, "Psychotherapy and Recovery of Repressed Memory." Is this a book chapter or an article, or what is that?
A. It's a book chapter done with Michael Yapco.
Q. Do you have a copy of that article?
A. I don't have the final draft of it, but Yapco does. He had it on his computer. He is in San Diego at the Erickson Institute.
Q. Do you have a draft of it that is pretty much the same?
A. I have an earlier draft.
Q. Are they pretty similar to the final draft?
A. I don't remember what changes we made, actually.
Q. Do you have earlier drafts that I could see?
A. I have an earlier draft that I could Xerox.
Q. How would I title that so you would know?
A. We are starting to get into an effort in Xeroxing here. Do you want to pay for this effort in Xeroxing, in which case I'm happy to give it to you?
Q. Well, I would like the articles.

87
A. Just tell me how you want to do this then.
Q. If we can do it after your deposition. I'm paying 1,400 bucks anyway.
A. I have to search for this stuff, is the problem.
***
Q. Then you have an article for *Psychology of Women Quarterly* called "Memories of Childhood Sexual Abuse, Remembering and Repressing."
A. Yes. That's the one that's the 19 percent study with Fullilove that you know about. I don't know if you have it or not.
Q. I just have that you wrote about it in the *American Psychologist* article.
A. Right, I can get that one and Xerox it, I have that one. I will have to have it Xeroxed.

Q. What do you call that one?
A. You could just say Loftus with Fullilove.
Q. Then you have Loftus and Belli, "Recovered Memories of Childhood Abuse,

88
A Source Monitoring Perspective." Is this a chapter in a book?
A. It's a book chapter; yes.
Q. Do you have that chapter?
A. That one I would have to get from Belli. He is at the University of Michigan.
Q. What's in that article?
A. Oh, it's theoretical discussion of the misinformation effect with a little bit of discussion about how it might be applicable to the recovered memory problem.
Q. Is there anything in that chapter that we haven't talked about today?
A. No.
Q. You have the last item under 1994 and in press, Loftus & Cohen–
A. That's the one you have on your list already, the NATO chapter, the five cases of the shopping mall, or the five cases of being lost, I should say.
Q. Are there any other articles or book chapters that you have written regarding repressed memories?
A. Well, I don't know if you saw my article in the ABA journal with Rosenwald.

89
Q. Yes, I've seen that.
A. My article with Lucy Berliner, we mention repressed memories in there.
Q. Where is that?
A. 1992.
Q. Page?
A. Page 17.
Q. Do you have a copy of that article?
A. Yes.
Q. So I could call that Loftus & Berliner?
A. Yes, Berliner & Loftus.
Q. Any other articles regarding repressed memories of sexual abuse or repressed memories?
A. I don't know if you have seen my piece in the Harvard mental health letter.
Q. Yes, I've seen that.
A. I think that's it.
Q. Is length of exposure or repeated exposure a factor that affects the accuracy of memory?
A. Yes.

Q. In what way?
A. The longer the exposure duration the better the memory, the more the repetition the better the memory, all other things being equal.

90

Q. Is there evidence to support the proposition that the essence of an event is better remembered if there is a traumatic element to the event, even if a lot of the details are distorted or lost?
A. There is some support for that, yes, in the work of Christianson.
Q. What is his work? Do you know what it's titled, Christianson's work?
A. He has done work that basically would show that you sometimes remember the gist of an event when it's highly arousing, even if a lot of the details are wrong.
Q. What is Christianson's first name?
A. Sven, S V E N. He is at the University of Stockholm.
Q. And you would agree that there is evidence that supports the idea that if you are a participant in an event you remember it better than if you are an observer; correct?
A. There are at least some studies that show that. Not all of them do, but at least some do.
Q. Is it your opinion that it's true that being a

91

participant in an event makes you remember the event better than if you are an observer?
A. I think it can be true, but there might be some conditions where it's not true, so if you are so traumatized by being a participant, that might begin to cause a deterioration in your cognitive functioning and make you worse.
Q. Are there studies to that, that show that?
A. I don't know that there are studies that show that, but there is certainly good theoretical reason to believe that you can become so traumatized that you have problems with remembering things.
Q. You might have problems remembering the peripheral details or the entire event?
A. Just the Yerkes-Dodson law is a law that essentially suggests that under very, very high levels of stress or fright you might see impairment–serious impairment in memory.
Q. Does that tend to be impairment of the central elements of the event or the details of the event?
A. Well, it depends on the study. I've seen studies where most of the details are impaired in a highly arousing event.

92

Q. I'm sorry, did you say where the details are impaired?
A. Well, yes, but sometimes they are pretty critical details.

Q. Dr. Loftus, have you had memories come back to you that were not corroborated but which you knew to be true memories?
A. Probably.
Q. Can you give any examples?
A. Oh, I can't think right now, but I think it happens to everyone.
Q. Do you have memories of being a child that cannot be corroborated but that you are sure happened?
A. Probably.
Q. You would agree, wouldn't you, Dr. Loftus, that there were discussions in [Plaintiff]'s therapy of events other than molestation?
A. Yes.
Q. And there is no evidence in this case, is there, that [Plaintiff] went to [Plaintiff's Therapist] and was talking about what was going on in her life and [Plaintiff's Therapist] said to her it sounds like you've been sexually abused?
A. I don't know what happened. It's my

93

understanding she went for job stress and to talk about difficulties with somebody at work, and this thing got linked to her father, and I'm not sure how the discussions went after that because the notes are very skimpy and the recollections are subject to retrospective biases.
Q. But you don't have any evidence to show that that is what occurred, do you?
A. Right.
Q. Right, you do not have.
A. Right, I don't, I don't.
Q. You would agree, wouldn't you, Doctor, that at least some percentage of children who are sexually abused are victimized when there are no witnesses to the abuse?
A. Yes.
Q. Is it your position that because there are no witnesses or other corroboration, that their memories of the abuse are not trustworthy?
A. It depends. I wouldn't say they are not trustworthy as a blanket statement; no.
Q. You couldn't say as a blanket statement either that someone who claims to have a memory of abuse after a period of not remembering has an untrustworthy memory, could you?

94

A. It might be a real memory.
Q. You would agree, would you not, that people can have a lot of mind control when they completely control an environment; correct?
A. I think I agree with that.

Q. And a parent of a small child pretty completely controls that child's environment; correct?
A. I would assume that happens a lot.
Q. Do you have any opinion regarding [Plaintiff]'s present psychological functioning?
A. No.
Q. You are not an expert in posttraumatic stress disorder; correct?
A. Right.
Q. And you are not an expert in dissociative disorders; correct?
A. Not from a clinical perspective; no.
Q. And you are not an expert in the sexual abuse of children, are you?
A. Not in a clinical or treating sense; no.
Q. Do you have any evidence to show that therapy clients are eager to discover that they were violated by people that they loved and trusted?

95
A. No.
Q. Do you know what the effect would be on someone who had to hide the experience of ongoing abuse and had to continue living with a person who was the abuser?
A. No.
Q. You can't say, can you, that [Plaintiff] wouldn't have had memories of sexual abuse return to her even in the absence of therapy, can you?
A. I can't.
Q. In some of your, well, at least in a prior deposition that I took of you, I think you gave an anecdotal example of Piaget having a memory of something that occurred and then he later realized that that event had not occurred.
A. Right. It's a classic example.
Q. Are you aware of whether or not Piaget had any posttraumatic stress disorder symptoms?
A. I don't have any idea.
Q. Did he ever talk about having flashbacks of this event?
A. Not that I know of.

96
Q. Or nightmares about it?
A. I don't have any idea if he did.
Q. Or phobias?
A. He might have. I don't know about his psychological state, other than his report of this memory incident.
Q. Are you aware of whether he had an exaggerated startle response?

A. I don't know.
Q. Or whether he had any affective disorders?
A. I don't know that.
Q. Or whether he dissociated?
A. I don't know.
Q. Even if every person in your test group, say of the mousetrap test group, had reported false memories, that wouldn't mean that [Plaintiff] had a false memory, would it?
A. Right, it wouldn't.
Q. You can't tell in any case whether or not there is false memory without corroboration one way or the other; right? You testified I think a number of times to that.
A. Right.
Q. All that you can testify to is what could be suggestive to a person.

97
A. Right. Well, actually a more accurate way of putting it, I have opinions that suggestive things are happening that might be responsible for the creation of false memories but they might not.
Q. They may not–can you say that last one again?
A. Well, for example in this case I believe that there are examples of suggestion that one can point to that could be in part responsible for the creation of false memories, if the memories are false.
Q. But they may not be responsible for any false memories?
A. Right.
Q. And the memories could be true?
A. I suppose it's possible that some or all of them could be true.
Q. The fact that there is no corroboration of memories does not mean the memories are false?
A. Right.
Q. And you would agree, wouldn't you, Doctor, that accused people are motivated to deny that they have abused a child?
A. I think that would be a motivation; yes.

98
Q. And so denials of abuse are not evidence that a victim's memories are not authentic; isn't that correct?
A. Right.
***
Q. I would like to ask you about the significance of what's been marked as Exhibit 3. Is that a January 19 conversation that you had with Floyd Ivey, apparently?

A. Yes.
Q. The first line says, "P's case history." Plaintiff's case history, I'm sure.
A. Plaintiff.
Q. What is the significance of that line?
A. I was taking notes while talking to him on the phone, and he just mentioned, I think, did I see the plaintiff's case history, so I made a note. It sounded like he wanted me to pay

99
special attention to it, I guess. I don't remember exactly.
Q. And you have reviewed her case history?
A. Yes.
Q. Had you reviewed it prior to this conversation?
A. I don't know if I had or not. I may not have. I didn't pay any special attention to it, anyhow.
Q. And then the next line is "She asked, 'am I a victim?' " What is the significance of that line?
A. I think Floyd said something to me that she was wondering about this before she recovered the memories.
Q. Does that have any significance to you?
A. It might. I don't know, that she was suspecting before she remembered.
Q. What does that mean to you? What significance is that, that she was suspecting before she remembered?
A. It's just a fact about her.
Q. Does that have any significance to you in terms of suggestibility or whether or not her memories are true or false?

100
A. I don't know whether there is any evidence that says if you suspect before remembering versus don't suspect it means anything one way or another.
Q. The first answers to interrogatories, "61 incidents, and then another 30 revealed in the next month." Where did you get that information?
A. I typed it, so it came out during this conversation.
Q. Did you get information from Mr. Ivey that [Plaintiff] had 30 memories in one month?
A. I don't remember. I just don't remember this conversation.
Q. Do you have evidence that [Plaintiff] had 30 memories in a month?
MR. IVEY: I think it should be 30 more.
Q. The document says, "30 revealed in next month." I'm trying to understand what that means.

A. 30 more revealed. The point he was trying to make, I believe, is that she at one point had 61, and then has continued to produce more, so now there are about 90 or so.
Q. Do you know over what period of time she had another 30 memories?

101
A. No.
Q. So you're not saying that she had 30 memories in one month?
A. I don't have–I haven't kept track of exactly when the extra ones came and over what period of time.
Q. Do you know when she answered the first set of interrogatories?
A. I don't remember the date.
Q. You're not going to testify that [Plaintiff] had 30 memories in one month?
A. I wasn't planning to.
Q. Then the next line reads "One case man defecate and put a snake on her. Later baby with white stuff coming out of coffin." What is the significance of that?
A. Some memories that he was mentioning to me.
Q. Were you told by Mr. Ivey that [Plaintiff] said a man defecated on her?
A. No, a man defecated and put snake on her.
Q. So you are not saying that she is saying a man defecated on her?
A. I don't think that's what this is about.
Q. What is your understanding of "Later baby with white stuff coming out of coffin?"

102
A. There is a memory involving a baby with white stuff coming out of it.
Q. And the baby is in a coffin.
A. Right.
Q. Are you aware that [Plaintiff's Sister 3] has a memory of her father taking her to a funeral parlor and [Plaintiff's Sister 3] seeing a dead baby at the funeral parlor?
A. I don't recall that.
Q. Did you read [Plaintiff's Sister 3]'s deposition?
A. I skimmed it.
Q. Does the fact that [Plaintiff] saw a baby in a coffin have significance to you?
A. Not in particular.
Q. Does it mean anything to you that a father takes children to a funeral parlor and lets them see dead babies?
A. I have no knowledge if it's true or why he would be doing it, if it is true.
Q. If it is true would that have any significance to you?
A. I don't know. It depends on the circumstances.

Q. Then the next line is "[Plaintiff] has read"–let me go back to that. What would be the

103

circumstances that would make it have significance to you versus not have significance to you?
A. I wouldn't have any idea. Maybe there is some legitimate reason to be at a funeral parlor, maybe there is not. He is a doctor. Maybe he is seeing somebody there.
Q. The next line is "[Plaintiff] has read sex books, porno while having intercourse. Claims she threw most away, but she produces three books, thus she has relied on porno for a long time." What is the significance of that?
A. Floyd Ivey was asking me whether I thought this would be significant in any way.
Q. And is it significant to you?
A. Well, only in that the claim is that one place that false memories comes from is books and other material, so just the fact that there are books could provide some material for the creation of memories.
Q. Are you aware of whether any of these books have anything to do with fathers molesting children?
A. I have no idea. I haven't seen the books.
Q. Then the next line, "One of lay witnesses met with [Plaintiff] for consciousness-raising

104

group. [Plaintiff] was inordinately preoccupied with porno She knew about books that others didn't know about." Is there any significance to that?
A. No, I don't have any further significance on that. That was just a question that Floyd Ivey had about whether that would be significant or not.
Q. And then the next line deals with [Plaintiff] having memories from age one, and we have already talked about the significance of that.
A. Right.
Q. Anything else?
A. No, I think we just talked about the childhood amnesia problem.
Q. Then the next statement is "Problem with sisters is the attempt to influence them. Plaintiff works on sisters. [Plaintiff's Sister 3]'s bad joke about girl playing with man's dolly got changed to be Dad. There were stories in the family about dolls hanging on the clothesline." Do you have evidence that plaintiff was working on her sisters?

105

A. Well, she was communicating with them a lot, she was trying to get them together for a meeting, she was telling them about her stories and her allegations and was telling them that they were abused, at least in the case of [Plaintiff's Sister 4], so . . .

Q. Didn't [Plaintiff] only say that she remembered the abuse with [Plaintiff's Sister 4] after [Plaintiff's Sister 4] told [Plaintiff] about that episode?
A. I don't recall which came first, actually.
Q. Does that make a difference to you?
A. It might make a difference in terms of who influenced who; yes.
Q. If [Plaintiff's Sister 4] said she had the memory of being abused with this wooden spoon, that's the memory [Plaintiff's Sister 4] is talking about; do you remember that memory?
A. Yes.
Q. If [Plaintiff's Sister 4] told [Plaintiff] about that memory before (Plaintiff) having that memory, then [Plaintiff] wouldn't be influencing [Plaintiff's Sister 4] to have that particular memory, would she?
A. Not that particular one; no.
Q. Is it unusual for a sister to tell her other sisters about memories of abuse after she gets.

106

memories of being abused by the father?
A. It might not be.
Q. Do you see that [Plaintiff]'s telling her sisters about her memories of abuse as an attempt to influence the sisters?
A. I don't know whether it is or not.
Q. You don't have evidence to show that it is an attempt to influence them, do you?
A. Well, not as I sit here right now, that I can recall. I do have the impression that she was trying to draw her siblings into this. That's the impression that I have from all of the material.
Q. So it's an impression, but you can't point to facts to support that impression?
A. Well, you know, the planning of the meeting, the communications before the meeting, the reading the list of memories, you know, one by one, these are all communications for some purpose, and the question is what was that purpose.
Q. It could be to get support?
A. It could be.
Q. Do you know who asked for the meeting of the sisters?

107

A. I don't recall.
Q. It could be that [Plaintiff's Sister 4] asked for the meeting of the sisters?
A. It's possible.
Q. Would that change your opinion at all regarding whether [Plaintiff] was trying to influence her sisters?

A. It's my impression that she was trying to draw them into this. That's my impression.
Q. What does that mean, draw them into this?
A. Get them to remember things.
Q. It's your impression, but–
A. That's my impression.
Q. I'm trying to see if there are any facts to support that rather than just an impression.
A. Well, I can't point to any facts right at the moment.
Q. Then you have "[Plaintiff's Sister 3]'s bad joke about girl playing with man's dolly got changed to be Dad." Do you know where that came from?
A. That came from this conversation.
Q. From the conversation with Mr. Ivey?
A. Right.
Q. So that's where you got that information?

108
A. Well, there is nothing about that in the materials too, but that's where it came from as far as that conversation is concerned.
Q. And you don't know where in the documentation this information came from?
A. Right. One of the sisters, but I just don't remember which one.
Q. "There were stories in the family about dolls hung on clothesline." Do you know where that information came from?
A. No. It's somewhere in the materials.
Q. Do you know what you mean by "stories in the family?"
A. No.
Q. What's the significance of that line to you, that sentence?
A. I don't know.
Q. Does it have any significance to you?
A. I didn't really rely on this very much.
Q. Do you intend to read the entirety of [Plaintiff's Therapist/Group Therapy]'s deposition?
A. Yes, before trial.
Q. If you reach any conclusions, any different conclusions or come up with any other

109
information based on reading the entirety of the deposition, can you write those down and give them to Mr. Ivey and ask him to send them to me?
A. Yes.
***

110
***

111
MS. LEVY: All right. That's all the questions that I have. Your turn, Mr. Ivey.
MR. IVEY: No questions. (Deposition concluded at 4:30 p.m.) ( It was agreed by and between counsel and the witness that the reading, examination and signing of the deposition were waived.)

## NOTES

1. Deposition taken on January 24, 1994, with Julie C. Oswald as certified court reporter. Barbara Jo Levy was counsel for the plaintiff, while Floyd Ivey was counsel for the defendants.

2. The original pagination is noted in this text to the upper left of each section; this is an edited and condensed version of the original deposition transcript. Sites of omitted text are indicated by asterisks.

# Appendix G: Selections, Cross Examination of Elizabeth Loftus, PhD

Barbara Jo Levy

*Lynn Crook vs. Bruce Murphy and Lucille Murphy*, No. 91-2-01102-5, Superior Court of the State of Washington, County of Benton

February 15, 1994

1607[1]

***

THE COURT: Mr. Ivey, you have completed your examination?

MR. IVEY: Yes, I have, Your Honor.

MS. LEVY: Your Honor, I move for the publication of the deposition of Dr. Elizabeth Loftus.

THE COURT: Deposition of Elizabeth Loftus taken on January 24th, 1994 is opened and published.

MS. LEVY: Thank you, Your Honor.

## *CROSS EXAMINATION*

BY MS. LEVY:

Q. Dr. Loftus, I've been waiting for a long time to be able to talk to you in a courtroom, so good morning.

A. Good morning.

Q. Dr. Loftus, you've testified on direct examination about a case you testified in a

[Haworth co-indexing entry note]: "Appendix G: Selections, Cross Examination of Elizabeth Loftus, PhD." Levy, Barbara Jo. Co-published simultaneously in *Journal of Aggression, Maltreatment & Trauma* (The Haworth Maltreatment & Trauma Press, an imprint of The Haworth Press, Inc.) Vol. 3, No. 2 (#6), 2000, pp. 349-372; and: *Sexual Abuse Litigation: A Practical Resource for Attorneys, Clinicians, and Advocates* (ed: Rebecca Rix) The Haworth Maltreatment & Trauma Press, an imprint of The Haworth Press, Inc., 2000, pp. 349-372. Single or multiple copies of this article are available for a fee from The Haworth Document Delivery Service [1-800-342-9678, 9:00 a.m. - 5:00 p.m. (EST). E-mail address: getinfo@haworthpressinc.com].

 

California murder trial of George Franklin. Is that correct?
A. I mentioned it, yes.
Q. And that was a case with repressed memory of a daughter remembering that her father had murdered her friend when she was a child. Is

1608

that correct, that was what the case was about?
A. Yes
Q. And in that case, a jury of twelve found George Franklin guilty beyond a reasonable doubt. Is that correct?
A. It did, yes.
Q. Now the experiments that you deal with, for the most part, are with subjects who are paid or who receive academic credit for participation; is that correct?
A. The majority of the subjects, yes, not all of them, but the majority–the majority of the studies I do involve that kind of procedure.
Q. And you also testified that there are people who are both in the clinical field and are a scientist, correct?
A. Yes.
Q. And Dr. Conte's one such person; is that correct?
A. Well, he does some research and publishes and also does clinical work.
Q. And you stated that, you testified, I believe, that part of your work is to use your studies and scientific knowledge for service in application of ideas to the public. Is that

1609

correct? Do you recall testifying to that?
A. Something like that.
Q. And today you are charging $350 for your testimony; is that correct?
A. That's my hourly rate, yes.
Q. Dr. Loftus, you charge $350 an hour for everything that you've done in this case; is that correct?
A Just about everything. I mean, I don't always bill all my hours, but that's my hourly rate for all time.
Q. And what is your charge in this case including your testimony today?
A. I'm sorry? $350 an hour.
Q. For how many hours?
A. Well, it depends on how long you keep me on the stand.
Q. Well, up to today, how many hours have you spent on the case?
A. I think I may have billed for approximately 15 or 16 hours, not counting the deposition time.
Q. And then your testimony today, in addition?

A. Right. Right. This is not counting the testimony.
Q. So you're looking at about, about close to

1610
$10, 000 in this case that you will earn?
A. It might approach that, yes.
THE CLERK: Defendant's Ident. No. 28 is marked.
Q. (By Ms. Levy) Dr. Loftus, I would like to use this chart that you drew for–during your direct examination. And I would like to–before I get to that–you say that you testified in approximately 10 to 15 cases on recovered memory; is that correct? In your deposition you said about 15. You think it's closer to 10?
A. Well, I haven't counted those so–
Q. Somewhere between 10 and 15 sounds correct?
A. It's just an estimate.
Q. And in all of those cases in which you've testified, you've testified on the side of there being suggested or false memory; is that correct?
A. In the cases that I testified, yes, I've been asked only a few times to consult on cases, you know, on the other side, and I have consulted on a few of those cases, but because my published opinions and my scientific opinions are so about the creation of false memories for the most part I don't think people would necessarily want that

1611
testimony on the other side.
Q. Now you talk about the acquisition phase, the retention phase, and the retrieval phase of memory?
A. Yes.
Q. And that the longer the time passes between the event and the retrieval, the more likely the memory is to fade–
A. There's more fading with the passage of time, yes.
Q. And the more likely the memory will be distorted by post-event suggestion?
A. It becomes more vulnerable to post-event suggestion.
Q. Now, Dr. Loftus, I would like to ask you a hypothetical question. I would like for you to assume that a doctor saw a patient one time. He's an ObGyn. He saw in eleven years of private practice approximately 55,000 client hours–or clients–patients, I guess he calls them, during that time. So this is one out of 55,000; that the patient was approximately 17 years old; she was a daughter of another doctor; and that the doctor that I'm talking about who treated her treated family members of other doctors in the

1612
community.

I would like for you to assume that the daughter came in because she had amenorrhea, and the doctor was checking her, as far as he was concerned, to see if she was possibly pregnant. He did an examination and found that she was not pregnant. It was a normal examination.

He had been in practice in the community for approximately three years prior to examining the patient and approximately eight years afterwards.

After those eight years of private practice, eight years following the examination, he went to school for three years in an entirely different subject matter, and then started teaching.

What would be the likelihood of that doctor remembering the details of the examination of one patient out of 55,000 hours, eleven years after the event?

MR. IVEY: I would object to the hypothetical unless it would include the facts or the contentions that the father of this particular patient was a physician within a very small group of physicians within the community at that time; that this doctor knew the family of

1613

the young woman to be examined; that the condition was unusual in that amenorrhea in a 17-year-old girl was an unusual condition; and that the doctor recalled the pathology of the event as opposed to names or faces; and that he taught the, as an example, in detail the particular condition from 1971 through 1986–

MS. LEVY: I would like to talk about the first time he taught. What will be the likelihood of his remembering this one patient out of 55,000? He never saw or talked to her–well, he never talked to her again. And he also treated other patients of doctors in this community?

A. Well, I couldn't put a probability on it, but it seems as if in that hypothetical situation there are some factors that would lead you to expect interference in memory particularly from other sources, so I don't know what kind of notes there were that could have been used to refresh their memory.

Q. I would like you to assume that he had no records to refresh his memories.

A. Well, you could expect in that kind of situation memory interference.

1614

Q. And then I would like you to further assume, Dr. Loftus, that over the next ten, 15 years, this doctor talked about this particular patient of his, and so had a rehearsal effect of saying the same thing over and over again. Is there the likelihood if he had a distortion of his details or his memory to begin with, that the rehearsal effect would make his confidence in those details more prevalent?

A. Well, I would expect based on the literature in that situation that he would–it would–the rehearsal would solidify that rehearsed version.

Q. And then I would like for you to further assume, Dr. Loftus, that 33 or 34 years after that one-time examination out of 55,000 patients, that doctor was asked to give his opinions about that examination and was given the same notebooks that you were given, including depositions of his friends whom he respected talking about other information regarding this patient.

Would you expect that post-event information and reading information from his respected friends to influence his opinions?

MR. IVEY: I would object to the

1615

hypothetical to the extent that it does not include the testimony that the physician had not received any of the materials related to this case when he was first contacted and recited in detail the–his recollection as he taught this case and as he did the examination and reported it to Mrs. Murphy immediately following the examination.

So the objection is that there was no materials in this physician's hands at the time he indicated what his examination had been over the telephone in October of 1991.

THE COURT: Well, that changes the nature of the question posed by the hypothetical, it seems to me. Your–I'm going the overrule the objection to the hypothetical. You can certainly add that in cross, or redirect, rather.

A. Well, my answer would be that post-event information can affect somebody's memory even if they are a doctor.

Q. (By Ms. Levy) And it would be likely that post-event suggestion 33 years after a one-time out of 55,000-time event could be pretty high; is that correct?

1616

A. Well, these same principals [*sic*] would apply with that situation too.

Q. Now, Dr. Loftus, most of your experiments deal with details of memory; is that correct?

A. Most of them but not all of them.

Q. And even in the example that you gave regarding the high school football game, which you characterized I think as being at least somewhat traumatic and to some people very traumatic, that some details in those memories that were changed. I think you said it was suggestions of blood and CPR that people were suggesting. Is that correct?

A. Right. The event happened and what was suggested to people was–well, in the case of blood, it is, I suppose it's a detail. In the case of someone administering CPR to the victim that never happened, but many people after the suggestion claimed that they had seen that.

So it's adding something to an event that already happened. You can call that a detail or call it a new chunk of information, whatever you want to call it.

Q. No one in that example said that they were at a 7-11 store instead of a football game, did they?

1617
A. No, not that I'm aware of.
Q. And your experiments have shown that it's easier to change people's memories of details than it is for the basic event. Is that correct?
A. I would say yes.
Q. You've never done an experiment, have you, Dr. Loftus, on the affect of someone having to live with trauma over a period of years, have you?
A. I'm not sure what you mean by that. I have done studies of victims of residential fires and other kinds of crime victimizations.
Q. You've never done a study of a person who has been traumatized over a number of years to determine what that person's memory is for the trauma, have you?
A. Well, no, that's not quite true because my collaboration with Dr. Mindy Fullilove involves women in New York who were traumatized and it looks at their memories for sexual abuse trauma.
Q. You've never done a study reporting people who were traumatized for a number of years to determine what the accuracy of their memory is for the traumatic events, have you?

1618
***
A. I think the answer is no. It depends on–I mean in most of these cases there's no way to know actually what happened because you don't know what the truth was. So when we study memory for on an event, a naturally occurring traumatic event, such as a victimization or a hospitalization, you often don't have the verification.
Q. (By Ms. Levy) But you don't know of such a study that you've done?
A. The only reason I'm hesitating is that I've done one major study with Group Health participants about their hospitalizations and doctor visits and doctor procedures and so on, and I'm just trying to think about whether that qualifies as an answer to your question or not.

1619
Q. Have you ever done a study, Dr. Loftus, regarding how a child deals with her memories, how she deals in the atmosphere of being traumatized for years, how she responds to the trauma, how she continues to live in a family where trauma is going on?
A. I personally haven't done that study, no.
Q. Do you know of such a study?
A. Well there are a lot of writings about this subject, but–

Q. Do you know of such a study?
A. Not as I sit here right now, an empirical study. I know there are a lot of writings about this subject.
Q. And you stated earlier that confidence in a memory is not necessarily correlated with accuracy, correct?
A. At best it's weakly correlated.
Q. So that if this doctor who is in the hypothetical that I was talking to you about a few minutes earlier was confident in his–in the accuracy of his memory, that would not necessarily mean that his memory was accurate. Is that correct?
A. Correct.

1620
Q. I think you stated, Dr. Loftus, regarding childhood amnesia, that there's a period of time before which most adults don't have concrete memories before age three. Is that a correct characterization of that testimony?
A. Well, three to three and a half is usually the period that we mark the offset of childhood amnesia.
Q. And some are later, some people have it later?
A. Some people's earliest memory is–
Q. Four, five?
A. Right
Q. Some people have it earlier than three, correct?
A. Well, some people think they have a memory that's earlier than three.
Q. You said in your testimony that there's a period of time before which most adults don't have concrete memories?
A. That's right. There's one new empirical study that suggests that maybe the birth of a sibling and a hospitalization in a few people might be recalled, if it occurred just before the age of three, say two and a half, two and three

1621
quarters or whatever. There's suggestive information but that study has other interpretations, too, that those memories might actually be family stories and not genuine recollections.
Q. Now Dr. Loftus, you talked about a study that you are conducting presently about a shopping mall; is that correct? You're presently conducting a study about being lost in a shopping mall and where you suggest a memory to someone as to whether they've been lost in a shopping mall?
A. Right.
Q. And presently, at least as of the time of your deposition, you had completed eight subjects?

A. Right.
Q. Is that still all you've completed?
A. No. Oh, gee, the last report from the chief research assistant was that somewhere between 15 and 18 percent of the subjects were, at this phase of the experiment, had come to develop this expanded memory of being lost in the mall. I'm not sure how many subjects that reflects. It's more than eight. Just a few more.
Q. At the time of your deposition, there had

1622
been eight studies completed and only one of the people had had the memory, the false memory implanted?
A. Well, in the formal study, not counting the five case histories that we've already published.
Q. And the five case histories are not a scientific study, are they, Dr. Loftus?
A. Well, they use the procedure and they document the existence of the ability to implant this particular false memory. That's what they stand for. They are existence proofs for the implantation of getting a lost memory
Q. But it's not a scientific study, doctor, those first five?
A. Well, it's not an experiment. Let's put it that way.
Q. And a number of those studies involved friends of yours, correct?
A. You mean the case–five individuals or the–
Q. Yes.
A. –I'm not sure what you're referring to.
Q. That part of the experiment, part of the people in the experiment were friends of yours?
A. Which experiment?

1623
Q. The one, the study that you did with five people being lost in a shopping mall.
A. Okay. That was not an experiment. It was a situation where we implanted in the minds of five people a memory for being lost.
Q. And going back to that particular study that you were doing, some of those people who were conducting this study were friends of yours, is that correct?
A. In the case of one subject, the father, who suggested the false memory to his daughter was an acquaintance of mine, yes, and actually did this in front of me.
Q. And in the Bellingham study that you were talking about, I write–
A. Himen[*sic*] is his last name.
Q. 20 percent of the subjects had false memories, approximately?
A. That was the figure that he reported at the psychonomics society meeting, yes.
Q. And 80 percent of the people did not?

A. Eight percent did not remember when they were asked, or when they received the suggestion about the overnight stay at the hospital for an ear infection, they said they didn't remember.

1624

Q. Now your testimony is that there's no way to tell a real memory without corroboration. You don't know one way or the other whether a memory is real?
A. Right, except in some–except in some circumstances where it's very likely false because of the childhood amnesia problem or it's very likely false because it's biologically, geographically or physically impossible. But in the vast majority of these cases, there's no way to know without some form of corroboration.
Q. Now you're an experimented psychologist, is that correct?
A. Yes
Q. You've had no experience in clinical work at all, is that correct?
A. I've had no experience in treating patients. I have done teaching, lecturing and workshops for clinical psychologists and other mental health professionals.
Q. You've never had a client or patient for a therapy?
A. Right.
Q. You've never diagnosed anyone with a mental disorder; is that correct?

1625

A. Not formally, no,
Q. Well, I hope you're not informally doing one on me right now. And you cannot give an opinion as to whether or not [Plaintiff]'s memories are accurate, can you?
A. Correct.
Q. Now you made some criticisms of the therapists in this case, or you testified that there were possibilities of suggestion in this case. Are you aware that [Plaintiff] had her first memory being sexually abused by her father after only four sections with [Therapist]?
A. Yes.
Q. Are you aware that she had only met him on two or three occasions prior to seeing him in therapy?
A. I don't remember the exact number, but–
Q. Are you aware that Dr. X testified here that it takes approximately more or less a year of therapy to really have a trusting relationship between a patient and a therapist?
A. I didn't–no, I wasn't aware of that opinion.

1626

Q. Are you aware that [Plaintiff's Therapist] testified that he's had clients who had repressed memories of sexual abuse and the offender has come forward and admitted the abuse?

A. I wasn't aware of that, no.

Q. And were you aware that Dr. X testified that he's had clients and has been involved in forensic situations in which there was repressed memory of abuse and the offender has admitted the abuse?

A. No, I wasn't aware of that. But it wouldn't surprise me if people could remember some things in therapy that they had not thought about for awhile and that they might be actual, might be actual memories.

Q. In fact, Dr. Loftus, you had a memory come back to you that you had not thought for a long time; isn't that correct?

A. Well, my personal case, it's something I had never forgot.

Q. You wrote a book called *Witness for the Defense*, didn't you, Doctor?

A. Yes.

Q. And you wrote this in what year? Do you remember?

1627

A. It was published in 1991.

Q. And I would like to read part of a page out of this book, Dr. Loftus, and I would like for you to tell me if I'm reading it correctly. You were asked in a case you were testifying in of the Tony Guerra case?

A. The pseudonym for the case to protect the identity of the people, but it's an actual case.

Q. You were testifying in a case. And you were asked the question on the stand, "You really don't know anything about five-year-old children who have been sexually abused, do you?" And then you wrote, "The memory flew out of me, out of the blackness of the past, hitting me full force."–And you testified then, "'Well, yes, I do.' I said, 'I do know something about this subject, because I was abused when I was six years old.' Brandard's finger"–and that must be the lawyer in the case–"stopped at mid curve, the thin smile disappeared from his lips and he looked at me, his eyes wide and astonished. It took him a few seconds to find his voice. 'You remember that,' he said. 'Yes, I do.'"

And then you go on to describe your memory

1628

of abuse, which I won't go into here.

And then you write, "After that, there is only blackness in my memory, full and total darkness with not a pinhole of light. Howard is simply gone, vanished, sucked away. My memory took him and destroyed him."

And then you write, "I realized Blanchard was asking me a question and my mind came back to the present."

Is that a correct rendition, skipping–

A. It sounds close or maybe it's right. I wasn't following the print, but it sounds familiar.

Q. So you remembered an episode of abuse when you were testifying on the stand. Isn't that correct?

A. I remembered that episode but it's something I remembered my whole life. It just happened to be the first time I ever spoke about it in a courtroom in front of jurors and television cameras.

Q. But you wrote "the memory flew out of me, out of the blackness of the past?"

A. Those were the words, but this is a memory I had had my whole life as evidenced by the various

1629

people I told.

Q. And no one was a witness to that episode; is that correct?

A. Correct.

Q. And no one could ever convince you that that episode of abuse did not occur; is that correct?

A. Well, I'm not sure of that. I believe it happened, but I have no idea if the details of my memory are accurate.

Q. Some of the details may not be accurate but you could be convinced that the episode in general took place; is that correct?

A. I believe it happened.

Q. Now you stated that some books that [Plaintiff] read could have been suggested to her, books such as *Courage to Heal* and *Secret Survivors*; is that correct?

A. Yes, just–I'm not criticizing the entire books, but the suggestion in pieces of these books are that if you suspect you were abused and you don't have any memories, then you probably were I think is an inappropriate suggestion.

Q. Do you know when Ms. [Plaintiff] read those books?

A. I don't remember exactly, but

Q. Do you know if she read those books months

1630

after her memory started coming back to her?

A. It's possible, but it's my understanding that there were also books and articles that were being read in conjunction with preparing presentations on child sex abuse. So that there was lots and lots of material and readings involved over an extended period of time. And I don't remember exactly what book was at what point.

Q. And you don't know what Ms. [Plaintiff] read when she was at the sexual assault center, do you?
A. Not specifically then. That *Courage to Heal* was published in 1988, so–
Q. But you can't testify that she read it prior to some of her memories returning, can you?
A. No. But that doesn't mean that it didn't have some influence when it actually was read
Q. But it couldn't have had influence before it was read could it?
A. Except on other people who may have read it and then created the influence.
Q. Are you aware when in [Plaintiff]'s therapy she started group therapy with [Plaintiff's therapist/GroupTherapy]
A. Approximately 1990. I have it in my notes of July 1990, approximately.

1631
Q. And so that would have been almost a year and a half after she had her first memory; is that correct?
A. Approximately. If you–
Q. And so the group couldn't have had an influence on [Plaintiff] prior to the time she was in the group, could it?
A. Well, but those groups could have an influence on the evolution of ever more bizarre or complex or questionable or expanded memories.
Q. But they couldn't have had–the groups couldn't have had an effect before [Plaintiff] participated in the groups?
A. On the things that emerged beforehand, no, you wouldn't cite the group as a source of influence.
Q. And you don't know what went on in those groups, do you, Dr. Loftus?
A. Not exactly, no.
Q. And you don't know that basically the groups were about giving each other emotional support and how to deal in present day life situations, do you?
A. That may have gone on.
Q. And that would be very different than people

1632
talking about their memories and giving each of their memories of abuse, wouldn't it, in terms of influence?
A. It would. George Janwis (phonetic), a psychiatrist at Emory University who has, others, worried about the impact of group, Paul McHugh, and others, have–really are worried that the ingredients in the stories that others tell in the group situation can influence the expansion or development of memories of any particular patient and also

are worried about the pressure to produce some memories that sometimes exists in these groups. I can't say without more information whether that happened in these groups.
Q. And in order to determine whether the group had influence, you need to know what went on in the group, don't you?
A. Well, that will be one way to find out, yes.
Q. And you also thought that, I think you testified that perhaps hypnosis or guided imagery could be a suggestive element in this case. Is that correct?
A. Well, those are two procedures that have caused some concern in the minds of me and others

1633
about this type of situation, yes.
Q. Are you aware that [Plaintiff's Therapist] testified that he only used hypnosis one time with [Plaintiff] and that was to try to uncover memories of happy childhood experiences, and that that attempted hypnosis was unsuccessful?
A. Well, I don't remember exactly if he said that, but there seems to be some controversy, given the different sources of information about just how many times the hypnosis was used and for what purpose.
Q. And if the testimony is that guided imagery was used for relaxation rather than to obtain or regain memories of abuse, that would be very different, wouldn't it, Dr. Loftus?
A. Well, if in fact that really were the purpose and not to unblock memories, which was in some place as stated as a purpose of this therapy–I mean, to now, years later, ask why did you use a particular procedure, the answer to that is subject to the same sorts of retrospected biases.
Q. [Plaintiff's Therapist] never testified that his purpose of therapy was to unblock memories, did he?
A. That is something that I took from either a

1634
letter he wrote or some other document that he used some Gestalt system for unblocking memories
Q. He said that Gestalt can be used to unblock memories. He didn't say that's that what he did in this case, did he?
A. I don't–just looking at the notes I have, I don't remember explicitly.
Q. It would be important for you to know what was involved in relaxation and suggestion to determine whether or not there was suggestion of sexual abuse, wouldn't it, Dr. Loftus?
A. It would certainly be helpful, yes.
Q. And if [Plaintiff's Therapist] said that he wanted [Plaintiff] to remember a peaceful place so that she could relax, that wouldn't necessarily be a suggestion of childhood sexual abuse, would it?

A. Correct.
Q. You can't find anything in the records that shows that [Plaintiff] was asked to do imagery work and as part of that work, she came up with memories of childhood abuse, can you?
A. I'm not sure if that's the way she got the memories or not.
Q. You can't point to anything in the records that shows that, can you, Dr. Loftus?

1635
A. Not that I recall
Q. I think you testified earlier that memory is more suggestible or suggestions of false memory are more likely if the people making the suggestion is an authority figure, versus a non-authority figure. Is that correct?
A. I don't remember if I testified about that here, but it is true that the source of the suggestion, at least in the studies, is important, can be important, that people can be more influenced by some sources than others
Q. And the repetition of suggestion also affects or can affect the malleability of memory. Is that correct?
A. Yes.
Q. And the implantation of false memory; is that correct?
A. It could play a role, yes.
Q. And you have studies, or there are at least three studies that show that the source of information is important. Is that correct?
A. Yes.
Q. And the studies, especially I think the Ceci study that you mentioned before, really talks about how children are suggestive to information

1636
from respected people or from adults. Is that correct?
A. Dr. Ceci was shown in particular, yes.
Q. And then there was–and that's the mouse trap study. Is that right?
A. Well, Ceci has shown that, you know, in a number of studies for many years, that the–he's done many studies of post-event suggestion, and the mouse trap is just one of them.
Q. And in that particular study, young children, I think these were pre-kindergarten children. Is that right?
A. Well, there are two studies now and they're approximately four to seven years old.
Q. And these young children had repeated questioning of them over a seven to ten-week period. Is that correct?
A. In one of the studies, yes.

Q. Now if a father suggested to a daughter over and over again that a snake was on her, he could make her believe that it happened. Isn't that correct?
A. In principle, I think it would be possible.
Q. And the same thing–effect?
A. Just I think that, with repeated suggestion

1637
you can get people to believe things.
Q. And especially of a young child?
A. Young children are especially suggestible.
Q. And that would be the same thing about suggesting to a daughter that she put her hand in a horse's anus. If her father told her repeatedly that that had occurred as a young child, he could make her believe that it had happened?

MR. IVEY: I believe this is in form of a hypothetical or asking the witness assume that that testimony has occurred and there's no testimony either in this case, either in depositions or a trial–that the father has suggested repeatedly about a snake or that the father had suggested repeatedly about a horse.

The memories have been testified in deposition as true memories occurring to the plaintiff in this case, but the question as propounded by counsel has not been suggested by any evidence or testimony.

MS. LEVY: Your Honor, I'm not stating that there's testimony to that effect. I'm asking a hypothetical question, if that could

1638
occur.

MR. IVEY: It's not probative then to this case, if it's not related–if it's off into some other case somewhere else in the world. That's a different thing.

THE COURT: Overrule the objection.

Q. (By Ms. Levy) Do you recall my question?
A. Yes. If somebody suggested something over and over, like a long time ago, you put your fist up the horse of an anus [*sic*], I, given what we know about suggestion and repeated suggestion, it would be possible to make some people, my prediction would be, believe that that happened. That's the whole point of this testimony.
Q. Now you have done some studies that show that people tend to remember in what you call a prestige enhancing way. Is that correct?
A. That's an area of research in the domain of memory, yes.
Q. And that means that people tend to remember things or themselves being better than what they actually did or how they actually were. Is that a layman's way of putting that?
A. Yes.

Q. In other words, people will remember that

1639
they did more housework in their house than they actually did or that they voted more often or that their children walked at an earlier age, that type of thing. Is that correct?
A. Yes. There are findings to that effect.
Q. And there's no study that you know of that shows that people will claim that they have post-traumatic stress disorder as a prestige enhancing memory, is there?
A. I don't know if it was a prestige enhancing memory but there's certainly people who have claimed that they have that to get out of having to be in the war.
Q. There's no evidence in this case that [Plaintiff] is trying to get out of a war, is there?
A. Not that I've seen.
Q. And there's no study that shows that people will try to have or claim to have a dissociative disorder as a prestige enhancing memory, is there, Dr. Loftus?
A. I wouldn't say there's evidence that people would claim this is prestige enhancing. There might be other motivations for it.
Q. And there's no evidence that shows that a person will claim to be a victim of incest as a

1640
prestige enhancing memory, is there, Dr. Loftus?
A. I'm not sure that people would talk about it as a prestige enhancing false claim, but there might be other motivations why someone would claim this victim status if in fact it weren't the case.
Q. Now you have no evidence to show that [Plaintiff] is claiming to be a victim of incest–let me try this again. You have no evidence to show that [Plaintiff] is fabricating her memories about being an incest survivor, do you, Dr. Loftus?
A. I haven't seen any evidence of a deliberate fabrication or deliberate lie, and in my opinion and the opinion of some other scientists and scholars in this area, the vast majority of these cases where there's a suspicion that the memories could indeed be false, the belief is that the people holding the memories and making the reports are at least sincere about them and not deliberately lying

MS. LEVY: Your Honor, I have a ways to go with my cross examination. This may be a good time to take a break.

THE COURT: Recess for lunch and resume at 1:30.

1641
(Following a lunch recess, the proceedings resumed, to wit:)

### *CROSS EXAMINATION (Continuing)*

BY MS. LEVY

Q. Good afternoon.

A. Good afternoon.

Q. Dr. Loftus, am I correct that you testified that you think that [Plaintiff's Therapist] had total acceptance of even bizarre memories of [description omitted]?

A. I don't know that I put it that way.

Q. You think that he believed everything she said as a memory was historically accurate?

A. Well, I'm not sure I would put it as everything, but he did express in a letter that he wrote that he believed that she was molested from the ages of one to 16 or something like that. And he mentioned a lot of very specific things in that letter, if I can just consult my notes, including the oral genital sex with the mother and the bestiality and other acts.

Q. Are you aware that in his testimony in this trial, [Plaintiff's Therapist] testified that he did believe [Plaintiff] was sexually abused, that she showed the signs of sexual abuse and post-traumatic stress disorder,

1642

that she's not psychotic, he saw no reason to believe that she was looking for secondary gain, that it was not easy for her to accuse someone that she loved and trusted, that it was not easy for her to talk about or acknowledge the abuse, that he did not have to believe every detail of every memory and what he was dealing with was an overall effect of sexual abuse.

Are you aware that that was his testimony?

A. I wasn't aware of his testimony on direct in this actual trial, only his deposition and earlier testimony.

Q. And even in cross examination, what he said is, I do believe that she was sexually abused. You're aware of that, aren't you?

A. That's my recollection.

Q. And it's your opinion that it's at least possible for someone to experience a painful memory or a painful event, excuse me, and if asked about it, they won't remember it?

A. That's possible.

Q. And there have been studies that have shown that people have been sexually abused and don't have memories of the sexual abuse, aren't there?

A. Well, there's been at least one study and

1643

there may be more, and they show that it's possible to be sexually abused and forget about it, at least, if it happens once.

Q. You have seen in the literature, have you not, doctor, literature that supports the theory that the more someone experiences a traumatic event, the more likely they are to repress the memories?
A. I'm not sure exactly what you're referring to by more. I've seen a claim in the literature that multiple sexual events get repressed, a claim, an unsubstantiated claim.
Q. You're not aware of the rehearsal effect of dissociation, are you, doctor?
A. I'm not sure what you mean by that.
Q. Do you know that there are therapists and experts in the field of sexual abuse who believe that a dissociative process can become a rehearsed event, that someone can disassociate from an event, forget it, and then, because they've learned to dissociate from one event, can dissociate from the next traumatic event and the next traumatic event, and the next traumatic event. In other words, they get actually better at dissociating?

1644
A. Wouldn't surprise me if people felt that way. Some people have held that opinion. I would like to see what proof there is for that, however.
Q. You agree, don't you, Dr. Loftus, that sexual abuse by a parent could be a very painful experience?
A. Yes.
Q. And you don't know of any study that shows that returned repressed memories are inaccurate?
A. I'm not sure that I know of any study where returned, supposed returned repressed memories were– at least there were reports of corroboration, so we would know whether they were accurate or not.
Q. You know that there are studies that show, excuse me, not studies that but that there have been cases that have shown that returned repressed memories are accurate?
A. I don't know of such a case. It wouldn't surprise me if there's–somebody could remember something that they had not thought about for a long time and it were ultimately to be corroborated. But as for even a few clear cases of active repression of a stream of traumatic

1645
events and an accurate recovery of those decades later, I don't know of absolutely corroborated cases where we know that repression was involved.
Q. Depends on your definition of repression, correct?
A. Right. I mean, if you use the, you know, the very, very liberal definition, that it's just I forgot, now I remember, then they do exist.

Q. Now you have memories of being a child which cannot be corroborated but which you know to be true memory, don't you, Dr. Loftus?
A. Probably, yes.
Q. And you have other memories in your life that cannot be corroborated but which you know to be true memories. Isn't that correct?
A. How are those different from the first?
Q. Well, some are as a child and some are later on in life.
A. Oh, yes.
Q. You have no evidence in this case to show that [Plaintiff] told [Plaintiff's Therapist] when she came in to see him that it sounded like she was someone who had been sexually abused as a child?
A. I don't have any evidence that he said those words, no.

1646
Q. Or any evidence that he told [Plaintiff's Therapist] that he thought that she had been sexually abused prior to her having memories of being sexually abused?
A. I don't know if he did that or not because his notes don't exist and there's information that's disappeared that we don't have. So–
Q. But you don't have that evidence, do you?
A. Right.
Q. And you would agree that at least some percentage of children who were sexually abused have no witnesses to that sexual abuse, wouldn't you?
A. Yes.
Q. And you can't say as a blanket statement, can you, Dr. Loftus, that a lack of witnesses makes a person's memory untrustworthy?
A. No, not necessarily.
Q. And even though a long time has passed in which a person didn't have a memory, it doesn't mean that it's not a real memory. Isn't that correct?
A. Could be real.
Q. You would agree, wouldn't you, Dr. Loftus, that a person can have a lot of mind control over another person when the first person has complete

1647
control of the environment of the second person?
A. Yes.
Q. And a parent of a small child would be someone who controls the environment of a small child. Isn't that correct?
A. I would say they–there is a lot of control possibilities there, yes.
Q. You have no opinion regarding present psychological functioning, do you?
A. No.

Q. And you're not an expert in post-traumatic stress disorder?
A. No.
Q. Or dissociative disorder?
A. No.
Q. Or the psychological conditions of children who are sexually abused?
A. I would not call myself an expert in those fields. My field is memory.
Q. And you have no evidence to show that people who are in therapy, clients who are in therapy, are eager to discover that they were violated by people that they trusted and loved, do you?
A. I'm not sure, I would put things quite that way, no.

1648
Q. So that's a "no" to my
A. I mean, I just wouldn't describe it as eager. There's a motivation there, in some cases.
Q. And you don't have any evidence in this case to show there was such a motivation, do you?
A. There may have been. It's an explanation for your problems and that's a motivation that has–that comes up in lots of these cases.
Q. But you don't have evidence in this case to show that there was a motivation, do you, doctor?
A. I don't have any concrete thing that I can point to.
Q. You don't know what the effect would be on someone who had to hide the experience of ongoing abuse and continue to live with the abuser, do you, doctor?
A. I'm not sure, what is your question about that?
Q. Do you know what the effect would be on someone who had to continue to live with an abuser and hide the fact that she was being abused?
A. Well, I'm not sure at what level you want an answer. What effect–it would be a very

1649
unpleasant situation.
Q. Do you know what the psychological impact would be in such a situation?
A. I don't–no. It's beyond my expertise.
Q. And in this case some of [Plaintiff's] memories could be true memories, couldn't they, Dr. Loftus?
A. It's conceivable.
Q. The lack of direct corroboration doesn't mean that the memories are false?
A. Correct.

Q. And are you aware that there is some indirect corroboration of other abuse and boundary violations that have gone on in this family?
A. I am aware of some sisters who are making some claims about different situations.
Q. Are you aware that one sister has testified that she always had a memory of her father sexually abusing her?
A. Well, I'm aware of some–I'm aware of some fact situation but I don't know that I would characterize it quite that way.
Q. Are you aware that there's a sister who has testified that she always had a memory of being

1650
sexually abused by her father?
A. I don't know what her testimony in the court here was. I do know about her claimed memory from the other documents that I read about, and I know there's some controversy about whether that memory was the same in history as it is today.
Q. You're aware, aren't you, doctor, that accused people are motivated to deny abuse of a child?
A. Yes, that people deny all kinds of crimes that they've actually committed.
Q. And denial of an abuse is not evidence that the abuse did not occur, is it?
A. Well, the abuse–a person can deny and the abuse could have still happened.
Q. Are you aware that there has been testimony in this case that one of [Plaintiff's] sisters, [name omitted], was taken to a funeral parlor and saw a dead baby in there?
A. I remember something about that in the documents in the book but I'm not sure.
Kazoontite (phonetic).
THE COURT: Thank you.
Q. (By Ms. Levy) You would agree, wouldn't you, Dr. Loftus, that it's not unusual for one

1651
sister to tell other sisters of her abuse memories, would you?
A. Might not be unusual. I wouldn't consider it that peculiar if it happened.
Q. And you wouldn't know in this case if [Plaintiff]'s telling her sisters about abuse would be an attempt to influence them, would you?
A. It might have been partly for that reason and she might have had some other reasons.
Q. Could have been just to get support, couldn't it?
A. Could have.
Q. You've done no studies on the effect of reading erotica, have you, Dr. Loftus?
A. Not in particular, no.

Q. And you've done no studies to date on traumatic memory and how traumatic memory may be different from other memory, have you?
A. Well, I've studied memories for lots of traumatic events, and I and many other memories experts, in fact most of the field in the field of cognitive psychology believe that these follow similar laws, the basic and fundamental laws of memory.
Q. You've done no specific study on how sexual

1652

abuse affects the memory of a child, have you?
A. Well, except for my study with Dr. Fullilove where we did study women who had been sexually abused and how they now remember it today.
Q. And in your study you found that 20–no–19 percent of the people in that study had reported to you that they had, at some point, forgotten memories of abuse and later remembered them. Is that correct?
A. In my study, they were given the three options when asked how would you characterize your memory: I've remembered my whole life, I've remembered part of the abuse but perhaps not all of it, or I've forgot for a period of time and later the memory returned. Nineteen percent checked that last option.
Q. Now in this case, you have not interviewed [Plaintiff], have you?
A. Correct.
Q. And you did not interview any of her sisters, did you?
A. Right. My material, my information comes only from the volumes and my conversations with Mr. Ivey.
Q. And you did not interview either Dr.

1653

or Mrs. [Defendant], did you?
A. Correct.
Q. That's all the questions I have. Thank you.
***
***
***

1666

## *RECROSS EXAMINATION*

BY MS. LEVY:
Q. I have a couple of questions, Dr. Loftus. Are you aware that in this case neither of the plaintiff's treating therapists nor did Dr. Shirley Feldmann-Summers nor did Dr. Jon Conte say that repression was a common way to cope with traumatic abuse?

A. I don't know if they did or not. It is a claim that you see in the loosely made literature, and perhaps they may have not made it. I wasn't aware of all of their testimony here.
Q. And are you aware that Shirley Feldmann-Summers has also done a study on repressed memory?
A. Well, actually, I came across this unpublished piece of work when reading her–a portion of her testimony in this case. But it's

1667
not published yet and I didn't know anything about it, her study of therapists and their memories, but from the description that she gave, I think that study is potentially similar to these others. It'll–it may be a contribution and may mean something. And I particularly found interesting her finding that physical abuse doesn't seem to be very different from sexual abuse in some ways in terms of how people think they remember it.

But it doesn't support this prolonged repression, at least not in the brief description of it that she gave here.
Q. Now in your study in which 19 percent of the people stated that they had forgotten abuse for a period of time, there are also people in your study who said that they had not been abused. Isn't that correct?
A. Yes.
Q. And some of those people could be people who had repressed memories of abuse and had not yet remembered it. Isn't that possible?
A. Well, it's certainly possible that those other people could be like the Linda Meyer Williams' people. They maybe have been abused and

1668
forgotten it and–but in Linda Meyer Williams' of course, those people who forgot haven't recovered and certainly the other half of my sample of women who said, no, they had not been abused, it's possible something happened to them and they had forgotten.
Q. Dr. Loftus, do you remember when you and I were on a television program last summer?
A. Yes.
Q. We sat next to each other in a little TV booth?
A. Right. "Sonia Live."
Q. Right. Do you remember that we had a conversation about Dr. Richard Ofshe as part of that when we were kind of chatting with each other before the program?
A. I don't–oh, I don't remember that in particular, no.
Q. Do you recall that Dr. Ofshe asked you to write an article with him?

A. No–no, that's not quite accurate. We were planning to write a–to possibly write something together on this phenomenon, maybe, oh, a year and a half ago, whenever I had–approximately about the time that I first met him

1669
personally.
Q. And you decided you did not want to write an article with Dr. Ofshe. Isn't that correct?
A. I felt that there were differences in the way that we wanted to express our ideas about this subject and that it would be too much of a compromise to try to come together and express them together in the same piece, that we could both–we just wanted to express ourselves differently, so–
Q. Would you say, Dr. Loftus, that Richard Ofshe's opinions on this subject of repressed memories are more extreme than your opinions?
A. Well, I would say that he–he's not afraid of being rude about how he feels about this topic.
Q. Would you say that his opinions are more on the extreme than yours are?
A. Well, it depends, I guess it depends on what you mean by extreme. I think he–he puts more of the blame on therapists and focuses more there than on other sources of suggestion, and he views the situation as one of massive influence in the sense that some cults can influence people to join, to stay, and to do things that they might

1670
otherwise not want to do. So it's a different focus.
Q. And he comes into a situation, hears that there's been repressed memory of many events over a long period of time, and knows before ever reading anything that it did not occur. Isn't that correct?
A. Well, I don't–I wouldn't character–I don't know that that's true of him.
Q. Thank you.
****

# Appendix H: Other Resources

For resources on each chapter topic, consult the author's bibliographic notes in each chapter. For additional, more general guidance, you may also find the following publications and national organizations helpful. There are many organizations not listed in this compilation who may be helpful, especially at the local level, and the inclusion of any organization here does not constitute a recommendation on the part of the editor or authors. Some of these organizations also offer information on the Internet; some such resources are listed below, but since Internet sites are constantly added and this is an incomplete list, we recommend that you check for other Internet resources with related organizations via telephone. To build your local resource network, ask for referrals from your state bar association or trial lawyer's association referral service, social service organizations, and other professionals who advocate for children and adults abused as children.

## *PUBLICATIONS*

American Psychological Association. *Violence and the Family: Report of the American Psychological Association Presidential Task Force on Violence and the Family.* Washington, DC: American Psychological Association, 1996.

Bowman, Cynthia Grant and Elizabeth Mertz. "A Dangerous Direction: Legal Intervention in Sexual Abuse Survivor Therapy." *Harvard Law Review* 109 No. 3, (1996): 555-639.

---

[Haworth co-indexing entry note]: "Appendix H: Other Resources." Rix, Rebecca. Co-published simultaneously in *Journal of Aggression, Maltreatment & Trauma* (The Haworth Maltreatment & Trauma Press, an imprint of The Haworth Press, Inc.) Vol. 3, No. 2 (#6), 2000, pp. 373-378; and: *Sexual Abuse Litigation: A Practical Resource for Attorneys, Clinicians, and Advocates* (ed: Rebecca Rix) The Haworth Maltreatment & Trauma Press, an imprint of The Haworth Press, Inc., 2000, pp. 373-378. Single or multiple copies of this article are available for a fee from The Haworth Document Delivery Service [1-800-342-9678, 9:00 a.m. - 5:00 p.m. (EST). E-mail address: getinfo@haworthpressinc.com].

 

Harrison, David L., Barbara Jo Levy, Michael S. Morey, Sherry A. Quirk, Rebecca A. Rix, and Anne P. DePrince. "Childhood Sexual Abuse-The Plaintiff's Perspective." *Shepard's Expert and Scientific Evidence Quarterly* 2, No. 2, (1994): 399-415.

Williams, Mary. "Memories of Childhood Sexual Abuse: Legal Issues for Psychotherapists." In *Construction and Reconstruction of Memory*, ed. Charlotte Procan. Northvale: Jason Avonson, 1997.

Williams, Mary. "Suits by Adults for Childhood Sexual Abuse: Legal Origins of the "Repressed Memory Controversy." *Journal of Psychiatry and Law* 24, (1996): 207-228

## *ORGANIZATIONS*

American Professional Society on the Abuse of Children (APSAC)
407 South Dearborn, Suite 1300
Chicago, IL 60605
(312) 554-0166

APSAC is a nonprofit membership organization for child advocates in all professions. Members receive the quarterly journal *Maltreatment*, and the quarterly newsletter *The Advisor*, which covers a wide variety of legal, clinical and other issues related to child abuse advocacy. APSAC also sponsors regular professional education seminars and an annual colloquium.

Center for the Prevention of Sexual and Domestic Violence (The Center)
936 North 34th, Suite 200
Seattle, WA 98103
(206) 634-1903

The Center provides training and training materials on dealing with sexual and domestic violence and clergy abuse to religious institutions and secular social service organizations across the United States, Canada, and around the world. Members receive a quarterly newsletter, *Working Together*, that covers emerging issues and publications related to The Center's mission. An annual resource catalog lists books, videos, and other training materials for preventing sexual and domestic violence, with a focus on religious and educational institutions.

Family Violence and Sexual Assault Institute (FVSAI)
6160 Cornerstone Court East
(858) 623-2777, ext. 427
E-mail: FVSAI@CSPP.edu

FVSAI is a nonprofit membership organization for child advocates in all professions. Members receive the quarterly *Bulletin*, which covers legal, clinical and prevention approaches to domestic and sexual violence as well as recent publications, and can access a comprehensive system of literature references on related issues. The FVSAI stays abreast of emerging literature on issues related to domestic and sexual violence, and maintains an inventory of recent books from publishers for retail, which makes them a centralized source of literature and information. The FVSAI also co-sponsors conferences on domestic and sexual violence. Non-members can call for books or other information.

National Alliance of Sexual Assault Coalitions
110 Connecticut Boulevard
East Hartford, CT 06108
(860) 282-9881
http://www.connsacs.org/alliance.htm

The National Alliance analyzes public policy and assists in legal research and *amicus* briefs on sexual assault related law, through its national organization and state organizations.

National Association of Counsel for Children (NACC)
Imhoff Pavillion, Suite 340
1825 Marion Street
Denver, CO 80218
(303) 864-5320

This is a nonprofit membership organization for child advocacy professionals. For its members, it provides legal resources and research assistance, as well as a quarterly magazine, *The Guardian*, which reports emerging legal news. Non-members can call for information and referrals to lawyers.

National Coalition Against Sexual Assault (NCASA)
125 North Enola Drive, Suite 205
Enola, PA 17025
(717) 728-9764

This is a nonprofit membership organization for survivors of sexual assault and their advocates. It emphasizes social change through education, legal and other forms of advocacy, and public policy analysis, and holds a national annual conference with caucuses for adult victim/survivors, women of color, and lesbians. Members receive a quarterly newsletter, *NCASA News*, which features articles on emerging developments in sexual assault prevention and survivor advocacy, as well as the membership's committee work. The coalition also has a library of fact sheets on sexual assault issues.

National Committee to Prevent Child Abuse (NCPCA)
332 S. Michigan Avenue, Suite 1600
Chicago, IL 60604-4357
(312) 663-3520

NCPCA is a nonprofit national organization dedicated to the prevention of all forms of child abuse. Perhaps best known for their public interest advertising in collaboration with the Advertising Council, this organization also works through state chapters to implement child abuse prevention programs developed and executed with governmental and professional organizations. An information packet, including an introduction to their programs to assist parents, teachers, coaches, social workers, and communities in preventing abuse, and their *Selected Child Abuse Information and Resources Directory*, is available by contacting them.

National Victim Center
2111 Wilson Boulevard, Suite 300
Arlington, VA 22201
(703) 276-2880
http://www.nvc.org

The National Victim Center is a nonprofit membership organization that provides resource referrals and advocacy for victims of all types of crime, including sexual abuse. Working with local, state and federal organizations, they provide direct services and resources, advocate laws and public policies that create resources and secure rights and protections for victims, and deliver training and technical assistance to victim advocates and service professionals. They offer a variety of publications that serve the needs of crime victims and offer information and referrals through their INFOLINK program for both survivors and professionals. Membership benefits include: a subscription to their quarterly newsletter, *NETWORKS*, which covers emerging legal developments, new resources and innovative programs; their quarterly public policy/legislation update, the *Pipeline*; priority access to their extensive legislative and service database; and discounted publications. MembershipPlus/Civil Justice Publications offers e-mail action alerts on relevant emerging information, and civil justice periodicals with monthly and quarterly updates on new cases and trends in civil remedies for crime victims.

One Voice: The National Coalition for Abuse Awareness
P.O. Box 27958
Washington, D.C. 20038-7958
(202) 462-4688

One Voice focuses on political advocacy and providing referrals and resources to survivors of sexual abuse and the professionals who help them.

Sexual Abuse Section, American Trial Lawyers of America
Stephen Rubino, Esq. (Chair)
Ross & Rubino
Sentry Office Plaza
Suite 100
216 Haddon Avenue
Westmont, NJ 08108
(609) 365-0500

The United States Congress has an Internet site (named THOMAS) at http://thomas.loc.gov/. It contains information on currently debated and recently passed legislation.

## LOCAL RESOURCES

Name, Telephone: ______________________________
Address: ______________________________
Resource Type: ______________________________

Name, Telephone: ______________________________
Address: ______________________________
Resource Type: ______________________________

Name, Telephone: ______________________________
Address: ______________________________
Resource Type: ______________________________

Name, Telephone: ______________________________
Address: ______________________________
Resource Type: ______________________________

Name, Telephone: ______________________________
Address: ______________________________
Resource Type: ______________________________

Name, Telephone: ______________________________
Address: ______________________________
Resource Type: ______________________________

Name, Telephone: ______________________________
Address: ______________________________
Resource Type: ______________________________

Name, Telephone: ______________________________
Address: ______________________________
Resource Type: ______________________________

# Index



 

For Product Safety Concerns and Information please contact our EU
representative GPSR@taylorandfrancis.com
Taylor & Francis Verlag GmbH, Kaufingerstraße 24, 80331 München, Germany

www.ingramcontent.com/pod-product-compliance
Lightning Source LLC
LaVergne TN
LVHW011107300926
849160LV00008B/296
*9780789011756*